Wedding Resource Guide

Over 500 Oregon & Southwest Washington
Wedding Sites & Services

Mary Lou Burton

BravoWedding.com

Bravo!® Publications, Inc.

630 B. Avenue, Suite 205

Lake Oswego, Oregon 97034

p. 503.675.1380

f. 503.675.1204

www.BravoWedding.com

This resource guide is comprised of paid advertisements. Although advertisers must meet a quality level of standards to be featured in this guide, Bravo! Publications, Inc. cannot and does not guarantee or take responsibility for services provided by said advertisers. No affiliation exists between Bravo! Publications, Inc. and any advertiser featured. Every reasonable effort has been made to provide the most accurate and up-to-date information.

Printed in the United States of America.

ISBN 978-1-884471-48-3

Table of Contents

© Katana Triplet

Table
of Contents

©FS Photography

Bravo!
Acknowledgements

Publisher
Mary Lou Burton

Account Managers
Kate Henry
Jennifer Maust

General Manager
Denise Hall

Production & Design
Jodie Siljeg
Bryan Hoybook

Web Sites & Optimization
Subpixel, Inc. - Subpixel.com
Don Richardson - Digitalpopcorn.com

Public Relations & Marketing
Heather Willig

Special Projects
Helen Kern
Michelle Clayton
Tina Monje

Intern
Adrienne Jarvis

Prepress & Printing
Consolidated Press

Cover Photo
David Barss Photographer

Back Cover
Powers Photography Studios

Mary Lou Burton - Bravo! Founder & Publisher

All great things begin with only a single thought. On her honeymoon, with the planning of her huge Italian wedding still fresh in mind, she relished in the thought of having a single resource to use when planning such an important event. Turning that into reality, Mary Lou and friend Marion Clifton crafted the first Bravo! Wedding Resource Guide in 1990 with an Apple IIe and a single-sheet bubble-jet printer. By 1994, the idea was taken a step further by publishing the first Event Resource Guide along with a meeting and hospitality trade show, Bravo! Live produced each October. In recent years, Bravo! has added the Bravo! Wedding Affairs in November and February and the Central Oregon Wedding Affair.

Graced with her large Italian family and four children: Alex, Nick, Will and Greta, Mary Lou is no stranger to the need for an organized, simple way to entertain, educate, and care for her family. She dedicates her life to acting with intention: if it is going to bring a smile upon a sad face, light the fire within a soul, or illuminate a cloudy path, she will find the time and energy to accomplish it.

If You Like Our Guide...
You'll Love Our Websites

BravoWedding.com

BravoCentralOregonWedding.com

The Entire Guide is Online With Links to Over 450 Services

Every client in the book is on our website with direct links to their sites and more details of their facility or service.

Virtual Tours & Galleries

Take a tour of Ceremony & Reception sites directly from our website. Hear a sound bite from musicians, or view a photo gallery from photographers.

Advanced Search

Search by area, capacity & price.

Sign Up to Win

Monthly prizes & drawings.

Calendar of Events

Our website has a comprehensive Calendar of Events that will let you know when and where the next bridal show and special events will be taking place in your area.

Wedding Blog

Find information on shows, industry events, tips & trends and testimonials from brides, grooms and local businesses.

Social Networking

Follow us on Facebook and Twitter for tips, trends, contests and more.

 **Bravoportland**

 **Bravopub**

Bravo! and Banquet & Event

Resource Guides

Bravo! Event Resource Guide

Portland • Vancouver • Salem
Outlying Areas & Regions

The 2010 edition is filled with important information and details about the area's finest businesses and service providers. Each page is presented in easy-to-read, resumé style format, alphabetically, by category. Designed to be user-friendly, the Event Resource Guide truly is your planning resource!

Suggested Retail Value: $9.95
(Complimentary to qualified meeting & event planners)

To Order, Visit: www.BravoEvent.com

B&E Event Resource Guide

Puget Sound & Beyond

The 2010 edition features more than 600 pages of easy-to-read, resumé style write-ups on over 400 area businesses and service providers, how-to's, checklists, plus lots of helpful hints!

Suggested Retail Value: $14.95
(Complimentary to qualified meeting & event planners)

To Order, Visit: www.BanquetEvent.com

B&E Wedding Resource Guide

Puget Sound & Beyond

The 2010 edition features more than 500 pages of easy-to-read, resumé style write-ups on over 400 area businesses and service providers, how-to's, checklists, plus lots of helpful hints!

Suggested Retail Value: $14.95

To Order, Visit: www.BanquetEvent.com

Bravo!
Wedding Planner

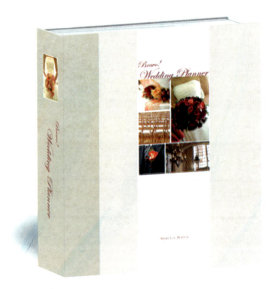

Unique Style With a Touch of Elegance

Everything from calendars and time schedules to contracts and lists for delegating duties has been put into one easy-to-use, centralized system. Guaranteed to guide you from your engagement to your wedding day looking calm, cool and beautiful. Rated as one of the nations five best wedding planners by Bridal Guide Magazine. The Bravo! Wedding Planner is what every bride needs to plan the perfect wedding.

FEATURING:

- Business card holder
- A sturdy 3-ring binder that is easy to customize
- 14 easy-to-find tabbed sections
- 40 detailed worksheets to record details
- Worksheets double as contracts
- Detailed budget, expense worksheets
- Time schedules, checklists and calendars
- "To Do" forms and "Delegating Duties" lists
- Pockets for receipts, swatches, and brochures
- Directs brides to ask all the right questions

Suggested Retail Value: $29.95

Order your copy today at BravoWedding.com or Amazon.com.
Or pick-up a copy at Borders, Barnes & Noble, and many wedding boutiques.

Planning Your Wedding

You're Engaged Now What?

Congratulations! He proposed, you've said yes - now where to go from here? You have to tell your parents, his parents, call all your friends, call the church, get time off for the honeymoon, buy a wedding dress, find a caterer.... STOP!

Work together so that you both agree on the same things, and then commit your thoughts to paper so that you will have a plan. Create a wedding "to do" timeline that will help you prioritize what needs to get done. See our helpful hint on this.

© Daniel Stark

First, take a deep breath. Organize a "wedding space" where you can keep everything related to the wedding in one area that makes you feel great about the person you are going to marry and the wedding you are planning.

Before all the hustle begins, do yourself a favor and sit down with your fiancé and ask yourselves the following questions:

- *Are your families large or small?*
- *What is your budget?*
- *What style of wedding would you prefer to have—do you like intimate gatherings, large parties, or impromptu, unique events?*
- *Do you want a romantic theme or a formal affair?*

Then create a "top ten" list outlining what each of you feel is most important. It may be the Music, Honeymoon then Ceremony Site for your fiancé... and Bridal Gown, Music and Cake for you. Sit down with each other's lists and cross-reference. You'll begin to see a pattern of what comes to the top—allowing you and your fiancé to make those difficult decisions based on your budget —easier to see.

Organize your thoughts and plans into a Wedding Organizer/Planner. The Bravo! Wedding Organizer is a great one filled with checklists, timelines, helpful hints, places to hold fabric swatches, business cards, etc.

Last, but not least, take time out for yourself at least once a week with an activity that is NOT wedding related. Go for a walk, swim, read a book, swing at the playground, see a movie or play – anything that will help clear your mind or body will cleanse and refresh your energy.

GETTING ORGANIZED

ONCE YOU MAKE YOUR PLAN, STICK TO IT!

Everyone seems to become an expert on wedding planning when they find out you're engaged. You'll receive loads of unsolicited advice, and everyone will try to sway your thinking. Don't let anyone steer you away from what's important to you and your fiancé. If you do, your wedding will be a combination of everyone else's dreams but your own!

A CONSULTANT CAN EASE THE STRESS

Hiring a consultant is a wise idea, especially if there is arguing between mother and daughter, between families, divorced parents and even attendants. This is an emotional time and if you can have an objective opinion of a consultant buffering between the two, it can sometimes ease the pressure. Money can be one of the biggest problems and obstacles. If a third party is involved, such as a consultant, they can collect the money without it being embarrassing. Many times these arguments result from lack of communication, emotional overload and misconceptions. The two parties just need to communicate; sometimes writing it down and having someone calm present to the other half is a good way to deal with it. They say you hurt the ones you love the most, the stresses of a wedding can truly test your relationships with family, friends and even your fiancé, remember to keep focused on what's important that day!

DELEGATE DUTIES

Every bride thinks, "If I don't do it, it won't get done the way I want it!" This may be true, but you'll soon realize you can't do it all and keep your sanity. You and your fiancé have figured out the plan, now delegate duties to family and friends.

Everything can and will be done the way you want it if you give a clear description of what you need accomplished and when. Family and friends will enjoy knowing they helped contribute to making your special day a success!

RELAX & ENJOY YOUR WEDDING DAY!

We suggest you get someone to coordinate all the details on the day of your wedding. Hire a professional or ask a trustworthy friend or family member who is not directly involved in the wedding party to oversee and coordinate delivery and setup of flowers, rental equipment, decorations, etc. Provide this person with a comprehensive list of everything he or she will need to keep an eye on, including the arrival of musicians and where they need to set up, where and when the formal photographs will be taken, phone numbers with a contact name for all the businesses providing services, etc. Your months of planning and coordination will pay off! You and your groom should be concerned and consumed only with the joy of the day and your love for each other!

11

You're Engaged Now What? Budgeting

SETTING A BUDGET & PRE-PLANNING

If you don't read any other page from top to bottom, make sure to read this one. The following suggestions will ensure that your wedding turns out the way you want it while keeping your budget in line.

The most important advice we can offer both you AND your parents is do not go into debt! Weddings come in a variety of types and sizes; one is not necessarily better than the other, based on the size or how much money you spend. Whatever you do, don't start your married life in debt.

Traditionally the bride's family has always been responsible for a majority of the wedding expenses. Today, however, the division of wedding expenses depends more often on the financial ability of the bride, the groom and their families. Many couples decide to split the expenses with both sets of parents or to pay for the wedding themselves.

It is important to sit down and discuss the type of wedding you want to have. Be specific about the services and what your budget is. Read any and all contracts thoroughly before signing to avoid confusion and unexpected expenses.

When attending bridal shows or collecting a large amount of information, fold down the corners of brochures from your favorite companies. This will make it easier to narrow down and organize information into your Wedding Organizer.

Do your research. Before choosing a photographer, caterer, or other vendor, ask to see or hear samples of their work. Ask specific questions and, if possible, check references, blogs from other clients and websites.

BE REALISTIC WITH YOUR BUDGET

Your wedding budget should be handled like a business budget. If your boss said, "The budget for the Christmas party is $5,000," you would use only those services that would keep you within your budget. The same is true for your wedding. Find the services that can accomplish what you want within the budget you've designated. Be realistic about your budget. If you have only $2,000 for your reception, it's unlikely you're going to be able to afford a full sit-down dinner for 300 guests, but a buffet with hot and cold hors d'oeuvres may work very well. Follow your budget allocations as closely as possible, this will eliminate financial stress.

SETTING UP A BUDGET

It is recommended you keep a spreadsheet of all your wedding costs. Create one ahead of time that shows what you are spending on which wedding categories. This will help you keep within your budget. If you have to go over on one category then you know you need to cut back on another. A wedding coordinator can help analyze your budget and give you helpful hints on how to cut back on a specific category.

12

Always pay businesses or services with a check or credit card for better records and tracking of expenses. Allocation of your budget depends on what is most important to the bride, groom and family contributing. Some spend more on music and entertainment or photography than others.

The Following Is A Percentage Break-out of What The Average Dollar Spent Is:

- Reception site rental, food & beverage: 37%
- Photography: 10%
- Florist: 10%
- Music: 10%
- Bride's & groom's attire: 10%
- Wedding Coordinator: 10%
- Invitations, programs, calligraphy: 5%
- Miscellaneous (clergy, guest favors, attendants gifts, transportation): 5%
- Ceremony site rental: 3%

Ways To Save Money

It's amazing how fast wedding costs can exceed the planned budget. If you find yourself in the position of needing to trim back to make everything fit within your budget, consider the following:

Avoid peak wedding days and seasons. You can save money by having your wedding during the months considered to be "off-season" (October through May) and on a Thursday or Friday evening or Sunday during the day. Because these times are in less demand, many businesses and services provide what you are looking for at reduced prices. You're also more likely to get your first choices!

Consider a daytime versus evening wedding. Considering a Friday, Saturday or Sunday daytime wedding gives additional options for your wedding date. Food and alcohol costs are considerably less for daytime events than evening events. People don't drink as much (if at all), and the food itself is far simpler and therefore less expensive.

Guest lists can be the first thing to get out of control. Begin by deciding what size you would like your wedding to be and be firm with your figures of how many guests each family can invite. Generally, if you have not been in contact with someone in the past year, you should not invite them to your wedding. Stick to family and close friends, adding other guests only if your budget allows. Remember that caterers charge per person, so consider having a buffet instead of a sit-down dinner as a way to cut costs.

Determine what is most important to you and put your money into that, but trim back on other areas. If fabulous flowers have always meant the most to you, spend a little less on your entertainment. If you've always wanted the most incredible dress in the world, cut back on the flower budget and have a DJ instead of a band.

Don't be afraid to shop around. A little time researching could save you a lot of money. There can be a considerable difference in prices between different businesses for the same items or services. Just make sure that you are going to receive exactly the same item or level of service from the less-expensive company and that no short cuts are being taken at your expense.

If you're very clear about what budget you have to work with from the beginning, you'll find that the people in the wedding industry can be very helpful with all kinds of clever ideas on how to save money. Don't be afraid to ask for suggestions or ideas.

Contracts

Contracts can be the most confusing and difficult part of planning a wedding. Keep in mind that this is a business arrangement. You're the customer and you are contracting with certain businesses to provide the services you request on a certain date, at a certain time, and within a certain budget. Contracts are a must when doing business with the many types of wedding-related services. Your wedding is an emotional experience, but remember—money is changing hands.

A contract will spell out everything in black and white, as well as clarify any grey areas. If the business doesn't have a formal

13

contract, write up your own and have them sign it. Estimates are a good first step, but they aren't final. Many brides have been shocked a week before their wedding when a supplier has said, "We had a price increase in the last six months; now it will cost this much for what you want."

Beware of contracts you feel pressured to sign! Make sure you don't sign something that you haven't thoroughly read or don't understand. Never sign a contract that makes you feel uncomfortable or that you can't afford. A contract is a legally binding document that commits you to the service or provider. Be well informed about what you are signing; ask questions, or take a copy of it home to look over if you have any hesitation at all.

Check Out References

The best way to research a business is to ask for references, check out their website, and then take the time to call them. This way you will rapidly discover if the services or merchandise were provided or delivered as promised. Getting recommendations from vendors you already trust is also a good place to start.

Deposits

In most cases a deposit is required to place an order formally or to reserve a certain date. Brides and grooms make the common mistake of assuming that the reception site is reserved based on a verbal commitment for date and time. The agreement is not always valid, let alone recorded, until after the deposit has been received.

You're The Customer!

Always remember that you're the customer! Even though this can be an emotional time, don't settle for less than what was contracted for. Insist on the best service and accept nothing less. You may be spending more money on this one day than most people spend in a year! Clarify your expectations and never make assumptions.

Wedding Expenses

The division of expenses depends on the financial ability of the bride, groom and their respective families. Sit down and discuss the type of wedding you want to have and use the following list of items so each participant can choose what he or she would like to pay for. Remember that the reception can sometimes amount to 50% or more of your total expenses. If your costs need to be reduced, you may want to change to a less formal reception.

The Bride & Her Family's Expenses Traditionally Include:

- The wedding gown & accessories
- Invitations & personal stationery
- Flowers for the church, reception & wedding attendants
- Photography & videography
- Reception, including room charge, food, servers, refreshments & wedding cake
- Music
- Transportation for wedding attendants to church & reception
- Gifts for bridesmaids
- Accommodations for bridesmaids, if necessary

The Groom & His Family's Expenses Traditionally Include:

- Groom's wedding attire
- The clergy or judge's fees
- The marriage license
- All honeymoon expenses
- Rehearsal dinner
- Bride's bouquet & both mothers' corsages
- Boutonnieres for groomsmen
- Groomsmen gifts
- Accommodations for attendants, if necessary

The Wedding Attendants' Expenses Are:

- Wedding attire
- Traveling expenses
- Wedding gift

The lists mentioned above are used as traditional guidelines, however, you don't have to follow tradition and can have those wanting to contribute pay for whatever they can afford.

You're Engaged Now What?

Managing Your Time

You've waited a long time to get married. Many reception facilities are reserved as far as a year in advance during the summer months and December. The size and formality of your wedding will play an important part in determining your date and schedule. Even if your wedding is small and less formal, allow yourself a minimum of three months. The more time you have to plan, the better your chances of reserving your first choices. With all you have to do, time will fly quicker than you think!

The following schedule and checklist provide you with the basis for organizing your planning time and ensure that all the details will be handled. These are strictly recommendations; we encourage you to look on the following pages to see when the businesses themselves say they need to be reserved.

AFTER ENGAGEMENT — SIX MONTHS & BEFORE:

- ☐ Select a wedding date and time — be flexible
- ☐ Buy a wedding notebook, such as the the Bravo!® Wedding Planner
- ☐ Figure out your budget and write it down
- ☐ Determine type of wedding and reception: formality, size, colors and theme
- ☐ Decide on the ceremony site and make an appointment with the clergy
- ☐ Reserve a reception facility; if there's no in-house catering, you will need to find a caterer
- ☐ Start compiling names and addresses of guests
- ☐ Decide on wedding attendants — bridesmaids and groomsmen
- ☐ Shop for your wedding gown and headpiece
- ☐ Select a photographer & videographer

- ☐ Start collecting favorite photographs from both of your childhoods through present that you'll want to use in your wedding video or multi-image slide program
- ☐ Select dresses for your bridesmaids
- ☐ Find a florist
- ☐ Mail out engagement announcements
- ☐ Send an announcement to your local paper
- ☐ Register at the bridal registry stores of your choice
- ☐ Reserve a band, DJ, or orchestra for your reception
- ☐ Decide on honeymoon destination; if it's a popular area, make reservations now

FOUR TO FIVE MONTHS BEFORE:

- ☐ Compile the final guest list; delete or correct as needed
- ☐ Make sure all deposits are paid for services reserved
- ☐ Finish planning the honeymoon
- ☐ Order bridal attire; some manufacturers require up to six months for delivery
- ☐ Order the wedding cake

15

- ☐ Have groom, groomsmen and ushers fitted for formal wear
- ☐ Purchase your wedding rings
- ☐ Order invitations, thank-you notes, imprinted napkins and programs
- ☐ Ask people to handle certain duties like candle lighting, guest book, cake serving
- ☐ Select musicians for ceremony

TWO TO THREE MONTHS BEFORE:

- ☐ Plan ceremony rehearsal and rehearsal dinner
- ☐ Address invitations (mail six to eight weeks prior to wedding)
- ☐ Organize details with service providers: reception facility, photographer, etc
- ☐ Check accommodations for out-of-town guests; send them information
- ☐ Make beauty appointments: hair, nails, massage, facial and makeup
- ☐ Arrange for final fittings for your gown and bridesmaids dresses
- ☐ Make your transportation arrangements for the wedding day
- ☐ Purchase gifts for your attendants
- ☐ Shop for your lingerie and going-away outfit
- ☐ Give a bridesmaids' luncheon or bachelor/ bachelorette party (optional)
- ☐ Send thank yous for gifts received early
- ☐ Get accessories: garter, unity candle, toasting goblets, ring-bearer pillow, etc

ONE WEEK TO A MONTH BEFORE:

- ☐ Change your name (if you choose) on your driver's license and Social Security card; organize which credit cards and bank accounts will be used
- ☐ Send change-of-address cards to post office if you are moving in together after the wedding
- ☐ Confirm accommodations arranged for out-of-town guests
- ☐ Get your final count of guests to caterer
- ☐ Delegate last-minute errands and details

- ☐ Make any necessary lists for your vendors
- ☐ Meet with your wedding coordinator to go over final details
- ☐ If you haven't hired a wedding coordinator, ask a responsible person to coordinate services and people on the wedding day; give them a list of who and what is supposed to be where and when
- ☐ Pack for honeymoon
- ☐ Get your marriage license. **Note:** if you were married before, you'll need to know the date and place of the divorce or annulment. You may also need to have paperwork proof of divorce or annulment
- ☐ Pick up your wedding rings; make sure they are the correct sizes
- ☐ Pick up wedding attire; try it all on one last time to make sure it fits
- ☐ Make sure bridesmaids have their dresses and they all fit
- ☐ Keep up on writing thank-you notes; don't let them pile up
- ☐ Pamper yourself and make sure you eat right and get enough sleep

THE WEDDING DAY:

- ☐ Eat a good breakfast
- ☐ Relax and enjoy getting ready for your big day
- ☐ Go to hairdresser or start fixing your hair a few hours prior to the wedding
- ☐ Put all the accessories you will need for dressing in one place
- ☐ If pictures are being taken before ceremony, begin at least two hours prior
- ☐ Just enjoy the day! All your months of planning will make your day perfect!

© Laszlo

16

Wedding Day
Survival Kit

You will want to put some things together a few days before your wedding to take to the church. We call it the "Wedding Day Survival Kit." It includes all those little odds and ends that you'll need for quick repairs and to cover the things others may have forgotten.

☐ Scissors

☐ Needles and thread (in the colors of your bridal and attendant gowns)

☐ Safety pins

☐ Iron and ironing board (if none are available at church or ceremony site)

☐ Makeup kit (for light touch ups)

☐ Hand mirror and makeup mirrors

☐ Kleenex

☐ Smock or towels to protect dresses from last-minute makeup touch-ups

☐ Curling iron or flatenning iron

☐ Bobbie pins and combs to anchor veils and headpieces

☐ Hair spray

☐ Deodorant or antiperspirant

☐ Dress shields

☐ A shower cap to protect your hair when putting on the gown

☐ Extra nylons in the appropriate colors

☐ Extra socks for groomsmen and ushers (someone is bound to forget)

☐ Toys to keep flower girls and ring bearers busy in a quiet way

☐ Smocks or old t-shirts for flower girls and ring bearers to wear over their wedding attire until it's time for the photos or ceremony (kids will get dirty!)

☐ Masking tape (for last-minute fix-up jobs on decorations)

☐ Scotch tape for taping cards to gifts so they don't fall off

☐ Lightweight wire (for last-minute repairs on decorations)

©Paul Rich

17

☐ Super glue

☐ Breath freshener and perfume

☐ Aspirin

☐ Refreshments (pop, ice tea, juice... everyone is bound to get thirsty)

☐ Straws (never drink directly from a glass or can; you will undoubtedly spill)

☐ A hand-held fan for those hot summer months

Put all your supplies for your "Wedding Day Survival Kit" into a carryall bag and put it next to the things that are going to the church. You'll be glad you have it!

ONE FINAL TIP

Find out whether your ceremony site has a stool that you can use in the dressing room. If not, bring one with you. You'll get tired of standing after you've dressed in your gown. If you sit in a chair, you'll wrinkle your gown. This is where the stool comes in handy! Drape your gown skirt and train over the stool, then sit; no wrinkles!

Notes

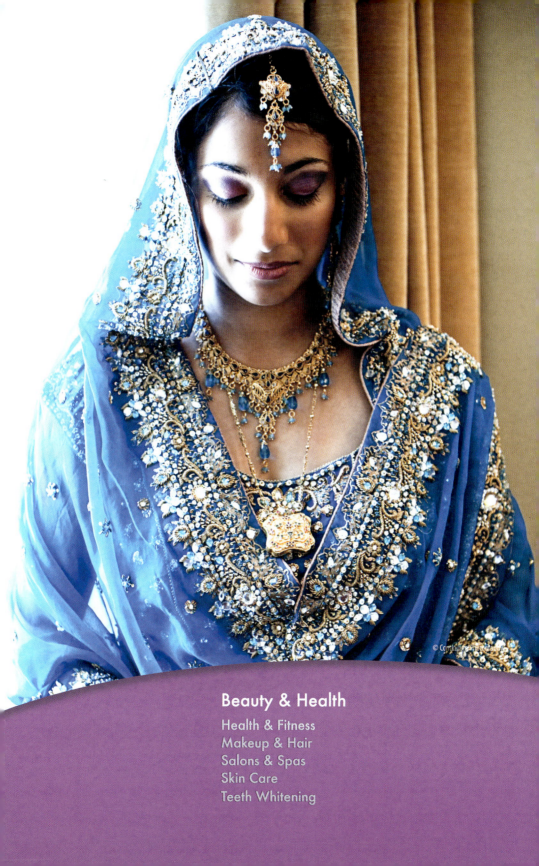

Beauty & Health

**the center for
medical weight loss**

11900 SW Greenburg Road
Tigard, Oregon 97223
p. 503.LOSE.NOW
e. Colly@swfamilyphysicians.com
www.swfamilyphysicians.com

The Diet with a Degree of Difference – a Medical Degree

Not only for your special day, but for a long, healthy and vibrant life, let us help you reach your desired body weight goal.

The Center for Medical Weight Loss is located at SW Family Physicians in Tigard, Oregon. Our team of providers, led by Dr. Cynthia Gulick, DO offer patients a proven, long-term weight-loss program managed with the full support of certified medical professionals.

Whether you are suffering from health issues that are worsened by excess weight, or merely looking to lose 10-20 pounds to fit into that dream wedding dress. You will receive a full Body Composition Analysis and a detailed report outlining the percentage of fat, muscle and water that you have in your body. Helping you lose only fat while maintaining muscle is an integral part of our program here at the Center for Medical Weight Loss and it protects against your metabolism going down from dieting, so you won't regain the weight. The program teaches patients how to maintain their weight-loss safely and permanently.

Our Center uses the latest techniques and medical research, and has access to high quality nutritional products and FDA-approved weight-loss medications that are available only by prescription.

We take great pride in the success of our program and look forward to assisting you with your weight loss goals.

Contact
The Center for Medical Weight Loss at Southwest Family Physicians

What Our Patients Say:

"I just got my wedding pictures and was thrilled with them! Losing weight through Dr. Gulick gave me the confidence to get married and plan a wonderful wedding."
– C.B.

"I have lost 50 pounds and have kept the weight off. The plan was easy and the accountability to the doctor kept me on track."
– P.W.

21

BRIDAL SPECIAL

Clinically proven to work. Take advantage of special packages and spend less per day than the average person spends on food. 10% for all Brides, Grooms and your entire immediate wedding party!

Bravo! Member Since 2006

Medically Proven

Fast

Effective

Safe

Permanent

therapy
state of the art wellness care

630 B Avenue Suite 201
Lake Oswego, Oregon 97034
p. 503.305.6135
f. 503.305.6137
e. info@therapy-lakeoswego.com
www.therapy-lakeoswego.com

22

Therapy Presents...A Healthy Way to Lose Weight & Start Married Life a New You!

Are you confused about all the weight loss plans out there?

Are you frustrated because no matter what you do, the fat won't go away?

Are you looking for a weight loss program that offers quick results and builds healthy habits for life?

Does that sound too good to be true? It's Not!!!

This program has been utilized effectively in weight loss clinics and hospitals throughout Europe for over 40 years. The research backs it up, this is the real deal. It kick starts weight loss by accessing stubborn fat stores that sometimes can't even be accessed by diet and exercise! The weight stays off, even after your program, because this is the only weight loss program that trains your body to maintain your new weight, instead of going back to the weight it was maintaining before. If you've been thinking about finally losing that weight, this program is for you! Call today for a consultation to find out more – mention the Bravo! Wedding Guide for special offers, including FREE SESSIONS in our Far-Infrared Sauna sessions. Burn 700 calories an hour—as seen on Oprah!

Contact

Dr. Kevin Misenheimer
Chiropractic Physician

Price

Starts at just $549 for basic program

You can lose 30 pounds in 30 days and:

- Eliminates stubborn fat - forever!

- Detoxifies your body so you can process fat normally again

- Resets your metabolism, erasing years of damage from yo-yo dieting

- Naturally decreases your appetite to normal levels & eliminates food cravings

- Trains your body to naturally maintain your new weight

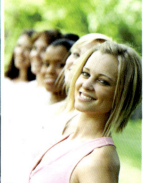

Bravo! Member Since 2008

77

1100 NW Glisan
Portland, Oregon 97209
p. 503.223.7331
www.seventyseven.us

About 77 Salon

77 offers the best bridal hair in the Northwest. Our staff will make you look your best for your special day. Whether it is the traditional look, or something with a more unique edge, we have the stylist for you. Our team of bridal experts have done numerous on-site weddings, bridal photoshoots and bridal fashion shows as well. Wedding day satisfaction is guaranteed.

Esthetic Services

Our estheticians offer a variety of facial and skincare services. Please visit our website for a full menu of waxing and facial services. If relaxation and beautification is what you need, you have found the place!

23

WHAT'S NEW

Please go to our website for a complete menu of services and prices
www.seventyseven.us

Bravo! Member Since 2005

Chris Wildschut
STYLIST

24

Beautiful and Distinctive Hair and Make-up

Would you like a fairy-godmother to pamper you on your wedding day or special event? Relax and let me do my magic! Enjoy the comfort and soothing personal attention which will enable you to feel, look and radiate your most elegant self on this memorable occasion.

Expertise and Versatility

I bring with me over 25 years of professional experience in national and international film, print and commercial video, providing hair styling and make-up for top models, actors and many celebrities.

Whatever your special wishes are... I can help them materialize into timeless visuals and the fondest of memories.

Contact
Chris Wildschut

p. 503.647.2688
f. 503.647.2688
pager 503.301.6486

Price
Varies on service, please call for customized quote

Services Include...
- On-site make-up, hair & styling for the bride & entire wedding party, including mothers & kids
- Complimentary consultation
- Specializing in long lasting photo friendly make-up and personalized hairstyles
- Optional make-up & hair trial run (bridal only)
- Styling & touch-ups for candid & professional photo sessions
- References provided

Remembrance Photography

Bravo! Member Since 2002

Event Cosmetics

© David Barss

About Event Cosmetics

Event Cosmetics is born from the passion of bringing out the most beautiful you. We offer a range of wedding services, both on location and in our studios to suit every need and wedding size. Our professionals are skillfully trained in makeup application, cosmetics and styling to give you an immaculate look from head to toe on your memorable day—when anything less than flawless is NOT an option. Your wedding day is one of the most definitive moments in your lifetime—Event Cosmetics can make it truly unforgettable.

At Event Cosmetics the Event Is You!

Event Cosmetics is founded by nationally-acclaimed makeup artist Katherine Sealy. With over 20 years experience as a makeup artist to celebrity clients and a corporate beauty educator, Katherine and her team of professionals have rapidly become Portland's "Must Have" beauty team for weddings and special events. The winner of Oregon Bride's Best of 2007 and 2009, and a founding member of the award winning Bridal Loft Group, Event Cosmetics prides themselves on being the best in the business.

With a full-time bridal beauty and special events coordinator on staff, Event Cosmetics has repeatedly become the city's favorite make up team not only for their warm, personalized service but for their expertise in creating flawless skin, impeccable eyebrows and long natural lashes. Katherine has become a leader in the cosmetics industry by developing her own product line and pioneering Custom Blend Makeup—a line that creates gorgeous coverage for all skin tones. Skilled in classic, cultural, vintage and avant-garde applications, Katherine and her team can achieve the perfect look for any occasion.

Contact

Bridal Beauty & Special Events Coordinator

Bridal Loft
2808 ML King Boulevard, Suite 3
Portland, Oregon 97212

p. 503.233.9076
p. 503.788.5280

e. beauty@eventcosmetics.com

www.eventcosmetics.com

Price

Quotes available with complimentary consultation

Quick Facts

- Over 20 years of experience
- Licensed estheticians, key & assistant artists
- In studio & On-site wedding day service
- Specializes in exclusive airbrush system, tattoo coverage, lash extensions & paramedical & pure mineral cosmetic products
- Makeup lessons for small & large bridal parties
- Featured makeup artist in Portland Bride & Groom

COMPLIMENTARY CONSULTATION

Call to schedule your complimentary consultation at our NE location or our new Downtown location at 503.233.9076.

25

OREGON BRIDE MAGAZINE BEST of 2007

OREGON BRIDE MAGAZINE BEST of 2009

Bravo! Member Since 2007

About Gypsyana Make-Up & Hair Services

Your wedding day is your day. You want to look your best in your wedding photos, but not like a different person. Let Tammy help to make this a lovely memory that lasts your lifetime. During a free consultation, she will take all your desires into consideration when planning your special day. Feel confident with her 20 years of experience with make-up and hair styling, NYC, film, video, print and runway.

Gypsyana Comes To You!

Don't run around to several locations the morning of your wedding day! Let Tammy come to you, where you're most comfortable. She can arrange for her team of trained professional stylists to assist if you have a large group.

Bridal Specials

Bridal clients receive 15% discount off their entire styling services when combined with a Wedding Photography booking with MistyBay Photography (Partner Company). Please see Pg. 289 for MistyBay ad.

Please visit Gypsyana's web site at:
www.gypsyana.com

Contact

Tammy Brant

515 Saltzman Road, #721
Portland, Oregon 97229

p. 503.810.8035

www.gypsyana.com

Price

Please call for price quotes

Services Include

- Make-up & Hair styling on location
- Free consultation
- Make-up & Hair trial run available
- Hair extensions & Fake eye lashes
- Reasonable package prices
- Assistance available for large groups
- Photography packages with Make-up and Hair included
- A soothing personality for that big day

See page 289 for
MistyBay Photography

Bravo! Member Since 2001

"Relax, Enjoy your Day!
Let us sculpt your hair into
A work of Art"

Deborah and her team of stylists are true "Hair Artists!" With 19 years of experience, they are exceptional at combining your ideas and their creativity to design a look that is right for you. Let "I Do" Artistic Hair Designs enhance your natural beauty to create confidence and peace of mind. With a consultation, you can explore different styles, from elegant or classic to contemporary.

- On-site, at your home or in the salon hairstyling
- Eliminate stress getting to and from the salon
- Consultation offered to explore different styles
- Make up artist available upon request
- Assistants available for large parties
- Pre-wedding salon services if desired

Let your Special Day be relaxed and enjoyable. No more stress trying to get to and from the salon. Let us bring our expertise and the salon to you.

Contact
Deborah Wright

p. 503.250.0871

e. idoweddinghair@gmail.com

www.portlandweddinghair.com

Price
Please call for pricing

Quick Facts
- Visit us at the Portland Bridal Show
- On-site hair & make-up services
- Extensive experience in runway, video & photo shoots
- A consultation to explore different bridal styles

27

WHAT'S NEW

For more information check our web site at portlandweddinghair.com

Bravo! Member Since 2000

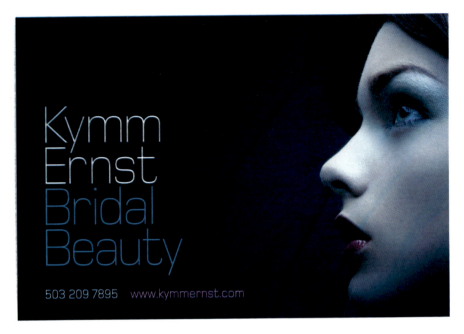

Kymm
Ernst
Bridal
Beauty

503 209 7895   www.kymmernst.com

Be Your Most Beautiful On Your Wedding Day.

Kymm has more than 21 years of experience on two continents styling for print and commercial advertising, having been signed by two of the world's most prestigious hair, makeup and wardrobe agencies. Allow an internationally recognized artist of this caliber to create your elegant and timeless look.

As a respected member of the Fashion Industry, Kymm's experience will be a part of your Big Day, no matter where it happens to be. Custom blended make-up is her speciality – she'll even provide you with a container of your signature lip color for touch-ups.

Contact
Kymm Ernst

p. 503.209.7895

e. kymm@kymmernst.com

www.kymmernst.com

Price
Packages starting at $250

Quick Facts
- Internationally recognized make-up artist

- Specializes in custom blended make-up

- Exclusive appointments available

- On-site make-up application, day of the wedding

- Eyelash extensions

YOUR BIG DAY

Your look is the focal point of your Wedding Day. Make it be the BEST it can be.

Call for an exclusive appointment:
503.209.7895

Bravo! Member Since 2006

About Portland Spa & Boutique

Portland Spa and boutique proudly introduces a new spa philosophy to Portland. A philosophy centered on service, convenience and solution-based treatments. A philosophy grounded in honesty and a desire to improve the lives of our clients in any way we are able. A philosophy of offering only the finest products and technologies without compromise.

What's New?

Organic Airbrush Tanning! Get your perfect bronze all year long! Portland's ONLY all natural, organic option to tanning! Custom airbrush tanning is perfect for all skin types and shades.

About Pink & White Nails

Our mission is to be the best Pink & White nail salon in the greater NW. Our goal is to offer the best quality, customer service and a clean environment. Our professional employees are great communicators. We will treat your nail needs as our personal responsibility. You will get exactly what you want, every visit. We encourage feedback and look forward to building a loyal relationship with each client.

What's New?

Featuring Creative Nail Design's newest colors & effects!

Bravo! Member Since 2008

Portland Spa & Boutique
Danielle Van Auken-Bussard

p. 503.222.0105
f. 503.222.0134
e. info@portlandspa.net
www.portlandspa.net

Quick Facts
- Voted best spa, best massage & best facial by Citysearch
- Complimentary valet parking
- Massage, facials, body treatments, pedicures, manicures, skin rejuvenation, body sculpting & more!
- Complimentry tea, wine & spa water to enjoy in our beautiful relaxation room

Pink & White Nails
Danielle Van Auken-Bussard

p. 503.222.2427
e. info@pinkandwhitenails.com
www.pinkandwhitenails.com

Price
$25–60

Quick Facts
- Voted Best Salon in Portland by Portland Picks for 2008
- Natural Nails, Acrylics, Gels. Bridal Parties, Bachelorette Parties, Birthday Parties, Tiny Toes Parties & More!

29

McMENAMINS EDGEFIELD

2126 SW Halsey Street
Troutdale, Oregon 97060
p. 503.665.1357
e. edspa@mcmenamins.com
www.mcmenamins.com

About Ruby's Spa

Our full-service spa offers an elegant array of luxurious treatments for brides-to-be, their partners, friends, family and guests! Try a Sun & Moon Facial so that your skin is clean and glowing. Or perhaps a "SpellBound" Aroma Massage to ease away stress and tension so you can enjoy your big day. Or have your hair and make-up done so you look perfect in your event photographs. Full bridal packages, combining an assortment of treatments and services, are also available for you and your guests. Don't forget your swimsuits to take a dip in our gently heated, saltwater soaking pool, perhaps while you indulge in a glass of wine or a pot of tea. Guestrooms at Edgefield are also available; book a girls' weekend for your entire bridal party! See mcmenamins.com for details.

About McMenamins

McMenamins Edgefield is a historic 1911 hotel surrounded by spectacular gardens and landscaping. Included onsite along with Ruby's Spa are a winery, brewery, distillery, movie theater, gift shop, two par-3 golf courses and more. Edgefield guests enjoy live music, wine tasting, recent-run films in the theater and beyond. The property is 20 minutes east of downtown Portland and only 15 minutes from Portland International Airport.

Contact
Spa Manager

Price
Depending on the treatment or package

Quick Facts
- Located at historic Edgefield

- Massage, facials, manicures, pedicures, make-up, hair styling & more

- Wedding packages available

- Services available for individuals, couples & small groups

- Complimentary use of the heated saltwater soaking pool

- Restaurants, golf course, pub & small bars onsite

Bravo! Member Since 1991

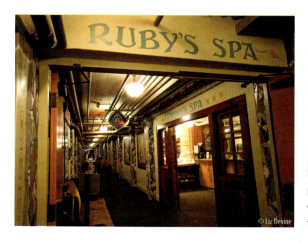

3505 Pacific Avenue
Forest Grove, Oregon 97116
p. 503.992.3406
e. glspa1@gl.mcmenamin.com
www.mcmenamins.com

About Ruby's Spa

You and your friends and family will enjoy a relaxing day at Ruby's Spa, located in the Grand Lodge. Arrange for a wonderfully luxurious massage to ease away any lingering wedding-planning tension or revel in a heated foot bath with friends as you enjoy a bottle of wine. Let the calming atmosphere inspire you during your treatment before heading outdoors to the soaking pool, bubbling with gently heated saltwater. Stay as long as you'd like. Afterwards, gather with friends and family in either of the hotel's restaurants for a meal or perhaps for cocktails in one of the small bars. Guestrooms are also available; see mcmenamins.com for reservations, photos and more.

About McMenamins Grand Lodge

This elegant 1922 Masonic Lodge-turned-hotel welcomes you to relax in cozy guestrooms, indulge in treatments at Ruby's Spa or take a stroll around the beautifully landscaped grounds. You will also enjoy the 10-hole disc golf course, movie theater, soaking pool, Yardhouse Pub and much more! See mcmenamins.com for additional information.

Contact
Spa Manager

Price
From $45 to $200+, depending on the treatment or package

Quick Facts
- Located at the historic Grand Lodge hotel
- Massage, facials & foot baths
- Services available for individuals, couples & small groups
- Complimentary use of the heated saltwater soaking pool
- Restaurants, wine bar, guestrooms & other small bars onsite

31

Bravo! Member Since 1991

SALON NYLA

THE DAY SPA

AVEDA

327 SW Pine Street
Portland, Oregon 97204
p. 503.228.0389
www.salonnyla.com

About Salon Nyla The Day Spa

At Salon Nyla The Day Spa we are committed to providing outstanding customer service. Our philosophy is to pursue advanced levels of education, training and teamwork to create a relaxed and serene environment. As an Aveda concept salon we are also dedicated to environmental concerns and community service.

32

Bridal Services

Special requests such as food, beverage and amenities can be added to any package.

Customize a package to fit your individual needs.

Bride Package

Wedding consultation (style and makeup) special day style, makeup and spa, manicure, spa pedicure

Groom Package

Haircut and style, spa manicure, men's deep cleansing treatment, one hour massage

Price

Depending on services

Salon Services

- Complete hair care
- Aromatherapy
- Vichy shower
- Bridal packages
- Massage therapy
- Spa manicure & pedicure
- Gift certificates
- Aveda retail center
- Esthetics: facial, skin care, makeup, waxing
- Body Treatments: bodywraps, saltglow, body polish, body waxing
- We are open seven days a week

YOUR WEDDING DAY

It is one of the most important days in your life. In the course of planning your wedding, don't forget one of the most important details...YOU! You deserve to be the most luxurious gift of all. After all, it is your day. Make sure you enjoy it, stress free.

Bravo! Member Since 2002

Call today! (503) 244-7717

SOLEIL
MEDICAL & BEAUTY SPA

7887 SW Capitol Hwy
www.SoleilMedicalSpa.com
Open Tues-Sat

Experience Portland's Finest Medical Spa... Soleil Medical & Beauty Spa

We invite you to experience the extraordinary difference of Soleil Medical Spa. We pride ourselves on providing advanced skin rejuvenation treatments & utilizing the most advanced lasers & cosmetic fillers, which our talented team of professionals can use to rejuvenate your youthful appearance.

Dr. Kathleen Myers MD
Board Certified Physician

Bridal Specials

- ZERONA Body Slimming Laser Treatment
  – Only $1,999 (Regularly $3,000)

- Laser Hair Removal
  – 40% OFF (6 or more treatment series)

- Soleil Collagen Signature Facial with Microdermabrasion & LED Treatment
  – Only $100 ($240 value)

- $250 OFF Any Laser Skin Rejuvenation Packages (3 or more treatments)

Contact
Soleil Medical Spa

7887 SW Capitol Highway
Portland, Oregon 97219

p. 503.244.7717
f. 503.244.8017

e. info@SoleilMedicalSpa.com
www.SoleilMedicalSpa.com

33

Price
$15–$3,000

Complimentary
Consultations

Services
- Clients coming from all over the west coast

- Threading available for clients that are allergic/sensitive to wax

- Offering ZERONA Body slimming treatments

WHAT'S NEW
We're excited to announce ZERONA Body Slimming at Soleil Medical Spa.
Lose up to 9 inches – in two weeks, effortlessly.

No pain, No surgery, No injections, No downtime!

Just 6 treatments in 2 week for only $1,999 ($1000 savings).

Drop 2 or more pant sizes, or up to 9 inches

Lose Up To 9 Inches in only 2 weeks.

ZERONA
Non Invasive Body Slimming

American Laser Centers
Hair Removal & Skin Rejuvenation

34

About American Laser Centers

American Laser Centers is the nation's leading provider of aesthetic services, offering Laser Hair Removal, Skin Rejuvenation, Skin Tightening, Since 2001, we have performed over 4 million treatments in our more than 225 clinics across the country.

We are committed to offering the newest and most effective treatment technologies to deliver the safest and fastest results. With a dedicated medical advisory team that is continuously exploring new technologies, we're constantly evaluating new therapies and procedures to ensure the best results and best value for our clients. See for yourself how we can help you look and feel your best!

Contact

Tina Viall
American Laser Centers

8625 SW Cascade Avenue
Beaverton, Oregon 97008

p. 503.227.2000
f. 503.227.2004
e. portland@americanlaser.com
www.americanlaser.com

Services
- Laser Hair Removal
- Laser Facial Hair Removal
- Microdermabrasion
- Skin Rejuvenation
- Skin Tightening

On your big day, everything should be perfect...
Especially You.

BRIDAL SPECIAL

Mention this ad and receive a 30% discount!

About Midori Lashes & Skin Care

If you're worried you'll cry at the ceremony and be self-consciously dabbing the mascara out of your eyes all night, consider lash extensions.

Midori knows the importance of looking your best on your very special day and she is here to help you look flawless when all eyes and cameras will be on you! We know how stressful it is to plan for an entire wedding and we want to make it easier for you when it comes to beauty!

Brides have no fear, these lashes will never smear!

For those of us who hate the clumped and unnatural look of mascara, lash extensions are the cure! During the big wedding day tears (of happiness) and honeymoon dips, maintaining beautiful long lashes is no longer a problem.

Contact
Midori DeBow

4839 NE ML King Boulevard
Suite 201
Portland, Oregon 97212

p. 503.282.2777
f. 503.282.2777

e. midorilashes@gmail.com

www.midori-lashes.com

Price
Varies on service
Lash extensions full-set $150
Bridal facial: $45 +
Bridal back facial: $45 +

Quick Facts
- Award winning professional aesthetician.

- 15 years of experience.

- Specializing in Eyelash extensions / Eyelash perm / Waxing / Skin care.

- Complimentary consultation (Sample eyelash extensions included)

- Language: Japanese / English

- Hours: Wed – Mon 9am – 8pm Tue – closed

35

Call today! (503) 244-7717

SOLEIL
MEDICAL & BEAUTY SPA

7887 SW Capitol Hwy
www.SoleilMedicalSpa.com
Open Tues-Sat

36

Experience Portland's Finest Medical Spa…
Soleil Medical & Beauty Spa

We invite you to experience the extraordinary difference of Soleil Medical Spa. We pride ourselves on providing advanced skin rejuvenation treatments & utilizing the most advanced lasers & cosmetic fillers, which our talented team of professionals can use to rejuvenate your youthful appearance.

Dr. Kathleen Myers MD
Board Certified Physician

Bridal Specials

- ZERONA Body Slimming Laser Treatment
  – Only $1,999 (Regularly $3,000)

- Laser Hair Removal
  – 40% OFF (6 or more treatment series)

- Soleil Collagen Signature Facial with Microdermabrasion & LED Treatment
  – Only $100 ($240 value)

- $250 OFF Any Laser Skin Rejuvenation Packages (3 or more treatments)

Lose Up To 9 Inches
in only 2 weeks.

Contact
Soleil Medical Spa

7887 SW Capitol Highway
Portland, Oregon 97219

p. 503.244.7717
f. 503.244.8017

e. info@SoleilMedicalSpa.com
www.SoleilMedicalSpa.com

Price
$15 – $3,000

Complimentary
Consultations

Services

- Clients coming from all over the west coast

- Threading available for clients that are allergic/ sensitive to wax

- Offering ZERONA Body slimming treatments

WHAT'S NEW

We're excited to announce ZERONA Body Slimming at Soleil Medical Spa.
Lose up to 9 inches – in two weeks, effortlessly.

No pain, No surgery, No injections, No downtime!

Just 6 treatments in 2 week for only $1,999 ($1000 savings).

Drop 2 or more pant sizes, or up to 9 inches

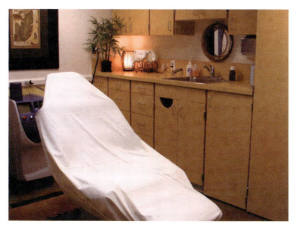

11900 SW Greenburg Road
Tigard, Oregon 97223
p. 503.597.1226
e. medispasfp@yahoo.com
www.swfamilyphysicians.com

About Medi Spa

Southwest Family Physicians is celebrating our 20th anniversary! We are proud to offer our Medi Spa services to help take care of all your skincare concerns. Our knowledgeable combination of both esthetician and physician staff can provide a variety of sevices that are safe, affordable and effective.

We offer the most advanced laser and anti-aging skin treatments to correct existing damage and prevent further damage. With Medi Spa treatments you can make sure you have no unwanted acne, rosasea, or hair for your wedding day. Commonly treated areas are lip, chin, underarms, bikini, and legs.

Dr. Michele Adamcak, D.O. is board certified in Family Practice. She is a certified injector in both Botox and Dermal Fillers. Look relaxed and youthful, not only for your wedding day but for a more relaxed and youthful 'happily ever after'. Call today for your free consultation or Botox appointment.

Check out our website for monthly specials and fun facts.
www.swfamilyphysicians.com

Contact
Southwest Family Physicians
Medi Spa

Price
Varies by service; call for our competitive prices and your free consultation about our services.

Medi Spa Services
- Laser hair removal
- Skin rejuvenation
- Vein therapy/rosacea
- Age & sun spot removal
- Non-surgical skin tightening
- Microdermabrasion
- Facials
- Chemical peels
- Waxing
- Home Care Products
- Clarisonic
- Latisse
- Revitalash

37

BOTOX & DERMAL FILLERS

A beautiful face for a relaxed and youthful you!
Dr. Michele Adamcak

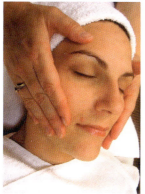

Bravo! Member Since 2006

An Ageless Smile

I am writing this with the recent wedding of my only child, my son, fresh in my mind! I surprised myself by how much I stressed out over every little detail. I even got three pedicures over a three week period to find the perfect toe color! My mother and my sister went through the same angst with hair, clothes, make-up, jewelry, you name it!

Attractive healthy smiles are always important, but never more important than on your wedding day or the wedding day of a loved one. The photographs will be enjoyed for decades to come, by family members, friends and thanks to the digital age, even complete strangers.

After months of preparation, the wedding is over in hours but your investment in your smile will continue to enhance your life and later the pictures you have taken with your grandkids!

Enjoy the moment,

Dr. Sue Wendling

Contact

karen@drwendling.com

340 Oswego Pointe Drive Suite 208
Lake Oswego, Oregon 97034

Testimonials

"When you changed my teeth, you changed my life! I'm so glad to have been one of your transformations. A lovely smile is the best gift a person can give to themselves (and to those being smiled at). Thanks for your artist's eye and great skill."

– Karen P.

"Every other dentist I saw for my bite problem said it could only be fixed with a combination of traditional braces and jaw surgery! Dr. Wendling performed a miracle with Invisalign only, I am thrilled with the result."

– Tiffany

SERVICES

Porcelain Veneers

Invisalign

Zoom Whitening

Night Guards

Implant Crowns

Bridges

Sedation

It's Your Day To Smile!

zehtab
FAMILY DENTISTRY

470 Sixth Avenue
Lake Oswego, Oregon 97034
p. 503.636.4324
f. 503.635.6978
e. administrator@zehtabdentistry.com
www.zehtabdentistry.com

About Zehtab Family Dentistry

Planning the big day? You've chosen the venue, selected your dress, decided on the guest list and thought about the food, flowers and the photographer. But have you considered whether the most important day of your life is really going to capture you looking at your very best in those smiling photographs?

Research has shown that one of the first things people notice when they meet someone new is their smile. Teeth Whitening has become an accessible and relatively easy way to instantly improve appearance, create a positive first impression and achieve a more youthful and radiant appearance.

Teeth can become discolored over a period of time. Discoloration can be caused by several factors including aging, smoking, consumption of staining foods and beverages, staining caused by medication and hereditary factors.

Safe and effective methods of achieving a whiter, brighter smile are now readily available.

We are able to offer a range of teeth whitening options to help enhance, improve and brighten your smile.

Whether it's tooth whitening or "smile design", your smile can transform your wedding photographs into a memory you will treasure with pride for a lifetime. After all, who wants a dress that's whiter than their teeth on their wedding day!

Please call about our specials for brides-to-be.

Contact
Hamid Zehtab DMD
or Dani

Testimonials
"Honestly, I continue to be more and more impressed with each visit and I started with a very high opinion of Dr. Zehtab and his practice to begin with."
– John

"You are all always the epitome of competence and professionalism along with the friendliness and kindness that you show me. You know I love all of you. Thank you for always taking care of me, in more ways than one."
– Debbie

"Linda and I always feel welcome and well taken care of at Dr. Zehtab's office... we get good care, excellent explanations and friendly people."
– Steve S

WHAT'S NEW
Invisalign
Zoom - Office whitening
Lumineers - No Prep Veneers
Laser
Sedation dentistry

39

Bravo! Member Since 2008

Helpful Hint

Looking Your Best

EAT RIGHT & GET ENOUGH SLEEP

It gets very hectic prior to the wedding with all the planning and parties. Be sure to take care of yourself! You'll need every ounce of energy. Eat right and get enough sleep to look your very best on this special day.

PAMPER YOURSELF

A couple of weeks before the wedding, take time to pamper yourself. To relieve tension and stress, schedule a massage, facial, body treatment, pedicure, manicure, foot therapy, eye lash and brow tinting, eye lash extensions, teeth whitening, and more. Some treatments might take a while to complete, such as laser body treatments or teeth whitening, so be sure and check with the spa or salon where you are receiving your treatment.

A facial is wonderful for your skin, but be sure to allow some time for your face to benefit from it. Avoid using unfamiliar products too close to the wedding in case your skin has an allergic reaction. Don't get your lip waxed less than three days before the big day - allow plenty of time for your skin to heal in case a skin reaction comes up.

HAIR CONSULTATION

When you have selected your headpiece, make an appointment for a consultation with your hairstylist. This allows time to experiment with different hairstyles that complement your face and work well with the headpiece. This way there are no "surprise" hairstyles the morning of your wedding. You and your hairdresser should agree on the style and look well in advance. Also make sure your hairstyle will look nice even when you take off the headpiece.

MAKEUP CONSULTATION

A makeup consultation can help you apply makeup in a natural and flattering way to highlight your features. The photographer may ask for a heavier application for the photos. Ask the consultant how to obtain the best look without overdoing it. Check out make-up artists who will come to you on the day of the wedding to apply your make-up, making it very convenient when you have so many other things to worry about on your wedding day.

BRIDESMAID LUNCH & MANICURE

A fun idea is to take your bridesmaids to lunch and then treat them to a manicure. This usually takes place a day or two before, or the morning of the wedding. For parties of three or more it is best to schedule an appointment at least three months in advance.

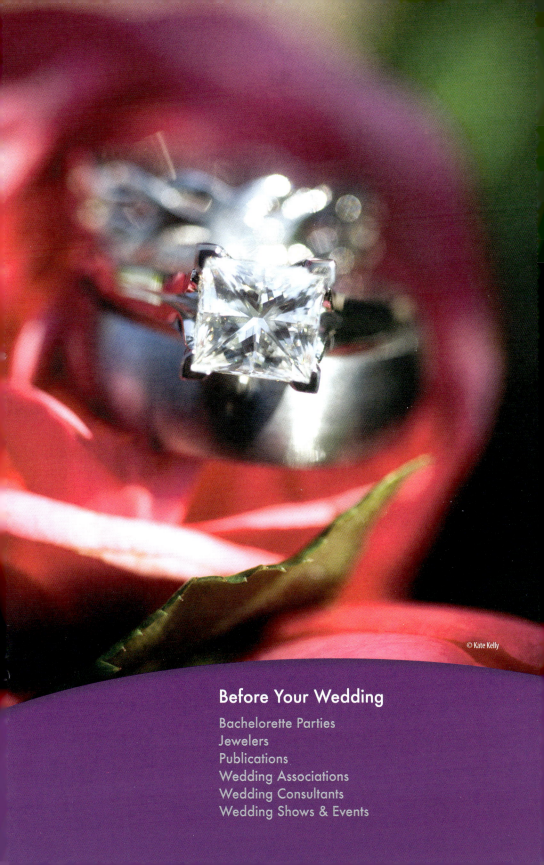

© Kate Kelly

Before Your Wedding

The Original

PORTLAND BRIDAL SHOW

Oregon's Premier Wedding Event

You are invited...

JANUARY 16 & 17

PLAN YOUR WEDDING WITH OVER 150 WEDDING RELATED EXHIBITORS

EXQUISITE BRIDAL FASHION SHOWS DAILY

Skamania Lodge

HONEYMOON GETAWAYS
GIVEN AWAY AT EACH SHOW

ADMISSION DISCOUNT COUPONS
AVAILABLE ONLINE OR AT
OUR EXHIBITORS

OREGON CONVENTION CENTER

Pre-register online,
receive valuable gifts:
portlandbridalshow.com
Info: 503-274-6027

No strollers or cameras allowed.

HURRY!
Shows sell-out early! Advance tickets at Safeway TicketsWest guarantee admission.

Tea is one of life's comforts that soothes the soul and warms the heart...

La Tea Da! If you are looking for a unique idea for a Bridal or Baby Shower, Afternoon Tea is a great choice. The Tea Room is a delightful place to spend time with family and friends to celebrate the milestones of your life. There is nothing more relaxing than a steaming pot of tea, accompanied by finger sandwiches, scones with jam and cream and an assortment of wonderful cookies and cakes.

Our Tea Room even has dress-up gowns and accessories that you can choose to use, if you wish. Take a group photo after spending some time "glamming" yourselves up!

The Doll House Tea Room is perfect for:

- Children's Parties
- Anniversaries
- Bridal Showers
- Graduation Parties
- Pampering Friends
- Birthdays
- Baby Showers
- Girls' Nights
- Celebrations
- Book Clubs

The Doll House Tea Room has been offering Fabulous Tea Parties for special celebrations since October 2000. Most often it is a birthday party but we have also done Fantasy Tea Parties for Brownies, Girl Scouts, granddaughters, etc. We look forward to seeing you!

The Doll House Tea Room

3223 SE Risley Avenue
Milwaukie, Oregon 97267

p. 503.653.6809
e. info@DollhouseTeaRoom.com
www.DollHouseTeaRoom.com

Quick Facts

- Minimum charge of $300 for up to 8 party participants plus $20 for each additional to a maximum of 25.

- Reservations should be made at least 2 weeks in advance, so call with you specific party need.

- A deposit of $100 is required to secure the date and time.

- In all fairness, the reservation will be given to the one who provides the earliest deposit.

- Parties last 2 hours.

43

p. 800.778.6214
p. 503.244.4653
f. 503.244.6558

e. info@premierewinetours.com

www.premierewinetours.com

About Premiere Transportation & Tours

Premiere is a local company with several vehicles that can handle our transportation needs for wedding transportation, guest entertainment, bachelor & bachelorette parties, wine tours, corporate shuttles, shuttle service for conventions, airport drop-offs, sporting events, casino trips, birthdays, and more. We offer one-way transportation, in addition to hourly or day rates.

Special Bravo! discount: book Premiere for your wedding transportation and receive 20% off a Bachelorette Party Wine Tour

Please visit our website to view our fleet and view all of the services offered.

Bravo! Member Since 1995

Contact
Premiere Transportation

Price
Charges vary according to circumstances and time duration.

Services
• Wedding transportation.

• Guest entertainment (wine tour, casino parties).

• Bachelorette / bachelor parties.

44

p. 800.778.6214
p. 503.244.7758
f. 503.244.6558

e. info@premierevalet.com

www.premierevalet.com

Have You Thought About Parking?

Let us do the thinking for you! When planning for your next big event, selecting the right parking service will add a great first impression, as well as smooth, convenient parking accommodations.

Consider the unparalleled level of personalized service and professionalism that Premiere Valet Service has been providing Portland residents and restaurants for more than sixteen years.

With our experience and knowledge, we have the ability to solve any parking problem. All valets are trained, screened and field tested to ensure that you will receive only the finest service available.

Bravo! Member Since 1995

Contact
Private Event Coordinator

Price
Charges vary according to parking circumstances and time duration.

Services
• Parking consulting services

• Lot attendants

• Light security

• Coat check

© Shahn Hughes

Sea to Summit Tours & Adventures

Sea to Summit Tours & Adventures is based out of Portland, Oregon. Sea to Summit specializes in transportation services and outdoor activities for weddings, B-days, bachelor and bachelorette parties.

We offer many activities including white water rafting trips, Oregon wine tours, Portland brewery tours, surfing lessons, sightseeing tours, personalized tours and more. In the winter season, Sea to Summit is Portland's Premier 4x4 Ski & Mountain Shuttle Service, available 7 days a week to all Mt. Hood ski areas.

Sea to Summit's 4x4 vehicles are highly equipped and our guides are knowledgeable and experienced. No matter what weather conditions prevail, Sea to Summit will get your wedding party to the destination of choice, without any worries!

Created, owned and operated by native Portland, Oregonians, est 2001

Simplify...make your reservation with Sea to Summit!

503.286.9333
www.seatosummit.net

Contact
Joshua Blaize

Portland, Oregon
p. 503.286.9333
e. seatosummit@qwest.net

www.seatosummit.net

Specializing In:
- Winery Tours
- Brewery Tours
- White Water Rafting Trips
- Sightseeing Tours
- Personalized Tours
- Ski Shuttles

Clients Include:
- Nordstrom
- Nike
- Adidas
- J.C. Penney
- REI
- Timberline Lodge
- Mt. Hood Meadows
- Intel, etc…

45

carl greve
Jewelry & Timepiece Collections

Downtown Portland - 640 SW Broadway, Portland OR 97205 - 503.223.7121
Bridgeport Village - 7387 SW Bridgeport Road, Tigard OR 97224 - 503.968.2868
info@carlgreve.com   www.carlgreve.com

About Carl Greve Jewelers

Since 1923 , Carl Greve Jewelers has had the pleasure of delighting a variety of brides and bride-to-be's. They recognize that there are as many unique bride personalities as there are unique wedding ring designs. Carl Greve has mastered the art of selecting award winning designers to match with each bride's personal style. Ask any stylish Portlander where their wedding rings are from and you are certain to hear "Carl Greve, of course!"

Carl Greve has two locations, Downtown Portland (on the corner of Broadway and Morrison) and Bridgeport Village. Each location has a bridal department that is meant to give each bride and groom a comfortable and relaxing environment to find the perfect engagement ring or wedding band. They also have an electronic wish list so that future brides-to-be can select their personal favorites, making it that much easier for grooms-to-be to find the perfect ring. Whether your wish list includes an emerald cut 2 carat diamond set in a Michael B. pave setting, or a Hearts on Fire 1 carat set in a platinum band, Carl Greve's bridal experts can assist you in navigating the process from beginning to end.

Some of the bridal designers that Carl Greve carries include: Coge, Furrer-Jacot, Hearts On Fire, Judith Conway, MaeVona, Michael B., Steven Kretchmer, and more.

Please enjoy complimentary valet parking at the Bridgeport Village location and complimentary parking validation at the downtown Portland location.

- Engagement rings
- Wedding bands
- Anniversary rings
- Eternity bands
- Celebration jewelry
- Bridal jewelry

Bravo! Member Since 2006

Contact
Downtown Portland Bridal Specialists: 503.223.7121

Bridgeport Village Bridal Specialists: 503.968.2868

e. info@carlgreve.com

b. www.carlgreve.blogspot.com

www.carlgreve.com

Price
Varies according to bride & groom's budget & preferences.

Please ask about Carl Greve's diamond trade-up program.

Quick Facts
- Carl Greve is a supporter of the United Nation's Kimberly Process which regulates conflict-free diamonds
- All center diamonds that are purchased at Carl Greve are eligible for the diamond trade-up program.
- Over 86 years as Portland's premiere jeweler
- Large, diverse, & creative bridal jewelry collections & wedding bands
- Specializing in the bridal jewelry selection process

SPECIAL FINANCING
Carl Greve offers a special 12-month no-interest financing program.

JUDITH ARNELL JEWELERS

Specialty

Judith Arnell Jewelers specializes in designer platinum jewelry, wedding bands, and engagement rings from antique estate-diamond jewelry to modern, custom-designed platinum wedding sets. We proudly feature the finest designer jewelry including the exclusive Daniel K. collection, Lazare Kaplan Ideal cut diamonds and bridal jewelry, Christopher Designs, The Royal Asscher Collection, Mark Patterson bridal jewelry among others.

Types of Jewelry Sold

Engagement rings, wedding bands, precious and semi-precious stone jewelry, earrings, bracelets, pendants and necklaces, custom–designed and handmade fine jewelry, pearls, cufflinks and studs.

Shapes and Kinds of Stones Available

We specialize in GIA-certified ideal-cut diamonds in all shapes, sizes, and qualities with prices comparable to the internet sites, with an extensive selection of Asscher-cut diamonds. We also carry a wide variety of sapphires, rubies, emeralds and other precious and semi-precious stones.

Custom Design

Designer Judith Arnell has been in the wholesale jewelry business for more than 30 years as a designer and manufacturer of fine jewelry. She will personally work with you to design the perfect, one-of-a-kind piece of jewelry…at a reasonable price! Please stop by our studio to view our work and discuss your jewelry needs in a comfortable atmosphere.

Contact

Judith Arnell Sales Associate

320 NW 10th Avenue
Portland, Oregon

p. 503.227.3437

f. 503.296.2466

e. judith@juditharnell.com

www.juditharnelljewelers.com

Price

$500 to $500,000

Quick Facts

- Couture designer bridal jewelry of the highest quality

- We have the ability to custom–design jewelry to your specifications

- Finest quality of colored gemstones & diamonds with the emphasis on ideal cutting

47

WHAT'S NEW

Now carrying the exclusive Star 129 Diamond. Visit us on the ground floor of the Elizabeth Loft Building on 10th between Everett & Flanders.

Bravo! Member Since 2001

About The Real Mother Goose

The Real Mother Goose is one of the Pacific Northwest's largest fine American craft galleries. A nationally renowned award-winning gallery, The Real Mother Goose represents nearly 1,000 American artists, most of whom are regional. For more than 35 years custom-design has been a specialty. Our on–staff designer is available by appointment. Imagine a year-round arts festival showcasing the Northwest's largest collection of fine art and craft, and you'll begin to understand what it's like to visit The Real Mother Goose.

At your convenience, come in and fill out a registry card with your favorite colors, themes and artists' work. Our creative and knowledgeable staff will gladly answer your questions and help you make choices.

From fanciful and functional tableware, to art glass stemware, unique kitchen accessories, creative lighting, garden accessories, furniture and other home décor, we have all the things you need to furnish your new home. We'll keep your information on file to guide your guests in selecting memorable wedding gifts.

901 SW Yamhill Street
Portland, Oregon 97205
p. 503.223.9510
www.therealmothergoose.com

Contact
Real Mother Goose staff

Price
Varies with selection

Quick Facts
- Nationally renowned, award-winning American craft gallery

- In-house custom jewelry designer with more than 25 years experience

- Hand-crafted, one-of-a-kind fine jewelry retailer

- Traditional to contemporary wedding ring styles in a variety of precious metals, in addition to titanium, damascus & stainless steel

- Loose diamonds & gemstones available

WHAT'S NEW

Visit our larger, remodeled store at the Portland International Airport

Bravo! Member Since 2006

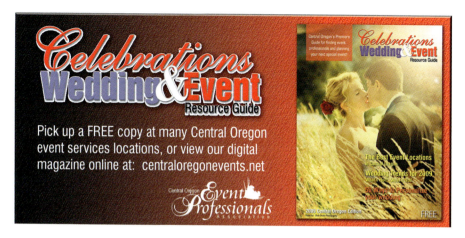

Celebrations Wedding & Event Resource Guide

The most trusted source in wedding and event planning in Central Oregon for 8 years. When it comes to planning your wedding we offer the largest source of event professionals in the Central Oregon area. You'll find everything you need to plan the perfect party in Celebrations Wedding & Event Resource Guide, the official publication of the Central Oregon Event Professionals Association. The magazine is filled with helpful articles, budgeting tips and ideas for every aspect of your special event! This full color resource magazine is sure to become your most valuable planning tool. Call or email us to request a FREE copy of the magazine or pick one up at wedding and event related businesses in Central Oregon.

Website: Central Oregon Events.net

Inside www.centraloregonevents.net you will find the Central Oregon Event Professionals member directory organized by services. All listings are complete with direct website links making this the only interactive resource of wedding and event service providers in Central Oregon. You can also enter the magazine link to view the digital version of the magazine on line for immediate information and inspiration.

The Central Oregon Event Professionals Association

Our association members provide quality services in the Central Oregon area. You will be glad you used our magazine and website as your source to find professional service providers and resources to help make your wedding a success beyond your dreams. Call us for assistance at any stage of your planning process…we call ourselves an association for a reason….it's service that sets us apart. Let us help you find the "perfect" match for your wedding or event.

Bravo! Member Since 2008

Contact

Central Oregon Event Professionals Association

Becky Wilkins, Association Manager

PO Box 3111
Bend, Oregon 97707

p. 541.598.8766

f. 888.899.0349

e. becky@centraloregonevents.net

www.centraloregonevents.net

Price
FREE

Services

- Wedding Apparel
- Event Coordinators
- Photography
- Floral Design
- Catering
- Cakes & Desserts
- Live Music & DJ's
- Event Locations
- Budget Guidelines
- Planning Tips
- Much, much more!

View our digital magazine and vendor web links at:
www.centraloregonevents.net

49

© David Barss

50

OREGON ABC
ASSOCIATION OF BRIDAL CONSULTANTS

Let a professional wedding consultant handle the details and plan your wedding with you. It's your big day. Make certain it turns out perfectly and enjoy your wedding day!

ABCOREGON.COM

Visit our website for upcoming events, a wedding planning directory, and information on hiring wedding professionals in Oregon.

ABC CODE OF ETHICS:

The ABC members agree to:

- Represent each client fairly and honestly; providing all agreed-to services in a timely and cost-efficient manner.
- Establish reasonable and proper fees for services and provide written estimates to each client.
- Use honest, factual advertising.
- Deal with employees and clients fairly, in an unbiased manner.
- Operate an establishment that is a credit to the community.
- Disclose to clients any payments received from suppliers.

Contact

Sue Corning, PBC

p. 503.449.5398

e. sue@purpleirisweddings.com

www.abcoregon.com

ABC MEMBERS INCLUDE:

- Bridal Shops
- Caterers
- Florists & Floral Designers
- Hair & Makeup Artists
- Honeymoon & Travel Specialists
- Ice Sculptures
- Invitation Designers
- Wedding Planners & Consultants
- Jewelers
- Ministers & Officiants
- Musicians
- Photographers
- Publications
- Receptions Sites
- Rental Services
- Videographers

© AJ's Studio

© KKayphoto.com

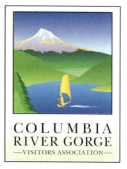

COLUMBIA RIVER GORGE
—VISITORS ASSOCIATION—

p. 800.984.6743
e. info@crgva.org
www.crgva.org

Celebrate the beginning of your journey into married life in the beautiful Columbia River Gorge. The breathtaking environment of the magnificent Columbia River Gorge offers romantic surroundings with spectacular ceremony sites to ensure that your extraordinary day is everything that you imagine.

You will find the ideal setting for picture perfect memories as you are surrounded by the Cascade Mountains, the Columbia River, Mt. Adams, Mt. Hood, lush forests or blossoming fruit trees. You can choose from a cozy bed and breakfast to luxurious mountain resorts for a venue and lodging. Fantastic dining and catering options, Columbia Gorge wines and every other service necessary to make your wedding dreams come true are available in the Gorge.

Visit our website at www.crgva.org to find the perfect wedding location to fit your needs. The Columbia River Gorge, spanning both Oregon and Washington, has it all. Make your day extra special by getting married in one of the most beautiful natural settings in the Pacific Northwest and the world!

Columbia River Gorge Visitors Association:

The Columbia River Gorge Visitors Association is a non-profit organization representing various businesses and organizations, in Oregon and Washington, that provide services and information to visitors throughout the Columbia River Gorge.

For a full list of CRGVA members, visit our website at www.crgva.org

The following categories will assist you in selecting all of the right services for your wedding:

Attractions & Services

Dining

Information Centers

Lodging

Meeting & Weddings

Recreation

51

© Portland Spirit

© Skamania Lodge

wedding network usa

About Wedding Network USA

Wedding Network USA (WNUSA) is a non-profit networking organization focused on industry business owners. The primary purpose and objective of WNUSA is to give wedding professionals a variety of opportunities for professional development through the sharing of business expertise, educational topics and networking.

Brides who chose members of WNUSA to be a part of their special day will know that they have chosen professional vendors who subscribe to a strict Code of Ethics.

Become a Member Today

Try a fresh approach to growing your business and adapting to an ever-changing market. Join today and start enjoying all the benefits of belonging to a national wedding network dedicated to bringing you the latest information affecting our industry, creating an environment of expertise which is readily shared, and forming lasting connections for greater continuity.

Check out our website for upcoming meetings throughout the area. www.weddingnetworkusa.com

Contact

Wedding Network USA
PO Box 1885
Clackamas, Oregon 97015
p. 888.509.6872
e. info@WeddingNetworkUSA.com
www.weddingnetworkusa.com

Chérie Ronning, Founder
& Executive Director
Uncommon Invites

Officers:

- Jennifer Taylor, President
  Taylor'd Events by Jennifer
- Brian Dale, Vice President
  Wave Link Music
- Cindy Rosen, Secretary
  Encore Events
- Linda Barclay, Treasurer
  Barclay Event Rentals

Board Members:

- Peter Barnett
  Premiere Catering
- Molli Barss
  Soireé
- Don Boshears
  Columbia Tower Club
- Donna Hoff
  The Wedding Genies
- Eric Newland
  Hybrid Moon Video
  Productions
- Gayle O'Donnell
  All About Weddings &
  Celebrations

52

© AJ's Studio

© Deyla Huss

Wine Country Wedding Professionals

PO Box 423
McMinnville, Oregon 97128
p. 503.868.9455
e. becky@winecountrywedding
   professionals.com
www.winecountrywedding
professionals.com

Contact
Becky Simpson

Amenities

- Yamhill Valley's best wedding professionals whose first priority is you!

- Price ranges to fit all budgets

- Oregon's most beautiful wedding sites

- The perfect destination wedding location for both you and your guests

Wine Country Wedding Professionals is made up of a group of skilled professionals from every facet of the wedding industry who specialize in you! We believe in providing the very highest quality of service to our brides.

Yamhill Valley is truly extraordinary, one of the most beautiful areas you could ever find. We have wedding venues located at inns, wineries, vineyards, ballrooms, farms, riverbanks, ponds and rustic lodges. With its 80 wineries and 217 vineyards, our valley is often compared to the wine regions of France & Germany.

Yamhill Valley also makes for a great destination wedding location. It has more than 25 inns, hotels and bed & breakfasts; wine-tasting tours; aviation & space museums; hot air balloon rides; nature hikes; golf courses; spa treatments; shopping and more.

Our professionals are the best of the best; it is our desire to help make your wine country wedding something extraordinary that will be talked about and remembered for years to come.

53

© Deyla Huss

An Affair To Remember

2400 Southeast Ankeny Street
Portland, Oregon 97214
p. 503.223.9267
f. 503.223.4746
www.anaffairtoremember.com

About An Affair To Remember

As the Northwest's premiere event planning and design company, we have been participants in some of the area's most creative and compelling wedding events, whether you prefer an intimate, graceful cocktail party or an elegant outdoor tented affair with chandeliers and silk chiffon draping. From exquisite cathedral ceremonies to formal, black-tie hotel ballroom receptions, we make your ideas, dreams and visions a reality. We are not merely wedding consultants – but wedding designers! Creating and designing your fantasy wedding is our mission.

Producing a Truly Memorable Event

In the same studio we later design your wedding day, from the rehearsal to the reception send-off. Together we create your invitation and announcement package, sample reception menu offerings, conduct cake tastings, listen to local and national musician demo tapes, coordinate floral and fantasy decor, script the ceremony, choose a photography ensemble and so on. We coordinate every detail to produce a truly remarkable event.

Contact
Mike Piper

Price
Please call to schedule your no-cost, no-obligation initial consultation

Attention To Detail
- Attention to detail & impeccable organization is what makes the difference between an ordinary event & a truly extraordinary experience
- Let us orchestrate the multitude of details to leave you free to live your dream wedding

CLIENT TESTIMONIAL

"The whole wedding weekend was a glorious success – you did a magnificent job. Everything was just lovely, the couple is married – the families got along – and the mothers are happy!"

– Mrs. Ann Gerache

See page 145 under Florists

Bravo! Member Since 1999

54

About Bella Notte Events

Wedding planning for the stylish girl ... A fun and fresh approach to your big day ... we specialize in beautiful & seamless weddings for the modern bride & groom ... your engagement stress free and your wedding day ... Flawless.

Contact

Cindy Danbom

PO Box 28036
Portland, Oregon 97228

p. 503.620.9656

e. info@bellanotte-events.com

www.bellanotte-events.com

Price Range

Day of Service $1,500 ++,
Partial & Full Planning call
for quote

Quick Facts

- Limit 15–20 weddings a year
- Recommended & published in Daily Candy, The Knot, Splendora, Grace Ormond, Your Wedding Day, Here Comes the guide, Todays Bride, By Recommendation Only
- Available for Travel, locally & International
- Have been in business for 8 years
- Believe you should enjoy planning your event

WHAT'S NEW

New office in Portland! Yes we are here full time, but also still planning in San Francisco and beyond!

© Joseph Milton

•b l u s h•

Bridal Consultation Group

1000 SW Broadway, Suite 1640
Portland, Oregon 97205
Office Hours are by Appointment Only
p. 503.224.7700
e. blush@blushbridalevents.com
www.blushbridalevents.com

Contact
Amy Nuttman

Price
Please call to schedule your complimentary consultation

Quick Facts
- More than 7 years experience in the industry

- Member of the Better Business Bureau & Association of Bridal Consultants

- Flexible Packages available to fit every level of coordination including Month-of to Full Service & everything in between.

- Hourly Consultation available

Here at Blush, it is our mission to provide uncompromising service, unlimited design, and unparalleled results. We believe that there are no limits to our creations. Our abilities to communicate with our clientele are unsurpassed, and we have the energy, stamina, and knowledge needed to succeed in making your most important day a memorable celebration. Your dreams and your ideas are why we are here. With helpful imaginations, we will ensure that your wedding is not only amazing, but also stress free. Let us untangle the details, so you can tie the knot!

"I do not even know where to begin, that is how amazing and flawless Blush Bridal is. They thought of every detail, were always there when we needed them and acted as a perfect liaison between the vendors and ourselves to ensure we did not have to deal with any issues on our big day. Blush went above and beyond their role in making sure our wedding was perfect! I will tell all of my friends about Blush and I hope you decide to use them as well. I highly recommend Blush and I know you will be thrilled with their experience, professionalism and attention to detail. They are 100% amazing!" – **Genny R.**

"If you could clone yourselves, you'd be planning every wedding in Portland!" – **Shelly M.**

© Altura Studio

© Impression Arts

Bravo! Member Since 2005

56

BLUSH BRIDAL
uncompromising service.
unlimited design.
unparalleled results.

© Joseph Milton

Bridal BLISS

17050 SW Pilkington Road
Suite #210 (Inside Anna's Bridal)
Lake Oswego, Oregon 97035
p. 503.804.4901
f. 503.636.1694
www.bridalbliss.com

Finding The Perfect Man Was Hard Enough, Planning The Perfect Wedding Just Got Easier!

Bridal Bliss is Portland's premiere bridal consultation group, and our goal is to make planning your wedding fun. We bring a fresh perspective and work with you and your budget to create innovative events with contemporary style and elegance. We are unique in that we give clients our undivided attention. Bridal Bliss will listen to your needs and ideas, offer creative suggestions, and bring your wedding dreams to life. We create events suited to a couple's unique style—a true expression of the bride and groom.

Save Time & Money

Through our experience in the industry, we have established extensive professional vendor relationships that enable us to produce a top-rate event in every aspect. By continually working with these contacts, special rates are passed on to you.

Planning a wedding should be a blissful time in your life, not one full of anxiety and exhaustion. Whether you are looking for assistance from start to finish or just a little help on the wedding day, Bridal Bliss is here to assist you.

Contact
Nora Sheils

Services & Fees
- Full-service event planning
- Day-of coordination
- Budget development
- Agenda & timeline prep
- Site selection
- Vendor research & selections
- Contract negotiations
- Décor & design
- Invitations & Printing
- Plus many more services customized to perfect your wedding day

57

© Joseph Milton

© Joseph Milton

Bravo! Member Since 1996

Bridal Recognition

OREGON
BRIDE
MAGAZINE
BEST
of
2006
2007
2008

© Garrett Grove Photography

Champagne
WEDDING & EVENT COORDINATION

p. 503.708.1142
p. 503.310.2357
e. info@champagnenw.com
www.champagnenw.com
www.champagnenw.com/blog

58

Champagne Wedding and Event Coordination

Take a moment and close your eyes. Picture the day of your much-awaited celebration unfold: the setting, food, music, attire, lighting, décor…everything as you imagined it would be. You…enjoying the moments that will soon become some of your most cherished memories. Now, open your eyes. Feel like some champagne? You've come to the right place. We might not serve you a glass of champagne, but we will serve you in ways that make you feel fun, happy, and light-hearted about your planning experience.

Champagne is a team of two experienced planners bringing you their creative, stylish approach in a professional and finished package. With Mandi and Rachelle, you can rest assured that your event is in the right hands. Their calm demeanor and attention to details creates the perfect setting for your wedding day to be exactly as dreamed.

Champagne's motto is live, laugh, love, and our team of event planners make it their goal to ensure you do all three while planning for your special day. Not a small feat when organizing such significant and memorable events, but the pleasure is all theirs. The result? You will minimize your stress while maximizing your joy. Now that deserves a toast.

Contact
Rachelle Bell or
Mandi Downs

Price
Please call to schedule a free consultation

Quick Facts
- Details- we love them! Organizing and bringing together the little details is what we thrive on

- Down to the wire? Don't worry, we can accommodate your last minute planning needs

- Packages AND A La Carte services are available to meet your specific needs

- Ask us about our Destination Wedding Package

© James Moes Photography

© Garrett Grove Photography

CHAMPAGNE SPECIAL

Mention that you found us in the Bravo! Wedding Guide and receive 5% off of any package.

CLASS ACT
EVENT COORDINATORS, INC.

Portland: 503.295.7890
Lake Oswego: 503.636.1083
Salem: 503.371.8904
Bend: 541.382.1816
f. 503.589.9166
e. events@classactevents.net
www.classactevents.net

About Class Act Event Coordinators, Inc.

We have been planning weddings for 20 years. Our unparalleled experience in the industry, innovative style, calm approach, and professional attention to detail combine to give you the highest quality of wedding planning services available.

Personalized Service

We are committed to personalized service. Your wedding should match your style, your vision and your budget. We spend time listening to you describe your preferences, your goals and your expectations regarding your wedding. Our job is then to make it happen – all the while making the planning process stress-free and a memorable experience for you and your fiancé.

A Unique Wedding Cannot Be Packaged

We feel you deserve individual attention and the opportunity to select from a range of services. Rather than package our services, we will meet with you to discuss your needs, your desires, your wedding dreams and prepare a services proposal unique to you. Contact us to schedule a complimentary consultation so that you can begin enjoying your wedding planning experience today!

Contact
Class Act Event Coordinators

Price
Custom quote per event

Quick Facts

- Celebrating 20 years as the area's premier wedding planning & design firm

- Extensive experience in destination weddings

- Visit our website for a complete listing of services & to view images from recent weddings

- Options range from day-of coordination to full-service planning

Member of ABC
(Association of Bridal Consultants)

Member ISES
(International Special Events Society)

TESTIMONIAL

"We appreciated your advice for decisions but also allowing us to make it 'our day.' We can't recommend you enough. Looking back at pictures and sharing memories, we have nothing but positive things to remember thanks to you!"

– Sandi & Michael Cox
Portland, Oregon

59

Bravo! Member Since 1998

Photo by Briel Johnson

60

Your Style – Your Way

Are you ready to make your wedding reflect who you are – classic to contemporary, traditional to trendy? Dazzling Affairé will work with you to create the wedding of your dreams.

Want an eco-chic wedding? We can help you explore sustainable options and plan a celebration that is both "green" and elegant, too.

Dazzling Affairé will be there to answer all your questions and make sure your wedding day is all that you have ever imagined!

Proper Planning is not an Option – It is a Necessity!

As you know, the planning for your wedding began as soon as you said "yes", but you may still be feeling a little overwhelmed and not sure where to start. That's where we can help. We will keep your budget on track and ensure that all the intricate details are being carefully looked after. Our staff provides several different services ranging from coordinating all the details, to managing specific areas of planning, or facilitating only the wedding day.

Love Letters

"You made our day flawless and you relieved so much of my stress. I never worried about a thing."
– Jamie and Trevor C. ~ newlyweds

"They are so passionate about what they do – I always felt like I was her only bride."
– Kristi B. ~ bride

"I cannot express how much we appreciate all Dazzling Affairé did for us. All their hard work resulted in the perfect wedding my daughter and her husband dreamed of."
– Lynn R. ~ mother of the bride

Bravo! Member Since 2008

Contact

Patty Hoppe
MaryAnne Miller

Portland, Oregon

p. 503.616.2393

e. events@dazzlingaffaire.com

www.dazzlingaffaire.com

Price

We'll be happy to provide a personalized plan and pricing structure that works for you.

Let Us...

- Give you our full attention
- Help you through your decisions
- Keep your budget on track
- Create a Green-Wedding
- SAVE YOU MONEY, time and worry!
- Turn your dreams into reality
- Reduce your stress level
- Customize a package for your budget

Member - Association of Bridal Consultants

COMPLIMENTARY CONSULTATION

Please call to schedule a no-cost, no-obligation consultation

Dreams Come True LLC
elegant entertaining and events

Dreams Come True Elegant Entertaining & Events

We'll guide you through the entire planning process, helping you to make appropriate selections and informed decisions without adding additional costs. From a simple and traditional to a luxury wedding, we can suit your needs.

Feeling overwhelmed while planning a birthday party? Relax. Think of Dreams Come True as your start-to-finish party planner. From invitations and arrangements, to decorations, menu items and event hosting, our friendly staff will help coordinate your party to ensure that your goals and budget are fully met. Your holidays will be just as wonderful.

Contact
Kathy Angelo

p. 360.600.7279
f. 360.254.6659

e. keangelo@comcast.net

www.dreamscometrueelegant entertaining.com

Price
Consultation is free, then I charge $75 an hour.

Quick Facts
- Wedding Planner
- Reunions
- Anniversaries
- Birthdays
- Holidays
- Wine Tours

61

© Flowers by An Affair to Remember

© Photos by Holland Studios

Love. Laugh. Celebrate.
We'll take care of the rest.

Just imagine…It's your wedding day, and you are laughing and smiling with your wedding party while getting ready. You arrive at the ceremony to find your fiancé in awe at the first sight of you. Just imagine… You move to the reception where everything is exactly as you had dreamed about and planned. Family and friends are full of happiness and love for you during this amazing celebration. Just imagine…You are stress-free and truly enjoying every moment of your wedding because someone else is taking care of your details for you. Just imagine…

You deserve that type of wedding day, even if you're planning something simple at home or elaborate downtown. You deserve to be catered to, and that is our focus. We are here to work with you as a team and to make your wedding as extraordinary and unique as you are!

We really do want you to simply love, laugh and celebrate while we take care of the rest.

WHAT'S NEW?

Encore Events has a new service called "Snapshot Sessions." Can't afford a coordinator but want access to their tips and resources? Meet with us for three hours and ask us anything you want about vendors, etiquette, budget, timelines, design, etc. Schedule one hour at the beginning of your planning, one hour in the middle, and finally one hour near the end. Or schedule all three hours at once, if you prefer. The choice is yours. Contact us for details.

Contact

Cindy Rosen

PO Box 82358
Portland, Oregon 97282-0358

p. 503.890.1249

e. cindy@encoreeventspdx.com

www.encoreeventspdx.com

Price

Starting at $1,300; hourly & special services also available

Quick Facts

- We love working with awesome couples who want their wedding day to be different & fresh!
- We pride ourselves in being inventive, organized, professional, compassionate & fun
- Any level of service available: from full service to month-of to simply helping you find that perfect venue or vendor
- Coordinating weddings since 2004
- Member of the Association of Bridal Consultants

Bravo! Member Since 2005

If you can dream it, we can create it!

- Creative, inspired, experienced
- We endeavor to exceed your expectations
- Seamless collaboration
- Define-the-edge design
- We manage all the details
- Flawless execution
- Network of savvy local sources

Environmental Commitment.

Special attention is given to the "greener" aspects of event stewardship, with an eye towards local and sustainable products.

Passionate drive to develop exquisite events is the elemental nature of the very fire that defines our work.

Contact

Teresa Beck

p. 503.224.1591

e. teresa@fireworkseventproductions.com

www.fireworkseventproductions.com

Quick Facts

- Weddings, showers, rehearsals, luncheons & cocktail parties
- Venue selection
- Menu planning
- Day-of coordination
- Vendor coordination & management
- Custom decor
- Rentals assistance
- Entertainment
- Gift Services
- Destination management for your guests

63

Hood River, Oregon 97031

p. 541.387.5502

e. leith@idoevents.com

www.idoevents.com

64

About I Do Events

Congratulations on your engagement!! Getting married is an exciting and magical time. But a wedding can also be an emotionally charged event where dreams meet a daunting to-do list. Whether a small intimate gathering or a grand affair, I Do will customize the details to meet your unique style.

Save valuable time and money by putting the logistics of your special day in the care of professional expertise. Let 20 plus years of event planning experience guarantee that no detail is neglected.

The I Do staff will do everything from bridal showers to honeymoon plans and all that is in-between. Your wedding is a time to enjoy the people who have come far and wide to share in your celebration. The day will go by so fast, free yourself of the to-dos so your "I Do" will be pleasant and stress free.

Contact
Leith Gaines

Price
Complimentary first meeting.

Packages ranging from "Day of" to full-service wedding planning

Quick Facts

- Range from full-service wedding planning to "Day Of" management

- Expertise in outdoor Gorge Weddings

- Plan rehearsal dinners & other wedding related events

- Vender referral

- Rehearsal Coordination

© Fritz Photo

© Millie Holloman Photography

Little House Events

PO Box 19674
Portland, Oregon 97280
p. 503.568.6368
e. faith@littlehouseevents.com
www.littlehouseevents.com

At Little House Events, the focus is on you.

At Little House Events, we want you to enjoy your special event. You can't do that when you are worried about every little detail, so we help take the pressure off. If you want someone to handle all the details or just need a little help doing it yourself, we are the ones to call. Whether you choose a green wedding, a rustic DIY celebration, or a lavish urban event, the end result will be a true reflection of you.

DIY: It doesn't mean doing it all by yourself.

Helping you do it yourself is our specialty. With our DIY package, you can save hundreds – even thousands – of dollars. Today, many brides are choosing to do some elements of their wedding on their own or with the help of friends and family. They want to save money or indulge their creative spirit. With years of experience as a special events florist and pastry cook, as well as experience in paper arts and stationary, we can help you design the look for your event, and then teach you, your friends, and willing family members how to execute your plan. Finally, we'll be there on your wedding day to make sure everything runs smoothly and looks perfect.

Contact
Faith Moisan

Price
Every event is unique. That is why we do not offer fixed prices. Please call us to set up a complimentary consultation. Then, if you like, we can create a customized budget for your event.

At Little House Events, we believe:

- It's your wedding – your event planner shouldn't get between you and your dream

- You should never be talked into spending more than you can afford

- Whatever your wedding colors, "green" is a nice accent. We can help make your wedding earth-friendly

- You don't have to sacrifice style for budget

- Doing it yourself should add pleasure to your wedding, not stress

65

© Millie Holloman

About Muse

As a full service wedding planning company, we pride ourselves in fashioning weddings of all sizes and budgets. With current statistics stating that couples are spending double or triple their original budgets, we believe that having a coordinator should save you money, not increase your budget.

Planning Should Be Fun!

Sit back, relax, and enjoy your big day. We'll look to the details, timelines and budgets while guiding you through the process. We do not use preferred vendors, here at Muse, but connect our clients to vendors who match their style, personality, and price range.

We bring solutions to the table. At Muse, we hold to the belief that our job is not simply to problem solve, but to prevent problems altogether. Our experience allows us to be attentive to every last detail and know the right questions to ask. Whether you have no idea where to begin, you have it all planned, or simply need assistance with a particular vendor, Muse has a package just for you.

Let us be the inspiration for your big day!

Contact
Christina Safford

20449 SW TV Highway #378
Aloha, Oregon 97006

p. 971.244.3555
f. 503.848.3813

e. christina@eventmuse.biz

www.eventmuse.biz

Price
Day-of services $500-$1,250
Full planning starts at $2,500

Quick Facts
- All Budgets, Sizes & Types
- Experience with Cultural & Destination Weddings
- 10+ Years in the Industry
- Consultation allows us to customize _your_ day to _your_ dreams!
- Member of ABC & Chamber of Commerce

FOR WEDDING TIPS:

Our Blog:
www.eventmuse.biz/blog
Twitter: MuseEvents
Facebook: Muse Event Planning

No Ordinary
Affair

PO Box 423
McMinnville, Oregon 97128
p. 503.868.9455
e. info@noordinaryaffair.com
www.noordinaryaffair.com

About No Ordinary Affair

Whether you're planning a large wedding or a small, intimate gathering, No Ordinary Affair can make your day one that won't soon be forgotten. We believe that you come first in every aspect; that means we work diligently on your behalf, putting everything in place to ensure you have the perfect day, exactly as you've dreamed it to be. We believe your wedding should be a unique reflection of who you are as a couple. We also work with you to help find creative ways to save you money without compromising quality. We believe in making your wedding a unique and extraordinary affair with many unforgettable memories.

Contact us for a **FREE** consultation… we would love to meet you!

Contact
Becky Simpson

Price
Please call for a free quote on your wedding

Amenities

- We work with you to create a wedding that is uniquely you

- Services range from full-service planning to day-of coordination

- We refer you to wedding vendors who fit your style, your needs and your budget

- Name Change Kits for Bride are available

- Some rentals available

67

© Jenny Hill

© Jenny Hill

WHAT'S NEW

Now selling The Name Change Kit for Brides. Let this kit take the stress out of changing your name! Kits come tailored for the state in which you reside.

Aisha Harley

Peter Paul Rubens

portland wedding planner, inc.

Careful • Creative • Calm

You and your fiancé should look forward to the big day with the least amount of stress possible. After all, this "business" of planning a wedding is quite an undertaking! It involves your closest friends, your loving families, months of planning, legal documents, decisions and deadlines, the hiring of many professionals, emotional overload …. and YOU …. The Star!

Our goal is to help you plan an affair that is true to your personality and is original in spirit. We will lift the load off of your shoulders and into our hands. Our careful behind-the-scenes guidance will put that extra special polish on your wedding day and allow you … THE STAR! … to shine.

"Oh my goodness where did you come from! Seriously, where would this wedding be without you? Good Lord, let's not think about it." — Sarah S.

"You are amazing! I adore you. I trust you completely. You are full of the best ideas and plans. I'd be lost without you." — Ashley P.

"You're making this experience a lot of fun and stress free. Exactly what we wanted." — Kari E.

"Marilyn had this wonderful calming aura about her. I needed that. I just knew she was the one." — Melissa M.

"Hiring a wedding coordinator was the best thing I ever did. Marilyn is a ROCK STAR!" — Michele R.

Contact
Marilyn Storch/Owner
p. 503.520.9667
e. info@portlandweddingplanner.com
www.portlandweddingplanner.com

Price
Introductory meeting & customized proposal – Both complimentary

Benefits
- 12 years of very specialized knowledge & experience in creating unforgettable events of all types & sizes
- Long standing relationships in the wedding industry
- A close working relationship with you to achieve the wedding day you envision

SPECIALTIES
- Private Home & Estate Weddings
- Last Minute Weddings
- Partially Planned Weddings
- Ethnic, Cultural, or Religious Traditions
- Vow Renewal
- Commitment Ceremonies
- Second Marriages
- Destination Weddings

MEMBERSHIPS

AJ's Studio

Peter Paul Rubens

Bravo! Member Since 1998

The Bridal Loft
2808 NE MLK Boulevard #3
Portland, Oregon 97212
p. 503.449.5398
f. 503.287.0985 (Call First)
e sue@purpleirisweddings.com
www.purpleirisweddings.com

About Purple Iris Wedding and Events

You will receive help with all the details of your wedding and receive invaluable advice when it comes to picking vendors and venues, saving you hours of research.

You will receive the benefit of our experience with local vendors, and help in deciding on the ones that will fulfill your dreams. You will receive advice on traditional etiquette and current trends.

You will receive all the help you need, wherever you are in planning your wedding. Whether you want information on vendors, day-of coordination, or help from start to finish, a package can be created for you.

You can schedule a complimentary consultation by email or phone.

Contact
Sue Corning
Professional Bridal Consultant

Price
Prices based on your needs

Quick Facts
- Purple Iris Weddings & Events is a full service wedding coordinating and event planning firm

- We are members of the Association of Bridal Consultants (ABC)

- You can be assured of receiving highly professional assistance with any type of event

- You will love the extras we can provide

- Your ideas, our leg-work

69

WHAT'S NEW

Visit our newly redesigned web site:
PurpleIrisWeddings.com

Sassitudes

EVENT PLANNING SPECIALISTS

PO Box 1138
Lake Oswego, Oregon 97035
p. 503.381.3528
f. 503.210.0994
e. info@sassitudes.com
www.sassitudes.com

70

sas·si·tude

– noun

1. sass + attitude = the ability to combine the values, goals, and traditions of the client and their event with a little spice of modern day sass.

Sassitudes is an event planning company specializing in personalized wedding management. From initial consult, to your big day, we ensure your wedding matches your vision and style. Our ultimate goal for your event is to leave your guests amazed, your budget intact, and you simply stress-free and 100% satisfied. We put our reputation into everything we do.

Sassitudes brings over 8 years of experience, knowledge, passion, and a tremendous sense of, well, 'sass' to every wedding we do. We would be honored to make your special day enchanting.

Contact
Stephanie Date,
Professional Bridal Consultant

Price
Call for complimentary consultation & customized quote

Quick Facts
• Budget development

• Vendor referral

• Site research & inspection

• Contract negotiations

• Rehearsal coordination

• Wedding & reception coordination

• Full-service event planning

Memberships
• Association of Bridal Consultants

Bravo! Member Since 2008

www.davidbarssphotographer.com

503.230.9311 **bonsoiree.com**

Soirée - Special Event Planning

Soirée was founded in 1998 and their specialty is weddings. They offer exceptional planning and creative design for local and destination weddings. They truly enjoy the emotional and personal relationships they build with all of their clients. Their mission is to take each individual couple's style and personality and help them create a unique and personalized celebration. Whether your occasion is an elaborate wedding weekend or a backyard celebration, Soirée will give you their full attention so you feel like you are their only client.

Soirée offers each of their prospective clients a complimentary consultation. By asking precise questions about your vision, Soirée is able to determine the goals and expectations of potential clients in which to create a custom proposal based upon the desired coordination services. Soirée invites you to view their Photo and Video galleries which demonstrate how dynamic Soirée's coordination abilities are. You are encouraged to contact past clients for feedback on their experience and relationship with Soirée.

Contact
Molli Barss

PO Box 5982
Portland, Oregon 97228

p. 503.230.9311
f. 503.230.9312

e. info@bonsoiree.com

www.bonsoiree.com

Price
Varies depending on planning assistance needed

Services
- 12 years experience in the Portland area

- Soirée manages all your wedding day details

- Works closely with client to make their vision come true

- Specializing in events of any size

- Complimentary consultation to assess your special event desires

- We will create a custom proposal for you

- Member of the Association of Bridal Consultants

WEDDING SHOWCASE

View our Wedding Photo and Video Galleries plus read comments from past clients at www.bonsoiree.com.

71

Bravo! Member Since 1999

© Emily Haven

p. 503.998.7644
e. heather@sorellaevents.com
www.sorellaevents.com

About Sorella Events

Congratulations, you have found the perfect person to share your life with! Now it is time to plan the day you have always dreamed of, your wedding day. This day is meant to celebrate your commitment to each other, your future together, and all the friends and family who helped you get this far. Planning, coordinating, and enjoying a day the represents so much can be an overwhelming amount of work. Luckily, Sorella Events is here to help you!

Sorella Events is a full-service wedding coordinating, event planning, and design company. From planning an extraordinary wedding to throwing a lavish party, we can accomplish it with style and elegance. Our always-expanding vendor list, constant research, and knowledge of design, ensures that we are up on the current trends as well as educated on the classic traditions. At Sorella Events, we offer a complimentary consultation to discuss your needs and our services. Let us help you take your dreams and turn them into a magnificent reality!

72

Contact
Heather Halstead, I.C.D.

Price
Price is based on individual client needs

Quick Facts
- Day of & full service wedding & event coordination
- Color scheme & theme design
- Pre-designed & custom packages
- Hourly Rates
- Complimentary consultation

© Paul Rich

© Paul Rich

Bravo! Member Since 2007

WHAT'S NEW
Follow us on Twitter at
twitter.com/sorellaevents

MEMBERSHIPS

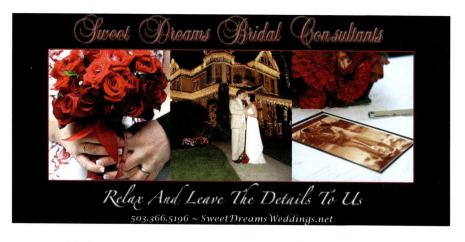

Sweet Dreams Bridal Consultants

Relax And Leave The Details To Us

503.366.5196 ~ SweetDreamsWeddings.net

We help you turn your dreams into an Extraordinary event!

Every bride dreams of what she wants her wedding day to be. She wants every detail to be perfect. She wants a wedding that everyone will be amazed by and will remember forever. Sweet Dreams can help you to achieve those dreams. At Sweet Dreams we specialize in planning unforgettable, uniquely stylish weddings on any budget. We allow you to relax and enjoy the planning process by not having to worry about all those small details. So, relax and leave the details to us and start enjoying your engagement!

Sweet Dreams is a full service planning and consulting company serving Oregon, Washington and beyond. Sweet Dreams will take your ideas and turn them into a truly one of a kind event just for you. We have packages to suit every budget, so whether you need full service planning, a little advice, or something in between, we have you covered.

Contact us today for your free "get to know us" consultation to see how Sweet Dreams can be of service to you.

Contact

Lisa Taylor
Professional Bridal Consultant

Conveniently located at
The Bridal Loft

2808 NE MLK Boulevard Suite 3
Portland, Oregon 97212

p. 503.366.5196

sweetdreamsbridal@hotmail.com
www.sweetdreamsweddings.net

Price

Pricing based on clients needs, check our website for details & current pricing.

Quick Facts

- Full & Partial Planning, Day of Coordination, vow renewals, commitment ceremonies.

- Professional Bridal Consultant through The Association Of Bridal Consultants since 2005.

- Please visit our website for a complete listing of our packages, current prices, and to view images from recent events.

WHAT'S NEW

We now offer Honeymoon planning with Sandals Resorts, along with Ask Me About Travel. Contact us today for more information about this new service.

73

Bravo! Member Since 2006

Taylor Events
Making your event memorable

PO Box 822158
Vancouver, Washington 98668
p. 360.882.6074
f. 360.882.6074

e. taylorevents@live.com
e. your.nw.dj@live.com
www.ataylorevent.com
www.yournwdj.com

74

About Taylor Events & Your NW DJ

Taylor Events is a full service event company. We offer many different services either together for a package price or a la carte! Our Brides are number one, & our references speak volumes for themselves.

Wedding Coordinators – We can provide assistance for the entire event or merely the day of, whichever the case our professionals are dedicated to fulfilling your needs.

Catering – We have many different menu options or we can custom TAYLOR our menus to please.

Servers, Bartenders & Security – Fully trained, licensed and ready to provide exceptional service.

Event Rentals – Buffet supplies, Slide show projectors, and more!

Your NW DJ – Complete sound system, lighting for dance floor ambiance, wireless microphones for formalities, & timeline coordination. Create a custom play list for a personal touch or leave the music to us! Our disc jockeys are experienced, professional and excited to get your party started!

Contact
Michelle
Taylor Events & Your NW DJ

Price
Call for specials.

Mention this ad for more discounts!

Quick Facts

- Wedding coordinators – Entire event or day of

- Catering – Servers & Bartenders

- DJ – Sound system, light for the dance floor, wireless mics & timeline coordination

- Security officers

Bravo!
2010 Calendar of Events

The Bravo! Central Oregon Wedding Affair

January 9th, 2010

10 am - 5 pm

Sunriver Resort - Great Hall

Bravo! Wedding Affair

February 21st, 2010

11 am - 4 pm

Embassy Suites Hotel Portland Downtown

Bravo! Live - A Showcase of the Hospitality & Meeting Industry

October 20th, 2010

11 am - 5 pm

Oregon Convention Center - Hall D

Bravo! Wedding Affair

November 2010

Time & Location to be announced

Visit BravoWedding.com for more information on planning your wedding

Salem & Eugene's Largest Bridal Shows

EVERYTHING FOR YOUR WEDDING

Save the Dates!

JANUARY 23 & 24, 2010
OCTOBER 2 & 3, 2010
Oregon State Fairgrounds
SALEM, OR

• • •

JANUARY 9 & 10, 2010
OCTOBER 16 & 17, 2010
Lane Events Center
EUGENE, OR

For more information call
1-800-317-6589

RICHARD ROMAN PHOTOGRAPHY

OREGON WEDDING SHOWCASE

Something for Every Bride

—— *Show Hours* ——
SATURDAY 10-5
SUNDAY 11-4

FASHION SHOWS AT 12:30 & 3:00 EACH DAY

• • •

SEE OUR EXTENSIVE LOCAL WEDDING RESOURCE DIRECTORY, GET ADMISSION DISCOUNT COUPONS, AND PRE-PURCHASE TICKETS AT

BR.OREGONWEDDINGSHOWCASE.COM

The Original

PORTLAND BRIDAL SHOW

Oregon's Premier Wedding Event

You are invited...

JANUARY 16 & 17

PLAN YOUR WEDDING WITH OVER 150 WEDDING RELATED EXHIBITORS

EXQUISITE BRIDAL FASHION SHOWS DAILY

 Skamania Lodge

HONEYMOON GETAWAYS
GIVEN AWAY AT EACH SHOW

ADMISSION DISCOUNT COUPONS
AVAILABLE ONLINE OR AT
OUR EXHIBITORS

OREGON CONVENTION CENTER

Pre-register online,
receive valuable gifts:
portlandbridalshow.com
Info: 503-274-6027

No strollers or cameras allowed.

HURRY!
Shows sell-out
early! Advance
tickets at Safeway
TicketsWest
guarantee
admission.

Rose City Bridal Showcase

October 2 - 3, 2010

Oregon Convention Center
Hall E

Show Hours: 10am-5pm
Fashion Show Times: 11:30 & 3:00

Tickets on sale at all TicketsWest (Safeway) and at the door
$7.00 Adult/Children
$2.00 Off admission ticket available on line

Register Online To Be Entered To WIN Fantastic Prizes!

www.RoseCityBridalShowcase.com

Everything you need to create your special day!
Top Vendors In The Bridal Industry Under One Roof

Alterations
Bachelorette Parties
Bakeries & Wedding Cakes
Balloons & Decorations
Bedding & Linens
Bridal Accessories
Bridal Registry
Bridal Resources
Bridal Shops
Catering

Childrens' Formal Wear
China, Cookware & Silverware
Day Spas
DJ Services
Florists
Health & Beauty
Hotels
Honeymoon Destinations
Invitations
Jewelry

Limousine Service
Music
Photographers
Rentals
Special Wedding Services
Travel Agencies
Tuxedo Shops
Videographers
Wedding Consultants
Wedding & Reception Venues

Media Sponsors:

Produced By:

Z100
K-Lite 106.7 60s & 70s
COMMUNITY NEWSPAPERS
Convention & Meeting Planners Of Oregon, Inc.

K103 fm
JAMMIN 107.5

WEDDINGS AT THE BEACH BRIDAL SHOW

FREE admission

FIFTH ANNUAL
WEDDINGS AT THE BEACH BRIDAL SHOW
SATURDAY FEBRUARY 20TH, 2010
10AM-4PM

SEASIDE CIVIC & CONVENTION CENTER
SEASIDE OREGON

Info:
503.738.5332
weddingsatthebeach.org

Helpful Hint

Bridal Registry

CHARITABLE DONATIONS REGISTRY

If you and your fiancé are set with household goods and items, consider the I Do Foundation, which allows you to make a donation (instead of party favors) in their honor or you can create a "charitable registry" in addition to your standard registry giving your guests the option to donate to your favorite charity.

UNIQUE SHOPS FOR REGISTRY

There are many wonderful stores where you can register. The china, glassware, flatware, and special accessories you select will be with you the rest of your lives. Look at the registry stores at BravoWedding.com and remember, you can register at more than one.

WHY YOU SHOULD REGISTER

By registering, you let your family and friends know the gifts you would most like to have, and will ensure that what you receive will complement both you and your fiancé's taste and style. Even if you and your fiancé can't imagine using fine china, stemware, and flatware in the near future, you'll appreciate them in years to come.

MIXING & MATCHING

Many shops allow you to mix and match your patterns to design your own dishware theme. Ask about ideas they may have.

WHEN TO REGISTER

Soon after you become engaged is the best time to register. If your friends want to send engagement gifts, you can tell them where you are registered. Or for showers, your guests can select from a variety of items that you have on your "wish list."

CHECK WITH YOUR REGISTRY

It is a good idea to check your registry list periodically and keep it up to date with items you have received. Some gift givers will be making purchases in your behalf from other stores or will forget to let the store you are registered or know whom they are buying the gift for.

© Bryan Hoybook

DAMAGED ITEMS

No business can be responsible for gifts that get broken after they leave their store. If gifts are damaged or broken, it usually happens in shipping. Packages that are carefully packed will reach you intact. However, if you find breakage upon unpacking, please call your delivery carrier (USPS, UPS or Fed Ex) for an inspection and claim. Leave the package intact if possible.

THANK YOU NOTES

It is important and proper etiquette to send thank you notes immediately after receiving a gift. This way you let the gift giver know that the gift was received. Keep up with the many thank you notes you will need to write, rather than waiting until after the honeymoon.

Helpful Hint

Choosing Your Ring

GEMSTONES QUALITY & VALUE

For most couples, the bride's engagement ring is the first major piece of jewelry that they have ever purchased. When you're making a purchase of this size and for something that you will wear for the rest of your life, it's nice to know what the jeweler is describing and what exactly you're getting.

The stone you select as the centerpiece of your engagement ring is judged by four distinct factors that combine in a number of ways to arrive at its value. These factors are commonly referred to as the "Four Cs."

CARAT WEIGHT

The weight of all precious stones is expressed in carats. Originally, the word carat was derived from a natural unit of weight, the seeds of the carob tree. Traditionally, gemstones were weighed against these seeds, but in more recent times, a standardized system has been developed by which one carat equals 0.2 grams, or one-fifth of a gram. The carat is then divided into 100 "points," so that a gemstone of 25 points equals a quarter carat, or a gemstone of 50 points equals a half carat, etc.

CLARITY

Virtually every diamond has some minute traces of noncrystalized carbon, the element from which they were formed. In most cases, these traces of carbon are not visible to the human eye but become apparent under magnification and are referred to as "inclusions." Therefore, the freer the diamond or other gemstone is of inclusions, the rarer the stone will be, causing a higher value to be placed on the stone.

COLOR

When it comes to diamonds, most of us don't think in terms of colors available, but diamonds do cover the spectrum of colors.

© Sikora

While the majority range in color from a barely perceptible yellow or brownish tint, the really rare stones are described as "colorless."

CUT

Of all the ways diamonds are rated, this is the one that man directly has an impact on. How each diamond is cut will directly affect its fire and sparkle, since it is the cutter's skill that ultimately releases the beauty of each stone. The better the cut, the more brilliance and sparkle you will see in the stone you select.

81

Helpful Hint
Hiring a Consultant

"WHAT WILL A BRIDAL CONSULTANT DO FOR ME?"

The question you may ask, "what will a bridal consultant do for me?" can simply be answered by stating that in addition to helping make your wedding dreams come true within your budget – and perhaps saving you from making costly mistakes – a consultant will save you time!

A consultant will be a major asset as you plan your wedding. By allowing you to spend time with your fiancé and your family instead of handling all the minute details, you will enjoy the fun of planning your wedding, instead of the stress.

On your wedding day, you and your fiancé can enjoy the day, while your Consultant and staff are working behind the scenes to make your dreams come true!

© Powers Studio

Helpful Hint
Planning a Bridal Shower

Give the hostess a complete and accurate list of guests to invite, including out-of-town family members who may not attend but wish to send a gift. Be sure to explain the relationship (e.g. cousin, college friend, great aunt) so that the hostess will know how to address the respondent when they RSVP.

Do not include the store where you are registered on your shower invitations. Let the hostess know so she can let the guests know when they RSVP.

SHOWER THEMES/GIFT IDEAS

- Kitchen Theme: Register at your favorite kitchen store

- Bathroom Theme: towels, soaps, shower curtain, etc.

- Beach Party: beach towels, sunscreen, picnic basket and supplies

- Garden Party: lawn furniture, hammock, flower pots, tools

- Spa Party: pamper yourself and bridesmaids at a local salon or day spa

- Coed Shower: a great way for friends to celebrate your impending marriage – use a theme such as travel, music, or barbecue

Bridal Attire & Tuxedos

Boutiques & Accessories
Bridal Attire
Dress Design & Custom Veils
Formal Wear & Tuxedos
Gown Pressing, Cleaning & Alterations

503.788.5280
AUGUSTVEILS.COM

August Veils

Craig Strong

www.davidbarssphotographer.com

b-mac photography

www.davidbarssphotographer.com

www.davidbarssphotographer.com

remembrance photography

Located at
The Bridal Loft

Enchanted Custom Corsets & Fine Apparel

Portland, Oregon
p. 503.522.5633
e. owner@enchantedcorsets.com
www.enchantedcorsets.com

An Enchanted Custom Corsets will give you the silhouette of your dreams!

From Snow White to Scarlett O'Hara, corsets are used to create the classic and elegant figure we all want. As women come in all shapes and sizes, a custom corset is essential to a flattering and comfortable fit.

A corset from Enchanted is handcrafted for *your* body and 24 of *your* measurements. Expertly made just for you - from the fabric of your choice and with flexible steel boning - an Enchanted custom corset will make you look and feel like a princess.

Full figured or considering a strapless gown? A corset worn under your dress provides the sliming foundation and support that allows you to focus on your beautiful day.

Tired of the same gown, different label? An heirloom corset and matching skirt can be worn again and again, rather than stored in a box in the attic.

For Paris couture from a Portland business, invest in an Enchanted Custom Corset and enjoy the rewards on your wedding day: slim, confident, and beautiful!

Contact
Lisa Marie
Proprietress

Prices
$750 and Up

What Enchanted Customers say:
"From start to finish, Lisa Marie was friendly, helpful, and excited about my corset. She never once lost patience with me–which I think is quite amazing, looking back. Her knowledge is amazing, from fabrics, to ribbon, to the construction of the corset. My corset is everything I could ever want - looks exactly like what was in my head, fits perfectly, and comfortable as a second skin. It's my first corset, and after this experience, I think I'd be hard pressed to go any where else for my next!"
- Brooke, Des Moines, Iowa

CASCADIA BRIDAL FASHION SHOW

Join Enchanted and other exciting designers at the Cascadia Bridal Fashion Show for bridal wear out of the ordinary!
When: Saturday, February 6th at 4:00 p.m.
Where: The Lotus Seed Center 4635 NE 9th Ave. Portland, Oregon
Cost: $5, cash only

About The Wedding Cottage

From the moment you get engaged to the day you walk down the aisle, The Wedding Cottage carries the largest selection of wedding accessories to complete and complement your wedding. Whether your taste is traditional or contemporary, our selection of accessories encompasses various unique styles sure to match your wedding theme and distinct personality.

From the latest fashionable wedding wear to the colors of the upcoming wedding season, The Wedding Cottage makes every effort to stay on top of today's latest wedding trends. Visit us for…

Guest Books & Pen Sets
Toasting Flutes & Cake Serving Sets
Flower Baskets & Ring Pillows
Garters, Hankies, Veils & Tiaras
Unity Candles & Cake Tops
Favor Boxes & Sweets
Bachelorette & Bridal Shower Items
Hoodies, Tanks & Tees
Attendant Gifts & MORE!

Contact

4775 Southwest Watson Avenue
Beaverton, Oregon 97005
p. 503.643.9730
f. 503.526.7677
e. info@theweddingcottage.net
www.theweddingcottage.net

What our customers say:

"Thank you so much for the amazing help and hard work you put into helping my husband and I plan a wonderful wedding. From save the dates and the individually tailored invitations, to the accessories and suggesting a marvelous photographer; our wedding and wedding planning experience was wonderful and perfect!"

– D.K.

Voted **Best Bridal Accessories**
2008 Oregon Bride Magazine

SHOP ONLINE

Shop our invitations, accessories & favors at www.theweddingcottage.net

See page 218 under Favors & Gifts and page 228 under Invitations & Calligraphy

Bravo! Member Since 1990

AniA Collection
Couture Bridal Boutique

419 SW 4th Avenue
Portland, Oregon 97204

(located in downtown Portland, on the corner of SW 4th & SW Stark)

p. 503.796.9170
f. 503.796.0008

www.aniacollection.com

A Full Service Bridal Salon

AniA Collection is proud to offer a unique selection of bridal wear for the modern and elegant bride. Our exclusive collection includes bridesmaid dresses, mothers' gowns, shoes, veils, custom jewelry and accessories.

We pay personal attention to each bride during this special time and strive to provide all assistance needed in fulfilling her wedding dreams.

Smart Park validation is provided with your consultation.

Contact
Ania Sales Associate
sales@aniacollection.com

We feature exclusive designer wedding gowns by:
- Amy Michelson
- Alvina Valenta
- Angelina Bridal Couture
- Augusta Jones
- Cymbeline Paris
- Jim Hjelm
- Lazaro
- Leaann Belter
- Maria Karin
- Pattis Bridal
- Tara Keely

…and many more.

MONTHLY TRUNK SHOWS

We host monthly Trunk Shows with our designers.

Please call us, check our website at aniacollection.com or follow our blog at aniacollection.blogspot.com for event details.

87

Bravo! Member Since 1996

17050 SW Pilkington Road
Suite 210
Lake Oswego, Oregon 97035
p. 503.636.1474
f. 503.636.1694
www.annasbridal.com

About Anna's Bridal Boutique

We are a full-service bridal boutique and feature elegant designer dresses and accessories. Our showroom is full of gorgeous gowns to accommodate any price range, style, body type, and color preference. Our goal is to assist you in finding your dream dress and making your experience as enjoyable as possible.

Wedding Party Attire, Accessories, and More

Anna's Bridal also offers a large selection of samples for the entire wedding party, including bridesmaids, flower girls, junior bridesmaids and mothers. In our showroom we showcase exquisite headpieces, tiaras, hairpins, veils, shoes and undergarments. Some of our headpieces feature real pearls and crystals which the bride can have made into a necklace after the wedding. Also available are gown preservation, expert in-house alterations, and of course, you will always be treated with impeccable customer care.

Our happy brides have been showcased on TLC's A Wedding Story and Martha Stewart Weddings and several of our sample gowns have been featured in Portland Bride and Groom and Oregon Bride Magazine.

Appointments are recommended.

Voted Oregon Bride Magazine's
Best Bridal Shop of 2008!

Contact
Anna Totonchy

Price
Attire to fit every budget

Designer Lines
- Melissa Sweet & Reverie
- Priscilla of Boston & Platinum
- Vera Wang
- Matthew Christopher
- Marisa
- Jim Hjelm
- Vineyard & Jewel
- Casablanca
- Pronovias
- Dessy & After Six
- Jade
- Winters & Rain
- Salon & Grace Shoes
- Manuel Mota
- Many more

BRIDAL BLISS

Anna's features an in-house wedding coordination and consultation service – Bridal Bliss. They will listen to your needs & ideas, offer creative suggestions & bring your wedding dreams to life.
See ad under Wedding Consultants

Bravo! Member Since 1996

Bella Brides

800 NW Wall Street #201
Bend, Oregon 97701
p. 541.330.7090
f. 541.330.7090
e. nicole@bellabridesbend.com
www.bellabridesbend.com

About Bella Brides

Bella Brides opened in a small location in Bend in 2005 for the sole purpose of helping the bride-to-be find the perfect wedding gown. Since then Bella Brides has more than doubled its size while relocating to our existing loft style boutique Downtown.

The process of finding the perfect gown isn't just about picking a color, fabric and size. It's about finding the perfect balance between cut, flow, shape and fit that complements your specific body type. Several of our brides have been unsuccessful at other shops in Oregon, Washington and California before finding the perfect gown at Bella Brides...*Find out why.*

Conveniently located in the heart of Oregon in beautiful Downtown Bend on the corner of Wall and Franklin. Downtown Bend is known for its beautiful parks, Mirror Pond, world class restaurants, breweries, accommodations and shopping.

Bella Brides' ever-changing inventory provides the most current fashions in a large and varied selection of styles and prices.

Contact
Nicole Sundsten

Price
$199 to >$2,000

Quick Facts

- Large selection of unique & designer wedding gowns to choose from. Styles ranging from elegantly simple to 'straight-from-the-runway' haute couture & everything in-between, allows you to find the perfect gown that reflects your personality & fit within your budget

- You'll work directly with the owner, Nicole, & have a fabulous experience choosing your gown while benefiting from her knowledge of gown design, fit & styles

- Carrying all the accessories you'll need on your special day from shoes & slips to veils, tiaras & jewelry. We also carry wedding-related gifts such as "future Mrs...." & "just married" apparel

- You'll also find a full selection of bridesmaids, flower girl & mother's dresses

89

8925 SW Beaverton Hillsdale Highway
Portland, Oregon 97225
p. 503.297.9622
f. 503.297.9061
e. bridal@charlottesweddings.com
www.charlottesweddings.com

90

About Charlotte's Weddings & More

Charlotte's Weddings & More is a full-service bridal boutique. We have a long standing reputation for great service, private bridal suites, large selection of gowns and knowledgeable staff. Your personal consultant makes finding the perfect gown, as well as shoes, jewelry, veil, bra, slip and more a fun and relaxing experience. Our goal is to assist you in creating the perfect look for your wedding day and your entire bridal party, even the groom. From the gown, to the accessories, to the invitations, we are here to help! Here are some of the things that Charlotte's has to offer:

- Private bridal rooms large enough for family and friends
- Your own personal consultant the stays with you
- Impeccable customer service
- Exclusive collections of gowns found nowhere else in the northwest
- A large selection of gowns to fit any budget

Reserve your private bridal room and personal consultant today.

Bravo! Member Since 1990

Price
Large selection to fit any budget

Quick Facts:
Oregon Bride Magazine Best Gown Shop 2009, Oregon Bride Magazine Voted Best Dress Shop of 2007, Citysearch best dress shop of 2007/2008, Proud Participants of Susan G. Komen Race for the Cure, Proud Donator to Brides Against Breast Cancer

Designer Lines:
2BE Bride, Aire Barcelona, Sophia Tolli, Maggie Sottero, Casablanca, Sottero & Midgley, Mon Cheri, Alfred Angelo & many more

WHAT'S NEW
Check out our website and create your own gallery where you can save your favorite dresses and email them to your consultant. You can even save your favorite dress to your facebook page. Also, sign up to receive monthly coupons and visit our blog for tips from your consultants and events in the store and around town.

MEMBERSHIP

**The Hostess House
&
The Bridal Arts Building
Est. 1984**

**Celebrating 26 years of
Trust & Service**

10017 NE Sixth Avenue
Vancouver, Washington 98685
p. 360.574.7758
www.bridalarts.com

The Hostess House presents
The Bridal Arts Building

Come visit and experience our truly elegant and completely stocked bridal salon.

Because you are so special to us, when you purchase your wedding gown we pay the sales tax for Washington buyers. We include a garment bag to protect your gown. We will store your gown until your wedding. We will professionally steam your gown. We will match any other full-service store's prices and services.

Select from more than 1,000 gowns in stock, in sizes from 2 to 32. Buy off-the-rack or place a special-order. Be sure to visit our magnificent sale room where you will find newly discontinued gowns from 25% to 75% off the original price.

Bridesmaids, flower girl dresses, mother suits and gowns, dyeable shoes, and accessories, special occasion and cruise wear, alterations available.

Directions: from I-5 take 99th Street Exit (Exit #5). Go west two blocks, turn right onto 6th Avenue.

Contact
Hostess House & Bridal Arts

Wedding Gown Pricing
$99 to $1,500

Featured Designer Gowns
- Alfred Angelo
- Allure
- Aurora D'Paradiso
- Bonny
- Casablanca
- Eternity
- Forever Yours
- Maggie Sottero
- Mary's
- Mon Cheri
- Venus
- We showcase "Temple ready" gowns
- We adore plus size brides

BUSINESS HOURS

Monday - Saturday
10 a.m. to 6 p.m.
Open until 8 p.m. on Thursdays.
Sunday Noon to 5 p.m.
Closed most Holidays.
Appointments available, but not necessary.

See page 358 Ceremony Sites, 435 Reception Sites

91

Bravo! Member Since 1990

Visit BravoWedding.com for more information on bridal attire & tuxedos

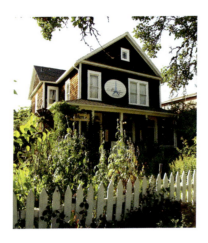

BOUTIQUE

8535 SE 13th Avenue
Portland, Oregon 97202
p. 503.236.7001
f. 503.236.7450
e. info@magnifiqueboutique.net
www.magnifiqueboutique.net

92

Welcome to Magnifique Boutique

Just beyond the white picket fence and gorgeous gardens, you will find Portland's hippest shop for brides to find their perfect dress or to plan their spectacular event and have fun doing it.

Magnifique Boutique will bring you designer and couture bridal fashions you are looking for in a relaxed and fun atmosphere that you deserve!

Gowns, Bridesmaids, Tuxedos, Accessories & More

Magnifique Boutique carries a unique selection of wedding gowns, bridesmaid's dresses, tuxedos, shoes, veils and hairpieces.

Many of our gown lines are new to the Northwest and exclusive to Magnifique Boutique. We also showcase bridal jewelry and headpieces from local designers.

Prepare To Be Pampered

When you come to Magnifique Boutique prepare for a unique shopping experience, browse the boutique while enjoying a glass of champagne or inquire about our Magnifique Fete' where you and your bridal party can have the entire boutique for your private shopping event.

(Walk - in's are welcome, but appointments are recommended)

Contact
Jennie Streitberger

Price
Call for Pricing

Designer Lines
- Casablanca Couture
- Lila Couture
- Tsarina Couture
- Stephanie James Couture
- Colet
- Blue by Enzoani
- Wtoo by Watters
- Ella Rosa
- Lynn Lugo
- Bill Levkoff
- Pink Shoes
- Jim's Formal Wear Tuxedos
- Headpieces by Austie
- Jewelry by Mandalena
- Jewelry by O'Pearl Art

WEDDING & EVENT PLANNING

Magnifique Boutique features in house wedding and event planning by Magnifique Events. We are your one stop for Gorgeous Gowns & Spectacular Events.

11545 SW Durham Road
Tigard, Oregon 97224
p. 503.603.0363
f. 503.443.6106
e. RosewoodBridal@verizon.net
www.rosewoodbridal.com

Exquisite Designs and Impeccable Service

Our genuine commitment to quality and service is the difference you will feel the moment you walk into Rosewood Bridal. Since 1995, we have been providing amazing women from the Northwest and beyond with our unique selection, enthusiasm and expertise, working with them to create their perfect day. We look forward to doing the same for you.

Your Bridal Party

Choose from our incredible selection of beautiful and flattering bridesmaid dresses, stylish tuxedos and enchanting flowergirl designs.

Visit us today for the gown you'll love and the attention you deserve!

Contact
Rosewood Bridal
Sales Associate

Hours
Monday & Tuesday
11 a.m – 7 p.m.
Wednesday - Friday
11 a.m. – 5:30 p.m.
Saturday 10 a.m. – 5 p.m.

Price
$300 – $1,800

Selection & Service
- Designer Gowns from Maggie Sottero, Mori Lee, Alma Novia, Impression, Essense of Australia, Eden & More!

- Beautiful bridesmaids

- Adorable flower girls' dresses

- Expert alterations

- Tuxedo rentals

- Tiaras, veils & jewelry

93

**NO APPOINTMENT
NECESSARY**

Bravo! Member Since 1997

Visit BravoWedding.com for more information on bridal attire & tuxedos

The Bridal Loft
2808 NE MLK Boulevard Suite #3
Portland, Oregon 97212
p. 503.788.5280
f. 503.788.5281
e. andrea@augustveils.com
www.augustveils.com

About August Veils

Let us help you create the headpiece or veil that is just right for your occasion. We will guide you through creative choices and playful suggestions to make your decisions a reality.

Headpieces may be embellished with Swarovski crystals, pearls, lace (new or heirloom) or whatever components you desire.

Off the rack veils are also available for purchase.

Appointments are highly encouraged to ensure personal service, however walk-in times are accessible: Tuesday, Friday and Saturday from 10 a.m. to 3 p.m.

Bottom Left Photo by Green Door Photography
Bottom Right Photo by Kate Kelly Photography
Gown by love, June
Make up by Event Cosmetics
Hair by FADA
Lashes by Midori

Contact
Andrea Hoyt

Price
Varies; $18 to $750
or more

Quick Facts
- All products crafted locally
- Custom design is our passion
- Large selection of veils & hair accessories
- Guaranteed craftsmanship
- Featured in Martha Stewart Weddings, Wedding Dresses Magazine, Portland Bride & Groom Magazine (front cover twice) & KATU's AM Northwest
- Quick turn arounds – as time allows

WHAT'S NEW
A proud member of an award winning group, The Bridal Loft. Best of Citysearch 2005 and Oregon Bride's Best All Around Wedding Vendor 2007.

Bravo! Member Since 1998

Member of Wedding Network USA

94

creating modern heirlooms

Adorn yourself:

Choose from our boutique collection, handcrafted right here in Portland, Oregon.

Inspired and elegantly designed pieces that gracefully flatter.

Or, splurge a little...

Commission the design of a modern heirloom, or restore one of your own. Love, June thoughtfully designs and reinvents gowns to be treasured for generations.

Love, June is excited to be offering our exclusive line of unique and sustainable bridal gowns — made without producing textile waste — now on Etsy! Visit us at www.lovejune.etsy.com!

Contact
Sara Temme
p. 503.997.2435
e. sara@lovejunebridal.com
www.lovejunebridal.com

Price
$800 & up for bridal design

Quick Facts
- Handcrafted in Portland
- Over 20 years of sewing experience
- Vintage gown restyling
- Mothers' ensembles, too!

95

WHAT'S NEW

Voted best custom design by readers of Oregon Bride Magazine 2009

OREGON
BRIDE
MAGAZINE
BEST
of
2009

Bravo! Member Since 2007

2010 suits are in, so check out the Catalina by After Six.
Colors include Black, Charcoal, Navy Blue and Tan.

A Formal Affair Tuxedo

4512 NE Sandy Boulevard
Portland, Oregon 97213
p. 503.287.2824
f. 503.287.4255
e. debbie@aformalaffairtuxedo.com
www.aformalaffairtuxedo.com

About A Formal Affair Tuxedo

You have every right to feel excited as it's not every day that you get to wear the most magnificent and distinguishing ensemble of Men's clothing.

If you appreciate incredible service and like to feel you are special, then we would be honored to help you achieve the "Perfect Look" you expect when renting tuxedos for your wedding.

When you visit our showroom you will notice that our tuxedos are of the highest quality and latest of fashion. No other company in Portland Proper can make this statement.

Let us spoil, pamper and amaze you! No one leaves our store with a tuxedo that just fits, but with one that fits great!

Contact
Debbie Drorbaugh

Price
Varies; please call for more details

Quick Facts
- **By appointment only**
- For your convenience, we also provide after-hour appointments
- Full service tuxedo & suit rentals
- All tuxedos are hand finished
- Ask about our downtown Portland hotel after event tuxedo pick-up service
- Proud members of the Association of Bridal Consultants

96

From After Six the White Carlisle new for 2010, always a classic!

Bravo! Member Since 2002

Visit our showroom at Winn Perry
2505 SE 11th Avenue, Suite 102
(entrance on 11th)
Portland, OR 97202
p. 503.281.6648
www.DuchessClothier.com

About Duchess, Clothier

For those not content with run-of-the-mill wedding fashion, Duchess Clothier provides the discriminating groom with a sartorial experience like no other. We offer a wide range of historically-inspired suits and tuxedo styles, every detail completely customizable to suit your taste. Have an exact idea for your wedding suit but unable to find it anywhere? Love vintage suits but have trouble finding one in appropriate condition that fits you? Every one of our suits is made-to-measure for the individual, unlike off-the-rack or rental offerings, which are made in standardized sizes and altered to fit as best they can, which rarely provides the ideal look.

We are a small local business indefatigably devoted to customer satisfaction. Additionally, for those located outside of Portland, our economical Scotch Basic Collection is available online for ease of ordering. Wedding party discounts are available on all made-to-measure suits, which take approximately six to eight weeks to complete.

Contact
duchess@duchessclothier.com

Price
$500 – $1,850

Quick Facts

- Your wedding offers a wonderful opportunity for you to invest in a custom suit which will serve you perfectly on the big day & for many years to come

- Duchess suits are available in a wide price range so that we may accommodate nearly any budget

- We cover all alterations for fit on suits for which we measure you in person

- Choose from hundreds of fabric offerings, from basic black or charcoal wool to vivid raw silk or striped velveteen

- We have created over 500 custom suits since our inception in 2005

- Please don't hesitate to call or e-mail us with any questions you may have!

97

Bravo! Member Since 2008

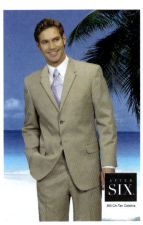

Mr. Formal

Grand Ave. 503.232.1542	Vancouver 360.253.9637
Clackamas 503.659.2337	Hazel Dell 360.574.7768
Hillsboro 503.640.1838	Gresham 503.667.6299
Beaverton 503.643.2661	Progress 503.620.2916
Kelso 360.501.6025	South Salem 503.399.7989
Lake Oswego 503.636.8911	East Salem 503.371.7970

More Brides Trust Mr. Formal's Wedding Experts

Trust Mr. Formal's Formalwear Experience

- Trust our 33 year commitment to Wedding Excellence
- Mr. Formal is the largest locally owned formalwear provider in the Northwest
- A Portland warehouse with an inventory of over 20,000 tuxedos
- Professionally trained Formalwear Consultants

Exceptional Quality and Selection

- Mr. Formal offers over 75 elegant tuxedo styles
- Tuxedos by top designers: Oscar de la Renta, Ralph Lauren, After Six, Calvin Klein
- The Northwest's largest designer vest collection with colors to match all dresses
- Tuxedo sizes from 4 to 70
- Suit rentals for informal/destination weddings

Mr. Formal's Commitment to Value

- We have tuxedo styles that accommodate every budget
- Generous discounts are available for bridal gown cleaning and bridal party gifts
- We offer a large selection of enhancement items to customize your look
- Our Price Promise: "We promise the highest quality tuxedos at the best price available."

The Time Saving Convenience

- 33 convenient locations throughout the Pacific Northwest plus SAVVI affiliates available nationwide for fittings
- Out-of-town ordering is easy with our custom measurement website form
- A local warehouse that guarantees that last minute changes are never a problem

FORMALWEAR COLLECTION

View our latest formalwear collection at:
www.mrformaltuxedos.com
and receive tuxedo discounts.

Bravo! Member Since 2002

Sewing Solutions

2808 NE MLK Boulevard
Portland, Oregon 97212
p. 503.788.5280
p. 503.869.6039
f. 503.788.5281
e. trickeykim@yahoo.com
www.thebridalloft.net
www.sewingsolutionsor.com

About Sewing Solutions

Sewing Solutions is a full-service bridal alteration business. Owner Kim Trickey has altered gowns by Maggie Sottero, Christos, Lazaro, Amsale, Vera Wang, Jessica McClintock, Rivini, Lena Medoyoff, Sue Wong, Reem Acra and Pronovias among others.

We have increased and decreased the size of many gowns; have added and removed sleeves, altered necklines, waistlines, bust lines and hemmed many different styles of gowns.

We like to talk with the bride and listen to what the bride has to say about her gown, and how she envisions changing it. Sometimes it's as simple as a hem, but, it can also be a complete reconstruction of the gown. The goal of Sewing Solutions is to do whatever is possible to make the wedding gown as close to the bride's vision as possible.

In addition to wedding gowns a large part of Sewing Solutions business is also altering bridesmaids, flower girl, and mother of the bride dresses. We want everyone to look their best and be pleased to be wearing a lovely dress. It is the bride's day, and she and her party should feel comfortable and beautiful in their wedding attire.

Sewing Solution's mission is to help each bride realize her wedding dream..

Contact
Kim Trickey

Price
$20 to $500

Quick Facts
- Quality alterations
- Fair & competitive pricing
- No job too large or too small
- Wedding gowns, bridesmaids, mother of the bride, prom & other special occasions
- More than 40 years sewing experience

99

CALL FOR AN APPOINTMENT

In the off season, October – April, we are happy to alter everyday wear and do small household projects.
Hours by appointment
Tuesday - Saturday

Helpful Hint

Choosing Your Dress

Bridal Gown Shops - Ordering A Gown

Selecting Your Bridal Gown

Take the time to try on the various styles available at different shops. Most importantly, pick the dress you feel the best and most comfortable in. NOTE: Allow at least six months to order your wedding gown.

Looking Good All Day Long

You may want to consider the fabric for your dress more closely, depending on how long you will be in the dress. There is no way to avoid wrinkling a dress once it is put on; however certain fabrics wrinkle more easily. Here are a few ways to preserve your dress: Have your dress pressed a week before the wedding, but make sure you wrap it in a sheet when it's finished – no dry cleaner or store bags; get dressed at the ceremony site, eliminate traveling in dress before ceremony, bring a stool to the ceremony site for sitting on, and make sure there is an aisle runner if you have a long train. Detachable trains and veils make it easier to travel about and dance at the reception.

Headpieces & Veils

Pick a headpiece that enhances your face and hairstyle; it should complement, not overwhelm. If you attempt to press your own veil, be extremely careful. Press the veil between white tissue – no steam.

Bridesmaid Dresses

There are several factors to keep in mind when selecting bridesmaid dresses. Colors and fabrics vary with the seasons. The style usually complements the bridal gown. The formality is based on whether it is a daytime or evening wedding. Choose a dress color and style that will be flattering on all the bridesmaids, and keep in mind that the main focus will be on the backs of the dresses during the ceremony. You can even have different styles for each bridesmaid, using the same color and fabric.

Important Note

The following recommendations are for your protection:

- Be careful about where you buy your wedding dress. Ask your friends and family about where they went and what their experiences were - check out our list of qualified bridal gown shops and dress designers.

- Make sure the delivery date of your dress is well in advance of your wedding. A helpful suggestion is to tell the the bridal gown shop your wedding date is a few weeks earlier than what it really is – ensuring you not only receive your dress on time, but have time to get it pressed before the big day.

- Get a copy of the order or receipt with a guarantee of delivery date to keep with your wedding records.

- If a contract is used, read it carefully (even the fine print) before signing!

- If you have any questions or concerns about the company, check it out with organizations that keep track of the reputations of companies, such as the Better Business Bureau.

© David Barss

DRESS DESIGNERS - HAVING A CUSTOM GOWN CREATED

WHERE TO BEGIN

Start by browsing through bridal magazines, web sites and shows to see a variety of dress designs and styles. Then try on as many different types and styles of dresses as you can before you contact a professional seamstress. That way, if you plan to have your dress made, you will know what length of sleeves, skirt and train you prefer as well as which neck and waist designs work best for your body type.

DESIGN

If you haven't found the dress of your dreams or if the dress you have in mind doesn't exist, take your ideas, pictures, and dreams to a dress designer. Designers offer a variety of options, taking a sleeve from one dress and a bodice from another to design a gown especially for you. Many expensive original designer dresses with designer prices can be copied, allowing you to stay within your budget.

HEMMING

Consult with a dressmaker on hemming your dress. Many dresses can be lifted at the waistline to avoid taking lace off the entire hemline, and without distorting the lines and design of the dress. Also ask about ways to bustle up the train so it is comfortable and convenient for you to get around in at the reception.

Note – Make sure you are wearing the shoes and undergarments you will wear to your wedding when making any decisions about hemming. A slight difference in heel height can change the measurements.

RESERVING ALTERATIONS SERVICES

As soon as you have selected your gown, be sure to make an appointment to reserve services for alterations. Many bridal-alterations specialists are booked months in advance. Your bridal shop can recommend a reliable seamstress or may have someone they work with. Brides should be prepared to pay for alterations and include this in their budget. They are seldom included in the price of the gown.

FORMAL WEAR

SELECTING FORMAL WEAR

There are a variety of formal wear styles available. The formal wear shop you decide to work with can offer suggestions for styles and colors that will appropriately fit the time of day. Accessories to match the bridesmaid dresses are available for rent or purchase, or can be special ordered.

QUESTIONS TO ASK

Is the formal wear stocked locally? Are the locations convenient for the groomsmen? What is the price, and what does that include?

FINAL FITTING & PICKUP DATE

You must instruct each member of the wedding party to pick up his own tuxedo. Make sure they try on the entire outfit at the store. This will avoid the most common problem with formal wear—proper fit. If adjustments or replacements need to be made, they can usually be done right on the spot, or arrangements for substitutions can be made.

OUT-OF-TOWN GROOMSMEN & USHERS

If some of the groomsmen and ushers live out of town, the formal wear shop can supply you with measurement cards to mail back to them. Any clothing or alterations shop in the groomsman's home town should be able to do a complimentary fitting. It is imperative that these gentlemen take the time to try on their entire tuxedos when they pick them up!

BRING EXTRA SOCKS

Have the groom buy a couple of extra pairs of socks to match the formal wear. Be sure these extra socks are on hand where the groomsmen plan to dress. It never fails that someone will show up with only white athletic socks. This may seem minor, but they stick out like a sore thumb in photographs.

GROUP RATES & DISCOUNTS

Many formal wear shops offer special group rates, discounts or rebates for black-tie or black-tie-optional events.

101

Notes

© AJ's Studio

Cakes & Desserts

PAPA HAYDN

WEDDING CAKES

ph. 503·291·8350
papahaydn.com

© JFab Photography
& Anna Mara Flowers

cup cake jones

307 NW 10th Avenue
Portland, Oregon 97209
p. 503.222.4404
f. 503.222.4494
e. lisa@cupcakejones.net
www.cupcakejones.net

Personalize Your Cupcakes

Cupcake Jones offers a seasonal menu, taking advantage of the flavors of the northwest. With dozens of cake recipes and hundreds of combinations of cakes, fillings, icings, and our famous handmade garnishes, you can create cupcakes that reflect your tastes and personalities.

Professional Friendly Service

We cheerfully walk you through the ordering process step by step, working with your event planner, reception site, florist, and YOU to create a stress free wedding day. We have wedding packages for every budget. Choose delivery, a personalized cupcake stand, and professional arrangement for the perfect "cupcake cake" of your dreams.

A bakery that shares your values

We use fresh berries from the local farmer's market, only rBST free dairy products, biodegradable non-aerosol cleaners, and 100% recyclable packaging. We donate all of our unsold cupcakes daily to a local service agency for the homeless. We recycle and compost everything we can.

Contact
Lisa Watson

Price
$1.50 and up

Quick Facts

- Cupcakes always baked fresh the day of your wedding

- Personalized friendly service to ensure a worry free wedding day

- Tastings / consultations scheduled at your convenience

- Handmade garnishes top our cupcakes like candied fruit ships, homemade marshmallows, candied rose petals, homemade sauces, and miniature cookies

- Jumbo and Mini sized cupcakes available in hundreds of seasonal flavor combinations each month

- No artificial colors or flavors, all natural, baking fresh daily

WHAT'S NEW

Ask us about our composting program!

105

© JFab Photography
& Anna Mara Flowers

© Amy Vining Photography

Dippity Doodads
Chocolate Fountain Rentals

8205 NE 91st Street
Vancouver, Washington 98662
p. 360.798.7395
f. 360.885.2036
e. shirley@dippitydoodads.com
www.dippitydoodads.com

106

$ THE FONDUE FOUNTAIN FITS THE BILL $

In our new economy everyone is looking for the most value for every dollar. The Fondue Fountain is the perfect way to provide great visual impact & a variety of scrumptious foods while adhering to the strictest budget!

Nothing is more fun, more elegant and more economical than a Dippity DooDads fondue fountain. The fountain experience encompasses delicious dipping items, entertainment, guest participation, and is most certainly budget friendly.

The tried and true will never let you down...dipping juicy red strawberries or puffy marshmallows into Milk, Dark or White premium chocolate fondue is the ultimate treat! A popular & economical idea is the "dessert buffet", where a chocolate and/or caramel fountain take center stage & many delicious dippers flank the main attraction.

Versatility? We offer several fondue options; Nacho Cheese, Creamy Caramel, Tangy Ranch Dressing & our latest addition, Hot Chicken Wing Sauce!

Please invite us to your wedding reception, corporate gathering, holiday party, fundraiser, Bat/Bar Mitzvah, graduation, prom....we can do it all!

Call today to reserve your fountain for ANY OCCASION!

Contact
Shirley Easton

Price
$185 – $495

Quick Facts
- Four fountain sizes to accommodate any size group

- Serving the Portland/ Vancouver area within 100 mile radius

- 10% Discount when renting two or more fountains

- Listed as a preferred vendor for many of the areas finest venues

- Price includes fondue, properly attired attendant, skewers, set-up, break-down & clean-up of all fountains

- Proudly serving our area for 6 years

WHAT'S NEW

Ask about our CHOCOLATE bullets, shot-gun shells and yes, hand grenades...really! Makes a great gift for your favorite sportsman.

Bravo! Member Since 2007

4733 SE Hawthorne
Portland, Oregon 97215
p. 503.234.8115
Business Hours:
Mon. – Sat. 7:30 a.m. – 6 p.m.
www.jacivas.com

Types and Styles of Wedding Cakes

If you're looking for a beautiful wedding cake, exquisite looking and luscious inside…A place where you can taste a variety of flavors and then select a different flavor for each tier…A place where you can get handmade mints to match your wedding colors…A place where you can get a special first-anniversary cake, just for the two of you, free…Then JaCiva's is your answer.

You can select a rich chocolate groom's cake or an assortment of Victorian tea pastries or chocolate truffles to make your rehearsal dinner or special-occasion event truly unique.

Cost, Ordering, and Delivery

Cost varies depending on the flavor, size, and style of cake. A deposit is required upon placing the order, with the balance due two weeks before the wedding. Early ordering is suggested, especially for summer dates. JaCiva's can deliver and set up your cake for an additional charge in their delivery areas.

Services and Honors

• We offer a wonderful selection of wedding favors, including customized boxes with European truffles or a selection of our Jordan Almonds, Initial Mints, chocolate dipped fortune cookies & etc.

• Featured on National Food Network's "Food Finds"

• United States Pastry Alliance – Gold Medal Winner

• Winner of the Austin Family Business Award

• Recipient of Master Chocolatier Award

107

Bravo! Member Since 1990

CONSULTATION

Call for a consultation with JaCiva's Wedding coordinator 503.234.8115. "The Perfect Place To Find Your perfect Wedding Cake."™

108

Sweet Masterpieces from La Joconde

Jutta Bach started La Joconde Cakes in 2006, after graduating with honors from the Le Cordon Bleu Pâtisserie and Baking Program at Western Culinary Institute in Portland. She also received formal training in architecture and design in Germany and applies this perfect combination of skills to creating her delicious works of art.

Her love of French cuisine, cultivated during extensive travels and study in France, results in a selection of innovative and modern flavor combinations that are based on classic French recipes.

All cakes are baked fresh, hand-crafted from scratch, using only finest ingredients to achieve perfect texture and exquisite taste.

At the personal consultation Jutta uses colored handdrawn sketches and her extensive design experience to create each couple's dream cake.

"Jutta, Awesome...everything was awesome. Start to finish it was just awesome. Your cakes were a huge hit, people were raving about them before they even ate them and then couldn't stop talking about them once we cut into them..."
— Mathew Braun

Contact
Jutta Bach

p. 503.481.4539
e. chef@lajocondecakes.com
www.lajocondecakes.com

Price
Varies depending on design; per-serving pricing scale.

Quick Facts
- Please schedule an appointment for a complimentary consultation & tasting

- Saturday & evening appointments available

- Many cake flavors & filling options; visit our website for complete menu

- No shortening, preservatives or substitutes; local ingredients used, when available

- Limited amount of cake orders taken to guarantee maximum quality; please secure your date early

DESIGNS
Classic or modern, simple or extravagant. Please view online portfolio at www.lajocondecakes.com

Papa Haydn Catering & Wedding Cakes

Papa Haydn first opened its doors in 1978 with outstanding food, impeccable service and a pastry case full of cakes, tortes and bombes. It was only a matter of time before loyal customers realized that nothing short of Papa Haydn's quality and innovation would do when it came to choosing a caterer or wedding cake. Papa Haydn Catering and Wedding Cakes is ready to help you create a flawless event, whether you are planning an elaborate wedding, a business gathering or an intimate dinner party.

Wedding Cakes

For weddings, the cake is the centerpiece of your celebration. Whether a unique cake from our portfolio, or one designed to your specifications, we guarantee that your cake will not just meet, but exceed your expectations. We make all our desserts from scratch using only the finest ingredients available.

We also have options available for VEGAN and WHEAT–FREE desserts. Please schedule a meeting with our wedding cake consultant and sample our wide variety of cakes.

Catering Services

Papa Haydn Catering and Wedding Cakes will handle all phases of your event from planning to clean up. Our catering menu is designed to accommodate your preferences: passed hors d'oeuvres, a buffet or an elegant seated dinner. We can work from our established menu or create one unique to your event. Our beverage service includes a full-service bar, as well as beer and wine selections. We have been recognized by WINE SPECTATOR MAGAZINE with an "Award of Excellence" for the past three years.

Contact

Papa Haydn
Catering & Wedding Cakes

p. 503.291.8350

e weddingcakes@papahaydn.com

e. catering@papahaydn.com

www.papahaydn.com

Price

Depends on menu selection; per-person pricing scale

Wedding Cakes

- Complimentary 6" anniversary cake

- We can custom design wedding cakes to fit your style

- Many cake flavors & filling options

- Complimentary consultations & cake tasting appointments available

- Discounts for larger cakes

STRESS FREE SERVICE

Papa Haydn's takes pride in making your event flawless. We will take all the hassle, headaches and stress out of the process so all you have to do is show up and have a good time.

109

The Party Scoop

- A unique dessert experience for your special event!

PO Box 3623
Tualatin, Oregon 97062
p. 503.539.0011
e. thepartyscoop@verizon.net
www.thepartyscoop.com

Be unique – break the tradition of just cake & frosting

The Party Scoop, Inc. was formed to fill a niche in the dessert catering industry. Our service comes to you providing the best in freshly scooped premium ice cream and customized toppings. We provide a customized service to meet your budget and size of reception.

We create a perfect marriage of ice cream and toppings for both you and your guests. Break the tradition of cake and frosting by serving our ice cream dessert, making your wedding reception stand out from the rest. Each guest can create his or her own unique sundae dessert. It is our passion to help make your event a very memorable experience.

Contact
Bea Thomas

Price
Customized quotes to fit your event and budget

Quick Facts
- A unique sundae bar service for your wedding reception
- Customize your special ice cream dessert
- We bring our special service to you
- Locally owned, fully licensed and insured
- Set-up and clean-up is included

(C) Tamara Orton & Evrim Icoz

WHAT'S NEW
Discounts available for booking our service on additional parties along with your wedding reception, i.e.: bachelor/bachelorette party, rehearsal, bridal shower, etc.

Bravo! Member Since 2009

110

419 SE 13th Avenue
Portland, Oregon 97214
p. 503.235.1415
www.pscheesecake.com

About Portland Style Cheesecake

Portland Style Cheesecake Company proprietor, Kim Haines, began her local specialty bakery in 1989 out of her home. In 1996, after kids and the bakery grew, the bakery moved to its current, larger location in Southeast Portland. Beginning with only one recipe, the bakery now offers over 25 different varieties. The cheesecakes are hand-crafted from scratch with the freshest ingredients. Our cheesecakes contain no preservatives and no partially hydrogenated oils. In 1998, Kim and crew joined talents with Bambi Sorenson to develop cheesecakes into unique one–of–a–kind decorated wedding cheesecakes. Discover for yourself the exquisite quality and flavor that has put Portland Style Cheesecake Company on the tip of everyone's tongue.

A Reason to Celebrate

During your consultation, we want to assist in every detail, working closely with your florist and event coordinator. Create your wedding cheesecake by bringing photos and, design ideas, along with color schemes to help our cake artisans design your one–of–a–kind wedding cheesecake. Fresh flowers, decadent fruit, silky ribbon and flowing fondant are just some of the items available to adorn your wedding cheesecake. So let Portland Style Cheesecake Company help you create a lasting memory for your very special occasion.

Contact
Portland Style Cheesecake Co.

Price
Varies on cake design & size

Varieties
- Vanilla
- Lemon
- Chocolate Grand Marnier
- Marionberry
- Chocolate Kahlua
- Italian Blackberry
- Tiramisu
- Red Raspberry
- And many more

Icings
- French Buttercream
- Rolled Fondant
- White Chocolate

111

WHAT'S NEW

Portland Style Cheesecakes are hand-crafted for your special occasion; please give us a call or visit our web site for more information
www.pscheesecake.com

Helpful Hint

Choosing Your Wedding Cake

You'll find many flavors and styles of cakes to choose from. Visit several shops and compare quality, style and prices. Also, sample different flavors of cakes to help in selecting the flavor you want. The baker is a specialist, so ask for advice and recommendations. Remember, each tier can be a different flavor.

© Amy Ouellette

ORDER YOUR WEDDING CAKE EARLY

Busy wedding months are June through September; you will need to order your cake four to six months in advance if you're getting married in the summer. At ordering time, you need only an approximate number of guests. Confirm the number two to three weeks before your wedding.

FIGURING THE AMOUNT

The baker will be helpful in advising you on the amount of cake needed based on the number of guests. The price is usually based on a per-slice amount. Be sure to ask about tier sizes and serving portions—are they pieces or slivers of cake?

CAKE KNIFE, SERVER & INSTRUCTIONS

Don't forget to bring a knife and server to cut the wedding cake or have the caterer supply them. Make sure your baker provides the service staff with instructions for cutting and serving your wedding cake. Because of their size and elegance, wedding cakes can be tricky to serve.

WEDDING CAKE TOPS & DECORATIONS

Most bakeries and bridal accessory stores have a large selection of cake toppers. Fresh-flower arrangements are another option and can be coordinated with your baker and florist. Cake toppers span traditional to funky designs. Many cake toppers can also be customized in a whimsical fashion patterned after the bride and groom. Some brides also choose cake toppers that are family heirlooms. When looking to achieve a dramatic look, some brides also opt to have a replica of their wedding bouquet as the choice for their cake topper often rendered in sugar or real flowers. For a cake topper with a humorous twist, some couples also select their favorite childhood heroes or characters.

112

Catering
Beverage & Espresso
Full-Service

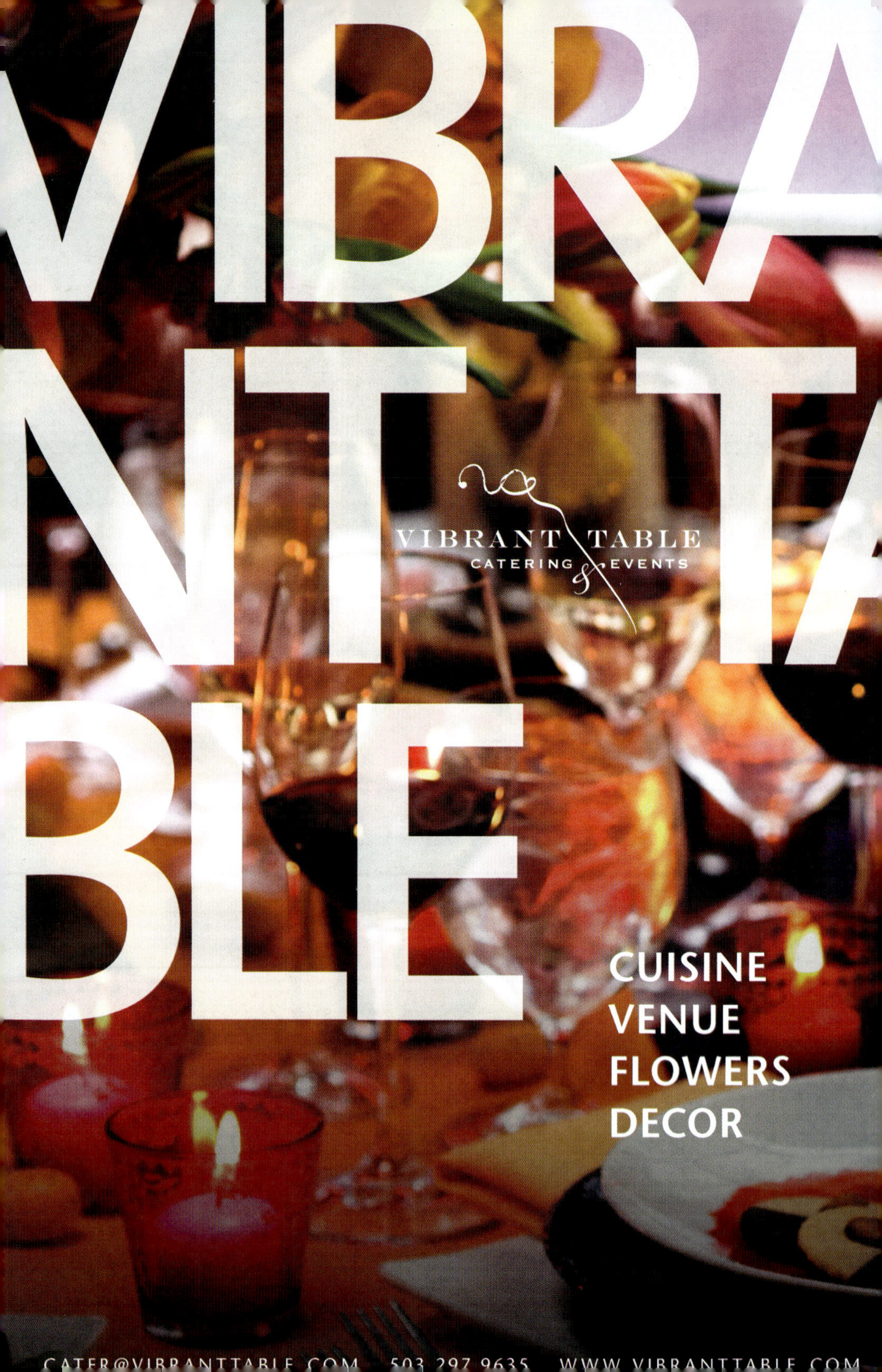
VIBRANT TABLE
VIBRANT TABLE
CATERING & EVENTS
CUISINE
VENUE
FLOWERS
DECOR
CATER@VIBRANTTABLE.COM 503.297.9635 WWW.VIBRANTTABLE.COM

About Espresso Arts Catering

At Espresso Arts Catering, we have our beans custom roasted for you by Stumptown Coffee Roasters just before your event. Using organic milk or soy, we then lovingly craft our lattes, cappuccinos, and mochas. We also offer exquisite coffee alternatives like our hot chocolate with homemade whip cream and spicy chai lattes. From Foxfire Teas we offer a large assortment of fragrant loose leaf teas. Whether you have an intimate wedding of 50 or a large event of 1,500, we have a package to fit every budget. We can accommodate small groups with our sleek, compact cart and be ready and rolling in minutes, while our large dual-machine package will efficiently serve large groups all day long.

"Their coffee is incredibly delicious, they serve it with a smile and love, they are the best."
– Pacific First Center tenant

"...this is a coffee cart like no other."
– Serena Davidson, Serena Davidson Photography

Bravo! Member Since 2007

Contact

Christine Herman-Russell
p. 503.475.3979
e. christine@espressoarts.com
www.espressoarts.com

Price

Affordable packages for any size event

Quick Facts

- Serving groups of any size in all of Oregon & Washington

- Espresso & French press services available

- Exclusively serving Stumptown Coffee Roasters, Foxfire Teas, & DragonFly Chai

- Please inquire about our current selection of Stumptown coffees

- Latest industry standard professional café equipment

- Iced espresso drinks, Italian sodas, orange juice, & pastries available upon request

115

"The Finest in Espresso Catering"

p. 877.281.8155
p 206.282.8155
e. Holly@EspressoElegance.com
www.EspressoElegance.com

Full-Service Espresso

When you choose Espresso Elegance, you are selecting a high-class espresso catering company that strives to enhance your special day by bringing a signature taste of the Pacific Northwest right to your wedding. Your guests will enjoy unlimited espresso drinks served to them by professional and friendly baristas. You are encouraged to customize the service to match your taste preferences, including selecting your favorite brand of coffee to be served.

Small to Large Weddings

From intimate receptions of 5 guests to extravagant weddings with hundreds of guests, Espresso Elegance handles every detail. We are equipped to serve events of all sizes with over 18 state-of-the-art espresso carts. With every event, Espresso Elegance is committed to exceeding your expectations.

"Espresso Elegance was a great addition to our wedding! Guests loved having unlimited espressos and they were great about accommodating our request for a special drink."

– Bride Michelle

Bravo! Member Since 2008

Contact
Holly Patton

Price
Customized affordable pricing to fit your wedding budget. Pricing is based on the number of guests & length of service.

Quick Facts
- Fully licensed & insured to serve events of all sizes in Washington & Oregon.

- Espresso Bars, Fruit Smoothie Bars, Italian Soda Bars and gourmet pastries are available to serve your guests.

- Eco-Friendly, Certified Kosher & Gluten Free packages available.

- Customizable service to fit your wedding theme & taste preferences from the brand of coffee to specialty menus.

WHAT'S NEW
Espresso Elegance is celebrating our 20th Anniversary of being the largest espresso caterer in the nation since 1989. To celebrate, we introduced our Eco-Friendly Espresso Catering package for earth friendly weddings & events.

116

Aarnegard's PREMIERE CATERING

2432 SE Umatilla Street
Portland, Oregon 97202

p. 503.235.0274
f. 503.235.8225

e. premierecatering@comcast.net

www.premierecatering.biz

About Aarnegard's Premiere Catering

Aarnegard's Premiere Catering offers fine dining in any location, customized to fit your style of entertaining, culinary tastes, and budget. We offer location catering at its finest...on the mountain top, at the beach, or in your garden... possibilities are endless.

Let Aarnegard's Premiere Catering make your event a true culinary success. We specialize in on-site cooking (ask for details). Nothing compares to freshly prepared foods for your event. Your guests will notice the fresh flavors and quality of your menu.

Aarnegard's Premiere Catering is a full-service caterer, providing everything needed for a successful event. Regardless of the type of event or service required, you can count on the reputation Aarnegard's Premiere Catering has earned, with over 20 years experience in the event business. With this experience, we are able to accommodate both large and small events. We will show you how experience pays off.

Contact
Michael Peters

Price
Please call for quote

Quick Facts
- Event planning & site selection
- Licensed to serve alcoholic beverages
- Rental coordination (china, glassware, silverware, tables, chairs, tents)
- Props & decorations
- Entertainment (bands, disc jockeys, musicians)

117

PROFESSIONAL & COURTEOUS

Premiere Catering prepares all entrees on-site to offer only the Finest and Freshest Entrees possible. Our professional & courteous service staff will assist in making your event successful. From set up to clean up, you will find our staff efficient and friendly.

Bravo! Member Since 2000

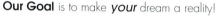

Always Perfect Catering

344 W Columbia River Highway
Troutdale, Oregon 97060
p. 503.465.0400
e. michele@alwaysperfectcatering.net
www.AlwaysPerfectCatering.net

Our Goal is to make *your* dream a reality!

Our Creative & professional team can assist with every aspect of your wedding. Exceptional service & hospitality above and beyond all expectations!

Our Knowledgeable catering planner will help coordinate menus, wine selection, specialty cocktails, staffing, rentals and other needed services.

We Have an amazing chef who can customize any menu to suit your taste & dietary needs.

Freshest Ingredients purchased locally whenever possible.

What People Say!

"Always Perfect Catering is Always Perfect...Whether it's taking care of 600 hungry party guests or an intimate dinner affair, the food is wonderfully prepared and the staff is top-notch."

– Linda & Junki Yoshida

"Extraordinary food! Fabulous service! Creative menu suggestions! Beautiful presentation! Ecologically conscious and they do the dishes too!...I can't say enough about them! They are my first choice in catering for all my catering needs!"

– Debbie Bishop ~ Port of Portland

Contact
Michele Blaine
Jason Rizzuto

Price
Based on menu, package & service style.
Free quotes & consultations.

Quick Facts
- Exceptional food
- Impeccable service
- Beautiful presentations
- Delivering an Always Perfect event!
- Wide selection of organic, vegan & free range products
- Environmentally friendly "GREEN" sustainable company
- Full service catering for 25 to 2,500 – plated, buffet, family style, etc

ALWAYS PERFECT!
Serving the greater Portland/ Vancouver area since 1992

118

Busy Bee Catering

PO Box 295
Welches, Oregon 97067
p. 503.622.6743
f. 503.622.0167
e. busybeecatering@hotmail.com
www.busybeecatering.com

About Busy Bee Catering

Busy Bee Catering is located in beautiful Welches Oregon, at the foothills of Mt. Hood. We provide service to many special local venues as well as service to the Metro Area, Hood River, Central Oregon and the Willamette Valley. We love the beauty and bounty that Oregon has to offer and like to showcase these aspects in the way we present our foods. We are available to provide a full array of services ranging from event planning and vendor coordination to delivery, set up or even drop off.

We have been busy catering weddings, corporate events, family picnics, and parties of every theme and type. We would love to work with you to create the kind of function that shows your personality and entertaining style. We have made lots of friends catering in the last 20 years and would be happy to provide a variety of references. Take the hassle out of your next ski trip or camp out with meals prepared in our local kitchen. Just stop by our convenient location on your way up the mountain. Whatever you're planning, please consider Busy Bee Catering...we love to cater and it shows!

Contact
Todd & Jan Ostrom

Price
Menus to accommodate all budgets

Quick Facts
- Over 20 years experience in corporate, social catering & event planning

- Long time relationships with local vendors to ensure freshest, high quality ingredients

- Creative presentation using clever props, fresh greens, flowers & herbs

- Caring, friendly & professional staff

- We are a fully licensed & insured off site caterer

- Fresh delicious foods that make even a simple menu elegant

- On site grilling & cooking

- Busy Bee Catering is a sustainable business

- Menu tasting available

119

Bravo! Member Since 2008

p. 503.238.8889
f. 503.238.8893
e. info@caibpdx.com
www.caibpdx.com

It's your Wedding Day

great food
impeccable service
lasting memories…

Catering At Its Best

We realize this can be a stressful time for couples ~

With this in mind, we have created complete, all inclusive Wedding Packages to help make planning your reception as easy as possible!

From a simple yet elegant hors d' oeuvre reception to a grand dinner buffet, these packages let you customize the perfect menu for your reception.

If "plated" service is more your style, one of our Event Planners will create a custom menu just for you.

Visit our web site to view our Wedding Packages.

Then call us to have a complimentary consultation with one of our experienced Event Planners.

Let our experienced professional team create a unique reception you and your guest will be sure to enjoy and remember!

Contact
Toni Robinson

Price
Based on package, menu selection & type of service

Services
- Personalized wedding planning & site location

- On site event manager & experienced service staff at every reception

- Vegetarian & special dietary menus available upon request

- Full service bars, experienced professional servers & OLCC licensed bartenders

- Complete rental coordination (tents, tables, chairs, dance floors etc.)

120

Portland Composts! Participant
RecycleWorks Award Winner

a proud participant

PORTLAND COMPOSTS!

a program of the city of Portland Office of Sustainable Development and Metro

Bravo! Member Since 1995

© Lyssia Coffey

12003 NE Ainsworth Circle
Portland, Oregon 97220
p. 503.408.8816
e. sales@chezjoly.com
www.chezjoly.com

About Chez Joly Catering

After the long success of Capers Café, we opened Chez Joly in downtown Portland's beautiful Pearl District on the corner of Broadway & Davis. Created by Christian & Annette Joly, Capers Café & Capers et Le Bar at Portland's International Airport, the company is family owned and operated, ready to fulfill all of your dining and catering needs. Our very talented chefs have a wide range of creativity and culinary skills, and the food is prepared using only the finest & freshest local ingredients.

Chez Joly is a custom caterer, specializing in foods and beverages tailor-made for its customers. You may choose from one of our "planned menus", or we can create a custom blend based on your special wishes or dietary necessities. By offering "A La Carte" pricing we can tailor our services and menu selections to fit into what you can afford, giving you the ultimate value for the money spent. Our Catering Director will be happy to meet with you and work to plan the perfect event.

At Chez Joly we can take care of all the arrangements for your functions. There are so many details to be addressed - date, time, guests, location, colors, the dress, the cake, the flowers. Our Catering Team pays close attention to those details of your day, covering all of the timing issues so that you can relax and enjoy time with your family and friends without stress. We provide experienced event staff, full beverage and bar service and any rehearsal dinner or reception style you'd like – plated, passed, buffet or a custom option. We never take shortcuts, and our work is 100% guaranteed.

We look forward to working with you!

Contact
Catering Team

Price
Budget conscious, ready to give you the best possible food and service for your event, specific to your needs.

Ala Carte pricing is available.

Services
- Over 25 years in the Restaurant, Catering & Event Industry.

- Preferred Caterer at many local venues.

- Tailor Made Menus specific to your special wishes, budget or dietary needs.

- Coordination of rentals.

- Event/Wedding Planning Services Available

- Professional, Licensed Staff & Bartenders

- Established 1990, A Family Owned Business

121

Bravo! Member Since 1994

CONNOR CATERING AT THE CROWN

Connor Catering at The Crown
The Crown Ballroom
918 SW Yamhill
Portland, Oregon 97205
p. 503.913.1040
f. 503.296.2057
e. connorrent@aol.com
www.connorcatering.com

About Connor Catering at The Crown

With over 10 years of impeccable service, Executive Chef and Owner of Connor Catering, Joseph Connor has garnered consistent accolades from bride & grooms of The Crown Ballroom, as well as from corporate clients and the industry at large.

"Thank you for all your hard work and expertise that you put into my daughter's wedding. That night will forever be special in part because of your culinary genius!!!!! The food was superb and your staff was professional yet very personable! "

We will highly recommend your services,
– Sandy Bailey

Chef Connor's legendary record of service at The Crown Ballroom is matched by his ability to provide exceptional catering at virtually any location in the Northwest. Connor Catering's esteemed list of corporate clients include Nike, Wacom Technologies, Intel, Marquis Companies, Warner Bros. Films and many more.

Contact
Joe Connor

Price
Please inquire

Quick Facts
- Menu price includes staffing, table & buffet linens, linen napkins, silverware & china

- Cake cutting service is complimentary

- Flexible bar packages

- Signature drinks per your request!

- Complimentary tasting & menu planning session for Crown clients

WHAT'S NEW
Please feel free to peruse their many menu, appetizer and dessert offerings on their website at www. connorcatering.com.

See page 404 under Reception & Wedding Sites

Bravo! Member Since 2001

122

CRAVE Catering

1324 SE 8th Street
Portland, Oregon 97214

p. 503.224.0370
f. 503.224.3919

e. catering@cravepdx.com

www.cravepdx.com

Think about the **BEST** party you've ever been to…what was it that made it so unique? Imagine what it would look like if every little detail went perfectly…

YOUR VISION + OUR PASSION = A symphony of local ingredients, crafted into mouth-watering dishes. Our events are always the talk of the town! We take great care in our ingredients, hand-picking produce & other local products to foster community support for local farmers, fishermen, and artisans. We are a Full Service Caterer that offers event set-up, equipment rental coordination, and full bar service. So you can relax and enjoy…let us do all the work. One could say Crave Catering is the quintessential Portland Catering Company!

"Crave Catering did an amazing job at our wedding. Our guests could not stop raving about the abundance of delicious food. The staff was very helpful and friendly, and they all had excellent attention to detail. They kept everything running smoothly and reduced my stress. I would highly recommend them."

– Kathleen Burns, Married August 2008

OUR EVENTS –

Weddings, Anniversaries, Auctions, Galas, Fundraisers, TV Shows, Movies, Luncheons, Company Picnics, Holiday Parties, Open Houses, Cocktail Parties.

Contact
Sales Department

Price
Call or visit www.cravepdx.com for ordering, menus, and pricing

Quick Facts
- Locally owned business with more than 25 years of experience

- Founding Member of the Sustainable Catering Association

- We use Local Seasonal Produce

- Naturally raised meats & poultry, and sustainable seafood

- Portland Compost Participant

- Portland RecycleWorks Award Recipient

123

CULINARY CRAVEings

Pacific Northwest
Rustic Italian
Traditional American
Asian Fusion
Caribbean Cuisine
Nuevo Latino
Old World French
Slow and Low Barbecue

WHAT DO YOU CRAVE?

Bravo! Member Since 1999

Catering and Events
DeAngelo's

9037 SW Burnham Street
Tigard, Oregon 97223
p. 503.620.9020
f. 503.620.3964
www.cateringbydeangelos.com

Catering Just For You Since 1983!

DeAngelo's Catering offers all types of menus from self- or full-service buffets to formal sit-down affairs. We offer the client the opportunity for full-service event planning including food, rental coordination, site evaluations, décor, and more. Our menus offer a wide range of food including Asian, Italian, Mexican, African, Caribbean, and Hawaiian; excellent service staff is available, attire is always appropriate.

124

Approved Caterer locations:

- Holy Names Heritage Center
- McLean House
- Wisteria Gardens in Brush Prairie
- The Party Room at Wild Bill's
- Museum of Oregon Territory
- World Forestry Center and Museum
- Marshall House
- Leach Botanical Gardens
- Oregon Square Courtyard
- Many more

Contact
DeAngelo's Catering

Price
Based on a per-person basis; however many other options are available

References
References provided upon request

Quick Facts
- Over 25 years experience ranging in all types of catering needs

- Food is scratch-prepared & exquisitely presented

- Fully licensed & insured to serve alcoholic beverages

- FREE consultations

- Complete flexibility to adapt to special needs & requests

- All full-service buffet décor is no-charge

Bravo! Member Since 1996

NEED IDEAS?
Visit our website at
www.cateringbydeangelos.com

Delilah's Catering

p. 503.243.3324
e. Linette@delilahscatering.com
www.delilahscatering.com

About Delilah's Catering

As artisans, we will craft your reception to reflect your style. Whether you talk to Linette or Heather at your first meeting, you can rest assured that we will see every detail through and be there on your wedding day.

We believe in beautiful food, both in taste and presentation. Our kitchen excels in Northwest cuisine and International cuisines as well. Tasty vegetarian dishes are always available. We strive to use local seafood, meats, fruits and vegetables, changing with the season. Our dishes are artfully garnished and arranged to be a focal point at your reception.

Services

We will coordinate your rental needs at no additional charge. This includes table settings and linens, as well as outdoor equipment such as canopies, tents, dance floors, tables and chairs in many styles.

Contact
Linette True

Price
Many variables determine price; we strive to work with your budget

Food & Beverage
- Full-service catering since 1985
- Northwest & International cuisines
- Wine, beer & full cocktail service available
- Espresso bar to treat your guests
- Chocolate fountain
- Professional waiters, chefs for on-site cooking or carving & on-site coordinators are available

125

DELILAH'S GIFT TO YOU

We know how exciting your wedding day will be, so we prepare a basket filled with goodies from your reception, for the two of you to enjoy when you're alone.

Bravo! Member Since 1996

www.DevilsFoodCatering.com

ring 503.233.9288

126

The Devil's in the Details!

We have years of catering experience and understand that no details can be overlooked. We roll up our sleeves and sort through the timelines and logistics. We make the rental orders and delivery arrangements. We are punctual, efficient and work to be sure there is no doubt that you are in expert hands and good company.

When you visit our kitchen you might see our chefs putting up pickled peaches or smoking bacon. We may be baking our handmade crackers or rolling out pasta… but there is always room at the table to sit down and begin planning your wedding menu. Along the process we will discover what food and styles you love and will design a menu to satisfy your tastes without offending your budget. Our comprehensive proposal will include menu ideas, rentals, staffing and bar options.

Devil's Food is a Green Business. We have a comprehensive recycling and composting program. We limit our power and water usage. And we source our ingredients locally.

Contact
Charles Stilwell

p. 503.233.9288

e. charles@devilsfoodcatering.com

www.devilsfoodcatering.com

Favorite Wedding Locations:
- The Gerding Theatre at the Armory
- The Oregon Historical Society
- Portland Classical Chinese Garden
- Blue Sky Gallery
- Jupiter Hotel
- The Wonder Ballroom
- Sauvie Island Farms
- The North Star Ballroom
- Wine Country Vineyards

Favorite Wedding Styles:
- Multiple small-plates stations
- Family-style Supper Club
- Tray-passed hors d'oeuvres
- Wine dinners at the Vineyard
- a Pig roast at the farm, or a clam bake at the coast
- Buffets and Seated dinners

Bravo! Member Since 2008

Eat Your Heart Out

1230 SE 7th Avenue
Portland, Oregon 97214
p. 503.232.4408
f. 503.232.0778
e. party@eatyourheartout.biz
www.eatyourheartout.biz

About Eat Your Heart Out Catering

You make us special. You're going to be whirlwinded, waited on, waited for, honeymooned, brided, groomed– kaazaam, you're married! And Eat Your Heart Out will be a part of it. Watch for our new book, We're Married Let's Eat, simple cooking and entertaining for your first year together.

Types of Menus and Specialties

Eat Your Heart Out Catering was created in 1975 by two brides, who produced three brides-to-be along the way. Maybe you want to be involved in the menu, or just sit back and be dazzled by choices ranging from Tuscan tenderloin of beef with Oregon Pinot Noir sauce and grilled baby lamb chops, to caviar eclairs with lemon cream and Gougere crab puffs with dried cherries, and Martini Bites.

Recommended by major facilities including The Aerie at Eagles Landing, The Marshall House, Crystal Springs Rhododendron Gardens, Leach Botanical Gardens, Elk Cove Vineyards, Ponzi Vinyard Home and Bridal Veil Lakes among others. We specialize in all cuisines: ethnic, traditional or more adventuresome with Northwest fresh products.

Contact
Monica Grinnell

Price
Varies, please call for quotes

Amenities
- 33 years of experience catering weddings & events including cooking with noted chefs such as Julia Child & Marcella Hazan

- We provide all rentals, linens, serving pieces both traditional & unusual, flowers, ice sculptures & design assistance

- Our staff includes talented chefs, charming bartenders & efficient servers

127

Portland Composts! Participant

WHAT'S NEW

For more information about us check out our website

www.eatyourheartout.biz

Bravo! Member Since 1995

Jake's CATERING

611 SW 11th Avenue
Portland, Oregon
p. 503.241.2125
e. lwolfson@jakescatering.com
e. ehight@jakescatering.com
www.jakescatering.com

128

Jake's Catering...A Tradition

Jake's Catering is part of the McCormick & Schmick's family of restaurants, including Jake's Famous Crawfish. Jake's is one of the oldest and most respected dining institutions in the Portland area, and Jake's Catering upholds this prestigious reputation.

Known for offering an extensive range of Pacific Northwest menu selections including fresh seafood, pasta, poultry and prime cut steaks, Jake's Catering has the variety, flexibility and talent to cater to your needs.

A Historic Gem

Listed on the National Register of Historic Places, The Governor Hotel is an architectural beauty. Built in 1909, the hotel has been completely restored to its original grandeur. The recently completed renovation of the Heritage Ballroom unveils Portland's best-kept secret, resurrecting this one-of-a-kind grand space for brides and grooms after a hiatus of more than 60 years. The classic design and ornate craftsmanship were preserved in the original Italian Renaissance styling. The room's high vaulted ceilings, marble floors and black-walnut woodwork and walls are truly unique.

Availability and Terms

Our Italian Renaissance-style rooms offer variety and flexibility for groups of 25 to 700. The newly renovated Heritage Ballroom, Renaissance Room, Fireside Room, Library and eight additional rooms gracefully complement the charm of The Governor Hotel. We require a 30% deposit to confirm your event and payment in-full 72 hours prior to event for estimated charges.

Contact
Linda Wolfson
Erin Hight

Price
$50 to $100 per person

Capacity
700 reception; 450 sit-down

Amenities
- Tables & chairs for up to 500
- Professional, uniformed servers
- Full-service bar & bartenders
- Cloth napkins & linens in variety of colors
- Fine china & glassware
- A/V available upon request
- Ample parking available

TYPES OF EVENTS

From stand-up cocktail and appetizer receptions to fabulous buffet presentations and complete sit-down dinners for groups and gatherings of all sizes.

See page 437 under Reception & Wedding Sites

Bravo! Member Since 1994

Pearl CATERING

206 NW 10th Avenue
Portland, Oregon 97209
p. 503.860.0203
e. carla@urban-restaurants.com
www.pearlcateringpdx.com

About Pearl Catering

Pearl Catering, delivers a menu of crowd pleasing favorites richly influenced by Northwest ingredients, beautifully presented and full of flavor! Whether you are looking to serve passed hors d'oeuvres at your wedding reception or a buffet dinner, Pearl Catering offers a variety of creative menus for any budget. Have something special in mind? No problem, we are happy to customize a menu to meet your specific needs and budget.

Pearl Catering is the exclusive in house full service caterer at Urban Studio, the Pearl District's quintessential event space. Ideal for wedding rehearsals, ceremonies and receptions, our experienced catering and event staff will make the planning process a pleasure and your wedding a success.

Price
Please call for quote

Quick Facts

- Full service and licensed caterer for both food and alcohol service

- Elegant or casual menu packages available (go to www.PearlCateringpdx.com)

- Setup & cleanup included

- China, silverware & basic linen included

- Friendly & knowledgeable event & serving staff

- Menu tastings available

129

WHAT'S NEW?

Rental cost of Urban Studio is waived with a minimum food and beverage purchase. Call for more information 503.860.0203.

See page 386 and page 511 under Reception & Wedding Sites

phresh
organic catering
503-313-0488

130

at **phresh** we cook passionately with respect to technique & creativity. we are dedicated to providing you with an exceptional culinary experience.

our professional event planning staff will coordinate all aspects of your event from rental & décor, to fully licensed bar service & vendor recommendations.

our courteous and gracious service staff will attend to your every need on site. with an eye for detail, **phresh** will help you plan & experience your most memorable moments.

sample menu:

hors d'oeuvres

- dungeness crab profiteroles with basil & heirloom tomatoes
- phresh salad rolls
- duck confit sliders with pinot noir-rhubarb salsa

dinner

- rose petal & peach salad
- farmer's market summer vegetable sauté
- olive oil roasted fingerling potatoes with chives
- oregon line caught salmon & organic basil – hazelnut pesto

JESSICAHILL PHOTOGRAPHY

Contact

Shelley Lomax,
director of catering & sustainability

3436 SE Milwaukie Avenue
Portland, Oregon 97202

p. 503.313.0488

e. events@phreshorganiccatering.com

www.phreshorganiccatering.com

Price

phresh services compliment all budgets

Quick Facts

- seasonal menus showcase the finest organic, local & artisan ingredients
- free menu tastings & full service event planning for bravo clients
- city of portland – metro certified sustainable caterer
- featured in the oregonian, portland tribune, willamette week
- client compliments: "perfect catering" "culinary ninja"
- customized, creative vegetarian & vegan menus also available

WHAT'S NEW?

- new seasonal menus
- preferred caterer at most portland venues
- specialized small plate & wine pairing menus available

7800 SW Durham Road
Portland, Oregon 97224

p. 503.620.8855
f. 503.620.3355

e. info@portlandcateringcompany.com

www.portlandcateringcompany.com

About Portland Catering Company

We offer thoughtful menus filled with dishes that are always fresh and well prepared and our gracious and attentive staff will take care of even the smallest details. Whether you're planning an intimate gathering for a family reception, an annual charity black-tie gala or a large, glittering holiday affair to celebrate with your corporate staff, Portland Catering Company will make your event a truly special occasion.

We will work with you to set the right tone, select the perfect menu and create an atmosphere that will make you and your guests feel pampered and completely at ease. From planning to perfect ending, let us help you every step of the way.

In addition to helping you plan your menu, we can assist you with so much more. Selecting a venue, handling the rentals, and coordinating with all of your vendors – we pride ourselves on making your event effortless – so you can relax and enjoy!

**There's No Better Way to Impress,
Except With the Best!**

Contact
Erin Cutlip

Price
Based on menu selection, guest count & type of service

Services
- Full-service caterer
- Customized menus to fit within your budget
- Friendly & professional staff
- Menu items prepared fresh daily & from scratch
- Free menu tasting available

131

Elegance in Catering

1410 SW Morrison Suite 600
Portland, Oregon 97205-1930
p. 503.248.9305
f. 503.243.7147
e. rafatis@rafatiscatering.com
www.rafatiscatering.com

132

Our Cuisine

Unique, inspiring dishes that compliment any theme or style. Specializing in Pacific Northwest, Pan Asian, South and Central American, Middle Eastern, Caribbean/ Island – we are ready to create the perfect menu for your event. Consider fresh Heirloom Tomato Gazpacho with Tortilla Skewered Shrimp, Tangerine Scallop Martinis with Cashew Crumble, entrée or small plates like our popular Painted Hills Tenderloin with Gorgonzola Risotto and Maysara Pinot Noir Wine Reduction Sauce, Chef's exhibitions of our famous Seafood Paella, or Wok Stations of fabulous Pan Asian Stir Fry.

Our Services

From the simplicity of everyday luncheon meeting needs, the formalities of white glove dinner service, the complexities of seminars and conferences, to themed corporate receptions or the selection of the perfect event location site, you can count on Rafati's. Our event coordinators will be happy to prepare detailed plans based on theme, décor, budget and other specific goals, then produce them with savvy style and flair.

Event Locations

Rafati's is located in and the exclusive caterer for the historic Tiffany Center. Our clients also enjoy our signature catering and event services at a wide selection of locations, facilities and private residences throughout Oregon and Southwest Washington.

Contact
Jessica Rafati
Event Manager

Price
The cost is determined by the menu selection, level of desired service and number of guests

Quick Facts
- More than 25 years catering to Portland's metro community

- Concentration on locally produced foods & sustainable products

- Unique, sophisticated presentations & themes

- Full bar services, local wineries, breweries & distilleries

- Highly trained & credentialed professional service staff

- Event planning included with full-service catering

With innovative menus, passionate focus on fresh local ingredients, edgy presentations & unparalleled service, you can depend on Rafati's each & every time to help you acheive the "wow" factor for your event catering needs!

REEDVILLE
CATERING

2975 SW Cornelius Pass Road, Suite D
Hillsboro, Oregon 97123
p. 503.642.9898
f. 503.642.5536
e. info@reedvillecatering.com
www.reedvillecatering.com

Your Vision

Reedville Catering understands the importance of your wedding day. Our professional culinary team and experienced event coordinators will help you create a memorable event with delicious, carefully prepared, and tastefully presented menu selections.

Your Menu

We are committed to creating a menu which reflects your tastes, satisfies and impresses your guests, and works within your budget. We specialize in the use of quality, local ingredients such as: Oregon bleu cheese, Northwest wild salmon, wild mushrooms, and house-made strawberry vinaigrette. In order to ensure that our flavors and your tastes are exactly what you've envisioned we invite you to a tasting of your selections.

Your Event

Reedville Catering will assist you in designing the right look and feel of your unique wedding reception. We provide a wide array of event services beginning with your event proposal and moving through a consultation, venue choices, florists, and event site visits. We're committed to making the planning of your wedding day as fun and as exciting as we know your reception will be!

Contact

Debbie Priest, *Event Planner*

Price

A proposal will be prepared for your approval based on menu selection, level of service required, & guest count.

Quick Facts

- Twenty years catering to the Portland/West Metro area
- Passed hors d'oeuvres, specialty food bars, tasteful buffets & elegant sit-down dinners
- Full bar services - including customized wine & beer lists & specialty drink packages
- Preferred caterer at World Forestry Center, Jenkins Estate, Walters Cultural Arts Center, Tuality Health & Education Center, & several wineries

WHAT'S NEW?

We offer "Wedding Boxes" and food trays that are great for feeding wedding participants, family and guests during the time leading up to your wedding ceremony, or for in-town guests to unwind after the wedding - perhaps picnicking or wine tasting together in the beautiful Northwest.

133

CATERING

134

14020 NE 4th Plain Road, Suite E
Vancouver, Washington 98682
p. 360.891.0584
f. 360.891.3087
e. kelly@simplythymecatering.com
www.simplythymecatering.com

Food is a central part of any celebration

. . . and we know it's important that any event reflects your taste and vision. Executive Chef Tamara Leibfarth CEC, and her culinary team will add the "savory ingredient" to the success of your celebration - by creating unique menus and giving attention to the quality and presentation of what we prepare. We offer menus for a range of budget considerations. Catering prices vary based on menu selections, guest count & level of service; we invite you to inquire.

Simply Thyme Catering provides catering for small, intimate parties to large, memorable events . . . from picnic pleasures to elegant times! We can cater at your chosen location - whether your dream is a wedding on the beach, in the Gorge or in your own backyard. We can also assist you with venue options from our extensive list of preferred sites in the Portland/Vancouver Metro and surrounding areas.

With our seamless service, we offer you the opportunity to be a guest at your own hosted event! We're able to assist in any or all phases of planning before your wedding day, as well as at your reception, with our on-site Event Manager.

Simply Thyme Catering is all about good food, exceptional service and creating a memorable day for you and your guests. We look forward to meeting with you and hearing of your ideas for your wedding day!

Chef Tamara & Kelly
Owners of Simply Thyme Catering

"One big thank you for making our special day SOOOO delicious. Blessings!" – JP

Contact
Kelly Hoeppner

Price
Please contact for pricing options.

Quick Facts

- Our menus focus on local, seasonal produce & products featuring globally inspired menus with a local focus.

- Vegetarian Entrees available, prepared with equal care to compliment Main Menu.

- In case you didn't have time at your reception to enjoy your selected menu, we provide a Dinner Box for you & yours to enjoy after the celebration.

- We're proud to be a women-owned business.

WHAT'S NEW?

Simply Thyme Catering has become well known for helping create beautiful weddings from the rehearsal dinner to "I do!"

VIBRANT TABLE
CATERING & EVENTS

2236 SE Belmont
Portland, Oregon 97214
p. 503.297.9635
f. 503.234.4051
e. cater@vibranttable.com
www.vibranttable.com

Catering

We believe it is possible to prepare extraordinary food in the smallest of quantities and on the grandest of scales. Whether your wedding is an intimate gathering or an extravagant celebration, Vibrant Table will help you create a memorable event that reflects your vision and personality.

Floral

Our floral design team is trained to see the perfect blend of form and color to compliment your event's overall look. We are adept at using color, texture, light and scent to highlight the unique attributes of every event.

Décor

Our staff skillfully combines flowers, candles, vases, trellises, lighting and other accessories that provide the greatest impact with the smallest details.

Venue

Our exquisite cuisine and dynamic services have earned us an exclusive spot at these fine venues: The Portland Art Museum, Zenith Vineyard, The Loft and The Treasury Ballroom. You will also find us on the preferred list at many other vibrant settings. Please visit our website for a complete list.

Contact

Kurt Beadell
Creative Director & Co-Owner

Price

Based upon guest count, food selection & service requirements.

Please contact us for a free consultation.

135

Quick Facts

- Our services range from fine cuisine & innovative décor to floral artistry & event theme creation

- Portland Caterer of the Year 2007, 2008 & 2009 (Oregon Bride Magazine)

- We follow sustainable event practices

- Recycleworks Award recipient

THE LOFT ON BELMONT

Our one-of-a-kind urban event space is ideal for rehearsal dinners, engagement parties or intimate weddings. Able to accommodate up to 100 guests, The Loft features large windows, a fireplace, lobby bar and striking, contemporary décor.

© Jaime Bosworth

Bravo! Member Since 2000

WILD CURRANT

201 South First Street
St. Helens, Oregon 97051
p. 1.866.330.9099
c. 971.533.2609
f. 503.366.9099
e. wildcurrant@ados.net
www.wildcurrantcatering.com

About Wild Currant Catering

"Be a guest at your own event!" Sit back and relax while we take care of the planning and preparation of your wedding feast. Our staff is ready to pamper you and your guests.

We love to entertain at the Wild Currant and we love good food. Our menu selection and food preparation are carefully thought out to provide you with the best quality food available. We strive to keep abreast of the latest food trends, while not forgetting the old favorites. We are versatile and can help you plan the menu you desire.

Your wedding day should be a day of lasting memories. We take the worry out of the wedding, leaving you to shine and enjoy. Let us share our secrets to a fun and successful wedding reception. Let's talk.

Contact
Doug Boyes

Price
Based on per person: many other options are available

Quick Facts
- Full-service catering & event planning
- Fresh NW ingredients
- Always freshly prepared
- Custom menus form traditional to exotic delights
- Wine, beer and full cocktail service
- Vegetarian & gluten free menus

136

WHAT'S NEW

Have another event coming up? We cater to weddings, receptions, corporate events, in-home catering, dinner parties (large & small), Celebration of Life, and anything else you can think of! Check out our vegetarian menu online at: wildcurrantcatering.com .

Bravo! Member Since 2008

800 NW 6th Avenue
Portland, Oregon 97209
p. 503.223.0070
f. 503.223.1386
e. candace@wilfsrestaurant.com
www.wilfsrestaurant.com

About Wilfs Restaurant & Bar

Wilfs Restaurant & Bar at Union Station, minutes from downtown, offers a unique, convenient location for all your events: lunch, dinner, meetings, wine tasting, family celebrations, to the perfect wedding! Our catering options range from informal cocktail parties to a formal sit-down affair with live entertainment.

Weddings as Easy as 1-2-3

Wilfs offers coordinating services to help unravel the complexities of event planning. Expert staff offers personal service and attention to the details, and Candace, our event coordinator, will create a seamless event. Our experience in asking the "right" questions from the start, assures you, your event for 10 to 1,000, will be effortless.

The Perfect Plan for your Perfect Day

Our packages are created for your moment. We offer reception-style, sit-down, or a cocktail party atmosphere; either at the restaurant or an event site. We source our ingredients from our NW backyard, creating contemporary cuisine with a classic touch for every palate.

Contact
Candace McDonald

Price
Starting at $15 per person

Quick Facts
- Capacity from 2 to 1,000
- Settings include Union Station Depot Lobby, Rose Garden, entire restaurant
- Outdoor urban roof top venue over-looking the city
- Off-site catering services
- Event coordinator
- Easy parking
- A sustainable company
- Open warehouse setting for up to 800
- Vegan & vegetarian options

WILF'S RESTAURANT & BAR
- Unique location
- Outdoor urban roof top venue
- Locally grown products from the NW
- Open warehouse setting up to 800

137

Bravo! Member Since 1992

See page 517 under Event & Meeting Sites

Helpful Hint

Choosing Your Caterer

DETERMINING THE TYPE OF MENU FOR YOUR RECEPTION

The time of day will help determine what you serve: for a morning wedding, you may want to serve a brunch menu; hors d'oeuvres are perfect for afternoon receptions; and a sit-down dinner or buffet is appropriate for evenings.

MENU SELECTION & THE WEATHER

Be certain that your menu selections will withstand your special day's anticipated weather. Avoid hot or heavy meals on muggy and humid days. High humidity may also wilt potato chips, cut cheeses and similar foods. On hot days extra care should be taken to protect easily spoiled foods. Be especially careful with mayonnaise-based items, raw shellfish and the like.

CATERING GUIDELINES

To avoid running out of food at your reception, it is important to plan your menu carefully. Your caterer will be able to help you determine the best style of menu, with the correct amount of food based on your budget. Be sure to ask your caterer if they

© Paul Rich

prepare any extra food for unexpected guests, and if there is an additional cost for this service. Always get a written estimate for the menu you have selected from the caterers you are considering. This estimate should include all food costs, rentals, labor, gratuities and taxes.

ESTIMATING HOW MANY PEOPLE

Determine your guest count as soon as possible, as all price quotes will be based on this number. Begin by requesting prospective guest lists from both your and the groom's parents. Then put together your own list. Once all the guest lists are combined, you can use the "rule-of-thumb" that 70–75% will attend to establish the final guest count.

WHAT THE CATERER SUPPLIES

When it comes to supplying china, flatware, glasses, cups, saucers and table linens, every catering company is different. Some will include the cost in their catering prices, while others will not. Ask each caterer you are considering how they handle this matter and make sure you fully understand all fees before signing a contract.

SERVING THE FOOD

After you have expressed your expectations for your reception, and have determined the flow of your party and time lines for the reception, your caterer will be able to suggest buffet table layouts and food start times. They may recommend that waiters serve hors d'oeuvres so that your guests can mingle, or offer you ideas about food stations which will create a more interactive reception for your guests.

LIQUOR LAWS & LIABILITY:

With today's strict liquor laws, it's always smart to check into who assumes the liability for any alcoholic beverage service.

a state-licensed bartender. Licensed servers have a permit from the State's Liquor Control Board. If you have a no-host bar where money changes hands, it is the law that you must have a server who has a permit from the State's Liquor Control Board showing that the bartender has completed alcohol-server education.

Advantages of hiring professional beverage servers: beverage and catering service companies provide professionally trained staff who can handle complete bar services at your event. They take care of the purchasing, bar setup and cleanup, serving, and liability. It costs a little more but may be worth it to ensure the bar will be handled in a professional and legal manner. These people are trained to detect if someone should not be served more, or if someone is underage. This service also allows you to enjoy the event without worrying about your guests.

Although the event facility and/or the caterer may carry liability insurance, the host or coordinator of the function may still be considered liable. Make sure all parties involved with the event are properly insured and consult with an insurance agent to make sure you have appropriate coverage for yourself.

Oregon and Washington Liquor Control Commission Laws: In Oregon private hosted bars featuring hard alcohol, beer, and wine do not require any special licensing. Private no-host bars may only feature beer and wine and do require a special day license. OLCC does not allow private no-host service of hard alcohol. Only OLCC licensed food and beverage establishments and caterers may sell hard alcohol. In Washington private hosted bars featuring hard alcohol, beer, and wine do require a WLCC Banquet Permit. The permit must be obtained one week in advance at any Washington state liquor store. Only WLCC licensed food and beverage establishments may provide no-host bars. For more information regarding these issues, contact: Oregon Liquor Control Commission or Washington Liquor Control Commission.

Private hosted bars: If you are serving hard liquor (alcohol other than beer or wine) at a hosted bar, you should consider having

Oregon Alcohol Service Laws: Any bartender contracted for pay is required to have the OLCC permit to serve alcohol. Volunteer servers do not need a service permit.

139

Washington Alcohol Service Laws: Bartenders are not required to have a permit to serve alcohol for a private function.

Beverages in bulk or case discounts: how do you get a good selection of beverages on a budget? Distributors, wine shops, and some stores offer variety and savings when purchasing in bulk. In some instances, unused beverages may be returned for a refund. However, keep in mind that some sites will charge a corkage fee to bring in your own alcohol and others don't allow outside beverages at all.

Control liquor and keep consumption costs down: have a no-host bar. Shorten the cocktail reception by 15 minutes. Serve beer, wine, water and soft drinks only; eliminate hard liquor from hosted receptions. Avoid serving salty foods during hosted bars (pretzels, peanuts, etc.). Instruct caterers or waiters to uncork wine bottles only as needed. As a healthy alternative, offer a juice bar or an espresso bar.

Wedding
Traditions

Something Old - to bring a sense of continuity

Something New - to add an optimistic note

Something Borrowed - the superstition that happiness rubs off

Something Blue - for purity, fidelity and life

Weddings make us all sentimental. By including a special item or tradition in your ceremony and reception that has been used by other family members, or that you yourself may wish to pass along to future generations, you allow family and friends to share in your joy as well as the traditions of your family.

© Bryan Hoybook

- Many brides choose to carry a family memento during their wedding. A handkerchief made from the lace of a family member's gown or veil can be easily carried or incorporated into your bouquet.

- Your wedding garter can be made from satin or lace used by other family members in their wedding attire. Just make sure you have a back-up garter for the groom to throw. Or use your mom or sister's garter from their wedding to wear for yours.

- Since the first toast at the reception signifies the celebration and coming together of two families as well as the beginning of a new one, crystal, silver or pewter toasting goblets make wonderful gifts to be passed on to future family brides.

- It is customary for the bride and groom to exchange gifts prior to the ceremony.

- If you are using a Bible in your ceremony, select one that you can comfortably carry down the aisle with you. At the completion of the ceremony, you and your groom can sign your names and your wedding date in the front of the Bible as well as the location and time of your marriage.

140

© Geranium Lake
& Kate Kelly Pho...

Design & Décor

Florists
Lighting
Wedding Design & Décor

A Blooming Bouquets

p. 503.254.3281 (Eastside)
p. 971.285.5628. (Westside)
www.abloomingbouquet.com

Weddings are our area of expertise

As an award-winning florist, A Blooming Bouquet has more than 20 years of design experience. We will take the time to listen to you needs, fit flowers to your style and help cover all the details for your wedding. We always remember that this is your special day.

Personal Service

A Blooming Bouquets is very conscientious about working within your budget to give you more flowers at a comfortable price. We are able to give you the best prices with the most flowers possible, as every stem we purchase is used for your wedding only. We never skimp on flowers!

Consultations

We offer personal consultations in a comfortable setting, with an extensive, full color portfolio for you to look through. With many original and creative ideas, your wedding and reception will be one of a kind. We always listen to you to create the effect you are seeking for your fairytale wedding.

Contact

Linda Negus (Eastside)
e. blmnbokays@aol.com

Kelly Cruickshank (Westside)
e. bloomingbouquets@juno.com

Services

- **Bridal Party Flowers**
  Bridal, bridesmaids & mother's bouquets, flower girls, corsages, boutonnières & hair flowers to compliment your desired color scheme

- **Ceremony Flowers**
  Altar arrangements, candelabras, unity candles, pew & chair decorations, garlands, topiaries, gazebos, arbors, chuppah & pagallas for an unforgettable ceremony

- **Reception Flowers**
  Head & guest table centerpieces, fresh floral cake decorations, buffet & serving table bouquets will add to the overall effect of your reception

- **Rental Items**
  If you're looking to add more to your day, we have many rental items to choose from to complement your own style

Bravo! Member Since 1997

About A Floral Affair

You desire the wedding of your dreams.
You want personal attention to every detail.
You need reasonable prices.

Our goal is to make your dreams come true! We know our clients schedules are full and we want to make your planning simple. We offer extraordinary designs, ideas and pricing!

Bridal Party

Brides Bouquet	$85.00 and up
Bridesmaids	$40.00 and up
Flower Girls	$20.00 and up
Corsages	$15.00 and up
Boutonnieres	$7.50 and up

Ceremony Decorations

Ceremony Bouquets	$75.00 and up
Unity Candle	$40.00 and up
Aisle Accents	$6.50 and up
Garland	Varies

Reception Decorations

Cake Top	$35.00 and up
Centerpieces	$15.00 and up

Contact

Angel Stegmann

Portland, Oregon

p. 503.794.9370

e. floralaffair@att.net

www.afloralaffair.com

Price

We welcome events of all sizes & budgets

Services

- Over 25 years experience
- Complimentary consultations
- Delivery & setup
- Out of area delivery available
- Rental items

Preferred vendor for:

- Gray Gables
- World Trade Center
- Arista Ballroom
- Acadian Ballroom
- The Aerie at Eagle Landing

VISIT OUR
FLORAL GALLERY

We invite you to visit our extensive floral gallery at:
www.afloralaffair.com

143

Bravo! Member Since 2005

p. 503.709.4375
e. info@affairsinbloomnw.com
www.affairsinbloomnw.com

About Affairs in Bloom

Affairs in Bloom is a by-appointment only floral design studio. From romantic English garden bouquets, to chic contemporary arrangements, we will tailor our designs to transform your event into a beautiful display of fresh flowers.

From intimate dinner parties to the largest weddings, we will work closely with you to create a vision that is uniquely yours. Our goal is to create an atmosphere beyond all expectations and leave lasting memories for our clients and their guests.

When you hire us, be assured that we are honored to be a part of your special day. We treat every client like family and your special day as if it were our own. We select only the freshest, most vibrant flowers for your event.

144

Contact
Cara Coates

Price
We work within our client's budget

Quick Facts
- Complimentary consultation
- Experienced design team
- Always fresh, innovative & elegant
- Rental pieces available
- We welcome events of all sizes
- Serving both Oregon & Washington
- Recommendations by request
- Complimentary tossing bouquet with booking

Bravo! Member Since 2006

AN AFFAIR TO REMEMBER

2400 Southeast Ankeny Street
Portland, Oregon 97214
p. 503.223.9267
f. 503.223.4746
www.anaffairtoremember.com

About An Affair To Remember

Designing spectacular weddings is what we are all about! With more than 10 years experience in wedding design and production, we combine gorgeous flowers with the most extensive collection of wedding props in the Portland area, and use our creative artistic skill to produce events of uncompromising elegance and style.

Color, Texture, Scent, and Scale

Attention to detail is what makes the ordinary wedding an extraordinary experience!

Color: What bride could resist falling madly in love with the classic color combinations: gorgeous hotel silver candelabras dripping with tones of white, cream and butter roses, lilacs, peonies and tulips on a table draped with pewter organza chiffon? We offer a myriad of color combinations. The fun will come in finding the right palate to suit your wedding.

Texture: Utilizing materials other than standard flowers gives your wedding flowers a feeling of depth and texture. We love to let our imagination run wild combining non-traditional elements into our work, such as moss–covered cake urns, birch trees full of hanging votives, fresh berries, citrus, kumquats, grapes and pomegranates gracing magnificent wedding cakes.

Scent: The freshest flowers provide the most exquisite scents – David Austen garden roses, lilacs and freesia to name a few. Our flowers excite the senses!

Scale: Understanding scale is of vital importance in wedding design. Your décor and flowers should fit the formality of the event, the size, scale and look of the event space, and the time of day and year.

Contact
Mike Piper

Price
Please call for more information

Quick Facts
- More than 10 years experience in wedding design & production

- We listen to the senses – utilizing the elements of color, texture, scent & scale to the fullest in each of our exquisite floral creations

145

CONTACT US

Please call for your no–cost, no–obligation wedding consultation.

See page 54 under
Wedding Consultants

Bravo! Member Since 1999

Artistic Floral Design by

Lillypilly

Specializing in Wedding and Event Flowers

p. 503.330.7672
www.lillypilly.net

About Lillypilly

Providing lush wedding flowers to ensure that your vision blossoms.

Our goal is to provide you with an upbeat and positive experience from the initial beginnings all the way through your spectacular wedding day. We are full of fun and creative ideas that we would love to share. Even if you know nothing about flowers, we will help you personalize an extraordinary floral package that will complement your own unique sense of style and imagination.

Terms

A $50 non-refundable deposit reserves your wedding date and will be applied toward your wedding order. 20% of your final balance will be due upon order approval and contract signing. The remaining balance will be due two weeks prior to your event.

Contact

Wendy Hosford
Lindsi Leahy

Price

Call for your personalized proposal & quote

Services

- Complimentary consultation

- Evening & weekend appointments available to fit your busy schedule

- Your designer will personally deliver & set–up your order

- We visit ceremony & reception sites before your wedding so that there will be no surprises

- Rental items & services available

- Mention this ad for a free toss bouquet with your wedding order

COMPLIMENTARY

From sublime bouquets to magnificent events, we invite you to contact us for your complimentary consultation. Congratulations on your upcoming wedding!

Bravo! Member Since 2002

17100 SW Pilkington Road
Lake Oswego, Oregon 97035
p. 503.635.6661
www.artisticflowers-decor.com

Premiere Service

Designing spectacular weddings is what we are all about: weddings with style, elegance, and timeless beauty.

We suggest unique and natural concepts combining unexpected elements: beautiful flowers and seasonal botanicals with fruits and berries, jewels, and/or other materials. Whether local or from around the world, we can provide it.

We are wedding specialists: from intimate dinner parties to the largest weddings, from romantic English garden bouquets to chic contemporary arrangements, we will work closely with you to create a vision that is uniquely yours. Together we can make your wedding dreams come true!

For over two decades, we at Artistic Flowers have committed ourselves to making your special day just that: the best it can possibly be.

Please contact us to make an appointment for a complimentary consultation.

Contact
Artistic Flowers
& Home Décor

Price
Varies depending on event; please call

Artistc Flowers
- Innovative
- Exquisite
- Striking
- Splendor
- Passionate
- Vibrant
- Energetic
- Tender
- Gorgeous
- Radiant
- Sensual & Brilliant

147

CONGRATULATIONS!

We look forward to meeting you and working together as we plan one of the most beautiful events of your life!

Bravo! Member Since 2006

Visit BravoWedding.com for more information on décor, floral design & lighting

Floral Package $349.00
Bride's Bouquet
Maid of Honor Bouquet
4 Boutonnieres   2 Corsages
2 Altar Arrangements

Becky's Country Garden

19244 Cantata Drive
Oregon City, Oregon 97045
p. 503.936.4737
e. weddings@bctonline.com
www.bctonline.com/users/flowers

A Floral Package for Your Wedding

Becky's Country Garden's floral packages begin at just $349 and includes bouquets for the bride and maid of honor, two mothers' corsages, four boutonnieres, and two large altar arrangements. "Brides are amazed at our prices," says Becky. "Most say they've been quoted $300 for the bridal bouquet alone." If you need more bouquets, corsages, and boutonnieres, Becky and Kathy will adjust the package to meet your needs.

The duo easily design flowers for large, elaborate weddings, or for smaller, intimate celebrations. No matter the size of the wedding, they put their hearts into creating exactly what each bride wants.

Contact
Kathy Brown
Becky McEahern

Price
Beginning at $349

Rental Items & Accessories
- Wedding accessories available: unity candles, frames, cake tops, pens, glasses, knife sets, & more

- Available for rent: aisle runners, candelabras, wedding arches, lattice pillars, Roman pillars, tall white wicker baskets, lanterns, brass baskets & free standing style altar holders

TERMS

Becky & Kathy recommend you bring pictures, swatches or any ideas that you may have to the complimentary consultation, so that they can best meet your needs. The terms & a $50 nonrefundable deposit to reserve your wedding day (applied to your order) with the balance is due two weeks before the wedding.

Bravo! Member Since 1999

148

www.blumfloraldesign.com

About Blüm; Design in Flowers

By combining beautiful blossoms with clean design Blüm has created a signature look that is both classic and modern. We take pride in creating floral decor that meets, and exceeds our clients' expectations!

Blüm; Design in Flowers was created by Jordan Gladow in 2005. Before opening Blüm, Jordan trained and worked in Portland, Salem, London and Boston, Mass. Our clients can rest assured that a highly professional designer will walk them through the creative process and develop their ideas into gorgeous reality. Whether creating décor for special events, holiday parties, weekly deliveries or weddings, we are excited and honored to enhance your environment with the most pristine flowers available.

Please take a moment to browse our web site and email or call us to set up your complimentary consultation. We look forward to sharing our passion for flowers with you!

Contact

Jordan Gladow

600 NW Naito Parkway Suite B
Portland, Oregon 97209

p. 503.851.1672

e. jgladow@yahoo.com

www.blumfloraldesign.com

Price

Please call for a
custom quote

Featured On...

Since her return to Portland Jordan's flowers have been featured on the WB's "Portland Wedding Style" & KATU's "AM Northwest." Images of recent weddings have been published in "Portland Bride and Groom," "Oregon Bride" & the "The Judith Blacklock Book of Floral Design."

WHAT'S NEW

Voted Best Florist

149

© Sidewalk Studios

OREGON
BRIDE
MAGAZINE
BEST
of
2009

Visit BravoWedding.com for more information on décor, floral design & lighting

Cannon Beach Florist

Basketcase, Inc.

123 South Hemlock
PO Box 1308
Cannon Beach, Oregon 97110
p. 503.436.2106
p. 800.611.5826
e. cbflorist@theoregonshore.com
www.cannonbeachflorist.com

Your Cannon Beach Florist

With more than 45 years of living at the coast, our experience is invaluable! A Cannon Beach native, owner Debbie Nelson knows the area and all it has to offer, and can provide complete floral services for the wedding you've always dreamed of. Our services include consultation, e-mailed bid for you to refer to, individually customized floral designs, delivery, set-up, and rentals.

Destination Wedding Consultant

We know flowers! We also know the other connections and vendors to make your wedding plans complete. We love to help, simply give us a call and schedule your complimentary floral consultation. Can't make it to the beach, that's O.K.! This is wedding destination central for the beautiful Oregon Coast. We do phone and e-mail consulting on a regular basis. This might be the first time you've ever planned a wedding, but it's not ours! We'll take care of the details so you don't have to. Call us and consider it done!

Contact
Debbie Nelson

Price
Complimentary consultation

Quick Facts
- Conveniently located in downtown Cannon Beach
- Complete floral services & rentals
- Local shop with beach theme wedding accents
- Individualized consulting & floral design

Sand Between Your Toes

From barefoot beach weddings to elegant events, let us make the arrangements for your perfect day. YOU... the BEACH...a WEDDING!

BEACH ACCENT

Take time to visit our downtown Cannon Beach shop to see our fun and unique line of wedding accessories. We even offer chocolate foil wrapped sand dollars in your wedding colors!

Bravo! Member Since 2006

824 NW Davis
Portland, Oregon 97209
p. 503.228.4700
www.cityflowerspdx.com

City Flowers in the Pearl District

Your wedding day should feel like your dream come true, and for the past 21 years City Flowers has been making dreams come true all over the Portland metro area! From classic to contemporary, with texture or clean simplicity, we can help you find the right fit for your wedding.

We make your ideas come to life!

- Please call or email us for a complimentary consultation.

- We utilize local, imported and exotic flowers to maximize the selection of materials available.

- Let us help you find the connection between your personality and your flowers.

- After booking with us, City Flowers will keep in regular contact with you to answer any questions or make any last-minute changes you may have.

- Our attention to detail will begin at the conception of your day and will carry through to the professional delivery and setup.

Contact
City Flowers

Price
Our pricing is individually based on your overall look; for more information, please contact us to make an appointment for a complimentary consultation

About Us
- Located in the trendy pearl district, City Flowers caters to the style-conscious brides of today

- Our name is synonymous with quality and a marked level of service

- Our down-to-earth approach will give you a sense of calm during the important process of selecting flowers for your special day

151

WHAT'S NEW

Voted most popular florist on Citysearch in 2006!
Visit us online at
www.cityflowerspdx.com

Bravo! Member Since 2004

CRYSTAL LILIES
exquisite flowers

134 SE Taylor Street
Portland, Oregon 97214
p. 503.221.7701
f. 503.200.1949
e. info@CrystalLilies.com
www.CrystalLilies.com

152

Crystal Lilies creates weddings with style, elegance and timeless beauty. We suggest unique concepts and unexpected elements that reflect each bride's unique personality and taste. In our studio you will meet with Kimberley to privately review extensive portfolios of our work. As a floral artist, Kimberley has the experience and expertise to make your wedding a success.

Flowers help define a mood, establish a sense of style and create texture. Whether you find yourself in a ballroom overflowing with luscious roses, or catch the scent of the bride's gardenia bouquet as she walks down the aisle, flowers invite our senses to depart from our everyday lives and transport us to a magical environment.

Crystal Lilies specializes in using only the most beautiful flowers, seasonal botanicals, fruits, berries, natural and unique elements, whether local or from around the world.

We are wedding specialists, from the concept and design to the finishing touches on your special day. Whether grand or intimate, Crystal Lilies is there for every detail to make your wedding truly memorable.

Exquisite flowers will make your wedding unforgettable.

Contact
Kimberley & Scott Lindsay

Price
Please call for a custom quote

Wide Range of Styles
- Romantic to contemporary
- Understated elegance to european opulence
- Natural hand tied or hand wired bouquets

Extensive Collection of Unique Props
- Aisle, table & floor candelabras
- Silver & glass compotes, vases & tall stands
- Iron arches, natural branch arbors, chuppahs
- Aisle runners, columns, & urns
- Custom made items for the discriminating bride

Consultations are complimentary and by appointment.

Bravo! Member Since 1995

DK Floral
Weddings & Events

Two Lives, Two Dreams, and a day when two become one

Your wedding day is one of the most important days of your life. Since 1997 DK Floral has been providing the expertise brides require to make their weddings truly memorable.

With such a diverse range of design choices and wedding venues available to the modern bride, our experience enables us to create a wide but exclusive range of floral designs that compliment each unique setting. Whatever venue you choose, our team will work hard behind the scene to make your flowers and your day breathtakingly beautiful. From the popular traditional setting of The Old Church, the whimsical fun of the Oregon Zoo, or the outdoor beauty of Bridal Veil Lakes, each venue presents a uniqueness that DK Floral can capture perfectly in our designs, ensuring that your wedding flowers will live on in your memories long after the guests have departed.

Contact
Kathy Pettigrew

p. 503.317.1061
e. weddings@dkfloral.com

www.dkfloral.com

Cost and Terms
- A 50% deposit is due at the time the wedding is booked.

- The remaining balance is due four weeks before the wedding date.

- Delivery in the Portland Metropolitan area is free. A small fee will be charged for those outside the area.

Rental Items Available
- Floor & Aisle Candelabras

- Unique Vases

- Columns & Aisle Runners

- Arches

153

Bravo! Member Since 2002

Visit BravoWedding.com for more information on décor, floral design & lighting

EastWest floral arts

503.235.5300
helene@ewfloralarts.com
www.ewfloralarts.com

154

This is your day, not ours.

What's your style?

Clean, simple elegance with square and sculptural forms; mossy, rustic northwest with branches and ferns; romantic, Old World charm, with jewel tones and flickering candlelight; fun, bright, hot, summer colors with a touch of whimsy; rich, fall colors with delectable fruits and berries; chic, understated, urban appeal with a modern edge; natural, organic wildflowers with grasses...

East West Floral Arts,

Our business, our passion

Defining your style and

Surpassing expectation.

Contact

Helene Goode

p. 503.235.5300

e. helene@ewfloralarts.com

www.ewfloralarts.com

Price

Varies, please call for more information

Services

- Complimentary initial consultation
- $200 deposit
- Rentals
- Delivery & set-up
- One wedding a day
- By appointment only
- Over 10 years of experience
- Member of American Bridal Consultants

DEFINING YOUR STYLE

Where the ordinary departs and the extraordinary starts.

p. 503.241.2225
e. floralevent@aol.com

www.eventfloral.biz

About Event Floral

Event Floral's studio is by appointment only, meaning that every flower purchased to use in your wedding is purchased new and just for you. We have no inventory that needs to be either 'used up' or wasted, so we can provide the freshest product to meet your particular budget or needs. We have a beautiful selection of silver and glassware available to rent, so when you come to the studio for your consultation we can work with our vases or with custom vases to create the look that you want.

Coming to Event Floral's studio is like a play date in a flower fairyland. Everything is 'hands-on' and we work hard to make you feel unique and special, so when you walk out of the consultation you know what everything is going to look like and can feel comfortable leaving the details in Cheri's hands.

Event Floral is a preferred vendor for Royce's Prop Shop, a Portland-based event design firm, and Portland's White House Bed and Breakfast.

Contact
Cheri Baber

Price
We can meet any budget need

Quick Facts
- Mission: work with other creative people to find the most engaging, rewarding ways to reach others through the art of floral design

- Over 20 years of 'thinking outside of the vase'

- Rose Festival float Floral designer from 2000 thru 2005, official Rose Festival floral designer in 2004

- Represented the West's Premier Wedding Florists in Martha Stewart Weddings magazine

- Wedding, reception, party, & holiday decorating

WHAT'S NEW

We also practice sustainability by turning old glass pieces into new art and have been chosen to show this art in the Cracked Pots Show at McMenamin's Edgefield, and other venues.

155

Bravo! Member Since 2008

floral dreams

where all your dreams flower

Weddings, Events,
GLBT Ceremonies

503.777.0800
www.floral-dreams.com

About Floral Dreams

When you come for your complimentary consultation, we recommend that you bring any pictures, swatches of material or color samples you might have. We will bring photos of our work and lots of clippings for extra ideas. We will ask you many detailed questions to help you pinpoint your vision of your own wedding flowers. When you leave the consult you will have an estimate of the cost of your particular wedding flowers to consider.

Our goal is to combine your ideas and dreams with our experience and artistry to create the look and feel you want for your wedding flowers. Whether you prefer timeless, traditional pastels and whites or brightly colored contemporary flowers, we do it all. We enjoy the challenge of the avant-garde or unusual wedding as well. Whether your wedding is small and intimate or large and spectacular, each wedding receives our full attention.

Contact

Selena Ross or
Peggy Hartman

p. 503.777.0800

e. Selena@floral-dreams.com

www.floral-dreams.com

Price

Call or e-mail for pricing specifics

Quick Facts

• Eight years experience in floral design for weddings

• Full service florist specializing in weddings

• We provide fresh, innovative ideas to create beautiful weddings, even with budget constraints

• We buy from local growers first

• By appointment only

Services

• We design your wedding & reception flowers, deliver them to your site, set them up, & stay to put on boutonnieres & corsages

• In addition to designing for the unique ideas of each bride, we offer three packages; please see our website for details

Bravo! Member Since 2006

156

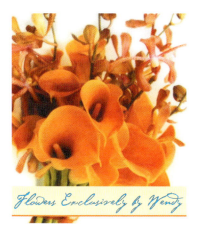

PO Box 257
25 NW 23rd Place, Suite #6
Portland, Oregon 97210
p. 503.288.1177
p. 360.993.4749
e. toflowersbywendy@aol.com
www.flowersbywendy.com

Personalized Attention for You and Your Floral Needs...

Designing quality wedding and event floral is our only focus. By not having a walk–in shop, it allows us to focus on designing your event floral without distraction. We purchase flowers for your event exclusively, leaving no question to the quality and freshness of our designs.

Because every event has different floral needs, we do not offer package pricing, which can limit the possibilities, instead focusing only on the floral you desire.

We offer complimentary consultations by appointment only. We know convenience is a must, so we can accommodate any schedule with day, evening and weekend appointments.

Contact
Flowers Exclusively by Wendy

Price
Varies

Services
- Focus on quality wedding & event floral

- Only the freshest & best quality flowers are guaranteed

- We are available for complimentary consultations; please call today to schedule your appointment

157

COST AND TERMS
A $100 deposit will reserve your date, with the balance due two weeks prior to the event.

Flowers For You LLC.

11226 SE 21st Avenue
Milwaukie, Oregon 97222

p. 503.318.6677

e. kay@flowerspdx.com

www.flowerspdx.com

Fabulous, Stylish, Fresh & Distinctive

Flowers For You is a by-appointment floral design studio that specializes in captivating designs for weddings and events. Dedicated to the highest quality, innovative creations and lush designs. We serve a unique clientele who seek out extraordinary fashions. Flowers For You is dedicated to designing creations that make an impression, cause a stir and will not soon be forgotten. Celebrating our clients' individuality and vision, we work hand-in-hand together to create incredible results!

As your floral designer, I work closely with Northwest growers and distributors to provide you with unbeatable quality and value. My passion for flowers and the art of custom designs will intertwine your personal style and dreams to create unforgettable wedding memories. By accepting only one wedding per date, you are guaranteed our exclusive attention to your event.

Relax and Celebrate......Come and experience the service and artistry of Flowers For You!

Contact
Kay Dietl

Price
Each event is custom designed to your individual style and budget

Quick Facts

- Complimentary Consultation

- Evening & weekend appointments available

- Welcome events of all sizes & budgets

- Flowers For You accepts only one wedding per date

- Rental of wedding & reception accessories

DETAILS, DETAILS... DETAILS!

We love, crave and depend on our obsessive compulsion for details!

Bravo! Member Since 2007

© Holland Studios

2335 NW 23rd Place
Portland, Oregon 97210
p. 503.228.3140
f. 503.778.5509
e. studio@flowerstommyluke.com
www.flowerstommyluke.com

Vibrant • Distinctive • Memorable

Impressions last forever, so for your special wedding day, trust the designers at Flowers Tommy Luke to express your true intent with beauty and style.

For over 100 years we have been handcrafting elegant, evolving displays that transform the most exquisite flowers into treasured memories.

At Flowers Tommy Luke we specialize in

- Bridal Flowers & Décor
- Corporate Accounts & Events
- Commercial Displays
- Unique Floral Gifts

We also offer delivery throughout the Portland Metro area. Visit our portfolio at **flowerstommyluke.com** or call us at 503.228.-3140.

Created by Nature,
Perfected by Flowers Tommy Luke.

Contact
Louella Scott

Price
Flowers to fulfill your dreams at a price that meets your budget

Quick Facts
- Portland's Premiere Florist since 1907
- State-of-the-art Design Studio in Northwest Portland
- We utilize water purification technology to assure long-lasting blooms
- Tropicals & Orchids received direct from growers to assure freshness
- Free Consultations with Brides and Bridal Party
- Serving the greater Portland/Vancouver region

159

4615 NE Emerson Street
Portland, Oregon 97218
p. 503.281.6163
e. info@gardenhouseflorals.com
www.gardenhouseflorals.com

160

Garden House Florals are experienced wedding professionals in flower design and consulting who specialize in creating beautiful wedding flowers. We work individually with you to create the wedding of your heart's desire.

We believe that your wedding is unique and that the flowers should be a reflection of your own personal style. We design your flowers to create romance, and enhance the spirit of the celebration, making your wedding day truly special and unique to you and your groom.

We look forward to sharing our passion for flowers and design with you to help you create a beautiful day to be cherished.

Consultation

Initial complimentary consultation to discuss your flowers, the size of your wedding, and the venue. We encourage you to bring swatches of fabric, pictures, and all your ideas.

Extra service

In addition to wedding flowers, we offer a separate wedding day service where we will take care of all the details of the event, so that your focus is on being a bride.

Contact

Janet Sisson

Price

Flower prices vary and all weddings are priced individually . Whether your wedding is large or small, it is our desire to provide you with beautiful flowers for your wedding. We will work with you and your budget to provide the most flowers possible... after all, it is about the flowers.

A 15% deposit reserves your date and is included with the total price.

© Kate Kelly Photography

555 SW Oak Street
Portland, Oregon 97204
p. 503.228.1920
f. 503.228.5567
e. kim@geraniumlake.com
www.geraniumlake.com
www.geraniumlake.com/blog

Geranium Lake's Flower Story

Geranium Lake Flowers is consistently recognized within the wedding industry as one of the city's best. Highly regarded and recommended by wedding professionals, venues, hotels and many happy brides city wide, they are frequently featured by local bridal publications and voted Oregon Bride Magazine's Best Wedding florist of 2008. They are also featured in Style Me Pretty's Little Black Book of florists and event stylists.

Owner Kim Foren is a fine artist turned florist who has more than 17 years experience and is recognized for her floral artistry, exuberance, and professional commitment to her brides. Her business has also been nominated by the City of Portland's Office of Sustainability for their commitment to the environment and running a "green" business.

Geranium Lake Flowers is overflowing with creativity and it shows. For fresh ideas with a twist, come visit us in "big pink" (the US Bancorp tower)!

Contact
Kim Foren

Price
Please contact us for custom pricing

What You'll Love
- Creative, fresh shop bursting with fresh, amazing & gorgeous flowers, ideas & inspiration
- Huge selection of luxury linens, lighting, chivari chairs, & more!
- Inspired designers & one-on-one, complimentary consultations
- Highly recommended by the NW's premier wedding vendors & venues
- Check out our revamped web site for inspiration! While you're there, check out our blog and visit us on Facebook!

161

WHAT'S NEW

STYLE
me
PRETTY
EST
2007

Geranium Lake is a member of Style Me Pretty's Little Black Book. Find us at www.stylemepretty.com

© Kate Kelly Photography

Bravo! Member Since 1996

Visit BravoWedding.com for more information on décor, floral design & lighting

About Gigi Floral Design

Gigi Floral Design is dedicated to take your vision beyond the ordinary. We are a studio-based company, which allows us to dedicate all of our time and creativity to your event. Creating a concept for an event is more than just looking through a series of photos; it is discovering who you are and designing a look that best reflects you. We've been working with an array of coordinators, brides, and venues for over five years and no challenge is beyond our creativity. Whether your inspiration comes from a color scheme, a family heirloom, or the outfit you wore on your first date, Gigi Floral Design is dedicated to bring your vision to life.

Contact
Natalie Mortimer

205 West 30th Street
Vancouver, Washington 98660
p. 360.909.1209
e. natalie@gigifloraldesign.com
www.gigifloraldesign.com

Price
Price upon request

Quick Facts
- Free consultation
- In business for over 5 years
- Wide range of style & location experience
- Consultant present at event

162

Kevan Inouye
private florist

p. 503.781.2485

e. info@kiprivateflorist.com

www.kiprivateflorist.com

About Kevan Inouye Private Florist – one of Portland's Premiere Wedding Florists

Kevan Inouye Private Florist is a design studio specializing in upscale weddings for the most discerning clientele. I am passionate about designing weddings that celebrate your unique personality in every aspect of your event.

Each wedding carries an unmistakable signature of quality that will exceed your expectations. Locally grown organic flowers are my first choice, although I also import flowers internationally from Holland, Asia, South America, & Europe.

What to expect from me:

- Simple, elegant and chic designs
- Your personal style in every detail
- Premium quality, imported and locally grown flowers
- A passion for perfection

Contact
Kevan Inouye

Price
Please call for details

Quick Facts
- Over 7 years experience designing fabulous wedding events
- I personally provide on site supervision & management of every detail
- I accept only one full service event per day
- Consultations are complimentary & by appointment only
- Your event is personally designed with grace, style & passion
- Fresh, locally grown organic flowers are my first choice
- I import tropical flowers directly from the grower in Hawaii

WHAT'S NEW
- My floral artistry has been featured in Portland Bride & Groom
- I have designed custom destination weddings in Hawaii, Washington D.C., and Boston

163

Bravo! Member Since 2007

© Jonathan Michael Studios

p. 503.228.1558
e. info@lavishflora.com
www.lavishflora.com

Inspired flora for extraordinary people and events.

Fresh flowers imbue a sense of mood setting the stage for an unforgettable event. Imagine chartreuse roses mingling with funky fuschia orchids, a bouquet of lemon tulips curving into a sensuous arch, or the simple perfection of a scented gardenia.

Lavish designers create custom works individually tailored to the personal style of our clients. With our passion for flowers and over 13 years of design experience we weave together distinctive and sometimes unexpected elements into innovative designs. From the tiniest of posies to the most extravagant display, our designers will attend to every last detail creating the distinctive event you envision.

Contact
Adria Lailer

Price
All of our events are one of a kind so we don't offer package deals. Instead we encourage you to set up a complimentary appointment to sit down and talk about the details of your wedding. We can help you establish a budget that will fit your fancy.

© Fae Edmonson

Organic choices are always available.
Along with exotic flora we offer a growing selection of fine organic and locally grown flowers to compliment your day.

Bravo! Member Since 2006

164

[541] 386.3666
[888] 363.4310
311 oak street
hood river, oregon

Lucy's
informal
flowers

flowers for all occasions
www.informalflowers.com

About Lucy's Informal Flowers

Lucy's Informal Flowers fuses creativity and innovation to build living works of art for the most discerning clients. Our wedding designs are masterfully planned and executed with only the finest attention to detail.

From the largest wedding to the most intimate gathering of friends and family, our talent ensures that the dreams and visions of our clients are exceeded each and every time. We begin each and every design process with an understanding of what your dreams and desires are and the results speak for themselves.

We will help make your wedding day special. From local and Northwest flower growers to certified organic flower vendors, we strive to design with the best products. If your tastes require something tropical or out of the ordinary, we can also provide.

Visit our blog at www.informalbliss.com

Contact
Lucy Gorman
311 Oak Street
Hood River, Oregon 97031
p. 541.386.3666
f. 541.386.3655
e lucy@informalflowers.com
www.informalflowers.com

165

Price
Pricing is based on a custom design to fit every budget.

Quick Facts
• Located in downtown Hood River.

• Have been doing wedding flowers in the Gorge for 20 years and we are familiar with every venue in the Gorge.

• Complimentary consultations, please call for appointment.

• Visit our web site to see galleries of our work and read a few of the many testimonials.

NANCY'S

Oregon Trail Center
2001 NE Burnside Road
Gresham, Oregon 97030
p. 503.661.0911, 800.645.9252
f. 503.669.0826
e. rcook@nancysfloral.com
www.nancysfloral.com

Fabulous Wedding Flowers

At Nancy's Floral, we strive to make your dreams a reality. Since no two weddings are alike, we do not have pre-set wedding packages, but instead make each wedding as unique as the bride ordering. Pay for only what you need. With over 75 years combined design experience we can accommodate any design request with the freshest and most beautiful flowers available.

Free Consultation

Please call and set up an appointment to meet with our wedding professionals to plan your special day. This free consultation will give you the opportunity to look through our extensive portfolio of personalized wedding designs and local wedding venues as decorated and discuss your ideas with our experienced designers. Please bring in fabric swatches, pictures, and sketches of your ideas. It is recommended that an appointment be made several months before your wedding day, but it is not uncommon to reserve our services a few weeks prior to the wedding.

"WHEN YOU WANT THE BEST... CALL NANCY'S!"

Contact
Rob Cook

Price
Varies - Based on individual needs

Quick Facts
- Complimentray consultation

- Prompt delivery & setup by an experienced designer

- Rental of wedding & reception accessories

- 2007 spotlight.com - best of Citysearch - highly recommended - best of florist 9.4 - Review highlights - "The flowers turned out better than I could imagine for my wedding day. Everyone commented on the flowers. Thanks for making our big day beautiful."

- We have a liquor license - wine & champagne

166

WWW.WEDDINGSBLOOMINOCCASIONS.COM

Weddings and Other Bloomin' Occasions

Weddings and Other Bloomin' Occasions can give you the personalized and extraordinary look that every couple deserves. Let designer, Sally Schneider help your dream wedding become a reality. With over 15 years experience in the bridal industry, her unique approach to the art of floral design can achieve either an exotic look with imported floral, or we can create a natural wedding style using materials found only in the Great Northwest

Weddings and Other Bloomin' Occasions has the flexibility to design the wedding you want, and stay within your budget no matter what it may be.

Your wedding day isn't about settling for the everyday. Your wedding should be unforgettable and timeless. We provide personal service to meet your individual needs, coordinating floral design from the rehearsal dinner, to your ceremony, to the reception. You can choose one service or all.

Weddings and Other Bloomin' Occasions will make your wedding "bloom".

Contact

Sally E. Schneider

67211 E Highway. 26 Space D
Welches, Oregon 97067

p. 503.380.9891

e. bloominoccasions@peoplepc.com

www.weddingsbloominoccasions.com

Price

Prices vary by budget
& design

Quick Facts

- Complimentary consultation by appointment. Evening & weekend appointments available to fit your schedule.

- Designer will personally deliver & set up your order.

- Visiting the wedding & reception venues to personalize your floral details.

- Serving both Oregon & Washington.

- Complimentary toss bouquet with booking.

WHAT'S NEW

Come visit our new shop! We've expanded our selection of unique gifts, art, candy, jewelry, and of course floral. Right next door to our old location in The Rendezvous Plaza!

167

Bravo! Member Since 2008

p. 503.970.0249
f. 503.281.0203
e dt@greenlight-creative.com
www.greenlight-creative.com

Why Lighting?

At last, your ceremony or reception can feature breathtaking lighting from an award-winning creative lighting designer and producer. Why spend the most important day of your life in a dull ballroom, or in a space that could look great if you just had the right lighting? Why spend thousands on gorgeous floral arrangements and decorations or a spectacular reception hall…only to have them hide away in the shadows? Let Greenlight Creative make your special day amazing!

Who We Are

Greenlight Creative is helmed by Dwayne Thomas, the Northwest's foremost expert in creative event lighting. You can rest easy and enjoy your special day, knowing you're in the hands of a design professional with over 25 years of experience. Our installers are courteous and professional, working safely and efficiently to ensure that your event is gorgeous.

How We Work

We do it ALL so that you don't have to! Our services include design, delivery, equipment rental, set up and teardown—you don't lift a finger! But best of all, our prices are very competitive. On a budget? Ask about our low-cost package options. At Greenlight Creative, our passion is in making your event memorable by utilizing the latest in lighting design techniques, modern, professional equipment, and friendly, attentive service.

Last (but certainly not least), Greenlight Creative offers a wide range of earth-friendly lighting options, and is a sustainably operated company.

Contact
Dwayne Thomas

Price
$495 and up

Your Source For:
- Bride-and-Groom Logo Projection
- Themed Color Washing
- Architectural Highlighting
- Stage or Dance floor Lighting & Effects
- Buffets, Bars, & Head Table Lighting
- Floral, Greenery, & Décor Highlights
- Thematic Pattern Projections

Hollywood
LIGHTING
SERVICES, INC.

5251 SE McLoughlin Boulevard
Portland, Oregon 97202
p. 503.232.9001
p. 800.826.9881
f. 503.232.8505
e. production@hollywoodlighting.biz
www.hollywoodlighting.biz

About Hollywood Lighting Services

Hollywood Lighting Services is proud to be the largest independent, locally owned and operated lighting provider in the Pacific Northwest. With our experienced design staff and complete line of state-of-the-art lighting equipment, we can make every event, large and small, truly memorable.

We have first-hand experience in hundreds of venues in the Northwest and can help you transform any room into the venue of your dreams. Hollywood Lighting also has an extensive inventory of low-energy lighting solutions, which are not only more environmentally friendly, but make lighting an option when power is limited. More than anything, it's our exceptional customer service that sets Hollywood Lighting apart and will make you glad you called.

Contact
Greg Eggen

Trust Us For:
- Weddings/galas
- Low-energy lighting alternatives
- On-stage entertainment, Stage & scenic lighting
- Digital scenery & projections

169

RecycleWorks Award Winner

Bravo! Member Since 1999

EXPERT EVENT LIGHTING

For over 60 years, Hollywood Lighting has been the Pacific Northwest's trusted leader in event lighting design, production, rentals, and sales. Whether your event is large, small, or in-between; bring your lighting challenges to us!

RECYCLEWORKS
2007-2008

PARADYM EVENTS
EVENTS WITHOUT PRECEDENCE

170

Paradym Events

A full-service event production company specializing in creating unique and highly personalized events. We can handle all of your event needs, from themed décor, floral, specialty linens, A/V and lighting. From design and management, logistics to execution, we can handle all your companies' event needs.

Design: Linens and flowers, metal and paper, glass and wood: all mediums are utilized to create your unique event environment. Just as your are one of a kind, so should your wedding be.

Price Range: No matter the budget, we work to ensure that you remain on target while providing the largest impact possible. There are no surprises at the end of an event, just a clearly defined cost for every aspect of the production.

Location: We have traveled everywhere, from Hawaii to the Mediterranean and back. We will accommodate your every need while providing you the comfort that every detail of your event has been taken care by our knowledgeable staff. You no longer have to work with a company from out of town and hope they can execute the event to your standards. Paradym Events will take the guess work out of the equation while adding the peace of mind and flexibility of a local and dedicated staff.

Specializing: In the details, no matter how small, we have it covered so you don't have to. We create custom events to highlight you and your company. We can handle all your event needs from, design and management, communications to the execution and logistics.

Contact
Mary Bennett

4060 SW Macadam Avenue
Portland, Oregon 97239
p. 503.219.9290
f. 503.525.0675
e. info@paradymevents.com
www.paradymevents.com

Price
Call for quote

Capacity
10 people to 10,000, we help you plan and fulfill all your event needs.

Expectations
Meeting your expectations is not good enough; Paradym Events strives to exceed them in every detail.

Your Event
Give us a call and let us show you the possibilities of your next event.

EXPERIENCE

Putting 50 years of design production experience to work for you, any theme, any event, any time, any place, you will know you have made the best choice.

Look for us on Facebook!

See page 311 under Rentals

Bravo! Member Since 1998

Peter Corvallis Productions

SINCE 1958

2204 North Clark Avenue
Portland, Oregon 97227
p. 503.222.1664
f. 503.222.1047
e. athena@petercorvallis.com
www.petercorvallis.com

About Peter Corvallis Productions, Inc.

Distinguished for our exceptional service and final results, Peter Corvallis Productions has provided quality tradition and experience in the event industry since 1958.

Our event specialists will help determine your wedding needs to create a unique style that will reflect your personality by applying our years of knowledge and expertise.

Wedding & Event Rental Inventory

We thrive to fulfill our customer's needs and as a full service event rental company we offer innovative and traditional products.

Our 100,000 square foot warehouse is filled with thousands of themed décor items plus we have an extensive wedding selection to choose from. In addition, we offer Lighting & Sound services to complete your event.

Contact
Athena

Price
Varies on size of event, call for quote

Services
• Tent & canopy rentals

• Party rentals

• Theme decorations & props

• Audio visual rentals & services

• Sound & lighting

• Trade show decorating & rentals

• Event planning services

• We deliver & setup

171

PROVIDES MORE THAN JUST QUALITY PRODUCTS

We not only have rental equipment, we also have many services to make your function run smoothly so you can enjoy your event along with your guests. Having an event will never be easier.

See page 312 under Rentals

172

ROYCE'S PROP SHOP

5406 North Albina Avenue
Portland, Oregon 97217
p. 503.283.8828
f. 503.283.3651
e. info@propshop.com
www.propshop.com

Contact
Royce Mason, CMP

Price
Customized to fit your budget

Quick Facts
- Award-winning event design
- Unique tabletop & floral
- Custom linens & chair covers
- Satin/chiffon swag & drape
- Complete production services: lighting, backdrops & fabrication
- Catering, rentals & entertainment assistance

AWARDS
- 2006-2007
  Meeting Professionals
  Int'l Supplier of the Year
  Award
- 2004
  Event Solutions Magazine
  Spotlight Award
  Designer of the Year
- 2003
  Oregon Restaurant Assoc.
  Award of Gratitude &
  Appreciation

See page 313 under
Rental Services

"Your visions are innovative and never cease to amaze…"

Mary Lou Burton
President
Bravo! Publications & Trade Shows

Event industry veteran Royce Mason and his dedicated team of professionals at the Prop Shop pride themselves on award-winning event design, décor, production and, most importantly, impeccable customer service.

Royce's Prop Shop is equipped with unparalleled resources and can produce an extensive range of formal to informal rehearsal dinners, wedding ceremonies and receptions at any venue — from elegant ballrooms to tented mountaintops!

Memberships include ABC, ACEP, ISES, MPI, and **Green Certified Member** of Travel Portland.

Bravo! Member Since 2001

503.294.0412   1400 NW 15th Avenue, Portland, OR 97209   www.WCEP.com

About West Coast Event Productions

It starts with a promise... a promise to make your wedding unforgettable!

At West Coast Event Productions, we believe your wedding should be the extraordinary and flawless occasion you've always imagined. For 30 years, our wedding specialists have been helping people say "I do" with premier consulting, design and rental services. Whether you are looking to create an atmosphere of simplistic elegance or one of true extravagance, our inspired team of planners, designers and technicians is committed to your unique vision. From concept to completion, our specialists work with you every step of the way to create an exquisitely romantic celebration.

Contact one of our specialists today to start planning the wedding of your dreams!

Photos: (Top) www.THEPHOTOGRAPHERS.us;
(Bottom, L-R) Holland Studios, www.THEPHOTOGRAPHERS.us

Contact
Pat Smith
e. pat@wcep.com

Quick Facts
- Consulting: venue selection, site planning & logistical layout, décor & floral planning, catering & musical selection

- Design: concept development, floral & centerpiece design, lighting design & special effects

- Rentals: elegant china & stemware, ballroom chairs & tables, heavenly tents & canopies, magical dance floors, enchanting lighting & much more

- Member of Association Bridal Consultants

- Our design specialists can customize any item to achieve your vision

BEHIND THE SCENES: AN EVENT BLOG

Be sure to visit our brand new event blog online at www.wcep.com... a forum full of inspiration, ideas and most importantly, events!

See page 315 under Rental Services

173

Bravo! Member Since 1996

Helpful Hint

Choosing Your Florist

SELECTING A FLORAL DESIGNER

Most floral designers have a portfolio of their work. Choose a floral designer who will spend time getting to know your style and desires for your wedding and who respects your ideas while offering their expertise. If you plan to arrange your own flowers, it is a good idea to consult a floral designer who can offer advice and help get the flowers you need.

SETTING A BUDGET

As with everything else, it is important to set a budget for your flowers. Your floral designer can inform you about what flowers will be in season and styles that will appropriately fit your theme and budget. Be honest about your budget so the floral designer can cater their services to fit your needs. One of the best ways to stay within a budget is to select a color scheme rather than specific flowers. For example, if you go to your floral designer saying you only want a certain type of orchid, you are subject to whatever the market price is at the time. Be open to a variety of flowers that will match your colors and theme.

DEVELOP A PLAN

Think about your floral design and decorations and write it down. Determine what you will need for the various people involved, arrangements for the church, and decorations for the reception.

MEETING WITH THE FLORAL DESIGNER

You should meet with your floral designer as soon as possible. A floral designer can only commit to a limited number of weddings or events, especially during the busy summer months. If it is not possible for them to see the wedding and reception sites ahead of time, it is a good idea to provide photos of the locations so the arrangements can best fit the surroundings.

BEING PREPARED FOR YOUR FLORAL DESIGNER

It is good to bring ideas to the first meeting with your floral designer. Although the floral designer may have photos of arrangements and bouquets or books of ideas, it is important to give a sense of what you are looking for. Take advantage of the floral designer's expertise. Be sure to tell the floral designer if there are flower types that you absolutely do not like; also let them know what you love!

FLOWER SHADES & COLORS

Colors and shades can be challenging when selecting flowers. Always use a fabric swatch or ribbon sample to show your floral designer the exact color you are envisioning.

BOUQUET TOSS

Consider having a separate, smaller bouquet for the bouquet toss. Many brides wish to have their bridal bouquet preserved.

BEYOND THE BRIDAL BOUQUET

Corsages and boutonnieres should be ordered for the wedding party and the mothers of the bride and groom. Also decide what type of arrangements you would like at the ceremony and the reception. If flowers will be near the food, be sure to choose mildly scented ones so as to not overwhelm the scent or taste of the food.

DELIVERY & SET-UP OF FLOWERS

It is very important that your flowers be delivered at the right time. Always put the location and date on your contract, as well as the desired time of delivery so to prevent questions or last-minute problems. They should arrive before the photographs are taken and kept out of direct heat or sunlight. Check to see if delivery and set-up are included in the contract. Be sure to read the entire contract before signing a final agreement with any floral designer.

174

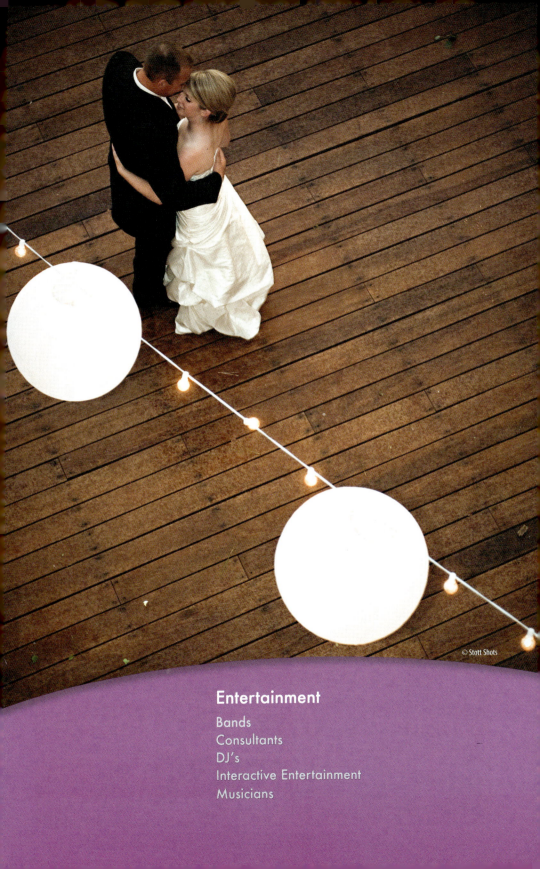

© Stott Shots

Entertainment

Bands
Consultants
DJ's
Interactive Entertainment
Musicians

world. chamber. jazz.

PO Box 42502
Portland, Oregon 97242
p. 503.235.0355
f. 503.235.0355
e. jessica@3legtorso.com
www.3legtorso.com

3 Leg Torso: Elegant, Joyful, Professional ... Just Right.

Offering a sophisticated blend of Klezmer, Latin, Eastern European gypsy, French café, Chamber music and American jazz, 3 Leg Torso has long been regarded as one of the Northwest's premiere ensembles for special events. With a unique sound, diverse repertoire and flexible ensemble size, the group appeals to wide audiences and covers all musical needs from stately ceremony music and tasteful background music to celebratory dance music that keeps the party going strong.

In addition to fulfilling the musical needs of private clients, the ensemble carries on an active concert and recording career. 3 Leg Torso has been featured on National Public Radio's "All Things Considered" and on Oregon Public Broadcasting's "Artbeat", has performed with several symphony orchestras and has completed successful East and West Coast tours. They are also recognized for their work with film makers, including Academy Award winner Joan Gratz, Sundance Film Festival award winner Rob VanAlkemade and two-time Oscar Nominee and Cannes Film Festival award winner Bill Plympton.

The consistent elements in all of 3 Leg Torso's musical ventures are the joyous nature of their music, the highest caliber of performance and the utmost of professionalism.

"All the beauty of Astor Piazolla's music, and all the spunk of Kronos Quartet's" ~ CMJ

Contact
Jessica Beer

Price
Call for a customized quote

Quick Facts
- Voted "Best Ceremony Music" by Oregon Bride magazine in 2006

- Diverse repertoire: from stately background music to celebratory dance music

- Flexible ensemble size (duo, trio or quintet) suitable for all sizes & types of events

- Instrumentation: violin, accordion, double bass, vibraphone, xylophone, glockenspiel, trumpet & various percussion

- Original compositions & arrangements of traditional world music. Special requests are welcome!

177

Bravo! Member Since 2008

David Cooley Band

swingin' hearts and rockin' souls

On The Most Important Day Of Your Life ...

David Cooley's onstage charm and blazing talent make his group one of the west coast's premier bands for wedding reception entertainment. The David Cooley Band delivers standout performances with swing, rhythm & blues, pop standards, and rock & roll classics. Whether providing background music "just right" for the occasion, or firing up the dance floor at the ideal moment, these professionals make it happen.

... Only The Best Will Do

Hired entertainment can make or break a reception. Brides and grooms have been absolutely delighted by the David Cooley Band for over 15 years, and their wedding planners know they can count on David and the band to bring the perfect blend of class, personality, fun and professionalism to the event of a lifetime. David is an outstanding singer and band leader. He's performed around the world, and it shows.

The Band

From a quartet to an eight piece group, the David Cooley Band complements any reception perfectly.

David Cooley Band Simply Offers More

Every booking comes complete with advance planning and key tips to make your reception flow smoothly, plus innovative ideas for an exceptional celebration. And don't forget – every David Cooley Band wedding package includes a complimentary dance lesson for the bride and groom.

"Our reception was perfect and your fantastic music made all the difference. Thank you!!"

– Katalin W.

Contact

800.364.1522
info@davidcooleyweddings.com
www.davidcooleyweddings.com

Price

Flexible, according to band size, venue & location

Performances

- Oregon Golf Club
- Portland Art Museum
- Sunriver Resort
- Multnomah Athletic Club
- University Club
- Portland Golf Club
- Benson Hotel
- McMenamins Edgefield
- Timberline Lodge
- Fairmont Olympic Hotel
- Seattle Tennis Club
- Waverley Country Club

ON YOUR SPECIAL DAY

The David Cooley Band is there for you – no detail is too small – creating superior reception entertainment with all the talent, versatility and experience to keep your family and guests smilin', swingin' and rockin'. Call or email today!

Bravo! Member Since 1994

THE HOUSE OF CARDS

7819 SE Henry Street
Portland, Oregon 97206
p. 503.231.1423
e. jen@thehouseofcardsmusic.com
www.thehouseofcardsmusic.com

About The House of Cards

Finding the right music for your wedding or special event can be a gamble. We can stack the deck in your favor with the hip, smart, eclectic bands we represent. From French gypsy swing to booty shakin' new wave, chances are we've got the band for you. We come straight from Portland's vibrant music scene, bringing years of professional event experience to the table.

Let's Face It

A lot of people aren't used to hiring a band, and most bands aren't accustomed to the business end of things. That's where we come in. Our agency takes the guesswork and the legwork out of booking music for your special event. Being musicians ourselves, with a decade of experience in the wedding and special event market, we have faced and problem-solved every scenario imaginable. We realize that the keys to a successful event are organization, communication and coordination of the myriad details that are bound to come up.

OUR EXCLUSIVE BAND ROSTER

The Ariel Consort	Evocative Chamber Music
Pete Krebs Gypsy Jazz	Smoky Parisian Swing
Amoree Lovell	Sultry Piano Chanteuse
The Stolen Sweets	30s New Orleans Vocal Swing
Dirty Martini	Trio of Stormy Pop Sirens
Vagabond Opera	Romantic Bohemian Cabaret
The Notables	Swinging Hits of Yesteryear
Cana Son	Traditional Cuban
Klezmocracy	Extreme Klezmer
Sneakin' Out	Frolicking Classic Rock Bluegrass
DJ Ango	Old-School Vinyl Spinning
Sassparilla	Dust Bowl Blues
Let it Bee Gee	New Wave/Retro Dance Hits

Contact
Jen Bernard

Price
Varies based on bands, duration of booking & travel

Quick Facts
- Our exclusive roster includes some of Portland's hippest, most artistically innovative bands
- Agency actually run by professional musicians
- Bringing years of professional event experience to the table
- Ceremony/reception packages available
- Personal relationships with all the musicians we represent

179

WHO WE ARE

The House of Cards Music is the brainchild of Jen Bernard and Pete Krebs, two hardworking, long-time fixtures of the Portland music scene. Who better to represent musicians than musicians?

PATRICK LAMB
PRODUCTIONS

6200 SW Virginia Suite 208
Portland, Oregon 97239
p. 503.335.0790
f. 1.866.720.9829
e. amy@patricklamb.com
www.patricklamb.com

About Patrick Lamb Productions

Patrick Lamb Productions currently represents Patrick Lamb - who tours internationally with Bobby Caldwell, Gino Vannelli & Diane Schuur, A Tribute to Ray Charles - an award winning show, and American Soul - which is Patrick's latest endeavor - a high energy horn driven band that's tailored made for your special event. American Soul will take you on a journey from Motown to 70's funk and high energy soul dance music. We can also provide a more traditional sophisticated feel of Jazz perfect for that cocktail hour. Patrick Lamb Productions is known for bringing the best and you will be amazed at the energy, vitality and quality we will bring to your event. We specialize in providing high-quality music, talented musicians, and years of experience in the event/music industry.

Testimonial

"Thanks for the great performance at Megan & Tom's wedding! The entire band was an absolute pleasure to work with and definitely kept the party hopping. The bride & groom were thrilled and several guests raved about how great you were. Thanks again and I will definitely be calling you for future weddings!"

– Nora Sheils, Bridal Bliss, Portland, Oregon

Contact
Amy Maxwell

Price
Starting at $800

Quick Facts
- Full production included
- Variety of music styles, jazz, R&B, soul, funk, disco & motown
- High-quality professional musicians
- Develop band selection tailored for your specific event needs
- Provide music for all occasions & events
- Provide specialty shows A Tribute To Ray Charles NW Gospel Project American Soul

Bravo! Member Since 1997

CONTACT US

Call us today for a promotional packet, demo CD, and a personalized price quote!

1414 NE 115th Avenue
Vancouver, Washington 98684
p. 360.254.3187
f. 360.604.8392
e. joe@swinglinecubs.com
www.swinglinecubs.com

About Swingline Cubs

Tarshene Daugherty: hailing from Vancouver, Washington, this young lady has been singing professionally since her high school days. One of her first gigs was with the popular Portland R&B band Body and Soul. She can sing styles ranging from Billie Holiday standards to knock-your-socks-off R&B and disco!

Michkael Baker: Michkael hails from Seattle, Washington, and is an accomplished choreographer as well as a singer. Sit back and listen to his repertoire of jazz standards…get up and dance to R&B, rock, and disco hits from the '60s to the present.

Quotable Quotes From Past Clients

"We don't want to jeopardize the business of other Portland-area bands, but after experiencing the Swingline Cubs at our wedding reception, we must give the following unsolicited advice: Hurry. Call the Swingline Cubs. Talk to them. Book them. Any season. Any year. If you want to party, call the Cubs. If you want to sleep, well, still call the Cubs. Yes, they're that good.
— Aaron & Jennifer Corpus

"Thank you so much for your wonderful performance…as usual, everyone was pleased and had a great time dancing the night away to the band's music. I look forward to working with you in the future."
— Nora Sheils, Bridal Bliss

"Your high energy, enthusiasm and great music was a fantastic pre-amble to the race kickoff and events. To say that Waterfront Park rocked is an understatement!!"
— Helen Williams, Race for the Cure

Contact
Joe Millward

Price
Varies, please call for quotes

Special Services
Ethnic music & special requests are gladly accepted; we can MC any activity from bouquet toss to door prizes; our PA & lighting systems are always available

Types of Music
We play all types of swing, '60s Motown, '70s hits, rhythm & blues, awesome renditions of standards & ballads & all varieties of rock 'n roll, as well as contemporary pop & jazz.

MODERN BRIDE

MAGAZINE'S 150 HOTTEST BANDS NATIONWIDE SELECTION

Swingline Cubs
Portland, 360.254.3187, swinglinecubs.com
The brass section behind this big band is "ripped with energy" according to wedding planners, who praise the group's extensive play list.

181

Bravo! Member Since 1990

THE BREAKFAST CLUB

The Breakfast Club

We are the Breakfast Club. As the name suggests, we play music from the 80's...all genres. Our message is simple: we rock, we have fun rockin', and people like rockin' with us.

Here's what our clients have to say:

"We hired The Breakfast Club 80's tribute band to perform at Widmer's 25th Anniversary Celebration, and they 'totally' nailed it. They were extremely professional and put on a great show...I received countless compliments about the music from guests and staff alike. I would definitely recommend The Breakfast Club for corporate functions, private parties, or any other events that require great live music!"

– Mindy Green, Field Marketing Manager
NW Region, CBA (Widmer)

"The Breakfast Club's ability to deliver 80's gems has made them an in-demand favorite throughout the McMenamin's Kingdom.

– Lisa Lepine, broker

"... You guys were a crowd favorite for sure. I never thought I would see hundreds of people singing along to "Jessie's Girl" on Alberta St. but you guys made it happen. Thanks again!!"

– Alberta St. Fair Entertainment Committee

"... They are totally professional and totally a blast. If you want a party, there's nothing like the 80's"

– Matt Roley, Booking Manager, Buffalo Gap

Contact
Jason Fellman

p. 503.288.6540

e. breakfastclub.pdx@gmail.com

Myspace: breakfastclubPDX

Twitter: breakfastclubOR

Price
Contact for pricing

Quick Facts
- We can perform as a full band, trio, or duo
- We have an offshoot 'Journey Tribute band' available for hire

Songs/Bands Covered
- Livin' on a Prayer
  – Bon Jovi
- Footloose
  – Kenny Loggins
- Walk like an Egyptian
  – Bangles
- Take on Me
  – A-ha
- Whip it
  – Devo
- I Love Rock n' Roll
  – Joan Jett
- Don't Stop Believin'
  – Journey
- Working for the Weekend
  – Loverboy
- Centerfold
  – J. Geils Band

© Scott Duvall

Northwest Artist Management
Musicians, Concerts & Fine Events

p. 503.774.2511
f. 503.774.2511
e. nwartmgt@bigplanet.com
www.nwam.com

About Northwest Artist Management Entertainment Consultant Services

Since 1989, Northwest Artist Management has been proud to offer the finest in classical, jazz and international music for weddings and all fine occasions. From arias to zydeco, soloists to elegant dance bands and hot jazz ensembles, we can accommodate just about any entertainment need or musical preference. We also represent fine DJs, children's entertainers, magicians, comedians and dance instructors.

Specialty

We represent only the finest Northwest artists whom you can select with complete confidence, knowing they are as dedicated to creating special memories as you are! We offer String Quartets, small Chamber and Brass ensembles, classical soloists and vocalists of all kinds, a wide selection of dance bands, DJ's, Jazz ensembles and International music such as Italian, Celtic, Klezmer, Country, Blues and R&B, Reggae, Greek, Hindu, Caribbean, Hawaiian, and Latin Salsa groups to suit most budgets. Weddings and theme parties are our specialty!

How Far In Advance Should We Meet?

If possible, we prefer to consult with you six to nine months in advance. To engage certain groups, booking one year in advance is advisable, especially if your wedding is on a Saturday evening in the summer.

Testimonial

"I think very highly of your professionalism, the people you represent, and your attention to detail. I never have to worry when it is an entertainer that we have secured through you. It is so appreciated!"
– Chris Blue, Art of Catering

"You have our business!"
– Kurt Beadell, Vibrant Table Catering

Bravo! Member Since 1992

Contact
Nancy Tice

Price
Ensemble averages begin at $300 to $2500
Soloists begin at $195
Price quotations gladly given

We Accept Visa & MasterCard

Save Money...Get Exactly What You Want
- Our commission is built into the artist's fee.
- We consult with you to determine exactly what your preferences are, & can usually offer several choices from which to choose.
- We provide complete, complimentary promotional materials, demo CD's references & whenever possible, live performance observation possibilities so you can be assured of making an informed & confident decision.
- Let us be your search engine. Booking direct doesn't guarantee you'll save money. Our service is priceless because of all the time & frustration we save our clients.
- Check out the new FAQ section on our website: www.nwam.com.

ABC Member

183

A Dancing Penguin Music

DJ & LIVE MUSIC
p. 503.282.3421
e. Kim@ADancingPenguin.com
www.adancingpenguin.com

Solo Piano With a DJ

Or add: sax, flute, cello, violin, drums, singers.

Specializing in weddings since 1989, The Penguins are often recommended by event planners, talent agents, photographers and venues. Most of their clients are referrals.

This outstanding reputation was built with great customer service and attention to detail.

Ask about our live ceremony and reception piano + DJ package!

We Listen to You

You'll have total control over music selection and volume. We'll e-mail our DJ song list, and you can pick every tune. Or, tell us your favorite bands, and we'll do the rest!

The Professionals Say...

"The Penguins are fun...I always enjoy seeing them here."
– Dennis Yamnitsky, Manager, Oswego Lake Country Club

"Always do a great job...highly recommended."
– Susan O"Neill, Waverley Country Club

"Whenever I need a DJ, the Penguins are my first call."
– Nancy Tice, NW Artist Management

"The piano and DJ combination really adds a touch of class to your event."

-Charlotte Seybold, event planner,
Special Occasion Consulting

Contact
Kim Ralphs

Services

- Since 1989, more than 1,000 happy brides
- Songs you want at the volume you prefer
- We'll email our song list, you can pick every tune
- Master of Ceremonies & event coordination
- Free demo CD or MP3s on our website
- Tux is standard attire
- Electric piano available
- Ceremonies are our specialty
- Wedding dance band with female singer

PROFESSIONAL PIANISTS WHO ARE ALSO GREAT DJ'S. A CLASSY COMBINATION!

Bravo! Member Since 1994

184

A Sound Choice ENTERTAINMENT
Professional DJs
Digital Photo Montages
A Higher Standard Since 1993

www.asoundchoiceentertainment.com

1665 Edgewater Court
West Linn, Oregon 97068

p. 503.557.8554
f. 503.742.1302

e. asoundchoice@awpdj.com

Contact

Anthony Wedin, *Owner*

Andy Gilbert, *Office Manager*

Are You Wondering How to Pick a Professional Disc Jockey Service?

Anyone can make promises on a page! To ensure you're hiring a professional DJ service, ask other wedding professionals for a DJ referral.

The price you pay for DJ services doesn't matter if the performance of the DJ is poor and your guests end up leaving the reception early. Rates vary, so ask other wedding professionals for the name of a DJ company they trust, because they see good and bad DJs week in and week out.

Entertainment experience has everything to do with the success of your special day. A Sound Choice Entertainment has been in the business of wedding services since 1993. Our professional and well-trained staff is experienced and motivated to guide you through your wedding day so you can relax and enjoy your day your way.

What will we do for you?

- Consult with you about the vision of your wedding & help you plan your day
- Assist with all Master of Ceremonies duties to make your event run smoothly
- Dress in appropriate tuxedo attire
- Play your requests & run the event, because that's what a good DJ does
- Ceremony music
- Video Services
- A/V Rental

185

MasterCard

VISA

CALL & BOOK YOUR DJ COMPANY EARLY

For one or all of these added services and references please feel free to call or visit us online and get more information to help you make an informed decision for this most special day – your wedding day!

Bravo! Member Since 1994

All About Music
Entertainment

The Evolution of Entertainment

Congratulations on your engagement. A wedding is one of the most important events in a lifetime. Let us help you make the decision regarding your entertainment needs a simple one.

Before your special day we will meet with you to go over all the details from the beginning to end; from the Grand Entrance to the First Dance, Father-Daughter dance, Mother-Son dance, toast, Cake Cutting, Garter-Bouquet and any other special activities you would like to do. We will answer all your questions, listen to your needs and share ideas from our experience.

At your event we will coordinate with all the other event staff to ensure your wedding flows beautifully. We will keep all your special guests informed and entertained. Our meticulous attention to detail will ensure that your reception proceeds according to your wishes.

Remember, your DJ should act as a "spokesperson" for you and your family at your reception so that you and your loved ones can enjoy the special day. And it is important for you to feel comfortable with and trust the person you are hiring. "I want to be that person."

- Anthony, All About Music DJ Company

Contact
Anthony Rice

p. 503.408.7857

e. info@allaboutmusicdj.com

Price
Packages starting at $495

Additional Services
- Thousands of Songs - List Available Online

- DJs with 11 years of Experience

- Photo Montage and Videography Services Available

- Written Contract

- Teach Group Dances

- Audience Interaction

- Professional Attire

- Ceremony Music

- Wireless lapel and handheld microphones

This is the first day of the rest of your life.

Let's get this party started!

Call for an appointment
503.408.7857

Bravo! Member Since 1996

186

About All Wright Music

From the first song to the last dance, All Wright Music will transform your wedding into an event your friends and family will still be talking about years from now. We have been performing for 16 years in the Northwest/USA and each week help create spectacular wedding celebrations. We truly enjoy working on wedding receptions because they are a complete celebration.

AWM DJs are experts experienced at reading crowds to determine the flow of the event in both timing and music flow. During our years of providing DJ service, we have worked on every level of wedding from beach casual to the most formal of affairs.

We have worked with the best wedding coordinators and have seen what it takes to make an outstanding reception. Our DJ attire is a black suit or formal wear, or we can dress in other attire to fit the event.

All Wright Music DJs have helped create lifetime memories of joy, excitement, elegance and fun. We look forward to making your event memorable.

You will remember your wedding day forever! Make your world a little more wonderful with quality entertainment from All Wright Music!

Contact
Eric Wright

PO Box 1991
Lake Oswego, Oregon 97035

p. 503.635.1115

e. eric@allwrightmusic.com

www.allwrightmusic.com

Price
Individual event pricing

Quick Facts
- Eric Wright chosen by Modern Bride Magazine as one of the Top 75 DJs in America for 2006/2007/2008
- All Wright Music has successfully created more than 3500 events
- We excel at handling large-scale detailed receptions
- Please call & request a copy of our outstanding Wedding DVD

WHAT'S NEW
Our Wedding DVD is all new for 2010! It is a spectacular showcase of our wedding work!

MEMBERSHIP

Bravo! Member Since 1998

187

© Chris Lewis

AA
BUST-A-MOVE
Oregon's #1 DJ
Entertainment Service

ANYONE CAN PLAY
MUSIC, WE ENTERTAIN!

PO Box 2902
Oregon City, Oregon 97045
p. 503.201.3710
f. 503.632.4233
www.bustamovedjservice.com

About AA Bust-A-Move DJ Service

Frank Bratcher, founder of Bust - A - Move DJ Services, has many years of experience in the Entertainment Industry. In the early 80's he was the front man and lead vocalist for a touring rock group that appeared with KISS, Fog Hat, the Scorpions, Quiet Riot, Head East, and too many others to list. Putting on a first rate performance is all he ever strives for, and expects out of his crew of DJ's.

"I don't care about being the biggest DJ company in Oregon, I just expect us to be the best. Whether it's a bride & groom, school function, or a business party, they all spend a lot of money to make their event special and fun, and we're gonna give them more than their money's worth."

– Frank Bratcher

"I cannot express how grateful we are to you. You made or wedding day the exact way we were hoping for. We had an incredible time. I will recommend you to every single person we know needing your services. You were fabulous! Thank you"!

– Anthony & Nikki Kurtz

Contact
Frank Bratcher

Price
Affordable packages which can be custom-tailored for each event

Starting at $495

Quick Facts
- 27 Years of entertaining experience

- Fun, tuxedo dressed DJs

- State of the art lighting & sound

- Thousands of digitally recorded music selections

- Karaoke available

- Ceremonies starting at $125 if added into hours of chosen package

- Other services available

188

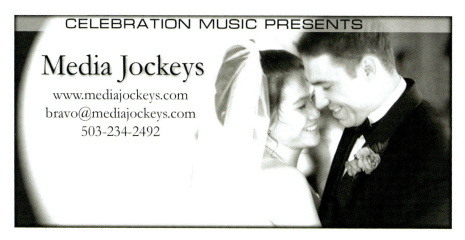

CELEBRATION MUSIC PRESENTS

Media Jockeys

www.mediajockeys.com
bravo@mediajockeys.com
503-234-2492

The Premier Mobile Entertainment Provider in the Northwest Since 1991!

Wedding reception entertainment has been a specialty of Media Jockeys DJ service for more than 15 years. Our DJs are experienced in playing music that reflects your musical tastes, making the appropriate announcements and helping to keep your event running smoothly. Our formally dressed DJs bring great equipment, a huge music library, and work hard to ensure you and your guests enjoy your special day.

Media Jockeys now offers discounted wedding ceremony services to its bridal customers. Book one of our DJs for your reception and you can order a second sound system for your ceremony at a significant cost savings, even if your ceremony is not at the same location as your reception. As part of this service, we will provide setup and operation of the sound system, allow you full control over the musical program, and provide you with quality microphone amplification so the ceremony can be heard clearly, even in the last aisle.

The Media Jockeys DJ service has a music library difficult for other DJ companies to match, in terms of size and variety. Covering all styles from classical to country, swing to salsa, rock to reggae, hip hop to house, soul to standards, pop to polka and contemporary dance to disco, our giant library is getting bigger all the time. We add music weekly and are very happy to take your requests and add those to our library as well. If you don't find your special music on the list, tell us in advance so that we can have it for your event. Our goal is to have every song that you or your guests want to hear.

Contact

Lynn Winkle

6916 SE 17th
Portland, Oregon 97202

p. 503.234.2492
f. 503.233.0835

e. bravo@mediajockeys.com

www.cmevents.com

189

Price

Please call or visit our website for more information

Services

- Offer digital projectors & screens for slide shows at competitive rates

- We use sleek laptop computers with digital sound processors to deliver a gigantic, searchable, CD-quality music library that never skips, pops, or degrades

- Multiple light & sound packages available

- References available upon request

- Free consultation

- Personalized dance instruction

VISIT US TODAY!

Please visit our website at www.mediajockeys.com or call at 503.234.2492

DW Duo

p. 503.642.9509
e. dawn@dwduo.com
www.dwduo.com

Elegance Of Live Music... Variety Of A DJ!

Wedding ceremony to reception, DW Duo has the flexibility to make your day unique and special.

Here is just one example...

The Celtic harp has a beautiful warm, full sound. It is a traditional harp that is a newly made version of harps that have been played in weddings for more than twelve hundred years, adding a romantic image and soft, meditative sound.

The classical guitar has a rich, complex sound that is full of soothing layers and tones that have a way of speaking straight to the heart.

Ceremony: classical guitar, harp and vocals.

Reception: (cocktails/buffet) smooth jazz, bossa novas and standards performed.

After dinner: smoothly merge into master of ceremony duties and DJ Dance Music.

Please contact us for booking information, referrals and options available. Thank you for considering us for your special day!

DW Duo ... Exceeding your expectations, not your budget!

Coast to Mountains ... We Always Arrive in Style!

Contact
Dawn Grishow
Harpist • Singer • DJ

Price
Packages starting at $495

Quick Facts
- 25 years experience
- Concert-quality equipment
- 10,000 + music library
- Complete wedding package
- HD professionally edited highlight video
- Match attendants colors
- Small sound system & cordless mic for ceremony
- Large sound system & lighting package for reception
- Wedding party dance

"WE LOVE WHAT WE DO... WE DO WHAT WE LOVE!"

WHEN IT'S TIME TO CELEBRATE... DW DUO!

Bravo! Member Since 2001

ENCORE
STUDIOS

Portland Metro Area
p. 503.255.8047
e. encore100@comcast.net
www.encore-studios.com

About Encore Studios

Experience and creativity! Let our professionals play at your wedding. Whether you wold like a DJ or a live band, duo, trio quartet or any other type of musician, we are here to help!

- Music by disc jockey pros with your style and favorites played for your ceremony and reception!
- With more than 20 years of experience, we can customize your event to your special needs.
- Master of ceremonies is our speciality.

Our professionals help you have a relaxed, playful and fun wedding day, just by doing what they do best in life!

To make your day the best it could be
call 503.255.8047.

Contact
Encore Studios

Price
Starting at $150 customized

Services
- We offer disc jockey, photography & videography services – all for less than photography alone at other studios
- Creative & passionate in making your wedding day a success
- Professional services with experience in thousands of weddings
- Customize packages to suit your style; we understand what budget means
- Local & traveling abilities

191

MUSIC STYLES

We have music of all styles & eras including: 20s through today, top 100, hip hop, R&B, country, jazz, classical, rock, motown, ballroom, big band, rap, reggae, alternative, disco, ethnic and more.

See page 271 under Photography

Bravo! Member Since 1995

Visit BravoWedding.com for more information on great entertainment

Why Choose Fish Productions?

Fish Productions understands this is YOUR big day! You have enough to worry about without having to stress over the music or the flow of your reception. When you hire Fish Productions you get an experienced Professional DJ who will work with your wedding coordinator, photographer, vendors, and guests to make sure everything goes as planned. We have over 20 years experience in hosting and DJ'ing concerts, corporate functions, radio events and weddings.

Music

It starts with the first dance. "Your song." From this day forward every time you hear your song you'll remember this day. Music is so powerful, and the right music can transform your wedding and reception into the one you've always dreamed of. Fish Productions will make sure this day is all about you and your fiancé. Get song suggestions for your father/daughter dance, bouquet toss etc. at www.fishprod.com.

Contact
Tim Fisher

p. 503.481.7744

e. tim@fishprod.com

www.fishprod.com

Price
Each wedding is unique & special, please call for a quote.

Quick Facts

- We can provide music for your ceremony for a small fee. We have traditional ceremony music as well as more contemporary options.

- Our greatest advertising has always come from past clients.

- You will have direct access to us as much as you need up until your big day!

TESTIMONIAL

"Dear, sweet, patient Tim, I was a total BRIDEZILLA! I called you thirty times before our wedding. You were a great MC! The reception was a blast, everyone is still talking about it. We will recommend you to everyone!"
- Cassie Johns, West Linn

Bravo! Member Since 2000

192

Jazz It - Up Productions

About Jazz It-Up Productions

Jazz It-Up Productions is a full-service entertainment company providing reasonably priced, professional mobile music, lighting, and rental services to the Northwest since 1993. We will guide you through all the steps of your ceremony and reception planning that will lead to a flawless special day. Jazz It-Up Productions has an extensive music library exceeding 20,000 selections.

Styles of music range from the 40s to what's current today in every genre. Requests from you and your guests are always welcome. Our disc jockeys are happy to act as master of ceremonies. We dress in the appropriate attire of the event.

We use only custom built sound and lighting systems to meet the stringent requirements of our industry. All packages include a wireless UHF handheld microphone. We offer packages that include small sound systems for your ceremony to concert sized sound systems for the largest of receptions. We will help you find the package that fits your needs and budget.

Ceremony and reception planner sheets designed by our planning staff help you to plan the music soundtrack for your special day. We find that most customers even circulate these planning sheets to other vendors as the basis for the event time line.

Reception package prices start at $489 for three hours of service. Our most popular packages don't exceed $589 for three hours of service and packages can be custom created. Each additional hour can be purchased for $60 at the time of booking or $100 at the event. There is no deposit required; a signed contract holds your date. Contact us today toll free.

Contact

Aaron Schumacher - Reservations
info@jazzitupproductions.com

p. 503.620.2606
p. 866.33.PARTY
f. 503.213.6072
www.jazzitupproductions.com

193

Price

Ceremonies starting at $159.00 & receptions starting at $489.00

Quick Facts
- Full-time professionals DJs
- DJ & master of ceremonies
- No deposits, pay the day of your event
- Wedding planner on staff
- Light show, video & karaoke services available
- Free planning guides & comprehensive website
- Video montage service
- Video production

SPECIAL OFFER

Free video montage with booking of a Rose package. Call now or check out our website for more information.

Level One DJ Services

Balanced.Responsive.Inspired

Portland & SW Washington
p. 503.648.0234
p. 877.625.3370
e. info@level1dj.com
www.level1dj.com

About Level One DJ Service

Our ethical services are backed up by an excellent team of DJ's where customer service is paramount.

We provide you with a "personally assigned DJ" that consults with you and answers all questions in detail before you "book" an event with us.

We can provide services for intimate events of 50 guests to grander events of 2,000 guests in a modern, fun and eclectic environment.

Our philosophy is to be minimalist DJ's that blend in with the environment without being over-bearing. The focus is on our clients and guests, NOT on the DJ. Our DJ's are experienced emcees and will provide the proper announcements and coordination to ensure your event is managed smoothly. We let our professional skills, proper coordination with venue staff and artistry of music choices blend together to provide an exceptional and memorable event for our clients.

194

Contact
Matthew Woolman

Price
Please call for pricing

Quick Facts

- Consultation meeting with personally assigned DJ prior to "booking" event

- Committed to providing clients with a responsive & ethical level of service

- We proudly & expertly serve culturally diverse & varied lifestyle clients

- 15 years of reliable & dedicated service

- Ceremony Service w/ wireless lapel microphone, separate audio system, plus FREE hour of service available with our "COMPLETE WEDDING PACKAGE"

- Video projectors & high definition plasma screens available

- "Eco/Green Friendly" LED lighting packages now available

MOBILE MUSIC ENTERTAINMENT SERVICES

Professional DJ Services...

SINCE 1978

www.mobilemusicentertainment.com

Type of Music

Mobile Music has over 300 hours of music we bring to each event. Music selection ranges from big band, '50s, '60s, '70s, '80s, 90's, current hits, cocktail, lounge, country, Top 40, rock, hip hop and jazz. We always play the music you want.

Equipment

The sound systems Mobile Music uses are custom-built for mobile use. You won't find any home gear in our systems. The systems are compact and can be set up in 20 minutes. We do have larger setups for functions up to 3,000 people.

Experience

Mobile Music has been in business since 1978. We provide music and entertainment at more than 1,000 events each year. We base our business on providing friendly, professional service to our clients.

Corporate Events

For corporate events, Mobile Music has a wide variety of activities, including karaoke, casino games, contests and games – all hosted by a professional master of ceremonies. Please call for more information and rates on packages.

Music the Way You Want It!

We at Mobile Music pride ourselves on providing quality music the way you want it played. We use only professional disc jockeys with experience who will help make your event everything you want it to be. If you have any questions or special requirements, feel free to call.

Contact

Brian Smith

p. 503.638.0624
c. 503.209.0413

e. smittyosu1@hotmail.com

Price

The basic package starts at $500 for three hours & $100 for each additional hour; price subject to change

Services

- Also serving the Salem Area: 503.380.6319.

- We have light shows & other special effects available for rent

- We also offer audio/ visual equipment

- A 20% deposit & a signed contract hold your date for you

Award

Voted Best DJ of 2009 by the Oregon Bride Magazine

SPECIAL SERVICES

Mobile Music uses only professional mobile disc jockeys from around the Portland area. Whether you want a life-of-the-party DJ or just music, we have the disc jockey for your event.

195

Bravo! Member Since 1990

NW Mobile DJ Service

NW Mobile DJ Service is completely dedicated to creating events as unique and individual as you. Our experienced mobile DJ's and MC's pride themselves on providing high end, state-of-the-art sound quality, a diverse music collection, and affordable prices to suit your budget. All this wrapped in a positive and personal touch guaranteed to make your wedding ceremony, wedding reception, corporate event, reunion, anniversary, birthday, school dance/prom, or Bar/Bat Mitzvah an event to remember.

NW Mobile DJ Service serves the Pacific Northwest (Oregon & Washington) with experienced professionals who are always courteous, friendly, energetic, and determined to make a difference.

The DJ/MC will gladly handle any announcements and activities during your event. Our level of interaction can be anywhere from conservative to out-going. At any level, our style never steals the spotlight – we strive to be part of the event and not the focus. We provide a professional, understated presence while engaging your group with music for all to enjoy.

196

Contact

Kevin Venables

PO Box 80896
Portland, Oregon 97280

p. 503.380.6319

e. Kevin@nwmobiledjservice.com

www.nwmobiledjservice.com

Price

$500 for 3 hours – $100 each additional hour – additional charge for out of Portland/Salem area

Our Services

- Full service DJ company – able to provide for both ceremony & reception

- Multiple services – karaoke, casino event contractors, interactive video games

- Video projectors & screens available

- Professional attire & attitude

- Approachable, reliable, & FUN!

© Eric John Photography

p. 360.909.6700
f. 360.571.3213
e. info@djpdx.com
www.djpdx.com

Paradox Productions brings a refreshing spirit and professionalism that is born from a passion for music and people. We will create a fun and entertaining environment without stealing the spotlight of your special day. We will make the planning process smooth, while maintaining consistent and open communication with you. We will meet with you personally in order to allow you a true feel for our unique individuality.

Your Paradox Professionals will act as Disc Jockey/Master of Ceremonies (MC) and Day of Event Coordinator. Both individuals will be available during the planning process, and present on your wedding day. We will organize and guide you through every aspect of your ceremony and reception. We will ensure that no detail is missed and no last minute needs are neglected. We will intuitively sense the energy level, and adjust the music to maintain an environment of celebration.

*"When Your Wedding Is Successful,
We Are Successful!"*

Contact
Jen Bardue

Price
$495–$995

Our Services
- Interactive Disc Jockey
- Master of Ceremonies
- Day of Event Coordinator
- On-line Reception Planner & Music Database
- Wireless Microphone
- Premium Sound & Lights
- Video Projector

197

Paradox Productions truly is..."The New generation in DJ Entertainment."

For more information and an instant price quote, visit www.DJpdx.com, or call Jen at 360.909.6700.

Barbara Pikus Caricatures
Since 1994

198

A caricature is a moment in time that you can keep forever

Let me capture the best of who you are as a caricature at your next event. My drawings are always meant to make people feel good, and are a unique addition to any occasion, corporate or private. I can draw anyone, age is no object, from newborn babies to 99 years. I've drawn them all.

Many guests will be fascinated just watching me do my 5 minute drawings. At your next event, as an ice-breaker and interactive entertainment, for wedding receptions or rehearsal dinner, please include Barbara Pikus Caricatures.

Praise for Barbara's Caricatures

"Thank you once again for bringing your superb talents to our Company picnic. Our employees truly appreciated you as indicated by the long lines.
– Spirit Boosters, Spirit Mountain Casino

"Thank you so much for being a part of our recognition event at the Portland Art Museum. We received many compliments on your work and it was such a pleasure to have you there!"
– Wells Fargo Recognition Committee

Contact
Barbara Pikus

p. 503.238.4301

e. sketch@involved.com

www.barbarapikuscaricatures.com

Rates
Please call for pricing

Some Clients
- Art Institute of Portland
- Hewlett Packard
- Spirit Mountain Casino
- Sephora USA, Inc.
- Yoshida Group

Corporate & Private Events
- Parties
- Picnics
- Conventions
- Bar/Bat Mitzvahs
- Weddings
- Rehearsal Dinners

CARICATURES
Caricatures that capture the best of who you are.

Bravo! Member Since 2002

**The Photo Booth without the Booth.....
Where Every Guest is the STAR!**

Your Solution for WEDDING FAVORS, GUEST ALBUM & RECEPTION ENTERTAINMENT.

Paparazzi Tonight Photo Booth is a mobile "paparazzi style" photo studio with a modern take on the retro photo booth experience. We take 4 shots 4 seconds apart. Your guests can either HAM IT UP or GLAM IT UP! Instant Prints for everyone in the shot. Unlimited Photos and Onsite Prints.

- **Live Photographers:** Ensure every shot is a winner.
- **Photo Wedding Favors:** The BEST Favors at any wedding. On Site Instant Printing allows EVERY guest an instant photo print, ensuring your wedding is memorable. Guests can return as often as they wish with different family/friend/spouse groupings.
- **Photo Guest Album:** Extra copy of each photo is printed and placed in one-of-a-kind guest album and signed by each guest. Presented to bride & groom at reception's end.
- **Creates Fun & Creative Reception Atmosphere:** Entertaining & Meaningful.
- **Instant Slideshow Projection:** Incorporate photos into reception via projection installations.
- **Web Gallery:** Public or password protected. All photos are online where guests are able to download, reprint & share studio quality hi-res images.
- **Cutting Edge:** Professional Lighting and Cameras.
- **High Capacity Printing System:** Perfect for 50 to 400+ guests.
- **Prop Kits & Themed Weddings:** 50% of our weddings have us bring out props sometime during the reception to accentuate and add a little fun. Hollywood and red carpet themes are our specialty.
- **Thank You Cards:** Created from Paparazzi Tonight photos & received by honeymoon's end.
- **Environmentally Friendly:** No harsh chemicals common in traditional photo booth rentals.
- **American Disabilities Act Compliant & Wheel Chair Accessible**
- **Locally Owned and Operated**

PAPARAZZI TONIGHT Photo Booth.....where EVERY Guest is the STAR!

Reservations and Information 503.939.6097

www.paparazzitonight.com • info@paparazzitonight.com

Bravo! Member Since 2007

Visit BravoWedding.com for more information on great entertainment

Party Outfitters

Party Outfitters offers a unique service for your special day. Utilizing photo booths, billiards, arcades and more; we can help make your wedding experience as fun and unique as you are. Don't settle for the same old same old. Keep your guests entertained and have them saying "this was the best and most creative wedding reception I have ever been to!" Call now to add the finishing touches to your most special day.

Photo Booths:

Add a professional photo booth to your wedding reception for all to enjoy.

- Guests enter the photo booth
- Select from many fun options
- Ask guests place one of the two photo strips in a nice box for you to keep & scrapbook.

Customize your photos. Add your names & wedding date or even your engagement photo to the bottom of each photo strip for your guests to take home with them.

Starting at only $695 CALL NOW to reserve your date. 800.853.5867

Kids Zone or Recreation Area:

Create a fun area for the kids (and the adult kids) to play and have fun during your wedding reception.

Wedding Reception Recreation Area:

- (1) Pool Table
- (1) Air Hockey Table
- (1) Classic Arcade Game (Pac-Man, Galaga, Frogger,etc.)
- (1) Pinball Machine

PACKAGE PRICE ONLY $995 (up to 3-hours)

Bravo! Member Since 1996

Contact

Justin Patenaude

Seattle, Washington & Portland, Oregon

p. 800.853.5867
f. 360.438.3614

e. justin@partyoutfitters.com

www.partyoutfitters.com

Price

Starting at $500

Quick Facts

You found the guy...

the ring...

the location...

now add the FUN!

PARTY OUTFITTER SERVICES

*Photo Booths
*Billiards and Arcades
*Kid Zones
*Batchelor/ette Parties
*Rehearsal Dinners
*Receptions

Celtic Kaleide

The Celtic Kaleide has the distinction of being the Portland area's most authentic traditional Irish ensemble. Spearheaded by fiddle virtuoso Brongaene Griffin, the band also includes the internationally recognized Irish Sean-Nós style singer and guitarist Nancy Conescu, acclaimed Celtic harpist and singer Elizabeth Nicholson, and award-winning whistle player Geraldine Murray. A foursome with ferocious instrumental and vocal chops, the band serves up lightning-paced dance tunes, bawdy songs, love ballads and contemplative airs with equal aplomb.

The Celtic Kaleide can provide traditional wedding standards for your ceremony, or allow you to personalize your music by choosing pieces from their extensive Irish and Scottish repertoire, or favorites from your own collection. For the cocktail hour, they can play relaxing waltzes and airs before kicking it up a notch when it's time to dance with some high-octane jigs and reels. The band is also able to pare up and down according to your instrumental needs; frequently they perform as a six-piece with the addition of acoustic bassist Mike Doolin and percussionist Bob Soper. You may choose to have a solo, duo, or trio, or the full quartet (or sextet) performing for any portion of your event.

Celtic Kaleide is also able to bring additional musicians into the line-up when needed, including Scottish and Irish pipers, flutists, accordionists, or any other instrumentation you desire. You may also choose to include Irish dancers for your reception, or a caller to teach guests authentic traditional dances during reception music, providing an enormous amount of fun. Various arrangements are available for all budgets to give you the best Irish or Scottish wedding imaginable.

Contact
Brongaene Griffin
p. 503.847.3566
e. brongaene@hotmail.com
www.myspace.com/celtickaleide

Musicians:
- Brongaene Griffin - fiddle/violin
- Nancy Conescu - guitar/vocals
- Elizabeth Nicholson - harp/vocals
- Geraldine Murray - Irish whistles/Irish dance caller

The band may also feature:
- Mike Doolin - acoustic bass
- Bob Soper - percussion
- Rob Barrick - highland pipes
- Channing Dodson - uillean pipes/flute
- Dancers from the Murray Irish Dance Troupe

Wedding duos starting at $250

201

PO Box 6411
Portland, Oregon 97228
p. 503.860.7688
e. contact@effesenden.com
www.effesenden.com

202

About Effesenden

Do you imagine floating down the aisle to the strands of Pachelbel's Canon in D? Or maybe you're not so traditional—you envision the train of your dress dancing to a rousing fiddle song that nobody has heard before.

You know what it sounds like in your dreams.

Effesenden music will make that dream come to life!

Coordinators say:

"Effesenden is absolutely amazing at personalizing and customizing your wedding music to perfectly fit your needs!"
– Rachel Goode, Cakewalk Events

"I have worked with Wendy and her team of professionals on numerous accounts. Every time she provides quality customer service and beautiful music!"
– Mandi Downs, Champagne Wedding & Event Coordination

On your wedding day:

"Every time we watch our wedding video we are captivated by your gift of music. Every song that you played just made the moment even more special. We still receive compliments to this day."
– Tina, July 2006

Contact
Wendy Goodwin

Price
Please call for current pricing

Quick Facts
- String Duos, Trios & Quartets in traditional & contemporary styles

- Jazz Ensembles perfect for cocktail hours & receptions

- Bluegrass & Celtic music

- Pop oriented bands with vocals for diverse, high-energy reception music

- Service & customization are our specialties

- Follow us on Twitter at: http://twitter.com/effesenden

WHAT'S NEW?

Effesenden Music is thrilled to offer a brand new demo for 2010, reflecting the versatility, quality and relevance we strive to bring to each event! Check it out at www.effesenden.com.

Bravo! Member Since 2002

1607 SE Ash Street #1
Portland, Oregon 97214
p. 503.984.8542
e. mlkern@email.com
www.matthewkern.net

About Matthew Kern

Matthew Kern has provided music for hundreds of weddings, receptions, rehearsal dinners, private parties and corporate events over the past ten years at nearly every Portland area venue. He began playing at the age of three and has an instantly recognizable style that encompasses many musical genres and eras from jazz and pop standards to rock classics and the hits of today. He has an intuitive sense of timing, atmosphere and what songs will be most enjoyable for you and your guests. Matthew's playing is unobtrusive yet engaging, and has been described by The Oregonian as "wildly romantic" and "wonderful." His versatility makes him the perfect choice for music lovers of all ages and the ideal musician for any style of event from the most traditional to the most casual. He will meet with you in advance if you wish to discuss your musical preferences. Friendly and professional, Matthew believes the music for your celebration should be as special as you are and will work with you to make sure your ceremony and reception are accompanied by the music that you love the most.

"Thank you for everything– the music was gorgeous and more beautifully played than we could have hoped for. We were so lucky to find you and so happy to have you as a part of our day!"
– Erin and Nathan

"Thank you, Matthew! The music during the ceremony and the reception was just perfect. You made the whole process really fun, and our guests all raved about your playing."
– Doug and Katie

Contact
Matthew Kern

Price
Sound samples, price quote & availability upon request

Quick Facts
- My music has been called "wildly romantic" & "wonderful" by The Oregonian.

- Over ten years of experience providing unforgettable music for weddings, receptions, rehearsal dinners, & private parties at nearly every Portland area venue.

- Served as house pianist for downtown Nordstrom for over nine years.

- One of Portland's most recognizable & popular musicians.

- Recordings have been featured on KINK 101.9 & KMHD 89.1 fm

- A distinct sound that encompasses many genres. Enormous repertoire of jazz, pop & rock standards as well as contemporary selections. Happy to learn new selections for your event.

203

Bravo! Member Since 2009

If you could have *anything you wanted* on your Unique Wedding Day, would Accomplished & Beautiful, 'tailored to you' Live Music be a part of your vision?

There is no replacement in emotion, quality, or class for the richness of Live Classical Strings. But that is just the beginning...

204

Envision:

- Beautiful flowing Prelude music greeting your guests as they arrive, make themselves comfortable, and enjoy the atmosphere.

- Timeless Classical Strings carry you and your loved ones down the aisle to pieces you have chosen yourself. (Any Song, Any Genre- I can help with song choice)

- A joyful request lifts your spirit past your community as you recess out- A Married Couple!

- Seamlessly transition to adding in Trumpet, Flute, Vocals, Even Percussion if desired- to provide an Up-beat backdrop, performing your favorite songs for a Social and Festive Reception/Cocktail Hour!

Using optional Live Looping Scott showcases his astonishing ability in multiple instruments, resulting in full sounds you might only expect from a duet, trio, small band, or combo piece, tailored uniquely to any segment of **Your Day.**

The possibilities are endless for creating the exact atmosphere you're looking for ~ Not to mention... All for the *price* of a Soloist!

Highly recommended, Scott's Experience, Professionalism, Musicianship, Flexibility, and Love of his Craft shine through from day one, making not just the Music one of a kind, but also working together a true pleasure!

Call, Send an email, or Visit Scott's Website to learn more and for booking an Unforgettable Wedding Performance- Your Style, on Your Day!

Bravo! Member Since 2009

Contact

Scott Head, *Musica Melodia*

p. 503.867.2697

e. scotthead@musicamelodia.com

www.musicamelodia.com

Price

Sound samples, price quotes, & availability upon request

Quick Facts

- Ten Years providing timeless Live Atmosphere to Weddings, Receptions, & Private Events in some of the Nation's finest Venues, to rave reviews & memories

- Currently House Musician for Portland's Andina, Fenouil, & del Inti Fine Dining Icons (Visit website for Schedule!)

- Enormous Repertoire & happy to work up custom arrangements & requests ~ Classical to Contemporary Favorites, Spanish style Guitar/Sultry Latin Jazz, Much more

"The music was absolutely beautiful- exactly what I wanted!... – Thank you for being so great and easy to work with!"
– Kara & James Cardwell

"...We simply loved Scott's choice of music and his versatility.... we could not have asked for a better experience."
– Camelia & David

For that perfect wedding...

The Stradivari String Quartet

Winchester Enterprises
p. 503.232.3684
f. 503.236.2920

About The Stradivari String Quartet

For that perfect wedding or event...perfect music by The Stradivari String Quartet for ceremonies and receptions in your church, synagogue, private club, residence or garden. The style is elegant, distinctive, and affordable. Information packet, including music list, available upon request.

Experience

Distinguished wedding music since 1972. Our clientele has included prominent Northwest social and business leaders, including Bravo's own Mary Lou Burton. In 1980 Stradivari String Quartet appeared in the Paramount motion picture "First Love" filmed on location in Portland.

Contact
Hugh Ewart, Assoc. Concertmaster Emeritus Oregon Symphony

Price
Call for current prices & availability

Quick Facts
- Consultations are complimentary

- Call for free demo CD

- Stradivari String Trio & Stradivari String Duo also available

Bravo! Member Since 1990

CHARMING AMBIANCE

"The Stradivari String Quartet added a charming ambiance to the event."
Barbara Jordan,
The Oregonian

Visit BravoWedding.com for more information on great entertainment

p. 503.231.1423
e. jen@lazybullmusic.com
www.lazybullmusic.com

Contact
Jen Bernard

Price
Call for quote

Quick Facts
- Hauntingly evocative chamber music for ceremonies & receptions
- Any combo of flute, violin, cello, harp, voice & classical guitar

The Ariel Consort is a multi-instrumental chamber ensemble featuring an enchanting blend of musical voices. Our instrumentalists fuse their unique textures to create a beautiful musical tapestry.

A consort is, by definition, a troupe of rotating musicians. We allow you to create any soloist, duo, trio or quartet from among the various instruments we offer.

Our eclectic repertoire includes classical, romantic, multi-cultural folk and jazz. We can adapt your repertoire completely to suit your taste.

Bravo! Member Since 1998

206

Contact
Susan Langenes
p. 503.317.5825
e. susan@collagetrio.com
www.collagetrio.com

Price
$300–$2,500

Quick Facts
- Variable ensembles to suit your needs
- Traditional classical, vintage swing, classic rock, & more
- Violin, cello, guitar, flute, mandolin, bass, piano, saxophone, & vocals
- Highly experienced & flexible musicians, happy to be adaptible!
- NEW Classic Rock cover band for receptions!

Your wedding deserves our experience

Founded in 2003, Collage Music is a group of highly experienced wedding music veterans. We love our work, love playing together, and are dedicated to enhancing your event with our craft.

We specialize in making it easy for you

Special request songs, vocals for ceremony and/or reception, sound system, emcee duties and more are all available. And always, unlimited consultation!

Visit www.collagetrio.com
to hear samples and get ideas!

Bravo! Member Since 2003

Duo con Brio

Contact
Corey Averill

p. 503.526.3908

c. 503.407.6256

e. singandbow@comcast.net

www.duoconbrio.com

Duo con Brio is a professional ensemble founded by cellist Corey Averill. The duo may be augmented to a string trio or quartet; guitar, trombone, flute, voice, harp, and trumpet are also available. We have a large repertoire from Classical to Pop, Jazz, Jewish, Holiday, and more. We pride ourselves at arranging up to two special song requests at no additional fee.

Price
Instant Quotes available on website

Solo cello $195 first hour ($95 each additional hour)

Duo $315 first hour ($165 each additional hour)

Trio $415 first hour ($210 each additional hour)

Quartet $515 first hour ($260 each additional hour)

We accept Visa/MasterCard/Discover

Experience
Formed in 1989, the Duo has performed more than 2000 events. Over the years we have performed both locally and abroad in Europe and Asia. Our memorable events include performing at Timberline's Silcox Hut, Oaks Pioneer Church, University of Phoenix Graduation ceremonies, Sammy Awards, and many beautiful weddings. We are members of Better Business Bureau, and the American Federation of Musicians Local 99.

Bravo! Member Since 1991

207

DW Duo

p. 503.642.9509

e. dawn@dwduo.com

www.dwduo.com

Elegance of Live Music...Variety of a DJ!

Wedding ceremony to reception, DW Duo has the flexibilty to make your day unique and special. Here is just one example...

Ceremony: classical guitar, harp and vocals.

Reception (cocktails/buffet): smooth jazz, bossa novas and standards performed.

After dinner: smoothly merge into master of ceremony duties and DJ dance music.

Please contact us for booking information, referrals and options available. Thank you for considering us for your special day!

"WE LOVE WHAT WE DO... WE DO WHAT WE LOVE!"

Contact
Dawn Grishow

Harpist • Singer • DJ

Price
Packages starting at $495

Quick Facts
- 25 years experience
- Concert quality equipment
- 10,000 + music library
- HD professionally edited highlight video
- Match attendants colors

Bravo! Member Since 2001

Eric Skye

p. 503.288.5493

e. min7b5@yahoo.com

www.ericskye.com

Acousitc Jazz Guitar Soloist

"A guitar maestro!"

- The Oregonian

"Talk about delicious subtlety…"

- Jazz Improv Magazine

"Eric Skye is a master Guitarist"

- Jazz Review Magazine

"Taste, tone, and technique"

- JAZZIZ Magazine

Classical repertoire also available for ceremonies.

Bravo! Member Since 2002

Styles
- Standards
- Ballads
- Bossa Nova
- And more

Also available as duo or trio

Notes of Celebration

Linda Smith, Piano Artistry

About Notes of Celebration

Not just a pianist, Linda is a piano artist, providing an uncommon level of musicianship and customer care to every event she performs at, going well beyond playing the notes on a page.

Whether playing music to make your spirit dance, classical stylings that relax and inspire, or music to create an elegant and romantic ambiance, the music Linda provides will frame your wedding or event with music that touches your heart!

"Linda, you were magnificent…your music added a significant element to the entire ambiance we were looking for…exactly what I wanted!"

- Debbie & Eric Rinell

Contact
Linda Smith

p. 503.645.2763

e. lindasmith@notesofcelebration.com

www.notesofcelebration.com

Quick Facts
- Over 20 years experience
- Customized piano programs
- Keyboard available
- Vocalist/strings can be added to the ensemble

William Jenks
Classical Guitarist

p. 503.654.0082
e. info@williamjenks.com
www.williamjenks.com

Contact
William Jenks

p. 503.654.0082

Price
Please call or email for a demo & quote

Highly sought after as a performer, Mr. Jenks has performed in countless weddings across the Northwest as well as a broad range of venues including a European tour in 2007 where he performed solo concerts in France, Germany, and Italy; two solo performances in 2004 and 2005 at the Portland Wine and Arts Festival; a performance on October 1, 2005 at the Newport Performing Arts Center; and a performance in 2005 in front of a crowd of 3,000 people at Cycle Oregon.

The beautiful tone of the Classical Guitar is perfect to provide the ambience needed for your wedding ceremony or reception. William's repertoire includes traditional classical guitar music including works by Bach, Pachelbell, Sanz, Sor, Guiliani, Albeniz, Villa Lobos and more.

209

Wedding Tradition

©JS Photographers

For centuries the month of June has been the most popular choice for weddings - but the original reason might surprise you. You see, during the 1400 - 1500's, May was the month in which the "annual bath" occurred. Yes, just as it sounds, back then people were only able to bathe thoroughly once each year. As such, since the over-all population was smelling relatively fresh in June, it was a good time to hold a special event like a wedding! Further, the month of June is named after the goddess Juno, who was the Roman counterpart to Hera, the goddess of the hearth and home, and patron of wives.

Helpful Hint

Choosing Your Music & Entertainment

If you're starting to think about bands and deejays for your reception - remember that music sets the tone for any event, and especially for weddings. Do you remember "the Chicken Dance" or "Who Let The Dogs Out" at the last wedding you attended... and the empty dancefloor? Set yourself apart from the crowd by planning your music with a couple of things in mind:

- First your budget. A ten-piece dance band will obviously cost WAY more than a two piece instrumental group. Deejays charge a lot less and a top-notch one may be a better choice than a "so-so" band, but there's something about hearing live renditions of favorite tunes that can be hard to pass up.

- If you'd rather your reception music was unique, consider budgeting for musicians - or make your budget go farther by hiring a band for the dining hour and a deejay for dancing, or play recorded music during the meal, then kick off the dancing with a live band.

- Ask around and get samples of music first. Utilize a consultant that represent everything from string quartets to International Music groups to deejays. They can assist you in providing complete and complimentary promotional materials, demo CD's, references and sometimes, if possible, live performance observation possibilities.

- Whichever you choose, read the fine print; including hidden charges, such additional costs for staging, number and length of scheduled breaks and what will be playing when they're on those breaks.

- What happens if the party is still rocking after the end of the scheduled time? Is there an allowance to extend beyond the timeframe? Overtime pricing?

- Do they assist as "master of ceremonies" announcing when the cake will be cut, toasts, first dance and buffet is open?

- Last, but not least, don't be afraid to ask about tailoring the playlist to the evening, but remember that while coming up with a range of music is one thing, scheduling every minute of the band's performance is something else. Bottom line? Provide the band with as much information as possible to increase the likelihood that they'll give you what you want.

DECIDING ON ENTERTAINMENT

Every entertainer should have a music list available for you to review. This will be helpful in deciding on what type of entertainment you would like. You may want to ask if the entertainer is currently playing somewhere, then you can listen to their music style live and see their stage presence before you make a final decision.

RESERVING ENTERTAINMENT

Reserve entertainment for your reception immediately. There are only a limited amount of Saturdays available, especially in peak wedding seasons. Popular bands and orchestras are often reserved up to a year in advance.

SET-UP REQUIREMENTS

The formality, facility, and size of your event will determine the type of music that is appropriate. Inquire about whether the site can accommodate dancing and has the area necessary for the musicians to set up and perform. Be very specific about getting the space and electrical requirements from the band so that you can accurately relay the information to your contact person at the facility.

CUT-OFF HOURS

When you make all the final arrangements with your facility, be sure to ask if they have any specified time cut-offs for music. Some facilities require that music be stopped as early as 10pm for the comfort of neighboring homes, businesses, or other guests.

BACKGROUND MUSIC & DANCING MUSIC

Remember when reserving your entertainment that the first hour of your reception is a time for mingling with guests. If your entertainment begins playing immediately, you'll want to

cake cutting, throwing of the bouquet and the garter toss. Your wedding coordinator is the best person for this job, however if you didn't hire one, the best man can be the liason. This will help the day to flow smoothly for the bride and groom.

BAND BREAKS

How many breaks will the band be taking and for how long? Will there be music provided during this downtime? Will the musicians require food and/or beverages? This could effect your total count to the caterer.

© Studio 190

make sure that the music is background-type music that doesn't overwhelm and interfere with mingling. The musicians can be instructed at a certain time or by signal to pick up the pace of the music for dancing.

KEEPING THE FLOW GOING AT THE RECEPTION

It is a good idea to have a coordinator between the bride and groom and the band. This person can instruct the band when it's time to play the "first dance" song. Many times the deejay or band leader will act as master of ceremonies, announce the

SAVING ON MUSIC

The best way to cut music costs is to have your wedding in off-season: January through March, Sundays, early in the day. Musicians will be more willing to negotiate prices if it doesn't conflict with another high paying booking.

Visit BravoWedding.com for more information on great entertainment

Notes

07/25/09

Bree & Chadd

WILDFLOWER SEEDS

Plant these seeds
and love will grow!

© Katana Triplet

Favors & Gifts

Irresistible Home
GIFTS FOR ALL SEASONS

p. 503.332.9591
f. 503.645.5614

e. IrresistibleHome@gmail.com
IrresistibleWeddingFavors.com
IrresistibleHome.com

214

We Can Do You a Favor!

- Boxes & Bags
- Favors & Tags
- Exquisite Packaging
- Gifts for the Wedding Party

Sharing a small gift with your wedding guests is a time honored tradition that symbolizes the blessings of good fortune for the lucky bride and groom. It's also a really fun way to creatively express your gratitude to friends and family for supporting you and your marriage! Create that lasting memory of your special day with an exquisitely packaged, gorgeous gift from **Irresistible Home.**

Whether your wedding style is lavish and extravagant, fun and frivolous, or hopelessly romantic, we have an extraordinary collection of gifts, favors and packaging options for both Do-It-Your-Selfers and Don't-Have-the-Timers! We can also help you custom design and package a one-of-a-kind forever keepsake that will be treasured for a lifetime.

Call, e-mail or visit us on-line and let's get started creating your wedding memories today!

Contact
Karlyn Gedrose

Products & Services

- Extraordinary selection of favors, keepsakes & gifts for the wedding party

- Miniature boxes, bags & specialty ribbon

- Moonstruck Chocolate truffles, Jelly Bellys & other gourmet treats

- Do-It-Yourself or pre-assembled options

- Custom designs available

- Order samples on-line!

Shop on-line at IrresistibleWeddingFavors.com and IrresistibleHome.com

See fabulous favors and order samples of your favorite styles

Visit our Photo Gallery for tips and ideas you can really use!

p. 503.954.7130
e. info@le-paperie.com
www.le-paperie.com

Favors should be fun and fabulous without breaking the bank.

As Oregon Bride magazine's winner of Best Wedding Favors for 2008 and 2009, we are dedicated to bringing you local northwest products and materials. Our favors range from fun and inexpensive edible favors to sophisticated customized favors made from local natural materials. We have the perfect favor to complete your place setting and complement your décor.

Contact
Le Paperie

Price
Favors start at $2.50 each with a $250 minimum order

Quick Facts
- Oregon Bride Best Favor Winner 2008 and 2009

- Inexpensive, fun and memorable favors

- Fully customizable, quick turn around time

- Specializing in local and natural products and materials

- Candy Buffet Service with endless selection of candies, decorative jars and unique favor boxes

215

See page 226 under Invitations & Calligraphy

Enjoy The Sweet Life!

We offer a candy buffet service complete with decorative glass jars, candies, bags and boxes for your guests. Our service also includes delivery, set-up and pick-up of your candy buffet. You've heard so much about candy buffets and candy bars and you've seen them in all the latest magazines. Here is your chance to have the perfect candy buffet to dress up your wedding décor without all the hassle.

Candy buffets are perfect as wedding favors during your reception or as a special treat during the hors d'oeuvres and cocktail hour. We have decorative all-glass jars in a variety of shapes and sizes sure to dazzle your guests and candies and chocolates sure to entice every taste bud. Our unique candy bags and boxes can be customized to match your wedding colors and can be embellished with wax seals, ribbon, crystals and charms to create that memorable favor your guests will talk about for weeks! Call us for a quote!

Contact

Petite BonBons
brought to you by Le Paperie

p. 503.954.7130

e. info@petitebonbons.com

www.petitebonbons.com

Price

Prices start at $300. Includes candy, bags/boxes to accommodate 100 guests, rental of presentation jars/containers, delivery, set up and pick up.

Treat Options:

- Customized M&Ms & Gourmet Jelly Beans

- Wrapped Chocolates in Assorted Colors w/ Optional Customized Labels

- Fun Novelty Candies, Lollipops & Assorted Mints

- Popcorn, Chips and Nuts

- Fruits, Jams, Jellies, Truffles & Baked Goods

- Specialized treats from the Northwest

SHOW AND TELL COOKIES
WWW.SHOWANDTELLCOOKIES.COM
503.699.1017

Show and Tell Cookies

Our cookie favors make a wonderful memento of your special day. We can take any picture, image or text and put it on a cookie. The images are made with edible food coloring ink.

Our cookies taste amazing and are individually wrapped in a cellophane bag. We guarantee they will leave a lasting impression on your guests!

Also great for save the date announcements and invitations.

Contact
Dawn Fisher

p. 503.699.1017

e. dawn@showandtellcookies.com

www.showandtellcookies.com

Price
$25 per dozen
Four dozen minimum

Quick Facts
• Cookies stay fresh for
  2-3 weeks

217

INVITATION & ACCESSORY
Boutique
"Everything but the dress."

THE WEDDING
cottage

218

Voted for **Best Favors**
2007 Oregon Bride Magazine

Looking for a sweet finish?

Your favor is not a only a small token of appreciation for your guests, but it is a great way to share your story. We have many themed favors perfect for destination weddings, the wine connoisseur couple and more!

Our distinctive favor line includes...

Colorful Favor Boxes & Truffles
Personalized Favor Ribbon
Napkins & Matches
Sparklers & Bubbles
Plantable Favors
Candles
Wine Stoppers

More about The Wedding Cottage

Beyond our favor selection, The Wedding Cottage is a wedding invitation and accessory boutique where you can find "Everything but the dress!" Visit us for all your wedding stationery needs.

Bravo! Member Since 1990

Contact

The Wedding Cottage

4775 Southwest Watson Avenue
Beaverton, Oregon 97005

p. 503.643.9730
f. 503.526.7677

e. info@theweddingcottage.net

www.theweddingcottage.net

What our customers say:

"The Wedding Cottage is one of the few "true" bridal shops in the Portland metro area where you can find all the things that make a wedding special--invitations, guest books, wedding favors, attendant gifts, the list goes on! Thank you for giving brides a beautiful place to shop with exceptional service!"

– L.B.

SHOP ONLINE

Shop our invitations, accessories & favors at www.theweddingcottage.net

See page 86 under Boutiques & Accessories, page 228 under Invitations & Calligraphy

© Artistique Photographie

Honeymoon & Travel

THE HONEYMOON EXPERT

2525 NW Upshur Street
Portland, Oregon 97210
p. 503.231.0796
c. 503.407.1651
e. jennifer@wtpdx.com
www.offtotheislands.com

About The Honeymoon Expert

"I would love to help answer your important questions, and help you design a honeymoon that exceeds your expectations." Please call me today to set up your free one-hour honeymoon consultation.

Our Services

- Professional service
- Fun, warm, caring
- Personal knowledge of resorts, restaurants and activities
- 16 years of experience
- Step-by-step, stress free guidance toward the honeymoon of your dreams!
- Thousands of satisfied honeymooners
- Sandals certified expert
- Maui destination specialist
- Hawaiian Islands destination specialist

Contact
Jennifer Zeman

Price
Varies on location, type of resort & time of year; please call for quotes

Destination Ideas
- Hawaii
- Mexico
- Caribbean
- South Pacific: Tahiti, Cook Islands & Fiji
- Sandals Resorts
- St. Lucia
- Bahamas
- Barbados
- Lots of all-inclusive packages

SCHEDULE YOUR CONSULTATION TODAY!
Call us at: 503.231.0796

See page 361 under Destination Weddings

503-620-0620

www.uniglobespectrumtravel.com

Uniglobe Spectrum Travel

Your Extraordinary Honeymoon or Destination Wedding—you expect and deserve the best, we make it happen! Creating the perfect lifelong romantic memory is our one goal.

Tropical Destinations: Luxurious and Romantic
- Tahiti, Fiji and the South Pacific
- The Caribbean & Bahamas
- Hawaii & Mexico
- Belize & Costa Rica

All-Inclusive Resorts: Fantastic Choices
We recommend the most romantic and upscale all-inclusive resorts in the world.

European Honeymoons: Independent & Cultural
- Italy - Greece & Turkey – France

We specialize in European honeymoon destinations. Leave all those details to us!

Exotic Honeymoons – Unique & Active
- Peru - Machu Picchu
- Thailand - Bangkok & the Beaches
- South Africa - Wildlife Safaris

Destination Weddings & Weekends
- Beach Weddings with your family & friends
- Cruises and Weddings at Sea
- Bachelor & Bachelorette Getaways

Contact
Mary Hanigan

15150 SW Bangy Road
Lake Oswego, Oregon 97035
p. 503.620.0620
p. 800.544.2575
e. honeymoons@unispectrum.com
www.uniglobespectrumtravel.com

221

Price
Cost-saving wholesale packages available.
All price ranges available to meet your budget.

Why UNIGLOBE:
- Free online Honeymoon Registry
- Convenient after-hours consultations
- Locally-owned, full service agency
- Certified Specialists: Sandals, Hawaii, Tahiti, Las Vegas, Mexico, & all Cruise Lines
- Friendly, professional & well traveled

WHAT'S NEW
Uniglobe Spectrum Travel is committed to offering sustainable tourism destinations and suppliers as well as being green in our operations to protect and preserve our environment.

Bravo! Member Since 2001

Helpful Hint

Guest & Bridal Party Accommodations

Attendants and guests arriving from out-of-town often stay with relatives or friends, but this may not always be possible. Hotel accommodations may be more comfortable for everyone. Don't try to have attendants or relatives stay with you before the wedding… things will be hectic enough without worries about house guests.

WHO PAYS FOR ACCOMMODATIONS

The bride and groom usually pay for the wedding attendants accommodations. Out-of-town guests, both relatives and friends, pay for their own accommodations. As a courtesy to these guests, facilities and costs should be researched by the bride and groom to ensure comfort, convenient location and reasonable price.

SPECIAL GROUP RATES

Most hotels offer a special group rate for your guests. Many have information, special cards that you can send to your guests in the invitations, or separately, or emails with links to the discounted rooms.

TRANSPORTATION

Inquire about transportation from the airport to the hotel. Some hotels provide complimentary service for your guest's convenience.

BED-AND-BREAKFAST HOSPITALITY

Most bed-and-breakfasts are private homes offering overnight accommodations. Traditionally, guests receive a homemade breakfast each morning.

222

Notes

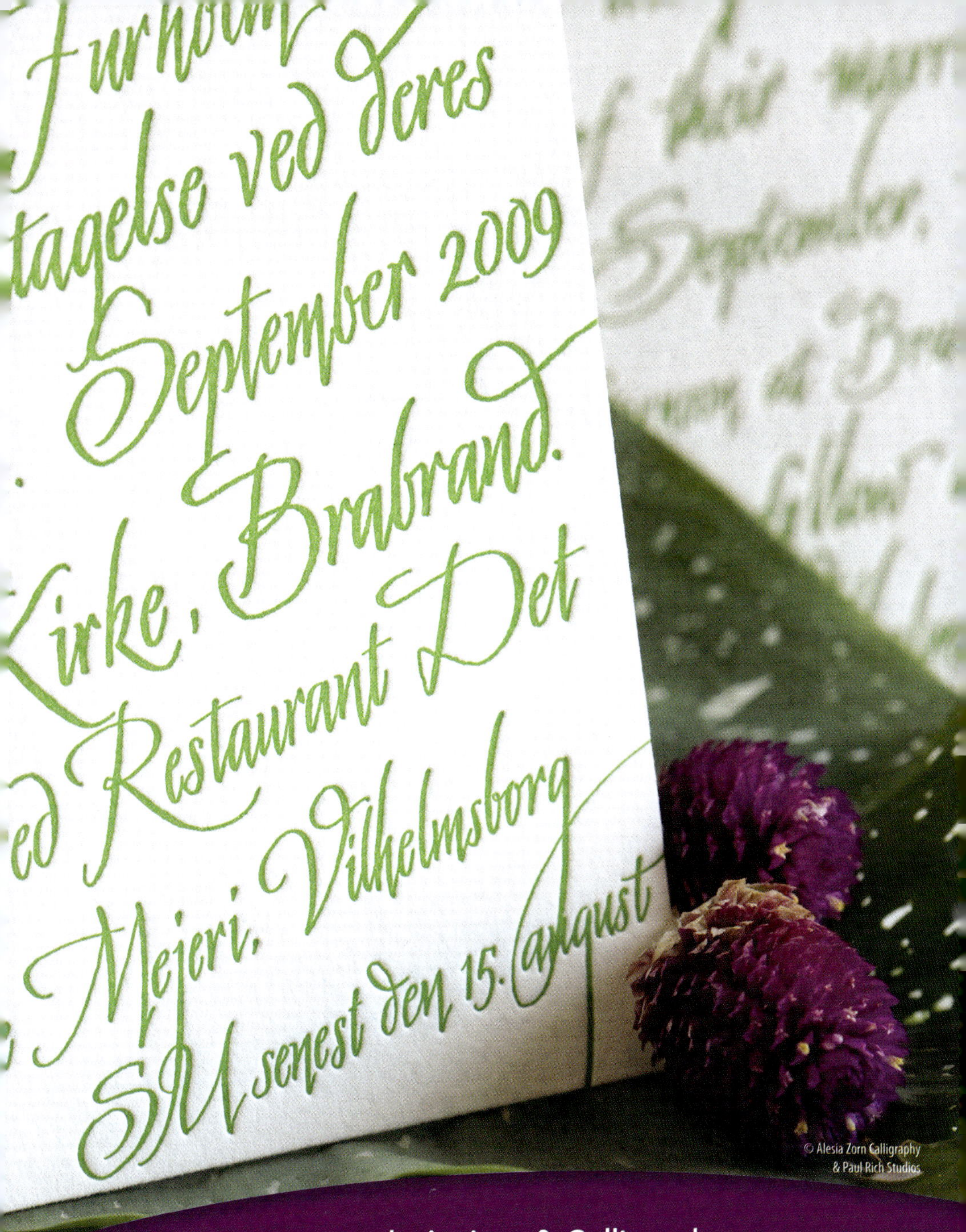
Furholm
tagelse ved deres
September 2009
Kirke, Brabrand.
ed Restaurant Det
Mejeri, Vilhelmsborg
SU senest den 15. august

© Alesia Zorn Calligraphy & Paul Rich Studios

Invitations & Calligraphy

Calligraphy
Invitations

Alesia Zorn
calligraphy

PO Box 12651
Portland, Oregon 97212
p. 503.287.3207
e. alesia@alesiazorn.com
www.alesiazorn.com

Contact
Alesia Zorn

Price
Varies upon service requested

Quick Facts
- Calligrapher since 1996 serving all your hand lettering needs
- Invitation design & addressing
- Place cards & table markers
- Programs, menus, vows
- Monograms
- Anything else you can dream up!

"Thank you for helping our wedding day feel like we are part of our own fairy tale!"

– Evelini P. - bride

"My wife and I could not have been more pleased with the personal service & attention to detail that Alesia offered. When working with vendors, the number one thing they can give is flexibility & expert opinion. We were offered both at an extraordinarily fair price. I could not recommend her more highly, and could not have been more pleased with her end product & her quality of service."

– Alex L. - groom

"I wanted to write you to thank you for the beautiful work you had done for us! Your work is truly a piece of ART; giving my wedding invitations that perfect final touch! Furthermore, it has been an absolute joy to work with you and I look forward to future projects."

– Kimberly C. - bride

WHAT'S NEW

Please visit my website for the latest samples, news and trends!

MEMBERSHIP

Bravo! Member Since 2006

1235 McVey Avenue
Lake Oswego, Oregon 97034
p. 503.697.4424
f. 503.697.4428
www.grandpapery.com

You're engaged...Congratulations!

Let us help you create your wedding's look and feel. When it comes to: save the date, bridal shower, rehearsal dinner, wedding programs, napkins, menus, placecards and thank you notes...we are your source.

Passionate Creativity and Outstanding Service

We have over 25 years of custom invitation design and event planning experience. One-on-one personalized service with experienced staff can help with wording etiquette, design options & all phases of your wedding.

Big Budget, Little Budget and Everything In-between

We understand all this wedding stuff can be a lot to deal with. We're here to help. Cranes, Vera Wang, Kate Spade, William Arthur, Rita Renning, Checkerboard, Prentis Douthit, Take Notice, Carlson Craft...just to name a few of our select albums. We pride ourselves on offering a HUGE selection with little stress. And of course we offer all printing methods: laser, thermography, letterpress, engraving......including "green" eco-friendly options.

In-house Typesetting and Printing with Same-Day Service Available.

In a hurry? No problem! We have Oregon's largest selection of boxed invites that print beautifully on your printer - or just let us take care of it. Calligraphy addressing services available.

The Grand Papery & Gifts is your one-stop location for invitations & gifts for any occasion.

Member: Association of Bridal Consultants.

Contact

The Grand Papery sales staff

Open seven days a week!
Mon - Sat: 10a.m. to 6p.m.
Sun: 12 to 5p.m.

Invitations & Gifts for ANY occasion:

- Engagement
- Save the date
- Bachelorette & bridal parties
- Rehearsal dinner
- Wedding invitations
- Accommodation & map inserts
- Baby announcements
- Anniversary

225

SET THE SCENE FOR YOUR WEDDING

We are passionate about invitations and are great at what we do.

Let us help you set the scene for the wedding of your dreams!

p. 503.954.7130
e. info@le-paperie.com
www.le-paperie.com

226

About Le Paperie

Invitations that capture your style, story and spirit. At Le Paperie, we specialize in exceptional invitations and designs that your guests will rave about. For traditionalists, we offer letter pressed and embossed invitations. Environmentally conscious couples can choose from recycled paper, soy inks and bamboo stationery. And for those looking to make a statement, we offer ring boxes, pocket folds and fan programs. We have that special invitation you are looking for. Your choice of wedding stationery is a representation of individual style, story and spirit. Allow your guests the pleasure of opening a Le Paperie invitation and the memories of a Le Paperie wedding.

Schedule a free consultation with us.

Contact
Le Paperie

Price
$300 minimum order

Quick Facts
- As seen in The Knot Best of Weddings 2008
- Invitations, programs, favors and more
- Unique and custom invitations and designs
- Wide selection of fan shaped wedding programs
- Distinctive selection of ready to order invitations

WHAT'S NEW

Bravo exclusive offer, receive $100 off of any order of $500 or more.

See pages 215 & 216 under Favors & Gifts

1321 NW Hoyt Street
Portland, Oregon 97209

p. 503.222.2355
f. 503.222.2551

e. admin@newandblue.com

www.newandblue.com

Wedding Invitations

New and Blue carries a huge inventory of invitations, favors, gifts, and more. Our experienced team has helped brides create extraordinary invitations that range from simple and traditional to one-of-a-kind works of art. Visit our boutique in the Pearl District to view this diverse selection of fabulous styles:

- Letterpress
- Nature inspired eco-friendly
- Traditional & elegant
- Destination or seasonally themed
- Exquisite silk box invitations
- Vivid colors & whimsical
- Unique shapes & pocket styles
- Quick printing
- Imprintables

New and Blue has much more!

- Guest books & pens
- Wedding favors
- Save-the-date items
- Bridal shower items
- Wedding party gifts
- Music & books
- Garters
- Cake toppers
- Unity candles & sand
- Wedding Supplies
- Place cards & holders
- Wedding decorations
- Bachelorette items

Mention you saw us in Bravo! and receive a free gift!

Price

Price varies;
New and Blue invitations range from elegant, affordable designs to extravagant, custom pieces

Quick Facts

- Proud member of the Better Business Bureau

- New and Blue has shipped invitations around the world for over seven years

- Located in Portland's Pearl District near the bus & Streetcar line

- Visit New and Blue's wedding blog for the hottest wedding tips and trends to assist in making your special day a dream come true!

227

VISIT US ON THE WEB

Many products are available on our websites. Check it out!

www.newandblue.com

www.savethedatemagnet.com

www.save-the-date-cards.com

About The Wedding Cottage

Looking to save the date, announce your engagement, or tie the knot? The Wedding Cottage offers brides the largest selection of invitations in the Portland area. With over 100 invitation books for viewing and more than 20 years of experience, we assist brides with tough etiquette and wording needs for the most traditional or contemporary invitations, as well as wedding programs, announcements, receptions and save-the-date cards (magnets too!).

• Selection & Style •

Whether you are jetting off to Maui for a destination wedding or looking for the perfect way to incorporate your engagement photo, we have the invitation to complement your distinctive style and wedding theme. From 100 percent cotton papers and engraved printing, to contemporary styles with a bit of flair, there are endless possibilities to help convey the most formal to whimsical occasions. Our lines include…TRU, Encore, Carlson Craft, William Arthur, Checkerboard, Crane, and more!

• Services •

When working with our staff, we will help you make selections while keeping inline with your budget, color scheme and style. Once you have decided upon an invitation, we will work with you in selecting the invitation wording that best suites you and your event. Appointments are not necessary to browse our selection; stop by anytime!

Contact
The Wedding Cottage

4775 Southwest Watson Avenue
Beaverton, Oregon 97005

p. 503.643.9730
f. 503.526.7677

e. info@theweddingcottage.net

www.theweddingcottage.net

What our customers say:

"They helped us almost better than a wedding planner. The Wedding Cottage helped us with many of our needs… invitations, programs, guest book, attendant gifts, etc. We consistently received excellent service. They went above and beyond our expectations; our programs arrived one week early when we were on a tight deadline. Finding you was like finding a gold mine."

– M.B.

SHOP ONLINE

Shop our invitations, accessories & favors at www.theweddingcottage.net

See page 86 under Boutiques & Accessories and page 218 under Favors & Gifts

228

Uncommon Invitations For All Occasions

We are a boutique stationer specializing in the art of creating custom invitations for all occasions. We believe that custom can be affordable, and that every client deserves to have the invitation that is perfect for them!

You have 3 great options with Uncommon Invites!

You can choose our 10 EASY STEPS to create your ideal invitation, at your convenience. From your ideas to our production, we make it stress free!

Choose...

1. size and shape
2. the invitation basics
3. a layout style
4. to add a graphic
5. to add embellishments
6. to add a backer card
7. additional cards
8. a packaging style
9. an envelope liner
10. an addressing style

You choose from pre-designed invitations by our design team or our industry partners that you can view in our gallery.

You can choose to do a totally custom design by working with a member of our design team.

Uncommon Invites We Love Weddings!

Bravo! Member Since 1992

Contact

Uncommon Invites

p. 800.676.3030

e. info@uncommoninvites.com

Price

Starting at $1.00

Services

- Save the date announcements
- Wedding invitations
- RSVP cards
- Accommodation cards
- Bridal shower announcements
- Rehearsal dinner invitations
- Wedding programs
- Reception dinner menus
- Place cards
- Table signs
- Favor & gift basket tags
- Favors - check out Uncommon Favors

Founding Board Member of Wedding Network USA

229

Helpful Hint

Invitations, Programs, Guest Lists & Thank You's

THANK YOU'S

Today wedding etiquette consists of good manners and a blending of traditional customs with contemporary ones. The following tips show you how to incorporate proper etiquette into every aspect of your wedding, giving you greater confidence in every situation.

ANNOUNCING YOUR ENGAGEMENT

Share your good news with your families as soon as possible - it's only right that they hear it from you. Create a website, blog on Twitter, Facebook, wedding websites or announce it formally in your both you and your fiancé's hometown papers. Check out their website links for forms and how to upload your engagement photo.

It is nice to let out-of-town guests know as far as a year in advance of your wedding, especially if they need to take time off from work, make arrangements for school leave, find a pet sitter, or save money for the trip. A simple "save the date" card, even a holiday card, with your names, the date and city and state of the wedding are all that is needed. Hotel information may also be included.

GUEST LIST

Where do you draw the line with the guest list?

The bride's family, groom's family and bride and groom generally each develop a "wish list". Then the list is narrowed down closer to the attendance you have budgeted for. Usually the attendance will be between 70 to 75% based on if family and friends live in town or not. A good rule of thumb to narrow down the list—if you haven't made contact with the person in the last year, leave them off.

INVITATIONS

Order your invitations at least four months in advance to give you plenty of time for printing, addressing and mailing. There are many different styles of wedding invitations - check out our clients for creative ideas and pricing. Make sure you shop around for the supplier who is going to give you the style, quality and price you are looking for. This is the introduction to your wedding and a representation of what your special day will be like. Are you having an intimate vineyard wedding, a large splashy ballroom event or upscale sit-down dinner? Your invites should reflect this theme with color, font, paper and wording.

ADDRESSING INVITATIONS

Create a master list of names in order to avoid duplication. Make sure names and titles are spelled correctly and addresses are accurate. Keep in mind that many women have retained their maiden names or prefer to be addressed by their titles or professional names. In these cases, put her name above his on the envelope. Follow the same rule for a couple with different last names or unmarried couples living together.

Adult members of a family over 18 years old should always receive seperate invitations. You may, however, send one invitation to two siblings living together at one address.

See Bravowedding.com for examples of addressing styles.

SINGLE FRIENDS & GUESTS

If friends are single and you encourage them to bring a guest, you can write "and Guest" on the invitation. If a couple is living together, you can send one invitation with both their names listed alphabetically.

© New and Blue

MAILING INVITATIONS

Invitations are usually mailed 6-8 weeks before the wedding. Do send invites to your wedding officiant, your fiancé's immediate family, all members of the wedding party, and a guest list made up of both your friends and his, as well as other relatives and co-workers with whom you want to share your day. Keep in mind your budget limitations and refrain from letting your guest list get out of control. Selection may be difficult, but it is best to stick as closely to your list. If you haven't received an RSVP by two weeks before the wedding, have a family member call and check. Do not put "Regrets Only" on a formal invitation - it's tacky. When each invitation is accounted for, let your caterer how many guests to expect.

231

DON'T FORGET TO INCLUDE THE WEDDING PARTY

Remember, even though special people are playing a role in your wedding you do need to send invitations to them: parents, grandparents, clergy, attendants and immediate family. A good idea is to even send an invitation to yourself to track the date guests will receive the invitation.

ORDERING INVITATIONS

Ideally, you should order your invitations three to four months before the wedding to allow enough time for delivery. Some shops offer quick-print service in one day to one week. Invitations should be sent six to eight weeks before the wedding.

When figuring the number of invitations to order, combine the lists from the bride's parents, the groom's parents, the bride, and the groom. When the lists are compiled, any additions, deletions, and corrections can be made by everyone. Be sure you are counting families or couples not individual guests for the number of invitations needed.

WORDING INVITATIONS

It's become common to list both your parents and his on the invitation - regardless of who's paying - but divorce and remarriage can make it sound more like a phone book than an invite. Simpler wording may be better: "Together with their families, Jane Smith and John Doe request the honor of your presence..." Or suggest listing one parent and his/her partner on the ceremony invite and the other parent and partner on the reception card.

CORRECT SPELLING OF NAMES

Etiquette books and websites cover proper addressing of both inner and outer envelopes. Before addressing your envelopes, make sure you double check on your master list for the CORRECT spelling of names.

© Studio 190

Programs - Do you Need One?

Programs are optional, but if you're planning a ceremony that guests may have a hard time following (like a lengthy inter-cultural service), a program will make everyone feel welcome and involved, as well as inform your guests as to "what's the groom's mom's name again?"

What To Include

A program is both a guide and a keepsake. Personalize with a photo or drawing that suits your venue. You can include -

- Your names, wedding date, time and ceremony location.

- The elements of the ceremony, such as prayers, readings, and musical pieces. To encourage participation, list the words to prayers, refrains, and hymns.

- An explanation of cultural traditions.

- The participants, including your officiant, attendants, readers and musicians.

- Thank you's to your guests and to your families.

- A tribute to deceased relatives (ex: "today we honor those no longer with us, especially John Smith, the groom's uncle").

Who Hands Them Out?

Groomsmen or anyone you'd like to honor (and who's not already in the bridal party). Programs can be handed out to each guest as they are being seated, at the front door, placed in a stack on the guest book table or on each seat.

Should You Make Them Yourself?

Your costs can be as minimal as the price of paper and ink, but if you already have too much on your plate, enlist the help of your maid of honor, bridesmaids or any other close friend or relative. This is also a nice way for them to participate in your special day and they can be responsible for making sure they not only get to the "church on time", but carried over to the reception as well, making sure everyone receives one. You can also get very creative with them - making paddle fans, scrolls, ribbon tied booklets - and not have to worry about something happening to the programs before the wedding - belated delivery, wrong spellings or color or crushed items.

Should You Order Professional?

If you are ordering your invitations from a company that also creates programs, they may be more cost-effective than you think. Anything other than a basic design can look amateurish if you make it yourself and don't really know what you are doing. Embellishments, multiple colors and graphic lay-out and design may be difficult to pull off. Home printers may limit the size and thickness of the paper you use and you could end up wasting not only beautiful, expensive paper in the process... but hours of your valuable time.

Thank You Notes - Rules & Etiquette

Send thank you notes to acknowledge everything from place settings to gifts of time or talent. Remember - a separate, handwritten note must be sent for each wedding present or act of kindness. Start sending thank yous as soon as gifts arrive, even if it is before your wedding (but make sure to use your maiden name). Gifts that you receive on your big day should be followed up with a thank you note no later than one month after you return from your honeymoon (now you can use your new last name). To ease the process, keep track of wedding gifts and thank-you cards on the same list of names and addresses used for your invitations. Personalize the thank-you cards by ordering them with your monogram or with a picture from your big day on the front.

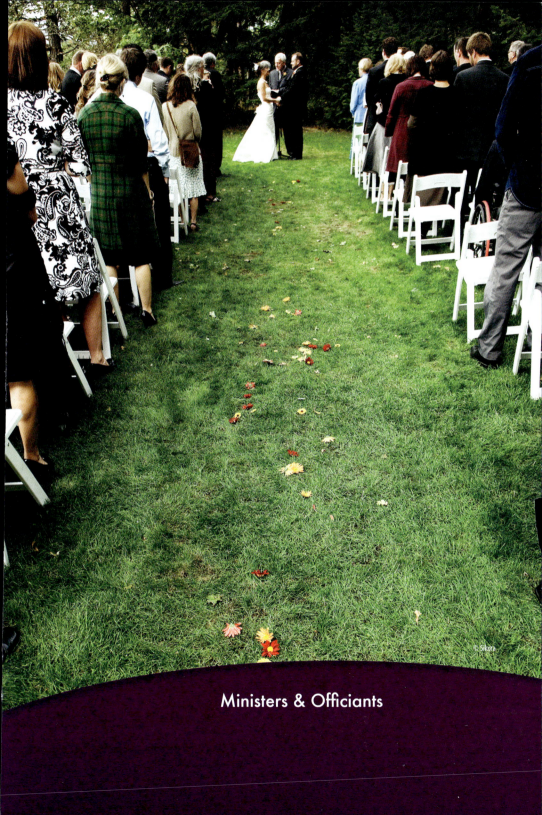

© Sikora

Ministers & Officiants

A Bonding of Love

"Your moment in time, a personal, sacred ceremony, in your own special way."

Congratulations on your upcoming marriage! I have served hundreds of couples in creating ceremonies that reflect their own beliefs, wishes and heart's desire. I perform a wide variety of ceremonies, such as non- denominational, Christian, interfaith, civil or other unique ceremonies. I can also provide such specials as the Unity Candle, the Rose Ceremony or Uniting the New Family with a Family Blending Ceremony.

It would be my privilege to assist you with your wedding.

Blessings,
Rev. Robert Bonds

Testimonial

"Our guests felt included in your every word throughout the ceremony, and that makes it really special."

– Dan & Sassa

Contact
Rev. Robert Bonds

p. 503.781.9482

e. revbonds@anytimeweddings.com

www.anytimeweddings.com

Price
Please call

Quick Facts
- Traditional or creative in a setting of your choice
- Family blending ceremonies
- Free consultation to assist in your planning
- Personalized to fill your wishes

Testimonials

"First and foremost, I wanted to thank you for an absolutely beautiful service - all of our friends and families have commented on what a great job you did."

– Sam Duncan
Chairman & Chief Executive Officer of Office Max

"We sincerely thank you for turning an ordinary ceremony into a cherished memory we will never forget."

– Matthew & Kristen

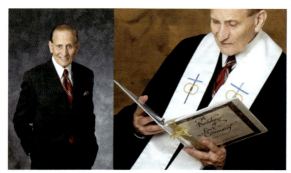

Bravo! Member Since 1990

Maureen Haley
Wedding Officiant

p. 503.888.9876
p. 503.550.1744
e. revmaureenpdx@aol.com
www.portlandministers.com
www.123oregonweddingofficiants.com

235

Maureen Haley - Wedding Officiant

Wonderful wedding ceremonies which will make your hearts sing!

- Warm and flexible, with attention to details
- Religious, non-religious, interfaith, in between
- Complimentary consultation
- Unity candle, sand ceremony, family blending or your choice
- Enjoy teamwork with coordinators and other vendors
- Preferred vendor at many wonderful venues
- Beautiful customized ceremonies according to your wishes

I love marrying happy couples!
What are your wedding wishes?

Let's talk. Maureen 503.888.9876
or email revmaureenpdx@aol.com

"Maureen is a wonderful officiant! She really knows how to work with couples to ensure that the wedding ceremony is just right for each couple's personality and style. I would recommend Maureen without reservation to anyone wishing to hire an officiant for their upcoming wedding ceremony."

– Susan Langenes,
Wedding Musician
www.collagetrio.com

Contact
Rev. Maureen Haley

Testimonials
"Dear Rev. Maureen, Pete and I loved having you in our wedding! You were so sweet, intuitive, and very compassionate (as well as very professional)! You made our ceremony feel so much more personal and loving... instead of just a formality. You truly listened and catered to our needs and wants... and not to your own beliefs and judgement. Thank you so much for making our wedding so memorable!"

Love,
Linh and Peter Hougard

www.portlandministers.com
or
www.123oregonwedding
officiants.com

9840 SW Clark Hill Road
Beaverton, Oregon 97007
p. 503.628.3486
c. 503.936.2553
e. rmoore007@comcast.net
www.moorecreativeweddings.com

Moore Creative Weddings - Rev. Roger Moore

Congratulations on your engagement. Every couple is unique, with different needs, style and preferences. Your wedding is about you, the bride and groom. You should be the center of attention. It is your day and you should feel special. Your wedding is a special moment in time and it is fun to create a ceremony that captures your special moment. The ceremony will be tailored to meet your vision for your wedding. Creative and unique weddings are always fun and your family and guests will enjoy what we create together.

I like being a part of the team for your wedding – bridal consultants, facility coordinators, caterers, florists, photographers, videographers, DJs – all working together to make your wedding flow smoothly.

I do have a sample that will give you a lot of ideas for developing your personalized ceremony. Since it is your wedding you should have a ceremony that reflects your ideas and your vision for your day.

I am an ordained minister and yet make the couple and marriage the focus of the ceremony. What you develop will be followed and you will not have any embarrassing surprises.

I do have my own portable PA system that allows the audience to hear what is being said. **For a small fee I** can also provide a lapel microphone for the groom so the couple can be heard when they are sharing their vows and placing the rings.

I can email you a sheet with references of vendors who will affirm my services.

Contact me and let's see if we are a good match in making your celebration a perfect day.

Contact
Rev. Roger Moore

Price
Please call

Quick Facts
- Willing to travel anywhere
- Free personal consultations
- Provides a sample ceremony
- Professional, knowledgeable, & experienced
- Flexible & yet organized
- Listens to your vision
- Provides rehearsal leadership but can work with any coordinator
- A team player to make your day flow smoothly

TESTIMONIAL
"We wanted to tell you thank you for performing our wedding ceremony for us. It was absolutely perfect, and we both really appreciated your sense of humor, kindness, and calm demeanor on our big day. We received lots of compliments on our ceremony and we owe that all to you and your help before, during and after the wedding. Thank you so much again."

– Kendall and John

Rhiannon Griffiths, M. DIV

503.631.4300

And they lived happily ever after

Kindred Spirit Ceremonials

Wouldn't it be great to have an officiant who takes time to listen, knows your story and understands your values so your ceremony reflects your unique relationship?

Your story is at the heart of the creative process as Rev. Rhiannon Griffiths delivers an intimate and unforgettable ceremony weaving together your values, beliefs and shared vision. Imagine your guest's excitement as they walk away touched and fulfilled by the heart opening experience shared by all.

Rev. Rhiannon delights in interfaith, alternative, blended family and Celtic handfasting ceremonies. With 18 years of experience, insight, humor and the Conscious Commitment process, she supports your journey to the altar and prepares the ground for a rich and rewarding union. Without fail every couple who has participated in Conscious Commitment has been glad they did!

Rhiannon Griffiths, M.Div., CHT, is an ordained minister, spiritual counselor, ceremonialist and dog lover. Known throughout the Northwest as the "Conscious Commitment Minister", she is adept at creating sacred space wherever she is. Rhiannon is guided by her faith in the ever evolving power of Love to connect and transform the human heart.

Testimonial

"Rhiannon's expert guidance through the Conscious Commitment process made our wedding extraordinary. My partner and I were amazed at how it brought us closer not only to each other, but to the shared values and desires we have – and a few of our differences as well! Most people splurge on the flowers and food, but the real beauty and nourishment for us was in the conscious creation of our marriage."

– Gwenn Cody Wald, bride & psychotherapist

Contact

Rev. Rhiannon Griffiths

p. 503.631.4300

www.ksceremonials.com

Price

Discussed at our free consultation over tea!

Testimonial

"Rhiannon captured our unique selves and brought to light our talents and our quirks, making our guests erupt in laughter and sometimes tears. She incorporated everything we wanted to represent us to share with our family and friends and it couldn't have been more perfect. We are still hearing from friends how awesome and unique our ceremony was, some say it was the best ceremony they had ever seen!"

– Morgan Pace,
bride & wedding photographer

237

A Creative Wedding Ceremony

By Rev. Sharon K. Biehl, M.A.

"Your Day Your Way!"

Contact
Rev. Sharon K. Biehl, M.A.

p. 503.653.2013

c. 503.805.7732

Wedding ceremonies are created and personalized for your special day. It is important for you to be comfortable with your officiant. There is no charge for an initial meeting to discuss your plans. For twenty years, I have helped couples design ceremonies reflecting their wishes and beliefs. During the consultation, we will determine exactly what you want and discuss the fee. A variety of options are offered for the rehearsal in order to honor your style. The result will be a wedding unique to the two of you. As a nondenominational minister, I can be flexible to the situation, and I will be glad to perform the ceremony at a site of your choice.

- Non-denominational Minister
- Licensed Professional Counselor

Ceremonies
- Religious/Spiritual
- Traditional/New Age

Services
- Licensed in Oregon & Washington
- Free Consultation
- Optional Premarital Counseling
- Call 8 a.m. to 8 p.m.

Portland/Vancouver area rates start at $150.
I'm happy to travel to surrounding areas
for an additional fee.

Bravo! Member Since 1990

238

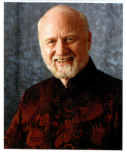

A Perfect Ceremony

Rev. Robert Griffen

p. 503.421.3213

e. r.griffen@comcast.net

www.APerfectCeremonyPDX.com

Rev. Griffen knows more about great weddings than anyone! He has been in "the business" for more than 30 years: as a formal wear specialist while a seminary student, 30 years as a Presbyterian Minister and 25 years as a wedding photographer. He is very creative and will accomodate a broad range of litergical styles and traditions, including those of non-traditional and alternative lifestyle couples.

"We couldn't have been happier! He was so sincere and has a warm sense of humor... I was very nervous, and he got me to relax. Our wedding was perfect!" — John & Julie R.

"Griff helped us plan our whole day, not just the ceremony. We avoided some big problems thanks to him, and the day was trouble-free." — Mary & Drew J.

Contact
Rev. Robert Griffen

Services
- Free consultation
- Licensed in Oregon & Washington
- Knowledgeable, experienced, professional
- Creative & accommodating to each couple's traditions & needs
- Email for sample ceremonies & complete information

Bravo! Member Since 2003

An
Event
To
Remember

Salem, Oregon
p. 888.652.0115
e. info@aneventtoremember.info
www.aneventtoremember.info

An Event To Remember Testimonials

"Johanna was absolutely fabulous, can't tell you how many wonderful compliments we got on the ceremony. She was really extraordinary, I can't recommend her highly enough!"

– Tiffany, Dayton, Oregon

"Johanna was exceptional! She far exceeded our expectations and provided us with a perfect wedding ceremony that my wife and I will always remember, as will every one of our guests.
– David Hillsboro, Oregon

Additional Referrals Available on Request.

Bravo! Member Since 2008

Contact
Johanna Respini

Price
Ask for Bravo! Discount

Quick Facts
- Civil & Spiritual Life Event Celebrant
- Member of Willamette Valley Wedding Professionals
- 'Day Of' Coordination Packages Available
- Rehearsal & all travel included in Day Of Package

239

p. 503.807.7927
e. willgables@wmconnect.com
www.aweddingyourway.com

Rev. Laurel Cookman

Love is both our highest achievement and life's most precious gift. The wedding ceremony is a commitment to honor and protect one another no matter what life places in your path. It would be an honor and a privilege to assist you as you begin your journey as a couple.

Rev. Laurel Cookman has been coordinating weddings for 17 years! She will help plan your rehearsal and wedding day.

"Thank you for making our wedding day so special, it was wonderful."
– Lynn & Mark

Contact
Rev. Laurel Cookman

Price
Call for more information

Services
- 17 years of experience
- Flexible, organized & on time
- Customized ceremonies
- Location of your choice
- Get acquainted meeting

Bravo! Member Since 1998

Custom Ceremonies
By Rev. Marky Kelly - and You

p. 503.282.2108
www.customceremonies.com

The coming together of loving individuals is a creative, dynamic process – and the expression of their commitment to one another is an ideal opportunity to mirror that joyful enthusiasm. As you've been reading through this resource guide, no doubt you've been fueled with many exciting ideas for the visual setting of your wedding...but what words do you want your family and friends to hear that day? How do you want your wedding to be? Solemn? Playful? Sacred? Serene?

Let me help you say just the right thing. I am a licensed non-denominational minister who enjoys taking time to find out about you. Together we can collaborate in designing your ideal ceremony, one which gives you and those who celebrate with you a true sense of your decision to share life's journey.

Bravo! Member Since 2000

Consultation
- Our first meeting will be no-cost, no-obligation & will allow us to see whether or not we are a good fit

Services
- My spiritual "un-focus" embraces many cultures, so I can help you blend elements of different faith traditions. We can also shape the ceremony content from alternative and/or secular sources.

240

Reverend Diana Evans–Baxter
Journeys of the Heart & Spirit

12501 SW 114th Terrace
Tigard, Oregon 97223
p. 503.590.7693
e. dianaeb@verizon.net

About Rev. Diana Evans-Baxter
Journeys of the Heart & Spirit

Your wedding ceremony is a rite of the heart, where you as a couple come before your family and friends to celebrate this very special time in your life. Let me assist you in creating a traditional or non-traditional ceremony that will make your wedding day a beautiful and memorable occasion.

Contact
Rev. Diana Evans-Baxter

Services
- Wedding ceremonies performed throughout Oregon & Washington, at a location of your choice

- Optional pre-marital preparation is available

- Call for a complimentary "get acquainted" visit from 8 a.m. to 10 p.m.

Bravo! Member Since 1999

The Heart of the Wedding is the Ceremony.

Jacqueline Mandell is dedicated to creating a ceremony that reflects the love of the bride and groom. She custom designs each ceremony to mirror the authenticity, connection and depth shared by the betrothed. Many couples like to write or choose their own wedding vows and commitments. Jacqueline has established a system to easily assist and expedite the choice of wedding vows. Respectful and enriching ceremony planning and collaborative conversations/meetings can be kept to a minimum of two or extended to as many as desired. Well traveled, adept at ceremonies and public speaking, Jacqueline is honored to preside over the ceremony of one of the most joyful days of your life. Jacqueline enjoys working with the creative process of designing a ceremony 'tailored to meet your dreams'.

Bravo! Member Since 2001

PO Box 2085
Portland, Oregon
p. 503.790.1064
e. info@pureheartsangha.com
www.pureheartsangha.com

Contact
Jacqueline Mandell:
Exquisite Weddings

Quick Facts
- Custom designed: heartfelt ceremonies
- Specializing in: Non-denominational, world faiths & Buddhist traditions
- Honoring cultural & family traditions
- Reflecting your authenticity & your wishes

Exquisite Weddings is a subsidiary of Leadership From A Pure Heart, LLC.

241

A wedding is an occasion of supreme transformation as well as a declaration of love and commitment. It is an intimate, timeless moment in a public setting.

I offer prepared and customized ceremonies presented in a thoughtful, eloquent manner, suitable for large or small gatherings. Nothing of a particular religious nature is included unless requested. I am available to conduct rehearsals. Ceremonies take place at your site choice.

Fresh Weddings
Http://home.teleport.com/~foxling

6614 North Knowles Avenue
Portland, Oregon 97217
p. 503.240.1780
e. foxling@teleport.com

Contact
Rachel Foxman,
Officiant

Price
Vary according to location & service rendered

Quick Facts
- Licensed officant since 1982
- I am available for last minute occasions
- Please call or write for an initial no cost consultation

Bravo! Member Since 2000

Cathy Hume
Interfaith Minister

Portland, Oregon
p. 503.957.9942
e. revcathyhume@comcast.net
www.revcathyhume.com

Interfaith Minister - Experienced - Flexible

I am an Interfaith Minister that believes that Love is sacred and holy. It is the words that you say to each other in your ceremony that you take forward into your marriage. This is a very special and meaningful day and should reflect who you are as people and who you will become as a couple. I can help you tell the story of your Love in a meaningful and creative way. We can together very easily create the ceremony that your family and guests will remember for years to come. I am happy to do ceremonies that are Nondenominational, Spiritual, Christian, or any faith tradition that you would like. I also do vow renewals and baby blessings.

Contact
Reverend Cathy Hume

Quick Facts
- Will honor all faiths
- Have the ceremony that is meaningful for your and your guest
- Can do short notice ceremonies
- Very easy to work with
- Beautiful, creative ceremonies

242

Lisa Kristen–Scott
Officiant & Artist

p. 503.460.9894
e. kristenscott@earthlink.net

As an artist as well as an officiant, I enjoy helping couples create a meaningful ceremony. The best weddings are the most personal, so I encourage you to include your own words, vows, stories, or spiritual symbolism. Most of my ceremonies are non-religious, focusing on you and the community created by your wedding. Some are very spiritual, from interfaith to non-denominational Christian. I'm relaxed and mindful on your wedding day, centered on you. I welcome all couples and respect all traditions.

"It was a pleasure meeting with you and developing our ceremony with you. Neither of us can imagine a more beautiful and meaningful ceremony...perfect for the setting, the day, and for us."

– Elise & Ken

Contact
Rev. Lisa Kristen-Scott

Price
About $300; rehearsal or travel outside of greater Portland would be additional, based on distance

Services
- Welcome all couples
- Respect all traditions
- Weddings, Unions, Commitment Ceremonies

PO Box 31075
Portland, Oregon 97231
p. 503.201.4484
e. james@manhattanmonk.com
www.manhattanmonk.com

About The Manhattan Monk

My philosophy is simple: Foremost, a wedding is a celebration. A celebration of two like souls, finding each other in this crazy world! A wedding is a declaration of your unifying love to both communities. The community of family and friends, and the community of the world at large!

Last, but not least, a wedding is about YOU! – the bride and groom. Your wedding ceremony should be a reflection of who you both are; saying things that touch your heart, your mind, and even your sense of humor! Let the Manhattan Monk help make your day fun and from the heart! L'Chaim!

Contact
James C. Lawrence, ULC

Price
$150 to $300

- Custom ceremonies that resonate with you!
- Contemporary & alternative ceremonies a specialty; funky, fresh style with an emphasis on the heart
- Free consultation
- The wedding alternative!

243

2115 Cunningham Lane South
Salem, Oregon 97302
p. 503.363.3156
e. brenggli@comcast.net
www.bobrenggli.com

About Bob Renggli, M.A.

Helping couples create a warm and memorable wedding celebration has been a great joy of my Catholic priesthood for over 30 years. Couples of all denominations are welcome. Generally two planning sessions and email correspondence is sufficient to assist couples in designing their perfect wedding ceremony. Today, many couples are eager to have their life moments captured in a way that truly celebrates their unique love story in a sensitive and spiritual way.

Contact
Bob Renggli, M.A.

Quick Facts

- Licensed in Oregon & Washington serving metro Portland, Vancouver & the Willamette Valley
- Wedding planning guide available
- Premarital relationship coaching available
- See my website for additional services

Bravo! Member Since 2002

Reverend Penny L. Johnsen
p. 619.929.9171
e. Asiadena@hotmail.com

One of the most meaningful dates in your life is the day you get married. This happy, sacred event will be captured forever in your heart. With so much time, attention and money going into planning of this very special event, the same care should be given when choosing the person that officiates your wedding.

I am an ordained Melchizedek minister and it would be my honor and privilege to officiate your sacred ceremony. If you would like help writing a more personalized ceremony that expresses who you both are, I would be happy to assist you with the writing. Or, if you prefer a more traditional service, I have a variety of examples from which to choose.

I promise to do everything I can to create a beautiful and memorable day for you, your family and friends. I look forward to meeting you.

Price
$150 and up

Services
- Free Initial consultation
- Non-denominational minister
- Licensed in OR, WA & CA
- Customized ceremonies
- Travel to your destination
- Available for rehearsal
- Feng Shui Master
- Author, public speaker
- References available on request

244

Reverend Robert H. Thomas

12820 NW 33rd Avenue
Vancouver, Washington 98685
p. 360.573.7725
e. charbobthomas@juno.com

About Reverend Robert H. Thomas
Inter-faith Pastor

Licensed to perform weddings in Washington and Oregon. I will be happy to perform your wedding at the location of your choice.

At our initial meeting, we will discuss whether you want a traditional Christian service or if you would prefer to create your own. Each wedding is personalized to suit the couple.

Pastor Bob Offers
- A variety of services to choose from
- Stress-free planning session
- Personalized vows
- Rehearsal information
- Attending your rehearsal
- Communication counseling available, but not required
- License information
- Each service is a celebration of love

Bravo! Member Since 1992

p. 503.206.9612
e. heather@the-wedding-officiant.com
www.the-wedding-officiant.com

About The Wedding Officiant

The words that you recite at your wedding ceremony will be treasured long after the DJ has stopped playing music and the cake has been eaten. In the end the vows you recite to one another will be the most intimate and authentic part of your wedding celebration. I have the education and experience to help you create a ceremony that will resonate with you and your spouse throughout your marriage. Congratulations on your engagement. I can't wait to meet you and start planning your ceremony.

I am a minister with the American fellowship church and a member of the Association of Wedding Consultants.

Contact
Heather Ann Mack, MA

Quick Facts

- I am the calm in the " wedding storm"
- I will help you create a personalized wedding ceremony
- My web site is helpful and beautiful
- I have an MA in Pastoral Studies and Spirituality

245

Wedding Tradition

American superstition claims that the day on which a couple buy their engagement ring holds important omens about their future. If it is on a Monday, for instance, they can look forward to a busy, exciting life; on Tuesday a peaceful and contented existence. Wednesday indicates a good-tempered relationship, while Thursday will able you to archive all you wish from life. Friday is a day which will demand much hard work, but there will be rewards in time, while Saturday is a day which will give much pleasure. Nice to know that there isn't a bad day among them! The custom of the bride being given away by her father has its origins in ancient times when women were considered to be owned by men. The marriage was treated as a property transaction, with the right of ownership being passed from one man to another.

Helpful Hint

Wedding Party Etiquette

MAID OF HONOR

Although she has no prewedding responsibilities, she is expected to assist the bride whenever she can. She lends moral support and plays a big role in making sure the other bridesmaids are dressed to perfection and they all make it to the ceremony on time. She is responsible for her

BEST MAN

His duties are many and varied and carry a lot of responsibility to ensure the wedding runs smoothly. The best man serves as the personal aide and advisor to the groom, supervises the ushers, carries the bride's ring and the marriage certificate, which he also signs, and acts as a right-hand man

© Artistique Photographie

own wedding outfit and pays for everything except the flowers. She also attends all prewedding parties and may even give one herself. The maid of honor is usually one of the witnesses required by law to sign the marriage certificate. Walking down the aisle, she precedes you and your father, arranges your train and veil, carries the groom's ring if there is no ringbearer, and holds your bouquet during the ceremony. If you have a receiving line, she stands next to the groom and sits on his left at the head table.

to the groom on his special day. If there's a head table, the best man sits at the right of the bride and, as official toastmaster of the reception, proposes the first toast to the new couple, usually wishing them health, happiness, and prosperity. His final duties are to ensure the new couple takes off for the honeymoon without a hitch and that all the ushers return their rented formal wear on time.

246

BRIDESMAIDS

Although they don't have any prewedding responsibilities either, it would be a nice gesture to help with any errands or duties that need to be accomplished. They are invited to all prewedding parties and may also give one if they wish. Traditionally they purchase their own attire.

GROOMSMEN / USHERS

Their responsibility is to seat guests at the wedding ceremony and act as escorts for the bridesmaids. To avoid seating delays, there should be at least one usher for every 50 guests. They also attend all prewedding parties the groom goes to and are required to provide their own wedding clothes, renting the proper formal attire if they do not own it. As guests arrive, each usher should offer his right arm to each woman and escort her to her seat on the left or right of the aisle, depending on whether she is a friend of the bride or groom.

THE BRIDE'S MOTHER

Your mother usually helps compile the guest list and helps with any other details you desire assistance with as well. It is her responsibility to keep the bride's father and future in-laws informed about wedding plans. She should also inform the groom's mother of her wedding attire so that their dresses are similar in length and style. The mother of the bride is privileged to sit in the very first pew on the bride's side. She is the last to be seated and the first to be escorted out after the ceremony. She can also greet all guests in the receiving line and sits in a place of honor at the bride's parents' table at the reception.

THE BRIDE'S FATHER

Your father escorts you down the aisle. He is also seated in the first pew behind the bride during the ceremony and later stands in the receiving line greeting and thanking guests. At the reception, he should dance the second dance with the bride and will usually make a short toast or welcoming speech to all the guests.

STEPPARENTS

If your parents are divorced or seperated, each set should host their own table at the reception. During the father-daughter dance, partner with whomever you're closest to, or share a dance with each dad, one at a time.

If your close to both your father and step-father and they agree, have both escort you down the aisle, or have one walk you halfway and the other walk you the rest of the way.

THE GROOM'S PARENTS

Your fiancé's mother should be invited to all showers and both his parents should be included in the rehearsal dinner, if they don't host it themselves. They should also contribute to the guest list for the wedding and reception and may or may not offer to share expenses. The groom's parents are honored guests at the ceremony and are seated, just before your mother, in the first pew on the groom's side of the aisle.

247

© David Barss

Notes

© Amy Ouellette

Photographers

Photo Booth

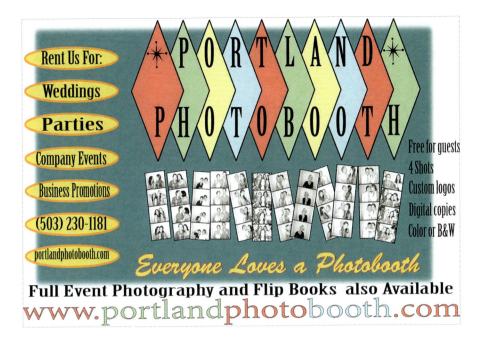

Rent Us For:

Weddings

Parties

Company Events

Business Promotions

(503) 230-1181

portlandphotobooth.com

Free for guests
4 Shots
Custom logos
Digital copies
Color or B&W

Everyone Loves a Photobooth

Full Event Photography and Flip Books also Available

www.portlandphotobooth.com

251

Our real photobooth is the best way to get great pictures of your guests. With no photographer in front of them your guests will be Fun, Relaxed and Creative. Entertain your guests and give them instant photostrips as gifts to help them remember your wedding. Strips can be customized with your names and wedding date, and can be color or black & white. All of the images from your event are saved and given to you in digital form, so you can view and print extra copies for yourself. A full time assistant is present to make sure your guests know what to do and to manage the crowds that will show up to use the booth.

What's New?

FlipBooks! We now offer real time creation of flipbooks to give to your guests. The books act like a stop motion animation film that your guests get on the spot to help remember your wedding. Learn more at www.portlandflipbook.com.

Contact

Soren Coughlin-Glaser

p. 503.230.1181

e. info@portlandphotobooth.com

www.portlandphotobooth.com

Quick Facts

- Photobooths make amazing guest books and the ultimate party favor.

- Unlimited prints means your guests can go in as many times as you like during your rental.

- Custom graphics and text can be added to your strips.

- Your guests get 2 photo strips, and you get a copy on a CD after the event

- Our booth is portable and can be set up in any space, inside or outside.

The Photo Booth without the Booth.....
Where Every Guest is the STAR!

Your Solution for WEDDING FAVORS, GUEST ALBUM & RECEPTION ENTERTAINMENT.

Paparazzi Tonight Photo Booth is a mobile "paparazzi style" photo studio with a modern take on the retro photo booth experience. We take 4 shots 4 seconds apart. Your guests can either HAM IT UP or GLAM IT UP! Instant Prints for everyone in the shot. Unlimited Photos and Onsite Prints.

- **Live Photographers:** Ensure every shot is a winner.
- **Photo Wedding Favors:** The BEST Favors at any wedding. On Site Instant Printing allows EVERY guest an instant photo print, ensuring your wedding is memorable. Guests can return as often as they wish with different family/friend/spouse groupings.
- **Photo Guest Album:** Extra copy of each photo is printed and placed in one-of-a-kind guest album and signed by each guest. Presented to bride & groom at reception's end.
- **Creates Fun & Creative Reception Atmosphere:** Entertaining & Meaningful.
- **Instant Slideshow Projection:** Incorporate photos into reception via projection installations.
- **Web Gallery:** Public or password protected. All photos are online where guests are able to download, reprint & share studio quality hi-res images.
- **Cutting Edge:** Professional Lighting and Cameras.
- **High Capacity Printing System:** Perfect for 50 to 400+ guests.
- **Prop Kits & Themed Weddings:** 50% of our weddings have us bring out props sometime during the reception to accentuate and add a little fun. Hollywood and red carpet themes are our specialty.
- **Thank You Cards:** Created from Paparazzi Tonight photos & received by honeymoon's end.
- **Environmentally Friendly:** No harsh chemicals common in traditional photo booth rentals.
- **American Disabilities Act Compliant & Wheel Chair Accessible**
- Locally Owned and Operated

PAPARAZZI TONIGHT Photo Booth.....where EVERY Guest is the STAR!

Reservations and Information 503.939.6097

www.paparazzitonight.com • info@paparazzitonight.com

Bravo! Member Since 2007

2026 SW Carolina Street
Portland, Oregon 97239
p. 503.516.2851
e. zuzubeephotography@gmail.com
www.zuzubeephotography.com

Your friends and family are an important part of your wedding day. Capture their sweet sassy, zany personalities with Zuzubee Photography's portable studio & Photobooth style pictures.

The Zuzubee Photobooth Studio is fun for everyone! Old or young, everyone loves being silly and mugging for the camera. You'll see guests bring out their best Zoolander impression, make everyone laugh, and have an unforgettable time!

These photos make amazing wedding favors, are perfect inserted into thank you cards, look gorgeous put together for a photo guest book or just make you smile seeing the true personalities of your loved-ones in individual prints.

Contact
Shane Shine Rutledge

Price
$150 – $500

Amenities
- Unlimited High Resolution Digital Photos.
- Groovy Props.
- Portable Studio Set-up.
- Disc of all photos.
- Unlimited digital downloads of photos for your guests.

253

Serving the Portland area   (503) 646-4710   www.RobPowellPhoto.com

About A Careful Budget Photography

All packages include a hi-res disc of your images, or the processed negatives and a set of proofs. You also receive a copyright release to make prints without the expense of ordering through a photographer.

A complete list of packages and prices can be found on my web site.

Digital: $750 summer, $695 off-season:

Five continuous hours of photography time, you receive at least 800 images on a hi-res disc, plus the right to make prints. You also receive fifteen 5x7s and four 8x10s.

Ask About:

- Digital proof albums as low as $3 per 8x10 page
- Real black and white prints from digital files
- Studio engagement portraits
- Adding film to digital packages
- Film-only packages

Important facts about Rob Powell:

I have been a professional photographer since 1975. I have never failed to show up as scheduled for a wedding. I have never ruined or lost anyone's images. I have never sent out a substitute photographer when the bride was expecting me. My wife and I have been happily married for 30 years. We believe in the sacredness and permanence of marriage vows. We wish the same joy for you.

– Rob Powell, PPA Master Photographer

rob@robpowellphoto.com

Aaronstadt Studios Photography
503-236-1871
[e]: p.lampton@comcast.net

www.aaronstadt.com

Playful Fine-Art Photography

- Award Winning Husband & Wife team with over thirty years experience. Fun, relaxed, spontaneous, personable.

- Style – 'narrative, unobtrusive, unique'.

- Online Preview Website for easy, convenient viewing and ordering.

- Digital Negatives (reproduction quality, copyright free image files) on CD/DVD with each package, for you to print 'wherever & whenever'.

- Engagement Session included with all Digital or Traditional Album Packages.

- Beautiful collaborately designed Custom Albums.

- Pre-wedding Planning Meetings and Unlimited Consultation.

- Extensive package options from 'time only' to 'all – inclusive'.

- Black & White, Sepia, Spot Coloring and other Special Effects are available.

"Can I just say,…HOT!…these are some of the most fantastic pictures on the web! Thank you for everything!" – Angela & Alan

"We LOVE our pictures. We have gotten compliment after compliment on the AMAZING photos! Thank you so much for bringing every moment to life." – Megan & Dustin

WHAT'S NEW

- DVD 'Video Album' Slideshow

- Photobooth

- Seasonal Specials pricing

Complete References, Resources, Package and Pricing Information online.

Bravo! Member Since 2000

Visit BravoWedding.com for more information on photo booths & photographers

255

Aden
Photography & Video Productions
503 625-8900

PO Box 1501
Lake Oswego, Oregon 97035
p. 503.625.8900
e. keith@adenphoto.com
www.adenphoto.com

About Aden Photography and Video Productions

Packages or a la carte plans are designed to suit weddings of all sizes. Wedding packages from two hours to unlimited time, as needed. Brochures listing services and prices can be sent to you upon request. Call for an appointment to see samples of photography and video.

"Sensitive, Creative and Experienced Photography and Video"

It's your special wedding day, a day to be remembered for the rest of your life. Through the years, your memories will become even more special, as will your wedding photographs and video. Your choice of a photographer is an important one. Since 1968, Keith Aden has been specializing in wedding and commercial advertising photography, including video production. His years of experience and knowledge of the very special art of wedding photography and video makes him sensitive to your needs and requests. Keith is a photographer who actually cares about you and your wedding.

Someone Who Cares About You and Your Wedding

You are not just another customer to Keith. Bridal couples and their families appreciate both his sensitivity to their "wants and needs" and his professional and unobtrusive style.

Contact
Keith Aden

Price
Custom packages available to fit all budgets

Digital or Film Photography
- A la carte or packages using only the finest professional digital cameras or Hasselblad medium format film cameras. It's your choice.

Video Production
- Basic to masterpiece wedding packages available.

DVD Albums or Traditional Albums
- DVD photo slideshow albums, DVD videos, montage DVD's including video & photo slideshow as well as traditional photo albums & video tapes.

Digital Photo Retouching, Restoration & Effects
- If you can imagine it we can make it happen.

travel
PORTLAND

See page 357 under
Video Services

Bravo! Member Since 1990

360.694.6684 ajsstudio.com

- Distinctive, unique style
- International award winning photographers
- Specializing in documentary photography
- Mat style albums, flush mounts and coffee table books
- All inclusive coverage, no restrictive packages
- Professional husband and wife team
- We Love Weddings!

Visit our gallery on the world wide web!

www.ajsstudio.com

Bravo! Member Since 1999

Visit BravoWedding.com for more information on photo booths & photographers

258

REAL. BEAUTIFUL.

One day you both realized you were better together. Sure, you were successful on your own. But there's something about being part of a twosome — an energy that brings out the best in each of you.

Our partnership, like yours, lets us reach new heights. An artist free to linger on the details; a producer to manage the myriad details. The result? Exceptionally rich and nuanced images. Wedding photography at it's best, from the first plans to the finest finished products.

John Valls' award-winning images have been featured in Portland Bride & Groom Magazine, Oregon Bride Magazine and The Knot. He was also recognized by PDN magazine as "Top Knot" honoring the best in America's "new school" wedding photography. Theresa Valls contributes her background in design management to produce timeless imagery and meaningful albums.

Stylish and affordable associate photographer packages begin at $2,000.

Visit our online portfolios, then call to schedule your personal consultation.

www.alturastudio.com
503.312.6400
theresa@alturastudio.com

amy ouellette photography

your wedding, your photos

About Amy Ouellette Photography

Amy's approach to photography is to capture the essence of you and your wedding day. She is committed to creating professional quality photographs and albums. In addition, she strives to provide the highest level of customer service to her clients. Her style is photojournlistic with a fine art flair. Photos are available in black and white or color. Amy Ouellette Photography also offers her clients a dvd containing all the high resolution images so that you can make additional reprints and preserve your memories. Hiring Amy insures that you will have a lovely collection of images from your wedding day.

Testimonial

"Just browsed through...and Amy, you rock!! I absolutely love the photographs (and can hardly wait to share them with Joel)! Your perspective is everything I dreamed it would be! And how fun it is to see photographs I had no idea were being taken. You are an indeed an incredible photographer!!"

– Alisha

Contact

Amy Ouellette

Portland, Oregon 97227

p. 503.313.4373

e. amy@amysgallery.com

www.amysgallery.com

Quick Facts

- Hire an experienced photojournalist to capture your wedding day

- Amy's photos have been published in New York Times Style Magazine, USA Today, Wine Country Living, Portland Monthly Magazine, Willamette Week & the Oregonian

- Focused on providing the highest level of quality & customer service

- Flexible packages

Portland | San Francisco | Seattle

Destinations Worldwide

Captivating Images... An Experience to Remember...

Your package will include (at least):

Two Photographers

Unlimited time

Unlimited images

Unlimited locations

Wedding Digital Negatives

Wedding Montage DVD

Engagement Portrait Session

Engagement Signature Album

Online ordering for one year

1 11x14 Portrait

2 11x14 Parent Portraits

Most packages will include a beautiful, hand-crafted wedding
story album in either a traditional matted style or a flush mount,
coffee table book

www.artistiquephotographie.com

503.310.9083

261

Images that tell the story of you

Blossom & Bee Photography is comprised of two photographers, Rosemary Ragusa & Jena Murray.

We combine years of experience with an eye for design and detail to make your wedding photography experience relaxed and beautifully captured.

Serving the greater Portland area, the Pacific Northwest, and the world beyond.

www.blossomandbeephotography.com

info@blossomandbeephotography.com

Blossom & Bee Photography

2505 SE 11th Avenue, #107
Portland, Oregon 97202
(by appointment only)
p. 503.287.3474

Price
Pricing starts at $3,200

All Collections Include:
- Complimentary engagement session
- Online ordering capabilities
- Bookbound proofbook
- Two photographers

Premium Collections Include:
- Your choice of a Leather Magazine-style Album or a Silk & Letterpress Eco Album, made locally in Portland.

Bryan Hoybook
photographer

Fun

Stylish

Affordable

503.453.5239

bryanhoybook.com

Weddings are supposed to be one of the most exciting times in a couple's life, but all too often the planning – choosing the dress, selecting the florist, the bakery and the photographer – can become a blur.

Are you having trouble comparing the Gold Edition Package from one photographer to the Prestige Album set from another? Or maybe three 8 x 10s and 40 4 x 5s just don't meet your needs. Well, Camera Art has a better way.

Since 1973, Camera Art has taken all the confusion and fuss out of pricing a wedding and allowed the bride and groom to have control of their budget and what they want to order. And, of course, breath-taking imagery of your special day.

Here Is How It Works

We charge a camera fee of $495 to photograph your wedding with one photographer and $595 with two photographers. We shoot your wedding from start to finish – no time limits – from getting ready through the reception.

You simply order what you want. Simple? Yes. We like it that way and so do our customers. Purchase the pictures you want in the sizes you want. You can also purchase your high-resolution digital images on DVD with release of copyright to you to reprint, share your memories or create your own album. Contemporary digital albums and traditional albums also available.

Contact

Carrie Leavitt
and Chandra Bickler

PO Box 2772
Hillsboro, Oregon 97123

p. 503.648.0851
f. 503.648.0851

e. cameraartphoto@live.com

www.cameraartphoto.com

Services

- Flexible pricing
- No time limits
- High-quality prints and internet proofing for viewing and ordering
- Breath-taking imagery – specializing in Traditional, Formal, Documentary and Photojournalistic styles to capture your special day
- Exceptional customer service at unparalleled value
- Complimentary pre-wedding/engagement photo shoot
- High-resolution digital images on DVD and photo slideshow

263

Bravo! Member Since 1991

Capturing Grace
photography

"Aubrie is an amazing photographer! We couldn't be happier with our wedding photos. Even our guests made comments to us about how dedicated she was, standing on chairs, lying on the ground, doing anything she had to do to get that special shot. And our photos definitely show her dedication paying off."

– Mary Allen 9.12.2009

"Her artistic eye is so unique and distinctive; I have received nothing but compliments from all who have seen my wedding album. Her ability to capture real and un-staged moments is what makes her special."

– Rochelle Jaques 6.13.2009

"I would highly recommend Capturing Grace Photography. There were so many details in our wedding planning and Aubrie made the photography part of our wedding appear seamless."

– Emily Olson 5.17.2009

Contact

Aubrie LeGault

19680 NW Pondosa Court
Portland, Oregon 97229

p. 971.563.2609

e. aubrielegault@gmail.com

www.CapturingGrace.com

Price
$1,200 – $2,600

Quick Facts

- Photojournalistic, candid and artistic style
- Member of WPJA (Wedding Photojournalist Association)
- All packages include a web gallery and digital negatives
- Engagement shoots, slideshows, albums and coffee books
- Easy and fun to work with

CONTINUUM
PHOTOGRAPHY

We are a husband and wife team of fine art photojournalists. We work together to create unique and poignant photographs that cover multiple angles and perspectives of every wedding we shoot.

Our Style

Our photography style is really a hybrid of documentary photojournalism and artistic concepts. We have many inspirations that come from a variety of sources that we try to implement into our images. Above all we love the raw emotion of photojournalism. The majority of the day we are focused on highlighting the laughter, tears and passion that you and your guests will be feeling while consciously remaining unobtrusive. We also love the seductive, mysterious look of fashion photography, and the classic look of older film processes. We are always on the look out for great backgrounds and interesting lighting. We never interrupt a moment or pose situations that are already magical on their own. We strive to capture the perfect combination of timeless elegance and fresh style.

Quick Facts

- We are fine-art photojournalists with a fresh and creative style.
- Full day coverage and two photographers always included in our base price.
- We offer a wide range of classic and stylish wedding albums.
- Photography add ons include our exclusive Fauxtobooth™, Bridal Boudoir Sessions, and Canvas Gallery Wraps.
- Base Coverage begins at $2,000

www.continuumphotography.com | 503.488.5800

Being a great Portland photographer means being creative yet laid-back and unpretentious, just like Portland's brides and grooms. I love Portland.

I work hard to create an artistic documentary of your wedding, and help you feel relaxed and comfortable the whole time.

I shoot fun, artistic and candid shots (in B&W and color), and know how to please the traditionalists in your family. Mom and Dad will still get the shots they really want from your wedding day, and you won't get stressed out.

I invite you to explore my photography style at www.portlandphotographer.com, or call me personally at (503) 230.1181

For something extra special, see our portable photobooth at www.portlandphotobooth.com

Soren Coughlin-Glaser

Owner: Coughlin-Glaser Photography

www.portlandphotographer.com

DANIELSTARK
photography

www.danielstarkphotography.com · 541.633.6135

I DO.

Do I promise to catch every little moment that reveals the beauty and fun, the crazy celebration and the touching scenes that you want to keep forever?

Do I promise to get that shot of your mom and dad (you know the one), those behind-the-scenes preparations of bride and groom and buddies from the old days?

Do I know how you feel about this absolutely amazing moment and how you want it to last forever in a photo-documentary that will always feel exactly right?

I do.

That's the way Daniel Stark Photography looks at your wedding — through your eyes, with your respect for the moment, in your hope for the best of all possible times.

Please give us a call and give us the chance to have you say, I do, too.

web: www.danielstarkphotography.com
email: daniel@danielstarkphotography.com
phone: 541.633.6135

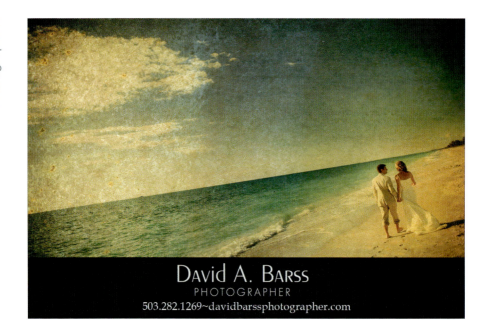

DAVID A. BARSS
PHOTOGRAPHER
503.282.1269~davidbarssphotographer.com

Your wedding day is planned with meticulous detail to embody your beliefs, personalities and to share those with your closest family and friends. The day is filled with the splendor of floral artistry, exquisite décor, delectable cuisine, a beautiful wedding cake, vibrant music and the beautiful sounds of laughter and joy. This grand moment will pass, but with extraordinary photography you can capture and keep the day alive forever.

We have been photographing weddings and events both locally and at unique destinations outside the greater Northwest for over 10 years. We try and offer a boutique style approach with many of our images and design work showcasing treatments exclusive to our studio.

Bravo! Member Since 2000

269

I believe in capturing your day as if you were reliving it every time you look at your photos! I think it's important to get to know each other during our consultation and engagement session, and one of the best things about my job is when a bride becomes a friend! I aim to create images as unique as you are so let's get ready to relive the most beautiful day of your lives!

"Deyla has a great energy. Her perspective as a photographer is amazing. Every shot she produces is beautiful. And, she's a heck of a lot of fun to work with!"

– Stacie & Mike

"You really are THE photographer to get, OMG Deyla I LOVE, LOVE, LOVE all the photos. I cried looking at them at work, but I couldn't wait until I got home. I was so excited and you did a fabulous job!"

– Love, Jedidah

What's New?

I am excited to have a brand new line of FABULOUS designer Albums and products for 2010, For recent E-sessions & Weddings, grab a cup of coffee and stop on by the blog www.deylahussphotography.com/blog I can't WAIT to meet you both!

Contact
Deyla Huss

p. 503.860.0630

e. contact@deylahussphotography.com

www.deylahussphotography.com

Price
Please visit my website for package info.

Quick Facts
- Fun & Fabulous creative flowing Wedding Photography.
- All images are High Contrast and full of life!
- I believe in life in the moment.
- Serving all over the US, available for Destination Weddings!
- Dance your socks off, I'll probably join you!

Don Frank Photography
Creative Photojournalism

Relaxed

Artistic

Cool

Fun

Love

Classic

Excellence

"Hey Don – Got the photos yesterday, and we were both absolutely floored. You are truly gifted. Thank you so, so much!" – Gary and Carla, 2009

Blue ribbon documentation of the beautiful, playful, cultural, romantic, and surprising details that make each wedding unique.

Your photos tell the story.

Worldwide since 1997.

About Don Frank:
Don is an award winning professional photographer based on the Oregon Coast. He is a regular contributor to Via Magazine and his images have appeared in Times Square New York and the Museum of Contemporary Photography Chicago, Illinois. Don has traveled around the world plying his trade and is currently living the dream.

503.738.5118

www.donfrankphotography.com

ENCORE
STUDIOS

Portland Metro Area
p. 503.255.8047
e. encore100@comcast.net
www.encore-studios.com

About Encore Studios

Experience and creativity! With more than 20 years of experience, Encore Studios offers the widest of selections of wedding packages in the Northwest, designed with your preferences and budget in mind.

- Photojournalistic, candid, traditional, documentary, and formal styles – what is desired today for your best wedding memories to be cherished for a lifetime!
- Videography capturing behind-the-scenes and vital moments of the most important day of your life!
- Along with traditional medium and 35mm formats, we also offer digital imaging.

Our professionals help you have a relaxed, playful and fun wedding day, just by doing what they do best in life! To make your day the best it could be, call 503.255.8047.

Contact
Encore Studios

Price
Starting at $150 customized

Services

- We offer disc jockey, photography & videography services – all for less than photography alone at other studios
- Creative & passionate in making your wedding day a success
- Professional services with experience in thousands of weddings
- Customize packages to suit your style; we understand what budget means
- Local & traveling abilities

271

FREE ENGAGEMENT PHOTO SESSION

For a free engagement photo session and consultation, call 503.255.8047 day or evening. Visit our website www.encore-studios.com

See page 191 under DJs

Bravo! Member Since 1995

e. info@fisherpicturesphotography.com | www.fisherpicturesphotography.com

About Fisher Pictures Photography

We have been in the wedding business for nine years now. We specialize in capturing the spontaneous moments of your one-of-a-kind event with photojournalism that can be candid, unique, traditional or formal.

We offer brides the economical choice and convenience of being able to make their own prints. As a bride you will have access to unlimited color and black and white pictures from your wedding (with complete copyright clearance) on CDs, as part of your package. There are no hidden costs. You make only the prints you want – in the sizes you want– yourself.

We are experts at blending in at your event, without interruptions.

Originals are usually available within ten days of your event.

Terms

A $200 deposit is required to hold the date, with the balance due two weeks prior to the wedding date.

Contact

Fisher Pictures
p. 503.699.1017

Price Packages

- 3 hours of coverage $750.
- 4 hours of coverage $850.
- 6 hours of coverage $1,050.
- 8 hours of coverage $1,250 (We will cover up to 18 hours @ $100/hour past the 8 hour price).
- Engagement Photo Sessions $250.
- DVD slide shows for ceremony/reception (Including up to 100 pictures) $200 ($3/ additional picture over 100).

Quick Facts

- All high-resolution digital negatives are given to you on CDs, giving you the ability to make as many copies, in any size, as you wish.
- Visa & MasterCard accepted.

Bravo! Member Since 2003

272

Five Gables Photography

(p) 503.550.7385
fivegablesphoto@comcast.net
www.fivegablesphotography.com
"Capturing the Moment"

Flexibility is one of the many advantages that we can offer you when capturing your special wedding moments. Whether your personal taste is for contemporary photojournalism, more traditional poses, or a unique combination of both, we are ready to serve you with creative, experienced professionals that are dedicated to making your wedding photographs a beautiful reflection of your personal style.

Affordable pricing is another aspect to consider when choosing a photographer. We offer many different options in our packages that start as low as $795. Packages of five hours or more come with 100+ 4x6 prints with preview album, enlargements and wedding album. All images can be viewed on your one-of-a-kind CD. All packages include two photographers for your event. Black and white photos are available in all packages at no extra charge.

More than 20 years of technical experience behind the camera and in the studio yield memorable images that you will treasure for a lifetime! Five Gables Photography is a member of Portland Metropolitan Photographers Association and you can be assured of the highest quality work.

Our friendly, easy-going personality draws genuine smiles from couples, their family and friends. We have a special gift for putting everyone at ease on a day that has so many details to be considered. Our desire to custom-design our work to your specific needs is evident in pre- and post-wedding consultations as well as during your ceremony and reception. We are passionate about our work and it shows!

Please call for available dates as soon as possible – our calendar fills in quickly. We invite you to visit our website to view samples of our work or call to schedule an appointment for a free consultation to view our portfolios. We look forward to serving you with top-quality work and affordable pricing for your very special wedding day! Having a destination wedding? Call for a quote to one of those special locations.

FS PHOTOGRAPHERS | RYAN & JOELLE FLOOD

RECOGNIZED AMONG THE TOP WEDDING PHOTOGRAPHERS
IN THE NATION BY *PHOTO DISTRICT NEWS'* TOP KNOTS

WE BELIEVE
THE FINE ART OF WEDDING PHOTOGRAPHY
IS CAPTURING THE JOY, NARRATIVE & DETAILS...
THEN SHARING THE COUPLE'S UNIQUE STORY
THROUGH FINELY CRAFTED DESIGN.

WWW.FSWEDDINGS.COM
INFO@FSWEDDINGS.COM
503.922.1677

Bravo! Member Since 2007

9420 SW 165th Place
Beaverton, Oregon 97007

p. 503.524.3544

e. gayle@gayleaman.com

www.gayleaman.com

Capture the Celebration...

The love, the joy, the once in a lifetime marriage event – all captured in extraordinary images to be enjoyed forever.

Gayle Aman believes romance is real, and it shows in the timeless treasures that her matchless photography delivers.

Gayle captures not only the traditional images you'll want to share, but also the rare moments that make your wedding experience unique. Relax and enjoy that extra special day – Gayle will capture all your magic and memories for you to remember for a lifetime.

Price

Packages are flexible & can be tailored to fit your individual needs.

Quick Facts

- Complimentary pre-wedding consultation.
- Engagement & pre-wedding event photography available.
- Eye for detail
- Specializing in relaxed, natural portrait & candid images in color, black & white or sepia.
- Enhanced photo editing & special effects.
- Well-respected with more than 20 years of experience.

275

Call to set up an appointment and get to know Gayle. Discover why hundreds of couples have chosen her to preserve the memories of their special day.

www.gayleaman.com

With your booked package, Gayle has a special bridal gift for you.

Bravo! Member Since 1992

276

Holden onto Memories
Photography by
Kisa C. Holden
www.holdenontomemories.com
kisa@holdenontomemories.com
503.804.0747

I take great pride in capturing the emotion and unique details of your wedding day. I will tell your wedding story, letting the day unfold naturally, with little interference. With a combination of color portraiture and detail-oriented black and white images and a photojournalistic style, I will capture the joy and excitement of your wedding day.

- Packages starting at $1,250
- Customized packages
- Complimentary engagement session
- Available for travel anywhere your wedding takes you!

Bravo! Member Since 2005

Holland Studios

277

- Giggling bridesmaids
- Anticipated walk down the aisle
- Dancing the night away
- Your dreams, your wedding, your reality

"When I look around our house, the only real things of value we
have from that day came from Holland Studios"
– Phil Avery, former groom

The light of afternoon falling on the most anticipated kiss. A grandfather's prayer. The
confessions of a lifelong accomplice. A night of dancing without shoes. These are the
blue-eyed moments, passed down through generations and we are there to capture them.
We are the visual biographers of extraordinary lives. Come to our studio, view our unique
wedding books, meet our photographers, and let us immerse ourselves in your story so that
we might help you share it with all.

*"The most important thing about photographing people is not clicking the shutter...
it is clicking with the subject."*

– Alfred Eisenstaedt

Bravo! Member Since 1998

IMAGES
by Floom
PHOTOGRAPHY
& VIDEOGRAPHY

(in Multnomah Village)
7843 S.W. Capitol Highway
Portland Oregon 97219
503.245.3676
www.imagesbyfloom.com

We are dedicated to providing beautiful, creative, unique images that capture the mood and emotions of your wedding day. The photographs are a blend of traditional and photojournalistic styles. Our packages start as low as $1,000.

We've made it simple...three packages to choose from, a package for every budget.

Ask about our VIP Lifetime Pass, good for one studio sitting and one 8x10 every year – for life!

Call now for details

www.imagesbyfloom.com
503.245.3676

"Images by Floom photographed three of my children's weddings beautifully. They are the best"

– Mrs. Pat Reser; Resers Fine Foods

"You are amazing, thank you so much for everything, the pictures are awesome, you exceeded our expectations!!"

– Scott and Jen Cannon

www.imagesbyfloom.com
503.245.3676

Bravo! Member Since 1995

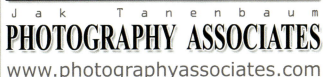

Jak Tanenbaum

PHOTOGRAPHY ASSOCIATES
www.photographyassociates.com

Classic Fine Art Black & White Film Photography

Looking for an exciting alternative to the digitized wedding album? Then let us share with you the wonderful time honored beauty of original film based black and white hand-crafted photographic images.

Photography Associates will create a wedding heirloom that will stand up to the test of time. Think about all of the beautiful black and white portraits that still adorn hallways and museums with no signs of aging.

Photography Associates specializes in presenting every client with a handcrafted, "One of a Kind," fine art, black and white wedding portfolio. We respect the uniqueness of each couple and offer a variety of options for presenting the finished work. Ever consider having your favorite photographs of your wedding day look like a work of art? We do. Your favorites can be museum mounted ready to showcase, presented in a contemporary album, or perhaps you have an idea of your own. Let's work together.

A Little About Us

Jak Tanenbaum received a BFA in Photography and Design from the University of North Carolina and an MFA in Photography from the Academy of Art College in San Francisco. He has been an active exhibiting artist for over 25 years and is currently an Instructor of Photography at Clark College in Vancouver, WA. Lynden Tanenbaum received a BFA in Photography from Humboldt State University.

Bravo! Member Since 1996

Contact
Jak Tanenbaum

PO Box 82758
Portland, Oregon 97282

p. 503.232.1455

e. info@photographyassociates.com

www.photographyassociates.com

Quick Facts

- We can customize a package to meet your specific needs.

- Specialized hand coloring, sepia toning, and archival museum matting.

- One of a kind hand crafted wedding portfolios.

- For these documentary style fine art portfolios we shoot film and custom print each exhibition photograph using traditional darkroom processes.

I have goosebumps looking at the pictures!
Michelle and Dave, August 2009

I have tears in my eyes!
I never could imagine that the photos
were going to be this beautiful!
THANK YOU!
Pernilla and Alex, September 2009

WOW, Jessica.....you truly captured our day.
The photos are amazing! We can't thank you
enough for all you did. You really rocked it!
Tiffany and Adam, September 2009

www.JessicaHillPhotography.com

info@jessicahillphotography.com

(503)415-1411

Jessica Hill Photography | 800 NW 6th Ave, Ste 340 | Portland OR 97209

The joy of your celebration
should be matched by the
artistry with which is it captured.

www.jonathanmichael.com
503.867.6486

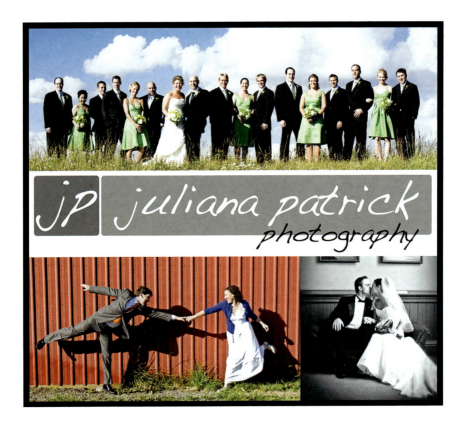

www.julianapatrick.com   503.318.5160

Let our EXPERIENCE give you confidence to relax
and enjoy one of the greatest moments in your life.
We are a PROFESSIONAL husband & wife TEAM,
We like to have FUN, and work seamlessly, capturing
YOUR DAY

INNOVATIVE Album Designs. CREATIVE Compositions.
Let us take care of you.

We want you to LOVE your images.

email: juliana@julianapatrick.com

Serving The Pacific Northwest and Destinations Worldwide

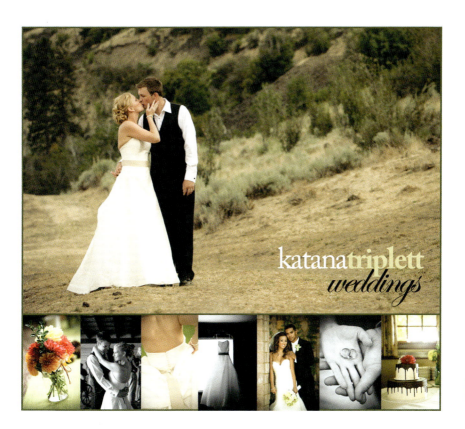

katana**triplett**
weddings

283

The wedding day is yours and I will be there to catch moments as they pass, make moments come to life, and make sure your memories of the day look as wonderful they will feel. I tell the story of the day, making sure that all of the beautiful things you worked so hard on will stay alive forever.

I am a commercial photographer and an artist with 15 years of photographic experience. I am technically trained and have an artist's eye. My training gives me the ability to combine technique, style, and creativity to capture your most precious moments. Your day will be in good hands, I promise!

My packages are flexible – Your satisfaction is my first priority. Come on by and we can chat!

Bravo! Member Since 2007

Contact
Katana Triplett

NE Portland, by appointment

p. 971.404.9311

e. katana@katanatriplett.com

www.katanatriplettphotography.com

Price
Custom built packages around $3,000

Quick Facts
- Top of the line professional digital Canon equipment
- Unlimited images
- Non-intrusive story telling approach
- I will not hold your images hostage – full resolution images on a disk
- I put my heart into every wedding!

WHAT'S NEW
Now offering HD videography!

WOW! You have truly outdone yourself, the pictures are incredible! You are incredible! We really can't express how much we are loving the images. We've already watched the slideshow four times! Thank you soooo so so so much for capturing our day for us! There isn't another person who could have captured our personalities so well. Thank you so much!

— Sarah & Jayson — 2009

Kate Kelly Photography
503.284.6035
katekellyphotography.com

Kathryn Elsesser
photography

Greater Portland Area
p. 503.335.9057
e. Kathryn@kephotog.com
www.kephotog.com

Artistic and Creative Wedding Photography Including Photojournalistic and Traditional Classic Images

Your wedding day is as unique as you are and your photographs should reflect your personality and individual style. I will record the memories of your day with a combination of both timeless classic as well as photojournalistic-style images that capture the spontaneous moments of this one-of-a-kind event.

It is important to me that we meet individually at least once and communicate often before your wedding to ensure that your wedding images reflect your day, not one preconceived by a photographer. Whether you want an all black and white photo essay or the addition of color portraits, I approach each wedding as a unique event and offer more than the standard formula of traditional wedding photography.

I take the utmost care to have your images developed with the highest quality processing available. Equal care is taken with presentation. Original photographs are presented in a rich archival album, yours to keep.

Contact
Kathryn Elsesser

Price
Please call for quotes

Quick Facts
- Flexible & customized wedding packages
- Film & digital formats
- Both mat & coffee table albums available
- Unlimited images

285

WHAT'S NEW

I am now offering Destination Wedding packages

Bravo! Member Since 2001

286

Two days of photography

Laszlo edits and finishes album for you

Photography for the select few

Laszlo Photographer

360-896-2637

laszlophoto.com

lauren brooks
- photography -

287

As a couple, you bring a unique style to your wedding celebration. We believe your photographs should reflect this style. On your wedding day, so much will happen in such a short period of time. Our journalistic approach to photography means that we document your entire wedding day as it unfolds, knowing that each image plays an important part in preserving your memories. We strive to capture the events of your day in a way that complements your personality and enhances the experience for you and your guests.

Lauren and Lincoln are a husband and wife team. Their wedding photography has been featured in local and regional wedding publications such as Portland Bride & Groom, and Oregon Bride, as well as national wedding resource websites including The Knot, Style Me Pretty and Snippet & Ink.

Lauren Brooks

SE Portland, by appointment

p. 503.467.9593

e. Info@LaurenBphoto.com

www.LaurenBphoto.com

Quick Facts
- International award-winning photography
- Documentary approach
- Husband and wife team
- Member of WPJA, ISPWP, WPPI and MyPortlandPhotographer.com
- Serving the Pacific Northwest since 2005

WHAT'S NEW?
We are excited to offer a full line of beautiful archival wedding books, boxes and folios that are hand-made locally by artisan book-binder Molly Lewis, owner of Hinged Strung Stitched.

Jonathan Ley
PHOTOGRAPHY

288

My goal is to capture the story of your wedding day with photographs that will bring back the memories and emotions for a lifetime. I offer a fresh and balanced approach to wedding photography; combining traditional, artistic and photojournalistic styles.

I'll work closely with you beforehand to make sure we're well-coordinated. I'll listen closely to learn about your plans, and will be happy to offer my perspective as an experienced wedding photographer. With good communication and a good plan you won't have to worry about the photos, and can focus on what matters – enjoying your wedding.

In the end, it's the photos that matter... so, visit my website to see what I can do. You can learn more about my services & styles, and book your date. I'd love to answer any of your questions by phone, e-mail, or in person.

Check out my website – www.leyphtography.com for the latest news!

Contact
Jonathan Ley

19065 NW Dorena Street
Portland, Oregon 97229

p. 971.222.6426

e. jonathan@leyphotography.com

www.leyphotography.com

Price
$1,200 – $2,000+

Quick Facts
- A balanced mix of traditional, artistic and photojournalistic styles.
- Flexible packages: Choose a package, or we'll customize one that works for you
- Option to purchase full-resolution "digital negatives"
- On-line proofing included
- Experienced & professional

WHAT'S NEW

Check out my website – www.leyphtography.com – for the latest news!

MistyBay Photography

Fun

Unique

503-627-0379
www.gypsyana.com

Artistic

**Capture your special moments to preserve for a lifetime
with our creative professionals.**

We customize packages to fit your finances and needs.

We offer interest FREE payment plans.

You own your negatives!

You keep all your proofs!

Convenient online viewing and ordering.

Elegant wedding story albums.

Color photos, black and white, sepia tone, metallic.

Pre-wedding engagement photo sessions, in-studio or outdoors.

Professional make-up and hair services also available.

Call for a FREE consultation and price quotes.

503.627.0379

Please visit our web site at
www.gypsyana.com

See page 81 under
Make-up & Hair

Fine Art Wedding Photography
by Oleg and Nataliya Sostin

Our Style of Photography

Our vision of photography has been influenced by the fact that we both grew up and received graduate education in Europe. Fine art approach to portraiture helps us to capture portraits that look modern and augment beauty of people whom we photograph. Simultaneous use of a photojournalistic style allows an unobtrusive capture of the story of your wedding day as well as genuine emotions and chemistry shared among people. We like to take many detail shots, which beautifully decorate our magazine-style flush albums.

Our Philosophy

Consistently high quality of the services that we offer is our gold standard because moments of the wedding day are unique and cannot be recreated. We consider it to be a great honor and responsibility to capture one of the most important events in ones' life.

"...I absolutely LOVE the pictures. I look at them over and over again. I can't even pick my favorites because they are all AMAZING! You are an incredible photographer..."
– Beth Rankin

Toll Free: 800-574-7976

www.SostinWeddings.com • Info@SostinWeddings.com

Bravo! Member Since 2007

PAUL RICH **STUDIO**

291

Imagine creative portraits, beautifully composed images, and stylish albums. Paul Rich will capture the specific details as well as the spontaneous moments that are unique to your wedding day.

Your wedding images will be personally edited, enhanced, and available to view within 4 weeks of your wedding. Every package option by Paul Rich Studio includes two photographers with all final images archived at full resolution onto disc.

"Your work leaves us speechless and the images will allow us to forever remember and relive every moment of our wedding. Your talent is matched by an equally great heart and personality..."

– Myra & Matt

Paul Rich has a degree in photography from Bard College in New York. He is a regular contributor to wedding sites such as "Style Me Pretty" and his wedding images have been published in Portland Monthly's Bride & Groom magazine. Recent destination wedding assignments include such locations as Kauai, St. Lucia, and Cozumel.

Contact us at 503.475.3306 to schedule a consultation and portfolio review.

Contact
Paul Rich

4930 SE 71st Avenue
Portland, Oregon 97206

p. 503.475.3306

e. paul@paulrichstudio.com

www.paulrichstudio.com

Price
Starting at $2,250

Quick Facts
- Innovative Contemporary Wedding Photography
- Flexible Wedding Package Options
- Gorgeous Gallery Wrap Canvas Prints
- Available for Travel

WHAT'S NEW?

2010 Special: 10% off all print orders placed within first 10 days of the launch of your wedding gallery.

Bravo! Member Since 2007

292

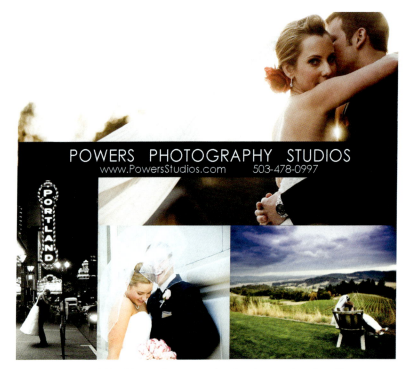

POWERS PHOTOGRAPHY STUDIOS
www.PowersStudios.com   503-478-0997

"Best Wedding Photography Studios in Portland"

Your excited to be married and totally in love! Your wedding photographs are very important to you and you do not want to settle for anything less than amazing.

Remember, your wedding photographs and albums will be family heirlooms that you hand to your grandkids. They will probably be one of the most valuable items in your entire house.

Each relationship is unique – let's work together to capture yours and spread it across a collection of amazing photographs!

OUR PACKAGE INCLUDES:
Up to Full Day Coverage
An Unlimited Number of Images
All Images Shot & Edited in RAW
DVD of All High Resolution, Edited Images
2 – 3 Artist Team
All Images Presented Online
Credit for Albums and Prints
Casual Engagement Session
Lots of Customization

Today we are considered one of the best and most ingenious wedding photography studios in the United States. We are committed to the art of wedding photography. In 2009 Oregon Bride Magazine named us the "Best Wedding Photography Studio in Portland"!

If you are truly interested in making an informed decision and carefully selecting your wedding photographer, please consider stopping by for a consultation.

1220 SW Taylor, Portland, Oregon 97205   503.478.0997

remembrance *Photography*

www.remembrancephoto.com   503.957.7758

- artistic, unique wedding photography since 1990

- modern, photojournalistic approach

- website and high-resolution CDs included with all packages

- unlimited number of images and locations

- custom-designed coffee-table albums

- all-inclusive packages starting at $1,500

- we travel

We are blown away by the beauty of our wedding photos. Thank you for your professionalism, care, and what can only be described as total heart and soul as an artist.

– Miles & Wendy Histand

I do not know how you did it, but you seemed to disappear...Your seeming invisibility meant that I am not camera conscious in any candid shot. I look natural and like I was having the time of my life...because I was!

– Cira & Patrick Collins

Bravo! Member Since 2000

Visit BravoWedding.com for more information on photo booths & photographers

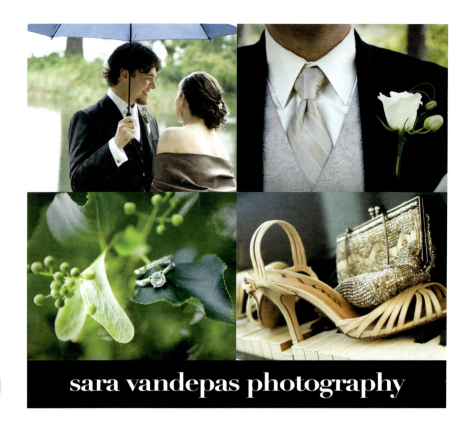

sara vandepas photography

blending photojournalistic spunk and portraiture romance

custom packages built around each client

couples typically spend from $1,500 to $2,000

digital images and printing rights included

i love weddings.

call me so we can talk about yours!

www.saravandepasphotography.com   ...   sara 541.990.6457

SIKORA PHOTOGRAPHY

CONTEMPORARY — STYLISH — CONCEPTUAL

Over several years we have developed a very unique approach to wedding photography, we are unobtrusive, yet fully immersed in the scene, we love to be creative and spontaneous. We are full of innovative, contemporary ideas and we will take on any photographic challenge. All of our image editing and book design takes place in our studio to assure the superb quality of the final product. We strive to produce the most distinctive and timeless memories for all of our couples!

"We can't say enough about the stellar duo that is Sikora Photography. From the impressive initial meeting to the unveiling of the stunning final results, Tom and Margaux were professional, fun and a blast to work with! We knew right off that we were in good hands, and the excitement only grew as the shutters started clicking and we saw how much passion they have for the art they create. Being both unobtrusive and markedly generous with their time, these two experts didn't miss a moment and effortlessly captured the magic of the most important day of our lives. The only bad part was saying goodbye, as we not only had an amazing time shooting with them, but also became friends along the way. Thank you Sikora!"

– Kambra and Adam – Summer 2009

Contact

Thomas Sikora

p. 503.866.2645

e. info@sikoraphotography.com

www.sikoraphotography.com

Price

Seasonal discounts available year round!

Quick Facts

- 2 fun photographers
- Hundreds of retouched images
- Color and B&W
- Online gallery
- Proof book or prints
- Designer albums
- Parent books
- Engagement photo shoot
- DVD of all images

Visit our blog for most recent projects: www. sikorablog.wordpress.com

"Illuminating the Essence of Love"
WWW.STOTT SHOTS PHOTOGRAPHY.COM
541-526-0563

BEGIN TO IMAGIN *with*
S T U D I O 190

297

Passion

A strong or extravagant fondness, enthusiasm, or desire for something.

Let our passion for amazingness become your reality locally and internationally, where your image is our everything.

www.s190image.com

www.studio190.wordpress.com

503.510.9623

stylewest photography

Stylewest Photography by Jennifer Costello

www.stylewestphotography.com
jen@stylewestphotography.com
503.816.0937

Elegant.   Timeless.   Natural.

Stylewest Photography specializes in professional, photojournalistic wedding photography.

Available for travel throughout Oregon and Washington.

Wedding Package Options Include:

High resolution CD
Second photographer/assistant
Online viewing of the event
Custom wedding album – flush or matted
Engagement session
Parent album
DVD slideshow
Rehearsal dinner coverage
Photo thank you cards
Photo wedding invitations

Please call or email for current prices.

Artistry...
Emotion...
Elegance...
Romance...
Sophistication...

Teresa Kohl Photography

503-430-5550

www.tfkphotography.com

299

TIMELESS ELEGANCE
Quite simply put...the best for LESS

*Digital capture with complete set of files for you to keep.

*Customized packages that work with your budget starting at $650 with specials and seasonal discounts.

*Choice of a wide variety of custom products including many album designs, slide shows, and unique print designs.

*Expertly coordinated plan for your special day at no additional cost.

** Teresa's gift to all Bravo! brides booking through Bravo! includes a detailed day plan for your wedding and a limited edition custom portrait.

Conveniently located in the Sunset Corridor. Call now for you free consultation and take advantage of Teresa's experience with over a thousand weddings to make sure your day is perfect.

www.tfkphotography.com
503.430.5550

Bravo! Member Since 1998

Visit BravoWedding.com for more information on photo booths & photographers

INNOVATIVE PHOTOJOURNALISM

To Jos and Jaysun, photojournalism embraces the essence of the human spirit. As storytellers, they capture the decisive moments that illuminate real emotion. The images say it all. Experience their website. Visit their studio. See their albums. Your love story is their passion.

"The Photographers have some of the most original and creative ideas in their field today. We highly recommend their services to anyone."
~Jamie & Yo

"Jos and Jaysun are SO fun! The photographs are beautiful and the album is amazing. The movie poster is brilliant!"
~Ken and Tracy

"There is no other photography team like The Photographers. You will never find anyone who takes as much time and care as they do."
~ Laura Schumacher

"Jos and Jaysun have so much to offer and really stand out in an industry swamped by 'photographers'... they are THE Photographers!"
~Christie Wilson

(Blush Bridal Consultant Group)

… let the images speak …

www.THEPHOTOGRAPHERS.us

800.758.5291

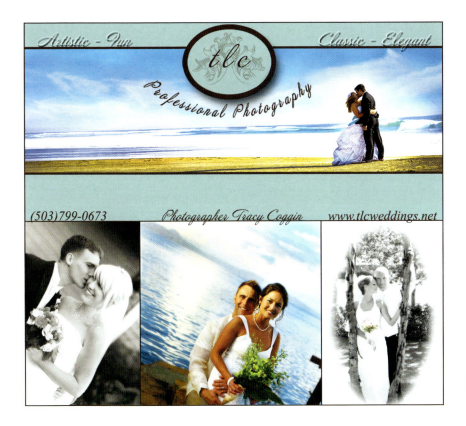

TLC Professional Photography offers a photojournalistic style with an artistic flair.

With TLC, the special moments of your wedding will be captured for future generations to see — and you'll have fun in the process.

Call Tracy today at 503.799.0673 to schedule your complimentary consultation.

Dear Future Bride and Groom,

When it comes to weddings, I am a true romantic. I love marriage and everything it stands for, and this love fuels my passion for wedding photography. With lots of TLC, I will capture on camera those moments that make your wedding day so special, so memorable, so uniquely yours. And this goes far beyond skill and an artistic eye — I take time to learn about your relationship, to hear about your hopes and dreams for the future and to discover why you fell in love. This allows me to create for you a treasured collection of images that you'll cherish for a lifetime.

May your marriage be blessed.

Sincerely yours,

Tracy Coggin

TLC Professional Photography

tracy@tlcweddings.net

Helpful Hint

Choosing Your Photographer

WHY ARE PHOTOGRAPHS IMPORTANT?

After the cake's been eaten, the tuxes returned, the flowers wilted, and you've shaken the last grains of sand off from the honeymoon, what's left of the wedding? Those treasured glimpses captured in photographs can in a moment rekindle the joy for both of you, bring back the friends, and show the love within families.

© Ajs

SELECTING A PHOTOGRAPHER

Find a photographer whose style you feel comfortable with. Look closely at his or her sample albums, website and don't be afraid to ask for references. A contract is important to reserve the date and should confirm that the estimate given will be the total cost excluding extra prints or specialty photographs ordered. Their prices vary from one photographer to another so make sure you understand what the "package price" is and what the extras are.

CONSULTING WITH YOUR PHOTOGRAPHER

When you finally select your photographer, sit down together so you can communicate what you imagine your photographs to be. Get specific about formal and candid photographs. Be sure you let the photographer know what you are expecting. Some provide a checklist for you to fill out.

To avoid family flare-ups during photos, discuss the shots with your photographer in advance. Make sure they don't try to force your divorced or seperated parents together into a family portrait. It may be tempting to exclude the stepfather you're not fond of, but a wedding is not the time for pettiness. Instead, pose for a picture with your mother and stepfather, and another one with just your mom.

ASSIGNING A PHOTOGRAPHER'S HELPER

You should submit a list of photographic requests to both the photographer and helper so that your helper can guide the photographer to the right people.

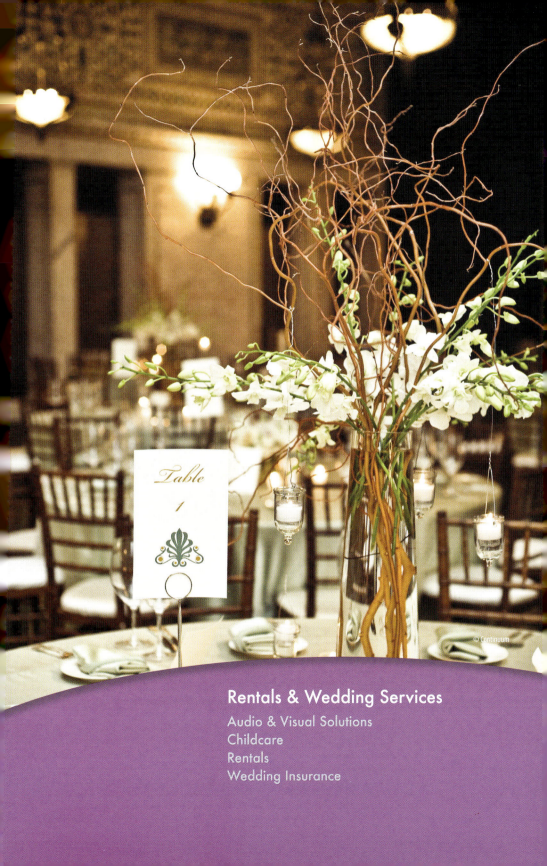

Rentals & Wedding Services

Audio & Visual Solutions
Childcare
Rentals
Wedding Insurance

304

Discrete • Efficient • High Quality Sound

About Ceremony Audio Service

Ceremony audio is more important than you might realize! Have you ever been to a wedding where you couldn't hear the ceremony? Now you know what we mean.

Your vows to each other are the most important part of your wedding day. Don't let them go unnoticed!

Your guests will thank you.

Our compact yet powerful sound system delivers clear, comfortable sound to all of your guests while you recite your vows. Most guests won't even notice the equipment! But, they will notice that they are able to hear the words you say to each other!

Imperative for outdoor weddings – Such as the beach, a winery, a country club or your own private property! Also very important for high guest count weddings!

A must for any venue that does not have an in-house sound system.

A veteran of Portland's music industry – Mark Storch – offers you years of experience as a professional musician and sound manager.

Dedicated solely to providing audio for your ceremony, with no other duties on his agenda at your wedding!

"I always smile when I see Mark at an event because he is courteous, professional and I know that with his help I will be able to get the best audio possible for my clients."

– Eric and Heather Newland; Hybrid Moon Video Productions

Contact
Mark Storch

p. 503.520.9667

e. mstorch2@gmail.com

Price
Varies according to location & services desired. Call for details.

Quick Facts
- Tech on duty the entire time
- Additional microphones available for readers, singers, & ceremony musicians
- We can work with your videographer to provide an audio feed for clear, flawless ceremony sound on your finished video
- Wind Guard, if needed
- Set-up & tear-down included
- Keepsake recording of ceremony available
- Sound system also available for cocktail hour & reception needs
- Play your iPod with your favorite music through our system at your reception.

creative childcare solutions
Professional on-site childcare at your event or hotel

Professional On-site Childcare at Your Event or Hotel

p. 503.518.2274
c. 503.819.5554
e. michelle@munchkincare.com
www.munchkincare.com

About Creative Childcare Solutions

Our company provides professional on-site childcare for events and for hotel guests. We are the only company in the state of Oregon that provides the services we do with commercial liability insurance. We are not a nanny agency or babysitting service but a group of professional women who work with children in places like schools, daycare centers, preschools and as social workers. The types of events we have worked at include, but are not limited to, conferences, meetings, holiday parties, wedding ceremonies and receptions, large and small corporate events and for individual families staying in local hotels.

The Venues

We have worked in all the finer hotels in downtown Portland, as well as hotels outside the city limits: Skamania Lodge, Crowne Plaza, McMenamin's, Columbia Gorge Hotel, Timberline Lodge, Resort at the Mountain, Oregon Zoo, and many more. Our clients include 100's of brides and grooms, Nike, Intel, Tektronix, TAPS, Edward Jones, Lewis & Clark Law School, OHSU, Department of Human Services Clackamas County, and many, many more. Check our website for a more complete listing of venues and clients.

Contact
Michelle Davenport

Price
Based on group's specific needs, call for quote

Quick Facts
- On-site childcare provided for your wedding & reception
- Hotel Guest childcare provided for individual families
- Professional, CPR/First Aid trained, criminal background checked caregivers
- Commercial liability insurance
- We bring all the necessary supplies to care for the children

305

LENDING A HAND

We have been asked to provide childcare services for the children under 5 years old attending a very special event in Washington, D.C. every Memorial Day weekend. This group provides support for families who have lost a family member while training for or in a war.

15266 SW 107th Terrace
Tigard, Oregon 97224
p. 503.515.7113
f. 503.684.0503
e. april.averys@verizon.net
www.averyschaircovers.com

Portland's Premier Chair Cover Company

Avery's takes pride in changing ordinary rooms into extraordinary memories. We specialize in Chair Covers that will truly transform any space. We have a variety of sizes to ensure a proper fit to each and every chair. Chair covers and sashes come in a variety of colors to personalize each chair with its own unique style. Avery's is committed to having the best prices in town and upholding exceptional quality.

306

Services

- We deliver directly to your facility.
- Setup is available upon request.
- Avery's has a large selection of colors to personalize your event.
- Consultation with designer to choose the perfect color and style to fit your needs.
- Avery's is a local company which means you can increase your chair count days before your wedding!

Contact
April Carter

Price
Varies; depending on style chosen

Extra Touches
- Oregon based business and all inventory is in stock.
- Visit Avery's showroom to help you choose the perfect look for your event.
- We have more than 60 colors to choose from.
- Different sized chair covers to fit every need.
- Best pricing in town, we can work with any budget!
- Aisle runners, table runners, napkins & tablecloths also available in a variety of colors & styles to accent your chair covers.

WE WELCOME YOU

Please visit our gallery at
www.averyschaircovers.com

Bravo! Member Since 2004

© Nataliya Sotin Photography

15515 SE For More Court
Clackamas, Oregon 97015
p. 503.656.9587
f. 503.656.4170
e. barclayevents@aol.com
www.barclayeventrental.com

About Barclay Event Rentals

Your wedding is one of the most important days of your life and Barclay Event Rentals understands this. We are a family owned and operated business, that prides ourselves on quality inventory and outstanding service. We are dedicated to making your special day exactly that – "special!"

Tables

- 36", 48", 60" and 72" rounds tables
- 4', 5', 6' and 8' banquet tables
- Bistro, umbrella and Serpentine tables

Chairs

- White and black wooden folding chairs with padded seats
- Samsonite folding chairs
- Chiavari chairs
- Stacking banquet chairs

Linens

- Countless colors, sizes and styles to choose from
- Chair covers, skirting, table toppers, aisle runners and napkins

China, Glassware, Flatware and Catering Equipment

- Choose from variety of different china patterns and styles
- Large selection of glassware sizes and styles
- Chafers, Cambro, beverage service, silver, portable bars, concessions and more
- Plate covers, chargers and decorations

Contact

Linda Barclay or
Robyn McManus

Price

Please call or visit our website for more details

Decorations

- Centerpieces, arbors and columns
- Garlands, silk flowers and trees
- Pipe and drape of many colors and styles
- Theme and holiday parties

Outdoor Equipment

- Tents
- Heaters
- Lighting
- Liners

307

EVENT FURNISHINGS

308

A Nationwide Rental Furniture Resource for the Event Industry

p. 888.CORT.YES (267.8937)

e. dawn.turner@cort.com

www.CORTevents.com

A Fresh Perspective

Remember the first time you toured your favorite event venue? How inspired your were by the new space and the fresh perspective it gave you toward event and meeting planning? Gain a fresh perspective every time with CORT Event Furnishing's visionary product line – quality products that deliver style every time.

Let CORT help you ensure a memorable impact with the right rental furnishings. You can create a mood and personality within an event space that echoes your style and fosters a sense of inspired awe. CORT can help you enhance your image while reinforcing your branding and marketing strategy. Making sure your vision gets through loud and clear – giving your audience a fresh perspective after every event and meeting!

About CORT Event Furnishings

CORT's contemporary product collections provide flexible design options that spark creativity and rouse the imagination. Visit www.CORTevents.com to view our photo gallery and explore our catalog to see the entire CORT Event Furnishings collection. All CORT Event Furnishings products are available for CAD download through the online catalog, or contact a CORT Solutions Expert who will create customized CAD drawings to bring your designs to life.

CORT Event Furnishings is a nationwide provider of high quality design-oriented rental furniture. Through our trusted solutions experts, we provides 24/7 service to answer the needs of event coordinators, meeting planners, and designers to help create events, meetings, and gala soirees. Get CORT and gain a fresh perspective.

Contact
Dawn Turner

Price
Please call for quote

Types of Events
- Sporting Events
- Movie Sets
- Exhibit or Display Houses
- Hotels
- Universities
- Weddings
- Parties
- Law Firms & Corporate Offices
- Conference Centers
- Convention Centers
- Special Event Facilities
- Corporate Meetings

AWARD WINNING

Event Solutions Spotlight Awards honored CORT with the Rental Company of the Year Award for 2007.

About Honey Bucket

Honey Bucket is the most experienced provider of portable sanitation services to Special Events in the Pacific Northwest. From the largest event with hundreds of units & on-site attendants, to a single unit for a wedding or company picnic, Honey Bucket is the right choice.

We take pride in our professional approach to Special Events. Our Honey Bucket name is "on the line" at each event & we expect attendees to have a pleasant experience when they use our units.

The "Event Planning Guide" on our website will help you determine the proper number of units, based on attendance, the length of the event & sanitary guidelines.

Honey Bucket continually adds new equipment to our extensive inventory & our units offer comfort, excellent design and appearance, & a variety of options. We only use our newest equipment for events.

You can go online to get a quote or information on products, event experience, & upcoming events. Or, You can call our Special Event experts who will be happy to help you with your specific needs.

Experience the CLEAR difference...

Bravo! Member Since 2006

Contact
Terry Nelson

1685 McGilchrist Street SE
Salem, Oregon 97301

p. 800.966.2371

www.honeybucket.com

Price
Please call or visit us online for more information

Mention Bravo! for a 5% discount at time of your order

Services
- Experienced provider of portable sanitation services for events in the Pacific Northwest
- On-site attendants available
- Committed to providing the best planning, assistance, equipment, services & value

VISIT US ONLINE

You can go online to get a quote or information on products, event experience, upcoming events, Honey Bucket "fun stuff" and much, much more at www.honeybucket.com

309

Interstate *Special Events*
"Portland's Premier Event Rentals"

1518 NE Lombard Place
Portland, Oregon 97211
p. 503.285.6685
e. becky@isevents.com
www.isevents.com

The History of Interstate Special Events

Joseph A. Dennis founded Interstate Rentals, Inc. in 1953. Initially, the first rental store was a converted ice-cream parlor consisting of a small 1000 square foot building. As the business experienced growth and success, other adjoining properties were purchased and new facilities were built. Between 1953 and 1983 the business mainly consisted of renting general equipment to homeowners and contractors.

In 1983 the Special Events division was established. Throughout the following years inventory has been expanded extensively. Professional expertise and an array of experience in the industry have also been acquired. In 1993 a canopy company was purchased allowing the Special Events division the capability of supplying canopies and tents for various events. In 1996 Special Events took over the current 22,000 square foot facility with one of the Northwest's largest inventories in canopies, flooring and other Special Event inventory.

As the Special Event division accelerated, the scope of the business has also expanded. Interstate Special Events has a friendly and professional staff with a broad proven background of expertise. The Special Events division now has the capability of handling the details for all varieties of social gatherings, supplying quality rental equipment and accessories for most any event from corporate gatherings to elaborate festive occasions. Our experience in many of the following types of occasions ensures our customer's

Contact
Becky Warrick

Price
Competitive prices

Quick Facts
- Excellent customer service
- Established business since 1953
- Quality equipment

WHAT'S NEW

Steamless wine glasses
Sofa's and ottomans
Natural wood chairs

Bravo! Member Since 1992

PARADYM EVENTS
EVENTS WITHOUT PRECEDENCE

Paradym Events

A full-service event production company specializing in creating unique and highly personalized events. We can handle all of your event needs, from themed décor, floral, specialty linens, A/V and lighting. From design and management, logistics to execution, we can handle all your companies' event needs.

Design: Linens and flowers, metal and paper, glass and wood: all mediums are utilized to create your unique event environment. Just as you are one of a kind, so should your wedding be.

Price Range: No matter the budget, we work to ensure that you remain on target while providing the largest impact possible. There are no surprises at the end of an event, just a clearly defined cost for every aspect of the production.

Location: We have traveled everywhere, from Hawaii to the Mediterranean and back. We will accommodate your every need while providing you the comfort that every detail of your event has been taken care by our knowledgeable staff. You no longer have to work with a company from out of town and hope they can execute the event to your standards. Paradym Events will take the guess work out of the equation while adding the peace of mind and flexibility of a local and dedicated staff.

Specializing: In the details, no matter how small, we have it covered so you don't have to. We create custom events to highlight you and your company. We can handle all your event needs from, design and management, communications to the execution and logistics.

Contact
Mary Bennett

4060 SW Macadam Avenue
Portland, Oregon 97239

p. 503.219.9290
f. 503.525.0675

e. info@paradymevents.com

www.paradymevents.com

Price
Call for quote

Capacity
10 people to 10,000, we help you plan and fulfill all your event needs.

Expectations
Meeting your expectations is not good enough; Paradym Events strives to exceed them in every detail.

Your Event
Give us a call and let us show you the possibilities of your next event.

EXPERIENCE

Putting 50 years of design production experience to work for you, any theme, any event, any time, any place you will know you have made the best choice.

Look for us on Facebook!

See page 170 under Wedding Concept & Design

311

Bravo! Member Since 1998

Peter Corvallis Productions

SINCE 1958

2204 North Clark Avenue
Portland, Oregon 97227
p. 503.222.1664
f. 503.222.1047
e. athena@petercorvallis.com
www.petercorvallis.com

312

About Peter Corvallis Productions, Inc.

Distinguished for our exceptional service and final results, Peter Corvallis Productions has provided quality tradition and experience in the event industry since 1958.

Our event specialists will help determine your wedding needs to create a unique style that will reflect your personality by applying our years of knowledge and expertise.

Wedding & Event Rental Inventory

We thrive to fulfill our customer's needs and as a full service event rental company we offer innovative and traditional products.

Our 100,000 square foot warehouse is filled with thousands of themed décor items plus we have an extensive wedding selection to choose from. In addition, we offer Lighting & Sound services to complete your event.

Contact
Athena

Price
Varies on size of event, call for quote

Services
- Tent & canopy rentals
- Party rentals
- Theme decorations & props
- Audio visual rentals & services
- Sound & lighting
- Trade show decorating & rentals
- Event planning services
- We deliver & setup

PROVIDES MORE THAN JUST QUALITY PRODUCTS

We not only have rental equipment, we also have many services to make your function run smoothly so you can enjoy your event along with your guests. Having an event will never be easier.

See page 171 under Wedding Concept & Design

ROYCE'S PROP SHOP

5406 North Albina Avenue
Portland, Oregon 97217

p. 503.283.8828
f. 503.283.3651

e. info@propshop.com

www.propshop.com

"Your visions are innovative and never cease to amaze..."

– Mary Lou Burton; President Bravo! Publications & Trade Shows

Event industry veteran Royce Mason and his dedicated team of professionals at the Prop Shop pride themselves on award-winning event design, décor, production and, most importantly, impeccable customer service.

Royce's Prop Shop is equipped with unparalleled resources and can produce an extensive range of formal to informal rehearsal dinners, wedding ceremonies and receptions at any venue – from elegant ballrooms to tented mountaintops!

Memberships include ABC, ACEP, ISES, MPI, and **Green Certified Member** of Travel Portland.

Contact
Royce Mason, CMP

Price
Customized to fit your budget

Quick Facts
- Award-winning event design
- Unique tabletop & floral
- Custom linens & chair covers
- Satin/chiffon swag & drape
- Complete production services: lighting, backdrops & fabrication
- Catering, rentals & entertainment assistance

313

AWARDS
- 2006 – 2007
  Meeting Professionals Int'l
  Supplier of the Year Award
- 2004
  Event Solutions Magazine
  Spotlight Award
  Designer of the Year
- 2003
  Oregon Restaurant Assoc.
  Award of Gratitude &
  Appreciation

See page 172 under
Wedding Concept & Design

Bravo! Member Since 1996

Visit BravoWedding.com for more information on rentals & other wedding services

Uniquely Yours
Chair Covers
Table Styling Linens

p. 360.624.0781
e. Lou@uniquely-yours.biz
www.uniquely-yours.biz

About Uniquely Yours

Our chair covers and styling linens cater to the individual style of each wedding. We pay close attention to every design detail so we can continue to reflect your personal style. Whether it is traditional, contemporary, vintage, garden party theme, we can help provide the linens and services to make your wedding a success!

The Reception

Uniquely Yours believes that your reception should be as elegant as your wedding and the bride's table should be the focus of the reception. We specialize in the unique requests and cater to the individual style of each bride, so that your wedding and reception is Uniquely Yours. Therefore, we pay close attention to every design detail so we can continue to reflect your personal style.

Personal Style

We specialize in chair covers. Chair covers make a stunning appearance and bring elegance to a bridal tea, engagement party, wedding brunch or any special event. Most appreciated about our chair covers is their ability to transform any conference chair to enhance your room decor. We have sashes and chair overlays in a large selection of fabrics and colors. We can accommodate special requests.

Table Linens

Uniquely Yours has an expansive selection of table styling linens to choose from, offering specialty table linens, overlays and runners.

Featured on Weddings Portland Style.

Contact
Louena Denny

Price
Depends on design chosen and guest count

Service
We at Uniquely Yours believe that our exceptional service towards the success of your wedding is our goal

Quick Facts
- Careful focus on attention to details so we can continue to reflect your personal style
- We are locally owned, so we're able to provide personal service for last minute guests
- We offer delivery & setup of rental itemsl
- We are continually adding new fabrics & designs to our linen selections

NEW ITEMS

Introducing Uniquely Yours, Too! Something old, something new...let us transform and personalize a legacy keepsake from generations past to you for your wedding day!

Bravo! Member Since 2001

314

starts with a promise...

503.294.0412   1400 NW 15th Avenue, Portland, OR 97209   www.WCEP.com

About West Coast Event Productions

It starts with a promise...a promise to make your wedding unforgettable!

At West Coast Event Productions, we believe a wedding should be the extraordinary and flawless occasion you've always imagined. For 30 years, our wedding specialists have been helping people say "I do" with premier consulting, design and rental services. Our 120,000 square foot warehouse houses the latest trends in wedding products, from hand-blown stemware, to beaded chandeliers, to white chiffon canopies.

Whether you require custom planning and design, or the guarantee of quality rental items, we work with you every step of the way to create an exquisitely romantic celebration. Contact one of our specialists today to start planning the wedding of your dreams!

Photos: (Top) Remembrance Photography
(Bottom, L – R) Stickeen Photography, Remembrance Photography.

Bravo! Member Since 1996

Contact
Pat Smith

e. pat@wcep.com

Quick Facts
- Full service wedding production: consulting, design & rentals

- Rentals include: specialty linens, centerpieces, elegant china & stemware, ballroom chairs & tables, heavenly tents & canopies, magical dance floors, enchanting lighting & much more

- Honored with Oregon Bride Magazine's "Best Rentals Award"

- Member of Association of Bridal Consultants

- Want to use your imagination? Our designers can customize any item to achieve your vision.

315

BEHIND THE SCENES: AN EVENT BLOG

Be sure to visit our brand new event blog online at www.wcep.com... a forum full of inspiration, ideas and most importantly, events!

See page 173 under Wedding Concept & Design

VIVE EVENTS
LINEN AND CHAIR COVER RENTALS

p. 503.933.8984
p. 503.771.7916
f. 503.772.1447
e. vive.events@hotmail.com
www.viveevents.net

316

Vive Events – Professionalism is Our Motto

Vive Events easily accommodates any size and style of wedding, from a casual gathering to an elegant celebration.

We have an extensive selection of Satins, Organzas, Silk, Chiffons, Taffetas, Cottons, Special Design and Embroidered materials. We can provide you with the finest products. The materials and services we provide are professional, and there are not order limits. All items are available in a variety of styles, colors, sizes, and prices.

Contact
Saturnino O.

Price
Price is based on individual client needs. Email us for a quote.

Quick Facts
- We offer delivery, and setup is available as well.
- We offer linens, chair covers, sashes, table runners, skirts, box table cloths in different styles.
- We have a variety of fabrics such as bridal satin, charmuese, poly satin, satin jacquard, solid taffeta, swirl organza, mirror organza, pintuck and polypoplin.

WHAT'S NEW

Visit us at ViveEvents.net for more details. We want your dream to come true!

© Wickens Photography

g GALES CREEK
INSURANCE SERVICES

800 NW Sixth Avenue, Suite 335
Portland, Oregon 97209
p. 503.227.0491 ext. 234
f. 503.227.0927
e. events@galescreek.com
www.galescreek.com
www.eventinsuranenow.com

Wedding Liability Insurance

Gales Creek Insurance Services has been offering speciality insurance for a variety of entertainment risks for more than 25 years. Our Wedding Liability Insurance policy is priced at a low $185, and this policy automatically includes protection for the insured when serving (hosting) alcohol. Unique features to this low priced policy are that it is offered with NO DEDUCTIBLE, and volunteers are also protected under the policy as Insureds.

Wedding liability insurance is designed to protect you, on this most important of days, against unforeseen incidents such as injury to an attendee due to a trip hazard or alcohol related accidents, such as an intoxicated driver leaving the reception site. This is the coverage most often required by rental facilities and metropolitan parks.

Our product is issued in the form of a Commercial General Liability policy with limits of $1 million per occurrence and a $2 million aggregate. The coverage limit for damage to rented premises is $250,000. This program typically meets or exceeds a rental hall or facility's requirement for special event insurance. The program rate also includes the naming of the location as Additional Insured.

Our wedding liability insurance can be quoted instantly online by visiting www.galescreek.com. Here, buyers can select Special Event Insurance, log in, and receive a full detailed quotation in minutes. If interested, you can instantly purchase the coverage and receive your Certificate of Insurance naming the facility as Additional Insured. A buyer may also choose to save their quotation and return to the site at a later time. If you choose to purchase the policy, there is no waiting for days or even hours to receive your certificate; it's instantly available for you to print, download or email.

Contact
Brigitt Whitescarver

Price
Premiums start at $185

Highlights
- No policy deductible
- $1 million dollars Commercial General Liability Limits
- Host Liquor Liability included at no cost
- Facility is named as an Additional Insured
- Volunteers are included as insureds
- Instant quoting online
- Instant online purchase
- Instant issuance of Certificate (proof) of Insurance

317

WEDDING INSURANCE

Quote and purchase online at www.galescreek.com
– click –
Wedding Liability Insurance

Bravo! Member Since 2006

Helpful Hint

Decoration and Rental Needs

Rental stores carry almost everything, from candelabras to coffee makers. They feature specialty wedding items for your ceremony and reception. You'll find such things as serviceware, portable bars, arches, tents, chairs, tables and all the tableware, dishes, glassware, flatware, and much more. Many shops also carry disposable paper products, decorations and a selection of bridal accessories.

© Black Swan

© Kate Kelly

VISIT A RENTAL SHOP WHILE PLANNING

It's smart to visit a showroom for ideas and to see the types and styles of merchandise and equipment in stock. Brochures describe all the different items available for rent: style, colors, sizes and prices. Rental shops are also a terrific place to obtain decorating ideas. Meet with one of the shop's consultants and go through your wedding plans step-by-step.

DECIDE ON FORMALITY & BUDGET

Keep in mind the colors and decor of the site. Pick linens or paper products and tableware that will complement the room.

DEPOSITS, DELIVERY & SETUP

Reserve your items as far in advance as possible, especially during the summer months when outdoor weddings are popular. A deposit will secure the order for your date. There is a charge on most items for delivery, setup and pickup.

TENT RENTAL

A tent often serves as an ideal back up location for an outdoor event, in case of unsuitable weather conditions. Many tents feature transparent vinyl siding that can be raised and lowered as needed. A tent supplier can recommend sources for any portable heating or air conditioning that you might need.

CHOOSING A TENT SITE

When arranging tents with a single transparent vinyl side, consider the position of the sun during your event; if the clear portion faces due west through an evening reception, the sunset may be blinding.

RETURNING ITEMS

If you don't arrange delivery and pickup services with the rental company, you will want to put someone in charge of picking up and returning the rented items for you.

© English Classic Limos

Transportation & Valet

ENGLISH CLASSIC LIMOUSINES

www.englishclassiclimos.com

320

Your Every Wish is Our Command.

Let Us Spoil You!

Featuring our:

1957 Bentley S1

1959 Bentley

1961 Bentley S2

1967 Rolls Royce Silver Shadow LWB

1947 Rolls Royce Silver Wraith

Including a Full Fleet of New Stretch Limousines

ONE HOUR SERVICE AVAILABLE

English Classic Limousines

PORTLAND'S ONLY WEDDING SPECIALIST!

Serving Portland since 1984.

Contact

4804 SE 69th Avenue
Portland, Oregon 97206

p. 503.736.1182
f. 503.736.0907

www.englishclassiclimos.com

Services

- Gift certificates available
- Customized wedding packages
- Hotel & airport service
- Memorable photo opportunities
- Bachelor & bachelorette parties

PLEASE VISIT OUR WEBSITE TO LEARN MORE.

www.englishclassiclimos.com

Bravo! Member Since 2000

LUCKY
LIMOUSINE & TOWNCAR SERVICE, LLC
503-254-0010

11824 NE Ainsworth Circle
Suite B
Portland, Oregon 97220
p. 503.254.0010
e. limo@besolucky.com
www.besolucky.com

Lucky Limo Fleet Includes

- 2006 14-passenger Stretch H2 Hummer
- New Lincoln Towncars
- Six, eight and 12 passenger stretch Lincoln Limousines
- 14, 16, 22 and 24 passenger Luxury Lounge Cruisers – fully equipped with a 42" LCD TV, Karaoke machine, XM radio, DVD player, CD exchanger, multiple bar areas.
- 19, 26 and 31 passenger Motorcoaches – for tours and shuttling. Equipped with bathroom, TVs and DVD player.
- Six passenger Executive Vans – plenty of cargo room

The entire fleet is beautifully appointed, detailed daily, well-maintained, smoke-free and fully insured.

Please view our website for viewing the entire fleet and services offered!

Contact
Customer Service

Price
Rentals starting at $70/hr

Services

- Experienced, professionally trained & attired chauffeurs
- 24-hour management staffing for all phone inquiries, experienced to help you design & coordinate your special event according to your needs
- One-way, hourly or day rates available

321

OUR GOAL

Our goal is to consistently exceed your highest expectation of what luxury transportation should be, at affordable rates, so everyone can...

...BE SO LUCKY!

Martin's Gorge Tours
Shuttles – Charters – Tours

About Martin's Gorge Tours

My shuttle and charter service will deliver your family and friends safely and comfortably to any venue that you choose. I take great pride in helping to make your event enjoyable and memorable for you, and your guests. Please call me at your earliest convenience to reserve your date, and allow me to accommodate your preferences.

I look forward to serving you.

Martin. 503.349.132.

Contact

Martin Hecht

PO Box 18177
Portland, Oregon 97218

p. 503.349.1323

e. Martin@MartinsGorgeTours.com

www.MartinsGorgeTours.com

Price range for shuttle and charter service

7 passenger vehicle at $69/hour, or 20 passenger coach at only $99/hour

WHAT'S NEW

Your family & friends can take advantage of my special Bravo! rate program to save 10% at the time of your booking.

Special rates are available for groups of 10 (or more), based on availability.

To reserve your date, call Martin at 877.290.TOUR (8687).

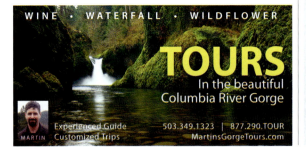

WINE • WATERFALL • WILDFLOWER
TOURS
In the beautiful
Columbia River Gorge
MARTIN
Experienced Guide
Customized Trips
503.349.1323 | 877.290.TOUR
MartinsGorgeTours.com

Parke Avenue Limousine

p. 503.750.3891

www.parkeavenuelimousine.com

About Parke Avenue Limousine

When intimate elegance and luxury are required, Parke Avenue Limousine is your choice.

We offer first class service, attention to detail and competitive pricing. Let us escort you in our stately, Rolls Royce Silver Cloud or one of our contemporary stretch limousines.

Our goal is to make your wedding a very special day with lasting memories.

Call today 503.750.3891 and make an appointment to see our vintage limousines or see them on our web site at:

parkeavenuelimousine.com
Specializing in Vintage Rolls Royce

Contact
Gary Parke

Price
Please call for more information

Choice of Luxury Automobiles
- 1958 Rolls Royce Silver Cloud, sliding rag top edition
- Eight passenger Tuxedo stretch Lincoln
- Nine passenger executive black stretch Lincoln

Services
- Your one stop complete wedding transportation specialists
- Rare classic car service
- Bachelor & Bachelorette parties
- Pre wedding day customized wine tours
- 50% discount for all past clients first anniversary
- Complimentary red carpet

YOUR FIRST CLASS VINTAGE LIMOUSINE SERVICE

Most major credit cards accepted.

323

Bravo! Member Since 2001

Sea to Summit Tours & Adventures

Sea to Summit Tours & Adventures is based out of Portland, Oregon. Sea to Summit specializes in transportation services and outdoor activities for weddings, B-days, bachelor and bachelorette parties.

We offer many activities including white water rafting trips, Oregon wine tours, Portland brewery tours, surfing lessons, sightseeing tours, personalized tours and more. In the winter season, Sea to Summit is Portland's Premier 4x4 Ski & Mountain Shuttle Service, available 7 days a week to all Mt. Hood ski areas.

Sea to Summit's 4x4 vehicles are highly equipped and our guides are knowledgeable and experienced. No matter what weather conditions prevail, Sea to Summit will get your wedding party to the destination of choice, without any worries!

Created, owned and operated by native Portland, Oregonians, est 2001

Simplify...make your reservation with Sea to Summit!

503.286.9333
www.seatosummit.net

Contact
Joshua Blaize

Portland, Oregon

p. 503.286.9333

e. seatosummit@qwest.net

www.seatosummit.net

Specializing In:
- Winery Tours
- Brewery Tours
- White Water Rafting Trips
- Sightseeing Tours
- Personalized Tours
- Ski Shuttles

Clients Include:
- Nordstrom
- Nike
- Adidas
- J.C. Penney
- REI
- Timberline Lodge
- Mt. Hood Meadows
- Intel, etc...

See page 45 under Bachelorette Parties

p. 800.778.6214
p. 503.244.4653
f. 503.244.6558
e. info@premierewinetours.com
www.premierewinetours.com

About Premiere Transportation & Tours

Premiere is a local company with several vehicles that can handle our transportation needs for wedding transportation, guest entertainment, bachelor & bachelorette parties, wine tours, corporate shuttles, shuttle service for conventions, airport drop-offs, sporting events, casino trips, birthdays, and more. We offer one-way transportation, in addition to hourly or day rates.

Special Bravo! discount: book Premiere for your wedding transportation and receive 20% off a Bachelorette Party Wine Tour

Please visit our website to view our fleet and view all of the services offered.

Bravo! Member Since 1995

Contact
Premiere Transportation

Price
Charges vary according to circumstances and time duration.

Services
- Wedding transportation.
- Guest entertainment (wine tour, casino parties).
- Bachelorette/Bachelor parties.

325

p. 800.778.6214
p. 503.244.7758
f. 503.244.6558
e. info@premierevalet.com
www.premierevalet.com

Have You Thought About Parking?

Let us do the thinking for you! When planning for your next big event, selecting the right parking service will add a great first impression, as well as smooth, convenient parking accommodations.

Consider the unparalleled level of personalized service and professionalism that Premiere Valet Service has been providing Portland residents and restaurants for more than sixteen years.

With our experience and knowledge, we have the ability to solve any parking problem. All valets are trained, screened and field tested to ensure that you will receive only the finest service available.

Contact
Private Event Coordinator

Price
Charges vary according to parking circumstances and time duration

Services
- Parking consulting services
- Lot attendants
- Light security
- Coat check

Bravo! Member Since 1995

Visit BravoWedding.com for more information on transportation & valet services

"World Class Transportation and Service"

VIP PDX can accommodate individuals, intimate groups, or events of up to 30 guests in luxury & style. For business or pleasure, VIP PDX offers first class fun in our executive party buses or choose our 'go anywhere' Land Rover or 7-series BMW for utmost in sophistication. Catering is available & special requests are always welcome. Our VIP staff is on site the duration of your event to ensure all your guest's needs are met. Our passion is customer service & exceeding your expectations.

Contact our friendly staff to customize your special event today & be sure to check out our website for further details!

VIP Coach Features

- Lounge Seating for 15 – 30
- 3 flat screen TV's & DVD/CD player
- iPod compatible sound system
- Spacious modern bathroom
- 2 beverages stations
- Professional driver
- VIP Host

Contact

Jennifer Berry

16869 SW 65th Avenue #238
Lake Oswego, Oregon 97035

p. 503.348.3233
f. 503.747.7202

e. info@vippdx.com
e. jennifer@vippdx.com

www.vippdx.com

Price

- Executive Cars
  $80 per hour
- Mini V starting at
  $130 per hour
- VIP Coach starting
  at $200 per hour
- Ask about
  seasonal specials

Ideal Transportation for:

- Corporate Events
- Wine Tours
- Sporting Events
- Golf Trips
- Brew Tours
- Ski/Snowboard Trips
- Holiday Parties

ABOUT VIP PDX

Try our new MINI V for up to 13 guests!
We are a locally owned and operated family business.

Bravo! Member Since 2007

Helpful Hint

Choosing Your Transportation

Everyone enjoys the experience of riding in a luxury limousine at least once in a lifetime. It can be the final touch that makes your wedding day complete, so be sure to include some kind of transportation category in your budget.

You may want to include transportation for your guests to and from the wedding. If you have a lot of out of town guests and your wedding location is hard to get to, you may want to rent a luxury bus for your guests. Renting guest transportation is also nice so

businesses will display or readily have available important information like a business license and liability insurance certificates. If you have any concerns or questions about the service, ask for references and check them out.

BE SURE TO GET WHAT YOU PAID FOR

Make sure the limousine will be cleaned and presentable when it arrives on your wedding day. Read the contract carefully before paying a deposit. Make sure the date, times, locations (addresses), and the

© Powers

327

that they can enjoy the wedding and don't have to worry about having to drive back to their hotel. This may be something else you want to include in your wedding budget.

DON'T RESERVE A LIMOUSINE OVER THE PHONE OR INTERNET

Go to the limousine service and personally inspect the vehicle you are considering renting. Be sure you're dealing with an established, reputable company. These

specific limousine you want are spelled out in writing on your contract. Remember that gratuities are usually additional. If the vehicle is not presentable and the chauffeur isn't professional, you are under no obligation to pay a tip.

Notes

© AJs Studio

Videography

Video Booth
Videographers

love
COMMITMENT
passion

Your story...

our promise to help you relive it forever.

Book Portland Video Booth For Your Next Event

Our closed-concept booths offer your guests an accessible, relaxed forum to share their greetings or messages with you.

The booths are simple to use for people of all ages. Simply push the start button and begin to record your message. The on screen display shows you that you are recording. Once the recording is complete, the booth will reset itself for your next guest.

$600 books the booth for four hours comes with a compilation DVD. Web hosting options are available.

Call Hybrid Moon at 503.295.1991 for more information.

http://portlandvideobooth.com/

Portland Video Booth is perfect for ALL occasions! Weddings, Bar/Bat Mitzvahs, Reunions, Parties, Dances and more! You name the event, your guests will love using our booths!

Contact

Eric Newland

1321 NW 17th Avenue
Portland, Oregon 97209

p. 503.295.1991
e. eric@hybridmoon.com
www.hybridmoon.com

Price

Please call for quote

Services

- Standard &
  high–definition options
- Customized DVD
  & menu creation
- Photomontage
  & sideshow creation

331

BRIDAL TIP

Do your homework! Meet the video artisan in person, and insist on watching several samples of finished product. A great video incorporates experience, talent, creativity and consistency.

MEMBERSHIP

About Hybrid Moon

At Hybrid Moon Video Productions, our work speaks for itself, and so do our brides. Here's what a few of them had to say when asked what advice they have for brides when it comes to deciding whether or not to hire a professional, as well as selecting a videographer…

"Hybrid Moon Video Productions is the best in the city. They are nice, reasonable and courteous."

– Nicki & Trever

"Our wedding day was a once–in–a–lifetime event; Hybrid Moon captured moments that we missed."

– Fred & Jennifer

"Hybrid Moon will give you not only your money's worth, but memories to last you a lifetime!"

– Scott & Erica

"Hybrid Moon was able to capture moments that the photographer did not, without being obtrusive. We hardly noticed them all night."

– Dan & Joan

"You have given the greatest gift. The quality and artistry of your work was better than any other videographers work we have seen."

– Will & Angela

Congratulations!

You're in love! You're having a wedding! Now, all you need is the perfect wedding video. Welcome to Hybrid Moon. No one else needs to tell you that your wedding is a big deal. You know…and so do we. That's why we view each wedding as a unique project – customized to fit your day, your needs, and most of all, your style. You've got a lot to look forward to, and with our skill and expertise – there's going to be a lot more to look back on too… with your new favorite movie!

Contact
Eric Newland
1321 NW 17th Avenue
Portland, Oregon 97209
p. 503.295.1991
e. eric@hybridmoon.com
www.hybridmoon.com

Price
Please call for quote

Services
- Standard & high–definition options
- Customized DVD & menu creation
- Photomontage & sideshow creation

BRIDAL TIP

Do your homework! Meet the video artisan in person, and insist on watching several samples of finished product. A great video incorporates experience, talent, creativity and consistency.

MEMBERSHIP

Bravo! Member Since 1996

332

Aden
Photography &
Video Productions
503 625-8900

PO Box 1501
Lake Oswego, Oregon 97035
p. 503.625.8900
e. keith@adenphoto.com
www.adenphoto.com

333

About Aden Photography and Video Productions

Packages or ala carte plans are designed to suit weddings of all sizes. Wedding packages from two hours to unlimited time, as needed. Brochures listing services and prices can be sent to you upon request. Call for an appointment to see samples of photography and video.

"Sensitive, Creative and Experienced Photography and Video"

It's your special wedding day, a day to be remembered for the rest of your life. Through the years, your memories will become even more special, as will your wedding photographs and video. Your choice of a photographer is an important one. Since 1968, Keith Aden has been specializing in wedding and commercial advertising photography, including video production. His years of experience and knowledge of the very special art of wedding photography and video makes him sensitive to your needs and requests. Keith is a photographer who actually cares about you and your wedding.

Someone Who Cares About You and Your Wedding

You are not just another customer to Keith. Bridal couples and their families appreciate both his sensitivity to their "wants and needs" and his professional and unobtrusive style.

Contact
Keith Aden

Price
Custom packages available to fit all budgets

Video Packages
- Basic to masterpiece wedding packages available

Video Production
- Only the finest in digital cameras & digital editing suites used in all packages

Digital or Film Photography
- Ala carte plans or packages using only the finest professional digital cameras or Hasselblad medium format film cameras; It's your choice

DVD Albums or Traditional Albums
- DVD photo slideshow albums, DVD videos, montage DVD's including video & photo slideshow as well as Traditional photo albums & video tapes

See page 290 under Photography

Bravo! Member Since 1990

Visit BravoWedding.com for more information on video booths and videographers

Ambient Sky specializes in Couture Wedding Films™ and our Signature Same Day Edit.

As winners of multiple international awards, we are Portland's premiere wedding cinematographers. Please spend some time on our web site and blog watching the numerous samples of our Couture Wedding Films™. To learn more, contact us for your personal consultation.

Testimonials:

"We never could have imagined beyond our wildest dreams how touching, beautiful and exciting you could have portrayed our wedding day. YOU GUYS ROCK!!! We cannot wait to see our Same Day Edit again. Everyone says it was the best wedding ever – due to the loving energy and YOUR AMAZING VIDEO. The two of you were so generous, gracious and sweet and our lives have become so enriched by coming into contact with you. From the bottom of our grateful hearts, THANK YOU!!!" – Sally & Matt

"You did an amazing job capturing all of the fun and memorable moments. Watching it last night made us want to do it all over again. We're so excited to show it to our parents and decided we're definitely going to have to watch it every anniversary. Thanks again!" – Danielle & Jeff

"Thank you from the bottom of our hearts for the amazing video you created for us. Heartfelt, beautiful, and classic! You captured all those moments and precious expressions that we were way too distracted to notice or appreciate on our very busy wedding day. Thank you so much for your attention to detail, perfectionism, and artistic approach. We have watched the video over and over, and will love and treasure it for years to come. You really were great to work with and that alone is a huge blessing when planning an event. By far, your service is the best we have seen. We are so grateful we chose you to capture our special day. We cannot sing your praises enough." – Susan & Kevin

- 2008 WEVA Creative Excellence Award winner.
- 2008 Telly Award winner.
- 2008 International DV Award winner, four awards.

Bravo! Member Since 2006

Contact
Scott Shama

p. 503.318.8314

e. info@AmbientSky.com

www.ambientsky.com

www.ambientsky.blogspot.com

Price
Please inquire for custom pricing

Quick Facts
- International Award Winning Cinematography
- Unobtrusive coverage
- High Definition and Blu-ray
- Multiple camera coverage
- Available for destinations Worldwide

THE SAME DAY EDIT
A stylized highlight film produced the day of your wedding and shown at your reception. Your guests will be blown away as they get a glimpse of all the days events just hours after they occurred.

Premium Video Services

It's Your Day!

Of all the days in your life, your wedding day will forever remain one of the most joyful and exciting. Bigler Productions is here to help you capture the memories you create so that you will always be able to relive that joy and excitement, year after year.

Bigler Productions specializes in high-quality wedding videography. We utilize the highest standards, striving for nothing but perfection. We offer you the flexibility of building your own video package or choosing from any of our competitively priced packages. With Bigler Productions you can rest assured your video will be enjoyed by all for decades to come.

Customer Testimonials

"I can't thank you enough for all of your efforts and expertise on our wedding day. Tyler and I couldn't be happier with our video. You were professional, fun and reverent of the most important event in our lives so far! It was our pleasure to meet you and spend our day in your company. Our sincerest thanks."

– Beth & Tyler (watch highlight online)

"We wanted to thank you for producing such a wonderful video that captures the memories of our wedding day. Your professionalism and artistic ability truly surpassed our expectations. You were very pleasant to work with and always responsive to our needs. We will be sure to recommend all of our friends and family to you. Thank you!"

– Todd and Chelsea (watch highlight online)

Contact
Dave Bigler

630 B. Avenue
Lake Oswego, Oregon 97034
(by appointment only)

p. 503.488.5896

e. dave@biglerproductions.com

www.biglerproductions.com

Price
Current prices online

Quick Facts
- Custom build for any budget
- Digital & high definition formats
- State-of-the-art HD editing
- Discreet & unobtrusive
- Free demo DVDs available

BIGLER PRODUCTIONS OFFERS BLU-RAY!

335

Bravo! Member Since 2007

Custom Wedding Videography

DreamCapture Media LLC produces wedding videos that exceed all expectations. We deliver an affordable, high quality journey through your special day that you can share, relive, and watch for a lifetime.

What our Clients say

"Out of all of the vendors that we used DreamCapture Media was by far the best. They did a phenomenal job, the video that they made turned out way better than we expected. They were very professional, and experienced. We have had people tell us that they spent twice as much using someone else and didn't receive near the quality as we did with DreamCapture Media."
– Jake & Amber

"I found DreamCapture easy to work with and very flexible. They were open to changes, showed up on time, made good suggestions and honestly, I never knew they were there. They worked quietly in the background and did not interfere with the wedding process in anyway. I highly recommend them."
– John (father of the bride)

"You're just so talented! I really enjoyed working with you! Thank you for helping make our special day!!"
– Jamie and Danielle

Contact

Serving Oregon and Washington

p. 360.608.9415 or
   360.921.9718

e. info@dreamcapturemedia.com

www.dreamcapturemedia.com

Price

Packages starting at $500

Custom packages available; please inquire

Services & Quick Facts

- No hourly time limits
- Unobtrusive
- Multiple cameras
- High quality audio
- Professional editing
- Cinematic highlights
- Online hosting
- Free demo DVDs

CUSTOMIZED

DreamCapture creates one of a kind customized DVD covers, menus, and labels. Our attention to detail enables us to achieve the most custom, creative, and high quality wedding videos.

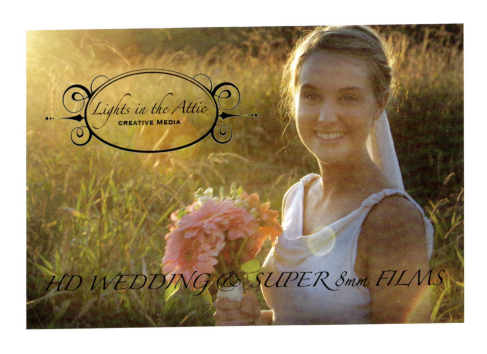

Wedding Films for the Discerning Bride

All weddings shot in HD at no extra cost to you
Super 8mm film available for the vintage bride
No travel fee throughout Oregon

*"You did such a fantastic job for us – truly above and beyond our expectations.
The production quality was first rate and you captured beautifully all the big moments
and the heartflet little ones too. This video is one of our most treasured keepsaks from
our wedding and we couldn't be happier with it. Thank you Jeff!"*
– Linda and Scott

Call for consultation 503.990.8669

LightsintheAttic@mac.com

www.LITAcreative.com

Visit BravoWedding.com for more information on video booths and videographers

Vintage Super 8 Film
HD Videography

"Nothing captured our day quite like our video! I felt like I was reliving it all over again. The editing, 8mm film sequences, music and sound quality are superior to anything I have seen!"

– The Kindsfaters

"Shields Films was great to work with! They do some really impressive stuff, especially with Super 8 film, which gives a really cool vintage effect."

– The Havens

"I would very strongly recommend to each prospective bride to budget money for a videographer; it felt like a splurge when I was planning the wedding, but is the one thing I am most happy I spent money on. (And Shields Films is the best as far as we are concerned!) Our video is a treasure – one our family (and future children!) will continue to enjoy for years."

– The Greens

shieldsfilms.com
503.516.8576

Bravo! Member Since 2003

© Miranda Celeste

A Team You Can Trust

Lets face it, planning a wedding is very demanding and requires much time and attention to make your day perfect. One concern you should be free of is the content and quality of your wedding video.

Our foremost goal is making sure you feel secure in knowing that we will capture your special day with the same care and consideration we would want if it were our wedding day.

Video Media places a high value on customer service and our priority is to work with you to produce something we are proud of and you are excited to show your friends and family.

Each wedding is different and requires awareness, experience and professionalism; we have that. Your wish, our next challenge.

Call us to set up a free consultation. We look forward to hearing from you soon.

Contact
Dan Pred

2580 NW Uphur
Portland, Oregon 97210

p. 503.228.4060

f. 503.228.0619

e. dan@videomediaportland.com

www.videoemediaevents.com

Pricing
Customized packages.
Please call for a consultation.

Services
- Blu-Ray
- Male/Female Team
- Multi-Camera Coverage
- "Our Story" Videos
- Photo Montage & Slideshow
- Customized Wedding Packages

339

© Miranda Celeste

WHAT'S NEW

Video Media is excited to now offer video wedding invitations. Send your guests a customized personal video invitation.

Helpful Hint

Choosing Your Videographer

WHY HIRE A PROFESSIONAL VIDEOGRAPHER?

Once their wedding is over, many brides say they regret not having hired a professional videographer. Your wedding day will be filled with thousands of emotional nuances, moments you'll savor forever, moments you'll undoubtedly forget. A professional has the skills and equipment to capture those moments that would otherwise be lost. Don't rely on a friend or family member to record your wedding day. While it might save you some money, it will also leave you with a video that's either too dark, too shaky, totally inaudible, or all of the above.

VIDEOGRAPHY HAS CHANGED

Gone are the days of big cameras, bright lights and long cables that would normally overpower a wedding. Rapid advances in video production technology have allowed videographers to become as discreet and unobtrusive as any photographer.

COSTS

Shop quality, then price. There's no reason to spend less money on a video that you won't be happy with. A well produced video takes many hours to piece together, therefore you should expect to pay at least as much for a good video as you would for a good photographer. If your budget is tight, eliminate love stories or photo montages. Top priority should be filming the day's essential events, including the nervous anticipation before the ceremony, the ceremony itself, and, of course, as much of your reception as possible.

FINDING THE RIGHT VIDEOGRAPHER

Much like photography, videography ranges far and wide in both quality and price. In general, the higher the price, the more polished your finished video will be. Start by requesting demo tapes or visiting the studios of candidates who make a good impression. Once you've narrowed the field, concentrate on those candidates you feel most comfortable with. Don't base your final decision on a slick demo video—ask to see full-length videos or check out their website from a variety of weddings. When you feel confident with a particular videographer's work, ask for references.

You'll want to make absolutely sure their presence will complement the atmosphere of your wedding day. More importantly, you'll want to be 100% certain your videographer will make your guests feel comfortable.

CLARIFY YOUR EXPECTATIONS

Be sure to discuss your ideal video with your videographer. Do you want something with a romantic edge or something slanted more toward the humorous side? Do you want a lot of black and white or do you want mostly color? Do you want a lot of guest interviews or would you prefer the videographer concentrate on other areas? Clearly, there are many options to consider. Your videographer should be flexible enough to accommodate your special requests and honest enough to tell you whether or not he'll be able to meet your expectations. A true professional should take time to collaborate with you beforehand so that he fully understands what elements you consider most important in telling your unique story.

PHOTO MONTAGES

The past few years have seen a growing trend toward projecting a photo montage or "love story" segment at either your rehearsal dinner or reception. Again, these options vary quite a bit in both price and quality. Be sure to investigate your options.

© Powers

Wedding Venues & Accommodations

Accommodations
Boats
Ceremony Sites
Destination Weddings
Reception & Wedding Sites
Rehearsal Dinner Locations
Wineries & Vineyards

stunning. romantic. unforgettable.

Abernethy Center

BALLROOM ◆ GARDENS

606 15th Street
Oregon City, Oregon 97045

503-722-9400
www.AbernethyCenter.com

1441 North McCellan
Portland, Oregon 97217

503.283.3224

www.QueenAnneVictorianMansion.com

About A Majestic Mountain Retreat

Serenity . . . This is your experience when you arrive at A Majestic Mountain Retreat – a handcrafted, three-story, luxury Log Home nestled in the forest of Mt. Hood, Oregon surrounded by towering trees, awe-inspiring mountains and a sea of blue skies. Every attention to detail has been made with your ultimate comfort and relaxation in mind.

This magical home is complete with pillow-top beds wrapped in 600 thread count linens, down comforters and Pendleton blankets. Melt into the deep-cushioned leather sofas and custom draperies surrounding you as you entertain your friends and family in the granite kitchen with top-of-the-line appliances and colorful china. The walls are graced with scenic photographs of the natural magic that is Oregon. The stairs are hand-carved from trees from the land and the second-story powder room's sink basin is carved by a local builder, and the stand is a tree from the land.

A Majestic Mountain Retreat

Mailing Address
38250 Pioneer Boulevard #602
Sandy, Oregon 97055
o. 503.686.8080
h. 503.622.0413
f. 503.622.0474
e. becca1st@gmail.com
www.AMajesticMountainRetreat.com

Contact
Rebecca Niday

Price
$250 – $875 a night

Capacity
12 Guests

Quick Facts
- Pillow-top Beds with Wonderful 600 Thread Count Linens
- Luxurious Bath Towels & Robes
- Gourmet Kitchen with Granite Counters & Stainless Steel Appliances
- The Kitchen is Generously Equipped by a Professional Chef
- Pine Log Beds, Table & Chairs
- 2-Story Wood Burning Stone Fireplace
- Game Room with a Poker/Game Table, Foosball Table & Games
- TV with Satellite and DVD's
- Wireless Satellite Internet Service

WHAT'S NEW
The Cedar House: A Retreat space that sleeps 61

Falcon's Crest Lodge
In Government Camp

p. 503.686.8080
Government Camp, Oregon
www.falconscrestlodge.com

About Falcon's Crest Lodge

This amazing 5,700 sq. ft. lodge, in the heart of Historic Government Camp, is walking distance to lifts, hiking trails and town. Craftsman style woodwork, granite counters and slate floors provide rustic charm and the luxury you desire. Falcon's Crest lets you relax in luxury and comfort.

Falcon's Crest sleeps 24 comfortably. There are 3 Deluxe King Master Suites with private baths and private decks and 1 Deluxe Family Suite that sleeps 4 with its own private sitting area and Jacuzzi tub. There are 2 bunk rooms, each sleeping 6, with full, private bathrooms. One even has its own 32-inch Satellite TV. Four families will feel right at home!

The Great Room has a custom Bar, the Dining Room a 15-foot log Family-Style table and your fully-equipped gourmet kitchen has a gas Viking 8-burner stove. The large decks have great views of Mt. Hood and the night lights of Ski Bowl.

The Game Room has a Foosball Table, Air Hockey, Poker/Game Table and plenty of Board Games for the whole family. The ski/snowboard tuning area has a large table and vice. At days end, relax in the new 6-person Hot Tub. Falcon's Crest Lodge is how life is meant to be enjoyed!

Contact
Becca Niday

Price
Varies, please call

Quick Facts
- Wireless Internet & Sirius Satellite Radio
- Big screen – HDTV with Satellite, DVD & VCR, X-Box
- Large laundry room with washer & dryer
- Slate foyer with convenient storage for ski gear

Testimony
"This house is Heavenly! It is amazingly well-equipped & I LOVED the kitchen. The beds were the most comfortable I have ever slept in. The kids enjoyed the games and we all had a fantastic time. Everything about this home is excellent."
– Jeannie C. Feb. 4, 2007

"I just wanted to thank you again for all your help in making our stay at Government Camp so wonderful. Falcon's Crest was a dream! Hope we'll be able to visit again."
– Cathy O. July 28th, 2007

345

© Cascade Photography

SUNRIVER®
R E S O R T

57081 Meadow Road
Sunriver, Oregon 97707
p. 541.593.4605
f. 541.593.2742
e. weddings@sunriver-resort.com
www.sunriver-resort.com

346

About Sunriver Resort

Located near the breathtaking Cascade Mountain range, just 15 miles south of Bend, Oregon, Sunriver Resort offers a unique experience for all ages. A unique Northwest resort destination for all seasons that creates togetherness and memories among families and groups, Sunriver Resort provides unmatched activities and experiences in a serene, natural setting.

With more than 44,000 square feet of flexible meeting and banquet space, guests can choose from a wide variety of flexible indoor space featuring Northwest style ambiance, or naturally gorgeous outdoor space, including the scenic Bachelor Lawn or the Great Hall Courtyard.

Whether planning a vacation, corporate meeting or a dream wedding, our state-of-the-art meeting facilities combined with the world-class recreation of Sunriver Resort will help execute your distinct vision with unrestricted flexibility and creativity that exceed your expectations.

Contact
Sunriver Catering Office

Price
Varies

Quick Facts
- Experienced professional staff to attend to every need
- Custom weddings
- Wedding packages are available for ease of planning
- Multiple locations, both indoors and out, that can accommodate weddings and groups of all sizes

© Tullis Photography

© Tullis Photography

See page 503 under
Reception & Wedding Sites

Portland SPIRIT ®

110 SE Caruthers
Portland, Oregon 97214
p. 503.224.3900
p. 800.224.3901
e. sales@portlandspirit.com
www.portlandspirit.com

The fleet and facilities of the Portland Spirit will provide a unique and memorable experience for your wedding or special event. Our knowledgeable sales staff and professional event planners will handle all the details, making your planning process easy and stress-free!

Portland Spirit
Ceremony: up to 200 guests. Reception: up to 400 guests

Willamette Star
Ceremony: up to 100 guests. Reception: up to 120 guests.

Crystal Dolphin
Ceremony: up to 80 guests. Reception up to 100 guests.

Columbia Gorge Sternwheeler
Ceremony: up to 150 guests. Reception: up to 300 guests

Thunder Island
Ceremony: up to 200 guests

Gorge Pavilion
Ceremony: up to 200 guests. Reception: up to 300 guests.

Contact
Group & Charter Sales

Price
Prices vary – please inquire

Vessel & Facility Amenities
- In-house catering
- Linen tablecloths and napkins provided
- China, glassware & flatware provided
- Servers and bartender included with food and bar service
- Full service cash bar available
- Clean-up provided
- Commercial parking and street parking available
- ADA limited with assistance – please call for more information

347

See page 401 & 484 under Reception & Wedding Sites

Bravo! Member Since 1996

Abigails Garden © womanphotographer.com

Abernethy Center
BALLROOM ✦ GARDENS

606 15th Street
Oregon City, Oregon 97045
p. 503.722.9400
f. 503.722.5377
e. weddings@abernethycenter.com
www.abernethycenter.com

About Abernethy Center

Abernethy Center is Oregon's all-season ceremony and reception site, located 20 minutes outside Portland in historic Oregon City. Our unique indoor and outdoor venues have all the amenities you need for a beautiful wedding experience.

Abigail's Garden

Enjoy a spring or summer wedding where gentle spring breezes shower your ceremony in cottonwood confetti and butterflies waltz on the warm wind of a summer's eve. Abigail's Garden encompasses a fairytale setting, complete with a gleaming white gazebo and a 60' by 70' reception tent.

Veiled Garden

Our Veiled Garden, nestled in a secluded one-acre woodland with filtered light, a stunning waterfall, and lacy white gazebo provides the perfect backdrop for an intimate wedding. Move effortlessly from your intimate woodland wedding to an elegant reception in the Abernethy Ballroom.

Contact
Sales Department

Price
Starting at $1,000

Capacity
Indoors up to 300;
Outdoors 300+

The Abernethy Ballroom
- Perfect for fall or winter weddings
- Soft color tones & chandeliers create ambiance perfect for 150 guests
- Bathed in natural lighting from expansive windows
- Services available: wedding cakes, ice carvings, expert menus & much more

COME SEE FOR YOURSELF

Take the virtual visit on our website, or set an appointment to see the real thing, and fall in love with this beautiful place.

See page 366 under Reception & Wedding Sites

© Holland Studios

© The Photographers

Bravo! Member Since 2001

Bell Tower Chapel

13360 SE Richey Road
Portland, Oregon 97009
p. 503.663.9333
e. kconnolly@bresnan.net
www.belltowerchapel.com

About Bell Tower Chapel

Built in 1907, the recently restored historic Bell Tower Chapel offers a dramatic, intimate setting for your wedding, reception or special event.

Featuring cathedral ceilings, gothic-style arched windows, original wood pews and floors, warm chandelier lighting and a working church bell.

The beautiful attached banquet room with tables, chairs, and manicured half–acre grounds are ideal for indoor or outdoor receptions any time of year.

The chapel includes candleabra's, sound system, organ, pulpit, unity candle table with holders, as well as gift and cake tables.

You may use your choice of vendors and catering, or choose from our vendor list on web site.

Located just 20 minutes from 1-205, east of Clackamas.

Call for weekly tours.

Contact
Kim Connolly

Price
$316+

Capacity
Up to 125 people

Amenities
- Reception Room
- Bridal dressing room
- Lounge area
- Kitchenette
- Air-conditioned
- Half-acre grounds
- Ample on-site parking
- Non-denominational
- Your choice of vendors
- Affordable pricing

349

Bravo! Member Since 2002

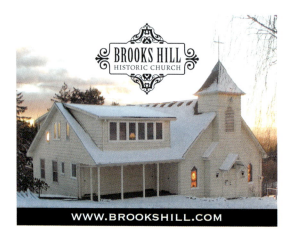

WWW.BROOKSHILL.COM

11539 NW Skyline Boulevard
Portland, Oregon 97231
p. 503.629.9700
e. cindy@brookshill.com
www.brookshill.com

We Love Small Weddings!

Built in 1933, our cozy neighborhood chapel is only 20 minutes west of downtown Portland, surrounded by beautiful farmland. Brooks Hill is the perfect place for your small wedding or event with a gorgeous view of the valley and a warm, friendly atmosphere. You are welcome to bring your own minister or we gladly provide you with a referral.

What's Included

A beautiful chapel, receiving hall, private bridal lounge, two private dressing rooms, guest book table, altar table, candelabrums, 8-foot table with linens, stereo and an old-fashioned church bell.

350

Contact
Cindy Banks

Price
Reasonable prices, call for a personalized quote

Capacity
Up to 100

Amenities

- Cozy & friendly
- Non-denominational
- Recently remodeled
- Stunning view
- Baby grand piano
- Dressing rooms
- Air conditioned

WHAT'S NEW

Brooks Hill Historic Church was chosen by Willamette Week for their 2006 'Best of Portland' awards.

Crystal Springs Rhododendron Garden

5801 SE 28th (No Mail)
Portland, Oregon 97202
p. 503.256.2483.

World-Class Botanical Garden

This world-class botanical garden, surrounded by a sparkling lake created by numerous natural springs, invites a wide variety of both land and water birds. Lush greenery of mature trees and shrubs combine with winding pathways to provide unsurpassed beauty throughout spring bloom and summer seasons, followed by outstanding fall colors. Three waterfalls enhance the garden's natural beauty. An atmosphere of peace, seclusion and solitude pervades the garden.

Availability and Terms

Events may be scheduled in July, August and until mid September. Weddings up to 50 may be scheduled in late April, May and June. Reservations are accepted up to two years in advance. A tent or canopy may be rented for shade or shelter. Maintain maximum flexibility by holding both your ceremony and reception on site in summer months.

Contact
Rita Knapp
Event Coordinator

Price
Calculated by size & hours; call for details

Capacity
Outdoor events only; 150 to 350 at the Meadow; other venues accommodate other sizes

351

Amenities
- Tables and chairs for 160 to rent for the Meadow

- Servers provided by caterer; champagne, wine & beer only (no kegs) with proper liability insurance; caterer must have bartender on staff

- Dance floor from rental company or dance on grass; 70 decibel sound restriction—no strobe lights

- Linens, china & glassware provided by caterer

- Small parking lot on site, plus across the street at Reed College

- Dressing areas on site for Meadow & Victoriana

- Welcoming overseas, out-of-state, and local clients

Bravo! Member Since 2002

909 SW 11th Avenue
Portland, Oregon 97205
p. 503.228.7465
f. 503.222.1903

e. kponce@fbc-portland.org
e. cbeard@fbc-portland.org
www.fbc-portland.org/weddings

First Baptist Church happily shares in the joy of the couples and families who unite their lives in our historic building. The church features tasteful and elegant surroundings perfect for weddings large and small and stunning details that your family and friends will remember.

The sanctuary's main floor seats more than 300 guests in a gently curving arc which faces the altar. Brides enter down a 40-foot center aisle which divides the room, accented by beautiful, original Povey stained-glass windows. Even the Bridal Parlor is a photo-opportunity, featuring an ornately carved floor-to-ceiling mirror fit for a queen!

Rare for an historic downtown church, First Baptist Church, Portland also offers a full sound system, air conditioning, and off-street parking.

You are welcome to have your officiant perform your wedding ceremony. Our pastors are also available to conduct ceremonies in English, Spanish and Cambodian languages. Our experienced staff is caring, helpful and enthusiastic in making your big day as special as the love you celebrate.

352

Contact
For date availability/tours –
Keith Ponce
p. 503.228.7465 x120
For otherv inquiries –
Chris Beard
e. cbeard@fbc-portland.org

Price
$1,000 – $1,200

Quick Facts
- Open to non-members
- We welcome your officiant to perform the ceremony
- Seating for 300+
- Stunning architecture enhanced by magnificent stained-glass windows
- Majestic pipe organ and grand piano
- Parking available

First Unitarian Church of Portland

1011 SW 12th Avenue
Portland, Oregon 97205
p. 503.228.6389
f. 503.228.2676
e. hnicknair@firstunitarianportland.org
www.firstunitarianportland.org

Nestled in the heart of downtown Portland, The First Unitarian Church offers three traditional ceremony spaces and the modern, newly built, LEED Gold Certified, Buchan Reception Hall, perfect for your dream wedding or commitment ceremony and reception.

The Eliot Chapel built in 1924, features Georgian Revival architecture and seats 200 people. For larger events of up to 650, the Sanctuary provides theater style seating, with a balcony and historic 1880's pipe organ and grand piano framed by a walnut and gold leaf presidium arch. Additionally, The Channing Room, a formal parlor, seats up to 30 guests and is ideal for intimate ceremonies and a perfect dressing room for bridal parties.

The Buchan Reception Hall, in our newly built, LEED Gold Certified Buchan Building, offers 2,600 square feet of modern and elegant space for up to 250 guests. Its floor to ceiling windows, city views, adjacent outdoor courtyard and two-story atrium add to its spacious ambiance.

View a virtual tour at www.firstunitarianportland.org

Contact
Holli Nicknair

Price
Between $550 and $2,050

Quick Facts
- Affordable, downtown, LEED Gold Certified venue
- Self cater or choose your own caterer
- Alcohol Permitted
- Our Music Consultants and Ministers are available, though not required for your event
- Onsite Event Coordinator and rehearsal time included in every package
- Two outdoor courtyards perfect for your photo shoot and reception

353

WHAT'S NEW

The Buchan Building was built in 2008 and is LEED Gold Certified by the US Green Building Council.

See page 418 under Reception & Wedding Sites

Bravo! Member Since 2001

Mississippi STUDIOS

3939 North Mississippi Avenue
(between Failing & Shaver)
Portland, Oregon 97227

p. 503.754.9619

e. events@mississippistudios.com

www.mississippistudios.com

About Mississippi Studios

Your alternative wedding venue, Mississippi Studios is the perfect setting for an intimate and unique ceremony or reception experience. The new roof-garden is included allowing for a variety of eclectic mixes and blending well with most styles.

We have State-of-the-art sound equipment and a warm ambiance, and will make your day a truly memorable experience.

We can provide as much, or as little, as you choose for your wedding event: Flowers, Cake, Catering, Ceremony and a Reverend, as well as beverages and musicians.

Please see our website: www.mississippistudios.com for details and testimonials. For those who seek a uniquely beautiful space, this is your urban chapel alternative.

Call us to arrange a tour today: 503.754.9619

Contact
Heather Bryse-Harvey

Price
Call to discuss your requirements – $1,200+

Capacity
160 (seated)
200 (cocktail-style)

Services
- Catering available: We welcome your favorite caterer & we recommend Mississippi Station
- Wedding cake custom designs available
- Officiant
- Musicians available
- We work with you to make it happen

WHAT'S NEW

Mississippi Studios has had a face-lift! We have remodeled the venue and can now hold 160 guests seated, or 200 cocktail-style! We now have a roof-garden too!

354

OLD LAURELHURST CHURCH

3212 SE Ankeny Street
Portland, Oregon 97214
p. 503.231.0462
f. 503.231.9429
www.oldlaurelhurstchurch.com

About the Old Laurelhurst Church

Old Laurelhurst Church, located at the center of 32nd and Ankeny in Southeast Portland, is centrally located and conveniently located. The church rose garden and beautiful Laurelhurst Park are favorite sites for wedding photography.

Built in 1923, Old Laurelhurst Church is an outstanding example of Spanish Colonial Revival-style architecture. With an arcaded entrance, curvilinear gables and domed corner bell towers with round-arched openings, the church features wrought-iron balconet and 11 magnificent cathedral-quality stained glass windows. The live acoustics and warm ambiance provide an intimate feeling complementing the long and stately aisle in the sanctuary, which features the ornate original, wooden beams and trim.

An independent Christian church, Old Laurelhurst Church seeks to be of service to the community. The church is available for weddings, receptions, concerts, seminars and community events.

Contact
Debbie Buckler
Coordinator

Price
Please call for details

Quick Facts
- Parking available one block east around the park & one block north on Burnside Street
- Attractive wheelchair access available through the rose garden
- The sanctuary acoustics have been acclaimed by musicians & speakers
- The church allows couples to bring in an approved Christian minister to officiate, or will provide referrals

355

For weddings, the church provides a five-hour time slot on wedding day, in addition to a one-hour rehearsal time, dressing rooms for the bride & groom, a snack room, gold-leafed unity candle table, grand piano, Allen computer organ, a quality sound system with CD player holding up to five discs, cassette player, gold-leafed table in foyer & guest book stand.

Bravo! Member Since 1996

1441 North McClellan
Portland, Oregon 97217
p. 503.283.3224
f. 503.283.5605
e. queenannevictorianmansion@yahoo.com
www.queenannevictorianmansion.com

A Magical Storybook Place

Every bride deserves perfection on her wedding day, whether it is formal, informal or a simple family ceremony. The Queen Anne staff is very detail oriented and will make sure you and your family are at ease knowing everything is taken care of start to finish. Easily accessible and very private setting on over two acres, the mansion is a beautiful and perfect location to create your special day. Built in 1885 by David Cole as a wedding gift for his wife, the mansion is truly a work of art. It features incredible original woodwork, chandeliers and one of the largest private collections of Povey stained glass windows in the world. Call to set up your appointment and allow our staff to dazzle you with a tour of the grounds and mansion. Appointments are made through the week.

Availability and Terms

The mansion is a 6,300 square-foot beautiful Victorian with a 42' round enclosed gazebo. Reserve as early as possible. Reservations have a 90-minute and six-hour time limit per function.

356

Contact
Event Manager

Price
Rates vary. Please call
for specific pricing.

Capacity
Up to 400 seated;
300 reception

Amenities
- Irresistable house catering
- Tables & chairs for up to 400 provided
- Gazebo is a perfect location for dancing
- Completely decorated in Victorian-era antiques, colorful floral garlands & arrangements throughout the home; meticulously landscaped gardens
- Full bar service available
- Plenty of free parking
- All inclusive in-house catering

Bravo! Member Since 1994

See page 486 under
Reception & Wedding Sites

First Christian CHURCH
a place for you
in the heart of the city

1314 SW Park Avenue
Portland, Oregon 97201
p. 503.228.9211
f. 503.222.1313
e. questions@fccpdx.com
www.fccpdx.com.com

For 130 years, First Christian Church (FCC) has been a favorite location for weddings. This historic church is nestled in downtown Portland. FCC is an open community of faith where members and nonmembers are welcome to be married. A First Christian minister will officiate at your wedding and our wedding staff will assist you with your ceremony plans. We strive to make your dreams come true, while accommodating your personal and financial needs.

FCC has a gorgeous renovated sanctuary that has the original Povey Brothers Art Glass windows. The sanctuary seats approximately 300 people. Our brand new 4,211 square foot reception space holds up to 600 people and is flexible for many uses

Bravo! Member Since 1992

Contact
Robyn Gett
Johanna Kennelly Ullman

Quick Facts
- Brand new 4,211Sq. Ft. reception space that holds up to 600 people.
- Full commercial kitchen for your caterer to utilize.
- A dedicated staff committed to making your wedding a memorable & beautiful occasion.
- All are welcome to be married at FCC.

357

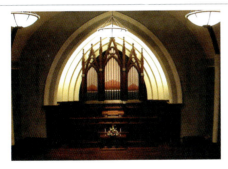

(Church Address)
1126 SW Park
Portland, Oregon 97205

(Office Address)
1137 SW Broadway
Portland, Oregon 97205

p. 503.228.7219
f. 503.228.6522
e. info@uccportland.org
www.uccportland.org

First Congregational United Church of Christ

For over a century, couples have selected First Congregational United Church of Christ as the perfect site for their wedding. The sanctuary of this historic landmark accommodates 800: 400 on the lower level, 250 in the balcony, with room for an additional 150 folding chairs if needed. The semi-circular seating and sloping floor, however, ensure clear views of the chancel for all. For small weddings, the chapel, with its lovely rose-colored windows, seats 40.

For receptions: A social hall with adjacent kitchen seats 80 – 100 at round tables.

For additional information about weddings and the church, please visit our website.

Bravo! Member Since 1991

Contact
Officer Manager or
Event Coordinator

Quick Facts
- Open to members & non-members
- Available for weddings as well as commitment ceremonies
- Known for its Venetian Gothic architecture, hand-carved woodwork & magnificent stained glass windows
- The bell in the 175 foot tower is rung in your honor

The Hostess House
&
The Bridal Arts Building
Est. 1984

10017 NE Sixth Avenue
Vancouver, Washington 98685
p. 360.574.3284
www.thehostesshouse.com

About Hostess House

The Hostess House is the only facility in the Pacific Northwest that was designed and built especially for weddings. The candle–lit chapel seats 200 guests and looks out onto a beautiful garden setting with a waterfall. Although we primarily provide our chapel as part of our complete wedding and reception packages, we also offer "ceremony–only" packages ranging in price from $200 to $650. Ceremony packages include our nondenominational house minister, or your officiant is always welcome. ADA accessible

Contact
Hostess House

Price
$200 to $650

Quick Facts
- Open seven days a week, please call for appointment
- Featured in Modern Bride as "the place" to have your wedding in the Pacific Northwest

See page 91 under Bridal Attire, 435 Reception & Wedding Sites

Bravo! Member Since 1990

358

OAKS PIONEER CHURCH
Portland's most popular wedding chapel-museum

455 SE Spokane
Portland, Oregon 97202
p. 503.233.1497
f. 503.236.8402
www.oakspioneerchurch.org

© Kate Kelly Photography

Located at the southern edge of Sellwood Park and overlooking the Willamette River, the historic chapel-museum was rescued from demolition in 1961.

Built in 1851, the chapel served the congregation of St. John's Episcopal Church. The chapel-museum is now managed by the Sellwood Moreland Improvement League (S.M.I.L.E), in partnership with the City of Portland Parks Bureau. A National Historic Landmark, the chapel-museum has been historically restored. Two original pews remain in use. The 1889 stained glass window, recently restored, provides a beautiful interior photo backdrop for day or evening weddings. Air conditioning keeps the chapel-museum comfortable year-round.

Contact
Lorraine Fyre

Price
Reasonable rates

Quick Facts
- Accommodates 75 guests
- Dressing rooms for the bridal party
- Nearby S.M.I.L.E. Station is available for receptions
- Antique pump organ available
- Christenings & memorials available

Bravo! Member Since 1990

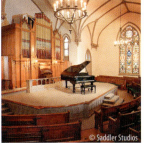

© Saddler Studios

The Old Church

1422 SW 11th Avenue
Portland, Oregon 97201
p. 503.222.2031
e. staff@oldchurch.org
www.oldchurch.org

The Old Church has been a Portland landmark since its completion in 1883. On the National Register of Historic Places since 1972, it no longer serves Portland as a dedicated church, but as an independent historical society. As a non-religiously affiliated church building, it allows each couple the opportunity to bring in the officiator of their choice. The Old Church stands as a striking example of Carpenter Gothic architecture with its Corinthian columns supporting a cathedral ceiling. The original stained-glass windows filter the afternoon light into the chapel. Hand-carved pews surround the center aisle and slope to the altar area, giving an intimacy to the chapel that belies its 300 person capacity.

Bravo! Member Since 1990

Contact
Trish Augustin

Quick Facts
- 1883 Victorian Carpenter Gothic church
- Romantic setting for any type of ceremony
- Centrally-located in downtown Portland
- A historic Hook & Hastings tracker pipe organ adds a warm ambiance to your wedding
- Now ADA accessible

359

Wedding Tradition

The Giving of an Engagement Ring was considered to show commitment on the groom's part to purchase the bride. The use of rings within the ceremony can be traced back to the Egyptians and Romans.

© Amy Ouellette

Helpful Hint

Choosing Your Ceremony Site

SEATING ARRANGEMENTS AT THE CEREMONY

For seating at the ceremony, there are two options: if parents are friends and they are not remarried, they can sit side-by-side in the front pew. Otherwise, the parent you have lived with would sit in the front row with his or her spouse, and the other parent sits in the second row with his or her spouse. Beyond that, your step-parents' involvement is up to you. You can honor your dad's wife by having her do a reading or, if that makes your mom uncomfortable, give her a less prominent role, like manning the guest book.

REMEMBER THE MARRIAGE LICENSE

Don't forget to bring the marriage-license packet to the wedding! Assign this task to a trusted friend, family member or your Consultant/Coordinator. A ceremony is not legal and complete without this.

MAKE YOUR CEREMONY SPECIAL

The officiant can help to make your wedding ceremony meaningful for both of you. Ask how you can personalize the ceremony—writing your own vows, selecting special songs, etc.

RING-BEARER PILLOW

Practice tying the rings to the pillow so that they will stay on during the walk down the aisle, but will slip off easily during the ceremony.

CHECK ALL THE RULES

Make sure you know all the rules and restrictions about the ceremony site. Some have strict rules about photographs or videotaping, candles and music.

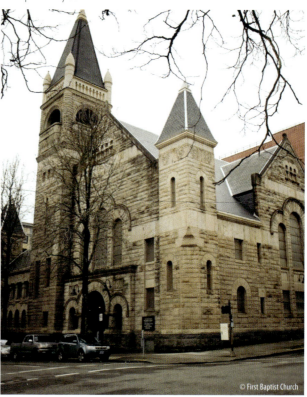

© First Baptist Church

OBTAINING A MARRIAGE LICENSE IN OREGON

You must be at least 17 years of age or have written consent from a parent. No exams or blood tests are required. Cost is $60 with a three-day waiting period. License is valid for 60 days.

Hawaiian Weddings & Tropical Honeymoons

2525 NW Upshur Street
Portland, Oregon 97210
p. 503.231.0796
c. 503.407.1651
e. jennifer@wtpdx.com

Thinking of Getting Married in a Tropical Paradise?

"This is what my husband and I did! We decided to get married in the beautiful Hawaiian Islands, and you can experience this unique and romantic way to get married too! I would love to meet with you and show you how easy, stress free, and inexpensive, your destination wedding can be! Please call me today to schedule your free consultation, and I'll share the many advantages of getting married in a way you will cherish forever!"

Professional Services

- 16 years experience
- Step-by-step guidance for the wedding of your dreams
- Personal knowledge of resorts, condos, restaurants, luaus and group excursions
- Coordinate family and group travel
- Arrange group activities including luaus and sunset/snorkel sails
- Sandals certified expert
- Maui destination expert

Contact
Jennifer Zeman

Price
Starting at $3,500 for a basic wedding & travel package

Locations
- Maui
- Oahu
- Kauai

All Sandals Locations Including:
- Jamaica
- St. Lucia
- Bahamas
- Antigua

361

©Nicole Wickens

SCHEDULE YOUR CONSULTATION TODAY!

Call us at: 503.231.0796

See page 220 under Honeymoons & Travel

Visit BravoWedding.com for great suggestions on destination weddings

© Robert Demar

SAN JUAN ISLANDS
VISITORS BUREAU

PO Box 1330
640 Mullis Street, Suite 211
Friday Harbor, Washington 98250
p. 888.468.3701 x1
p. 360.378.9551 x1
f. 360.378.9585
e. info@visitsanjuans.com
www.VisitSanJuans.com

362

About San Juan Islands Weddings

The San Juan Islands – Lopez, Orcas and San Juan – are the perfect location for a romantic and memorable destination wedding! The San Juans are located 90 miles northwest of Seattle, nestled between the coast of northwest Washington and Victoria B.C. Getting here is half the fun – enjoy a cruise aboard a Washington State Ferry (from Anacortes), passenger ferry (from Seattle and several locations), airplane or seaplane. The San Juans average 247 days with sunshine annually, and about half the rainfall of the Seattle area, making them a year-round destination for weddings, honeymoons, anniversaries and getaways.

Choose a wedding setting that is intimate or grand – get married on a beach, on a boat (or kayak), in a quaint church or at a waterfront resort. Request our "Wedding Planning Guide," which lists all three islands' wedding services: wedding and reception sites, wedding planners, officiates, cakes, catering, flowers, hair/makeup, musicians, party rentals, photographers, spas and more. The San Juan Islands Visitors Bureau is happy to help make your wedding day in the islands perfect.

Contact
Bettye or Deborah to request a Wedding Planning Guide

Price
Varies, depending on location

Services
- The San Juan Islands offer a unique range of wedding sites from beaches & parks, to boats & kayaks, to quaint churches & resorts

- The San Juan Islands offer more than 300 unique accommodations including resorts, inns, B&Bs, vacation rentals & camping

- Wedding guests will love having an excuse to visit the San Juan Islands, to enjoy their scenic beauty, watchable wildlife (including orca whales), outdoor recreation, history, arts & culture – or just kick back on "island time"

WHAT'S NEW

The San Juan Islands are consistently named in the "Top 5 islands in the continental U.S. and Canada" in Travel + Leisure magazine's World's Best Awards.

© Kathleen Ballard

© Steve Horn

503-620-0620
www.uniglobespectrumtravel.com

Uniglobe Spectrum Travel

Your Extraordinary Honeymoon or Destination Wedding—you expect and deserve the best, we make it happen! Creating the perfect lifelong romantic memory is our one goal.

Tropical Destinations: Luxurious and Romantic
- Tahiti, Fiji and the South Pacific
- The Caribbean & Bahamas
- Hawaii & Mexico
- Belize & Costa Rica

All-Inclusive Resorts: Fantastic Choices

We recommend the most romantic and upscale all-inclusive resorts in the world.

European Honeymoons: Independent & Cultural
- Italy – Greece & Turkey – France

We specialize in European honeymoon destinations. Leave all those details to us!

Exotic Honeymoons – Unique & Active
- Peru – Machu Picchu
- Thailand – Bangkok & the Beaches
- South Africa – Wildlife Safaris

Destination Weddings & Weekends
- Beach Weddings with your family & friends
- Cruises and Weddings at Sea
- Bachelor & Bachelorette Getaways

Contact
Mary Hanigan

15150 SW Bangy Road
Lake Oswego, Oregon 97035

p. 503.620.0620
p. 800.544.2575

e. honeymoons@unispectrum.com
www.uniglobespectrumtravel.com

363

Price
Cost-saving wholesale packages available.

All price ranges available to meet your budget.

Why UNIGLOBE:
- Free online Honeymoon Registry
- Convenient after-hours consultations
- Locally-owned, full-service agency
- Certified Specialists: Sandals, Hawaii, Tahiti, Las Vegas, Mexico, & all Cruise Lines
- Friendly, professional & well traveled

WHAT'S NEW

Uniglobe Spectrum Travel is committed to offering sustainable tourism destinations and suppliers as well as being green in our operations to protect and preserve our environment.

Bravo! Member Since 2001

Helpful Hint

Choosing Your Reception Site

RECEPTION HELPFUL HINTS

Begin looking for your reception site immediately. As soon as the engagement is announced, the first decision that needs to be made is where to hold the reception. Meet with your officiant to find out the days and times that are available for your church or wedding site. After setting a tentative date, begin to look for your reception site.

BE FLEXIBLE

If you are insistent about a certain date and time, you may spend weeks searching all over town for a place that can accommodate your needs. By the time you finally discover that no options are available on that day and time, your first choice in reception areas will probably be booked on your alternate dates also.

DEPOSITS ARE IMPORTANT

Remember that when you reserve a facility, a deposit is usually required. Even though you thought your date was secure, it may be that the site is not formally reserved until a deposit is received. Many brides have lost their reception site by overlooking this fact.

HOST OR HOSTESS FOR YOUR WEDDING

Ask someone to be the host or hostess for the reception if you don't have a Wedding Consultant or Coordinator. The family usually doesn't arrive at the reception until after the guests. If you have a host or hostess to greet the guests and direct them to the guest book, coat rack or bar, then they will feel more comfortable.

RECEIVING LINE

Sometimes it is difficult to get the flow of a receiving line started at the reception. You may want to alert four to five couples to watch for the bride and groom's arrival. Then they can quickly form a line to get the flow of the receiving line started. If you choose not to do a receiving line, it is your obligation to greet each guest at the reception.

GIFTS

Assign a reliable person to be in charge of gifts at the reception. He or she should have scotch tape handy to tape cards securely to packages. It is very frustrating and embarrassing to open gifts and not know who they were from. Make sure you have a vehicle (or two) to take the gifts to a safe place after the reception – especially if you are staying somewhere other than home for your wedding night.

23800 NW Flying M Road
Yamhill, Oregon 97148

p. 503.662.5678
f. 503.662.5626

e. christy@5rockranch.com

www.5rockranch.com

About 5Rock Ranch

5Rock Ranch is a Christian non profit ministry. Our 108 acres are located in the beautiful mountains in Yamhill, Oregon…just 50 miles from Portland. Our mission at 5Rock is to help build and restore families with a focus on the fatherless child. Throughout the year, we offer free camps for fatherless children and their moms. We give them tools to re-build and restore their lives. Since we believe that healthy families begin with healthy marriages we want to make 5Rock Ranch a place to begin and keep your marriage relationship strong. We require a 3 hour pre-marital training class at the ranch for couples who use the facility for their ceremony. We also offer optional relationship classes and retreats throughout the year.

Testimonial

"The remote location provided us with a elegantly private and spiritual setting for our creekside ceremony."

– Christina

Contact
Christy Bradley

Price
$1,000 – $12,000

Quick Facts
- Beautiful new amphitheater on the river
- Newly remodeled bunkhouse rooms & cabins
- Rustic log ranch house
- Indoor & outdoor site options
- Family style meals
- Catering also available

WHAT'S NEW?

Everything!!! 5Rock is the old Flying M Ranch. We've not only changed names, but we've changed the whole feel of the ranch. Our purpose is to share a place full of love in a way that restores the mind, body, and soul so each person who experiences the ranch grows in their personal relationships, and becomes part of God's family.

Abernethy Center

BALLROOM ♦ GARDENS

606 15th Street
Oregon City, Oregon 97045
p. 503.722.9400
f. 503.722.5377
e. weddings@abernethycenter.com
www.abernethycenter.com

About Abernethy Center

Abernethy Center is Oregon's all-season ceremony and reception site, located 20 minutes outside Portland, in historic Oregon City. Our unique indoor and outdoor venue have all the amenities you need for a beautiful wedding experience.

Abigail's Garden

Our 60' by 70' tent on the hill serves as the perfect outdoor wedding reception site. On warm days, open the sidewalls to let in a cool breeze off Abernethy Creek. On cooler days, close them and let light filter in from the expansive, clear windows. You and your guests will enjoy dancing the night away on the classy checkered dance floor.

The Abernethy Ballroom

The Ballroom's charm is unique. An elegant marble entry ushers guests into a breathtaking ballroom, complete with recessed ceilings and chandeliers. In the summer, pull back the curtains of our floor to ceiling windows and flood the room with photograph-enhancing light or wander out to our intimate, floral patio.

Contact
Sales Department

Price
Starting at $1,000

Capacity
Indoors up to 300;
Outdoors 300+

Amenities
- Table, chair & dance floor setup included in site rental
- Wait-staff, linen & china service included in exclusive on-site catering packages
- Staging & Bose sound system (Ballroom only)
- On-site & street parking
- ADA – fully accessible

VISIT US TODAY

Take the virtual visit on our website, or set an appointment to see the real thing, and fall in love with this beautiful place.

See page 348 under Ceremony Sites

Abernethy Ballroom   © The Photographers

Bravo! Member Since 2001

ABIQUA

COUNTRY ESTATE

That Special Day

You're planning for that special day, and you want it to be perfect. What better location to celebrate than a stunning 100-acre retreat? You will find charm and tranquility in this very unique country setting that is yours exclusively for the day.

The Ideal Outdoor Setting

Abiqua Country Estate, with its variety of settings, is the ideal outdoor location for your ceremony and reception, with its towering firs, heart-shaped lake and lush lawns bordered with a multitude of flowers.

The Bride's Entrance

What a beautiful entrance for the bride as the music plays…either descending the staircase to the West Lawn and Island or walking a wooded path to the expansive and woodsy East Lawns.

The Party

See the guests strolling the grounds with a glass of wine. Or sitting by the reflecting pond, enjoying the music. Or on the dance floor, under the stars.

Contact

Jude Strader – Events Coordinator

18401 Abiqua Road NE
Silverton, Oregon 97381

p. 503.829.9280

e. jude@molalla.net

www.abiquacountryestate.com

Price

Varies depending on event; please call for information.

367

Capacity

Up to 400 guests

Location

- Your guests will enjoy the country drive to the foothills of the Cascades, past our horses grazing in the pastures.

- A convenient 50 minutes from Portland, 30 minutes from Salem, & 10 minutes from two hotels & ten Bed & Breakfasts.

THE TOUR

Abiqua Country Estate is something you must see in person and we would love to show it to you. Please call for an appointment.

Bravo! Member Since 2004

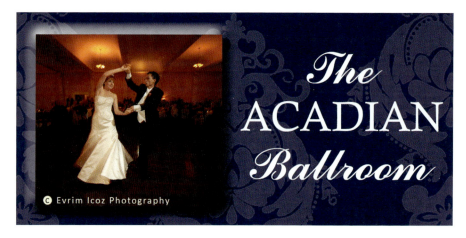

© Evrim Icoz Photography

The ACADIAN Ballroom

Historic Palladian Ballroom

In the heart of the Alberta Arts District, The Acadian Ballroom is a beautifully restored 1925 formal ballroom with a modern slant. Elements like our dark mahogany floors accented with white lacquer woodwork and marble pillars, an 18-foot barrel-vaulted ceiling and with our midnight bar and private mezzanine make The Acadian Ballroom uniquely suited to host your formal wedding reception.

At Your Service

Competent, experienced event designers will adjust every detail to fit your specific vision. Our expert event managers keep your event flowing smoothly throughout the entire evening. A classically-trained wait staff and doorman in formal attire will attend to your every need. Executive Chef MacLane Thurston evokes flavors that dance on the palate and soothe the soul.

Contact

Zack Smith – Event Designer

1829 NE Alberta Street
Portland, Oregon 97211
p. 503.546.6800
e. events@theacadianballroom.com

www.theacadianballroom.com

Price

Complete wedding reception package pricing begins at $30 per guest; a portion of the room cost may be waived with a minimum food & beverage purchase; special discounts available for Fridays & Sundays

Capacity

Luxury butlered dining for up to 330 guests; cocktail receptions up to 600

Amenities

- Custom event design
- Ceremonies & receptions
- Exclusive on-site catering
- DJ, sound, & multimedia
- All-inclusive pricing
- Private showings
- Formal red carpet entry
- Elegant lighting & room décor
- ADA accessible

WHAT'S NEW

Lux Groom's Suite, complete with multimedia.

Bravo! Member Since 2002

The **A**DRIANNA
GRAND **H**ILL
BALLROOM

918 SW Yamhill, 2nd Floor
Portland, Oregon 97205
p. 503.227.6285
f. 503.227.5158
e. info@adriannaballroom.com
www.adriannaballroom.com

About The Adrianna Hill Grand Ballroom

The Adrianna Hill Grand Ballroom is an elegant grand ballroom with beautiful restored hardwood floors, suspended u-shaped balcony, 55 foot-long stage backed by a high cathedral-style wall, large ornate brass chandeliers and a 35 foot high beamed and vaulted ceiling.

Built in 1901 and located in the Historic Pythian Building, this storybook setting with distinctive architecture has been completely refurbished. Elaborate Old World designs along the sculpted balcony are highlighted by white lights and tulle. Large gold framed mirrors, elegant artwork, antique foyer furniture, statuary and specialty lighting further enhance this unique setting.

We are proud to provide you with a treasured and unforgettable wedding day!

Contact
Philip & Linda Sword

Price
Fully inclusive packages vary

Capacity
75 to 350

Amenities
- Full service in-house catering & event planning
- Full bar available
- Available for ceremony & reception or reception only
- Linens, china & glassware included in packages
- Set-up & clean-up included
- Packages include ceremony & reception coordination
- Convenient downtown location

369

(c) Evrim Icoz Photography - www.evrimgallery.com

YES, CINDERELLA, YOU SHALL GO TO THE BALL!

Our full service set-up provides complete help and coordination throughout the entire process to ensure a stress-free event! We work with you to design the wedding day of your dreams.

Bravo! Member Since 1991

The *Aerie* at EAGLE LANDING

10220 SE Causey Avenue
Happy Valley, Oregon 97086
p. 503.698.8020
f. 503.698.8060
e. info@elventures.com
www.TheAerieAtEagleLanding.com

370

Minutes Away, Worlds Apart

The Aerie at Eagle Landing is situated atop Mt. Scott on The Eagle Landing Golf Course. Our French chateau-style facility, located just 20 minutes from Portland, is the perfect setting for your special occasion year round.

The Aerie, meaning "eagles nest," offers exquisite indoor and outdoor venues for wedding ceremonies, receptions, anniversary parties, and family reunions.

The Ballroom – Featuring vaulted ceilings, beautiful wood beams, generous windows, soft, neutral tones and dimmable chandeliers, our indoor ballroom combines classic sophistication and innovative Northwest design. West facing glass accordion doors open to accommodate event space between the ballroom and gardens.

Bellevue Gardens – As one of Oregon's premier outdoor wedding sites, the Bellevue Gardens and The Grand Pergola, offering breathtaking views of the West Hills, is framed by stunning floral gardens, manicured lawns and beautiful sunsets.

The Marquee – The Marquee tent, surrounded by majestic oak trees and our beautiful golf course, is a perfect haven in summer months or as an outdoor ceremony rain-plan option. In October through May this venue is fully enclosed with pleasing windowed sidewalls, heating and chandelier lighting.

Contact
Wedding/Event Sales

Price
Varies according to date, please call for details and to reserve your special day.

Capacity
Indoor seating for dinner/ dancing up to 160 guests. Indoor and Outdoor seating for dinner/dancing up to 300 guests.

Amenities
- Exclusive use of The Aerie for your wedding
- Free parking
- Beautifully appointed bridal lounge and groom's room
- Facility Equipment such as tables and chairs and use of three flat screen T.V.'s with DVD Player

Complimentary
- List of Preferred Professionals
- Additional photo session
- One hour rehearsal
- Cardio room or golf pass for bride and groom

Also Available
Tailored packages to fit your individual needs including Hotel/Limousine Packages, Wedding Coordination Package, dance floor, audio/visual equipment and discounted miniature golf.

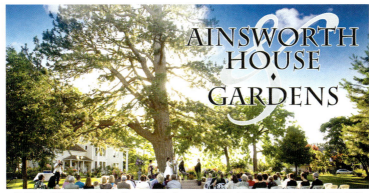

19130 Lot Whitcomb Drive, Oregon City, Oregon, 97045 / 503.656.1894 / 800.551.1716
[e]: information@AinsworthHouse.net / www.AinsworthHouse.net

The Elegant Ainsworth House and Its Magical Garden

We're a world away and yet just on your doorstep.

From the classic portico of the Greek revival-style Victorian Mansion to the ethereal woodland gazebo; from the spreading arms of a 200+ year old Ponderosa Pine to the Garden Room and spacious Conservatory, this site has everything. And, because we never double book, they're all yours. Please come visit us on the web or in person.

Availability and Terms

This elegant 1851 Victorian Mansion, with over two acres of perfect grounds and numerous ceremony sites, is fully restored and furnished and is available all year round. Only ten minutes from either exits #9 or #10 off of I-205, and 25 minutes from Portland Airport, we provide superior and separate preparation rooms for bride, groom and your family. A $1,000 security deposit is required to secure a date. A horse-drawn carriage and other extra services are easily provided.

Types of Events

Receptions, corporate events, weddings and meetings. Please come visit us on the web and in person. www.AinsworthHouse.net

Contact
Kevin Yell
19130 Lot Whitcomb Drive
Oregon City, Oregon 97045

p. 503.656.1894
p. 800.551.1716
e. information@AinsworthHouse.net

www.AinsworthHouse.net

Price
See website for guide

Capacity
We specialize in small to mid-sized events. No minimums.

Catering
Exclusive preferred caterers to suit your needs

Amenities
- Dance floor, linens, napkins, china & glassware are all included
- Many decorations are included
- Servers, bar facilities & clean-up are provided by caterer
- Audiovisual can be rented or provided by your DJ
- Ample free parking in Ainsworth lot for 30 cars & on adjacent road

SPECIAL OFFERS
Please see website for Special Spring Offer, also low mid-week rates all year.

372

ALBERTINA'S
RESTAURANT AND SHOPS

424 NE 22nd Avenue
Portland, Oregon 97232
p. 503.231.3909
f. 503.408.5060
e. margarets@albertinakerr.org
www.kerrshops.org

About Albertina's Restaurant & Shops

Listed on the National Register of Historic Places and a
Portland landmark, the stately 1921 Old Kerr Nursery
is conveniently located a mile from downtown Portland.
Refurbished in 2001, the Nursery is equally beautiful inside
and out. The charming, homelike building and garden
patios are the perfect setting for your special occasion.

With our four beautifully appointed rooms and two
garden patios we can host a broad range of events from
weddings, receptions and rehearsal dinners to business
meetings, showers and birthday parties.

Experience the history of the Nursery building and the
gracious attention to detail provided by Albertina's
dedicated volunteer staff. Albertina's Restaurant and
Shops are helping Kerr provide stability and support to
children, adults and families.

Contact
Margaret

Price
Varies with event & menu;
please call for information

Capacity
Up to 200 for receptions;
Up to 90 for formal dinners

Quick Facts
• Champagne, wine & beer
  service, bartenders, servers
  & hostess/host provided

• China, glassware, silver
  service & linens supplied

• Dance floor available
  upon request; ample
  electrical hookups

• Clean-up included

• On-site & free street
  parking available

• ADA accessible

• Beautiful fresh floral
  arrangements, including
  service tables, fireplace
  mantels & more

Bravo! Member Since 1996

ALDERBROOK
RESORT & SPA
—

10 East Alderbrook Drive
Union, Washington 98592

p. 360.898.2200
f. 360.898.5528

e. sales@alderbrookresort.com
www.alderbrookresort.com

Where Exceptional Gatherings Are a Natural

Nestled on the scenic shores of Hood Canal, Alderbrook Resort & Spa is two hours from Portland or Seattle. Yet it's a world away from the everyday. Established in 1913 and reinvented in 2004, Alderbrook is a breath of fresh air for meetings, retreats, social gatherings and special events. A place where groups from 8 to 200 come together to learn. Play. Share ideas. See things in a new light. Celebrate in one of the most scenic wilderness areas on earth.

Our incredible outdoor venues or our private yacht Lady Alderbrook are ideal for entertaining in the natural beauty of Hood Canal. The extraordinary views of mountains, trees, and gardens throughout the resort set the stage for a relaxing getaway. Numerous recreational opportunities for making your stay a complete event are offered, including golf, kayaking, swimming, and pampering services at The Spa.

Types of Events: We can accommodate all types of meetings, conferences, team building, conventions, and social events.

Capacity: Ten meeting rooms from 520 to 2,250 sq. ft.; we offer over 7,000 sq. ft. of flexible banquet and meeting space with additional outdoor venues for up to 200 and our Lady Alderbrook.

Contact
Marty McCormack

Price
Varies according to group size & date of event or meeting

Amenities
- Totally ADA compliant
- Ample complimentary on-site parking
- All tables & chairs for up to 200 guests are provided
- Courteous & professional staff committed to making lasting memories
- Full-service, in-house catering provided
- Full-service bar for hosted or no-host functions
- Dance floor available upon request
- Linens & Napkins: Select from a range of options
- Silver, china, & glassware are provided
- Decorations: We are delighted to help with recommendations
- Cleanup provided by our staff

373

Amadeus Manor

"Voted Portland's most romantic restaurant"

~ The Oregonian

About Amadeus Manor

Amadeus Manor is the perfect setting for weddings, rehearsal dinners and annual, monthly or quarterly business meetings. You and your guests will enjoy fine continental dining in a wonderful old mansion overlooking the Willamette River on two wooded acres, filled with antiques, fireplaces, crystal chandeliers, candlelight and fresh flowers. We offer a full bar with a wide variety of Oregon and international wines. Outdoor dining and wedding ceremonies on our patio are also available. Piano music is included.

Availability and Terms

Reservations should be made as soon as possible to ensure availability. A deposit is required at the time of booking. Half the deposit is refundable if cancellations are made at least nine months prior to your event.

No cost for using the facility, bartending services, linens, flowers, candles, valet parking or classical piano.

Contact

Kristina

2122 SE Sparrow
(North River Road. Exit/22nd Street)
Milwaukie, Oregon 97222

p. 503.636.6154
p. 503.659.1735
e. kpoppmeier@aol.com

www.amadeusrestaurants.com

Price

Full course buffet-style dinners

Saturday evening: $40 per person

Friday, Saturday day & Sunday: $35 per person

Add $5 per person for served, sit-down, three-course dinners

Capacity

Up to 300 people

Quick Facts

- Full-service in-house catering or off-location catering.

TYPES OF EVENTS

Individual rooms for conferences, day-long seminars, private meetings and large group luncheons. Holiday parties and celebration dinners. From small intimate events up to 300. Weddings and rehearsal dinners.

Bravo! Member Since 1994

Anderson Lodge

Mailing Address Only
18410 NE 399th Street
Amboy, Washington 98601
p. 360.247.6660
f. 360.247.6661
e. lodge@andersonlodge.com
www.andersonlodge.com

About Anderson Lodge

Nestled just north of Portland, in the heart of a luxurious forest is a charming Swedish lodge offering a perfect site for an indoor or outdoor celebration. The usual concept of a wedding and reception is limited to an afternoon. However, weddings at Anderson Lodge take place over one day or several days. Anderson Lodge provides the luxury of lodging and a ceremony/reception site all in one, allowing your family and friends to be more of a part of this wonderful event.

So Much To Offer

Our wedding couples have exclusive use of our facility. We have two locations for your event. Our Hilltop House provides a picturesque apple orchard with gazebo as an outdoor site and the Main Lodge consists of a garden terrace in a lush forest setting for the outdoor event. Both our facilities have conference rooms, reception pavilions and lodging included in the package price. Our catering staff provides on-site cooking to make your event a success. Guests appreciate our homey Scandinavian atmosphere, scenic views and natural beauty. Our quaint Swedish cottages are perfect for the happy couple. You owe it to yourself to make your wedding a truly memorable occasion. Call for an appointment today to begin planning your special day at Anderson Lodge.

Contact

Arvid Anderson
Vicki Anderson

Price

One & two day packages
Seasonal Rates

Capacity

Indoor: Small groups
Large groups up to 200
Outdoor: more than 200

375

Amenities

- Exclusive use of facility
- Lodging for family & friends
- Beautiful outdoor wedding sites
- Indoor reception pavilions
- Indoor conference rooms
- Indoor & outdoor dining
- Catering available
- Chalet cabins
- Lush forest setting
- One hour from Portland

ANDERSON LODGE

Where Natural Beauty is the Icing on the Cake!

Bravo! Member Since 1999

andina

1314 NW Glisan
Portland, Oregon 97209
p. 503.228.9535
f. 503.228.0788
e. jennifer@andinarestaurant.com
www.andinarestaurant.com

About Andina

Tupai, Andina's newest private event space, is located directly above the restaurant in the heart of Portland's vibrant Pearl District. Tupai is a diverse, open space that can be customized for any type of event, including distinctive rehearsal dinners and wedding receptions with live music and dancing. The dedicated kitchen and full-service bar make it a perfect spot to experience Andina's renowned Peruvian cuisine, extraordinary cocktails and award-winning wine program.

Featuring Inca-inspired architecture, eucalyptus floors, high ceilings and natural light, Tupai can accommodate up to 65 guests for a seated dinner and 100 guests for a standing reception or cocktail party.

Andina features three additional rooms perfect for smaller weddings, rehearsal dinners or other events surrounding the big day. We are delighted to tailor a variety of prix fixe, family style and tasting menus to ensure that every event is beyond memorable.

Contact
Jennifer Anderson

Price
Food & Beverage minimum per room & price according to menu

Capacity
Tupai – 100 guests
George V – 50 guests
Tourmaline – 20 guests
Pearl Wine Shop – 16 guests

Highlights
- 100 Favorite Restaurants Worldwide – *The Robb Report 2008.*
- 2005 Restaurant of the Year – *The Oregonian.*
- Award of Excellence 2006, 2007, 2008, 2009 – *Wine Spectator.*
- "Big Deal in Portland" – *Gourmet Magazine 2004.*
- James Beard House Invitee – 2006, 2008.
- Distinctive Peruvian Cuisine.
- Extraordinary cocktails.
- Friendly & knowledgeable staff.

BEST REHEARSAL DINNER LOCALE
Oregon Bride 2009

Bravo! Member Since 2007

376

© Randy Kepple

A special place for a special day . . .

The beautifully adorned Antonia Ballroom, with its warm, intimate atmosphere, is the ideal setting for your wedding celebration. Our vintage chandeliers accentuate the wall art and copper accents, illuminating the ballroom with its original hardwood floors, perfect for dancing. At the entrance and lobby, unique hand-painted murals provide an amazing backdrop for photographs. Elegant and distinctive, our décor complements your individual style.

From providing the reception site to coordinating a complete custom package, whatever your needs, our dedicated staff will help make your dream wedding a reality. Call today for a personal tour. You will love what you see.

Contact
Anfisa or Toni

221 North Grant Street
Canby, Oregon 97013
p. 503.263.2085
e. info@antoniaballroom.com
www.antoniaballroom.com

Price
Call for current pricing

Capacity
Up to 139 sit-down
Up to 199 reception

Amenities
- Custom packages upon request
- Friendly & professional staff
- Setup of tables & chairs included
- Original hardwood floors – ideal for dancing
- Surround-sound, CD player & microphone
- ADA accessible

377

TYPES OF EVENTS

Wedding ceremonies and receptions, reunions, anniversaries, birthdays, corporate events, holiday parties and more!

FS Photography | www.fsweddings.com

Historic Classical Ballroom

An icon of the exciting Hawthorne District, The Arista Ballroom is a restored formal 1920's ballroom. With hand finished mahogany floors, 18' faux sky coffered ceilings, hand-blown Murano chandeliers, sky bar with giant 3-story windows, and extensive white lacquer woodwork, The Arista Ballroom is specially designed to host your formal wedding reception.

At Your Service

Competent, experienced event designers will adjust every detail to fit your specific vision. Our expert event managers keep your event flowing smoothly throughout the entire evening. A classically trained wait staff and doorman in formal attire will attend to your every need. Executive Chef MacLane Thurston evokes flavors that dance on the palate and soothe the soul.

Contact

Zack Smith, Event Designer

3862 SE Hawthorne Boulevard
Portland, Oregon 97214

p. 503.288.3600

e. events@aristaballroom.com

www.aristaballroom.com

Price

Complete wedding reception package pricing begins at $30 per guest; a portion of the room cost may be waived with a minimum food & beverage purchase; special discounts available for Fridays & Sundays

Capacity

Luxury butlered dining up to 200 guests; cocktail receptions up to 250

Amenities

- Custom event design
- Ceremonies & receptions
- Exclusive on-site catering
- DJ, sound, & multimedia
- All-inclusive pricing
- Private showings
- Elegant lighting & room décor
- Air conditioned

WHAT'S NEW

Now featuring a plush bridal suite.

www.sjharmon.com

Bravo! Member Since 2002

© Rhonda Addison

The Banker's Suite

1215 Duane Street
Astoria, Oregon 97103
p. 425.417.6512
e. bankerssuite@bluemars.com
www.thebankerssuite.com

About The Banker's Suite

Located in Astoria's downtown historic district The Banker's Suite consumes the entire top floor of the historic Bank of Astoria building. The suite's 4500 square feet of formal style was inspired by its original ornate plaster columns and capitals. Whether you are planning a romantic getaway for two or a social gathering for 50 the Banker's Suite is the perfect venue.

Opening on our main floor in January of 2010 will be The Banker's Ballroom and The Banker's Gift Shop. The Banker's Ballroom will mimic the formalness of The Banker's Suite in a 1920s grand style with hardwood floors, tall plaster columns and silk drapes.

The Banker's Gift Shop will carry unique gifts, custom cake toppers, and couture dresses and accessories by Boudoir Queen.

Contact
Trish Bright

Price
$650 – $750

Quick Facts
- The Banker's Suite occupancy 50
- The Banker's Ballroom occupancy 150
- Overnight Accommodations for 2
- List of approved caterers available uponrequest
- Air conditioned

© Mark Younger-Smith

© Mark Younger-Smith

WHAT'S NEW

The Banker's Ballroom and The Banker's Gift Shop opening January 2010

bay13

701 NW 13th Ave
Portland, Oregon 97209
p. 503.227.1133
f. 503.227.1155
e. ginger@bay13restaurant.com
www.bay13restaurant.com

About Bay 13 Restaurant

Located in the historic 1909 Crane Warehouse Building in the heart of Portland's Pearl District, Bay 13 is the ideal location for your Portland wedding. Bay 13 is a modern seafood restaurant, featuring a sushi bar, oyster/raw bar and open kitchen. With high ceilings and exposed brick walls, this contemporary restaurant is decorated simply to allow you to create the perfect atmosphere for your event.

Work personally with our Event Coordinator and Executive Chef to choose the perfect menu from our world class cuisine and extensive wine list. Conveniently located, Bay 13 is within walking distance of all major downtown hotels, galleries and boutiques. Many options are available for rehearsal dinners or receptions, from private to semi-private spaces and an outdoor patio. Bay 13 can accommodate parties from 10 to 350 guests. Valet parking available upon request.

Contact
Ginger Cates

Price
Varies – based on type & size of event

Quick Facts
- Can Accommodate Most Wedding Sizes
- Private Event Coordinator
- Award Winning Architecture
- Sustainable Seafood

WHAT'S NEW

We are now offering a fantastic winter 'happy hour' cocktail party for the very reasonable rate of $150 for 15-20 people. Perfect for your bachelorette party!

© Kris Stalnaker

300 Reuben Boise Road
Dallas, Oregon 97338
p. 503.831.3652
f. 503.831.3279
e. info@beckenridge.com
www.beckenridge.com

381

Celebrate Your Special Occasion Nestled In the Beauty of the Vineyard.

BeckenRidge Vineyard was specifically designed for weddings, receptions and special occasions. The beautiful and private setting of the vineyard together with the friendly staff offers a warm, welcoming atmosphere for you and your guests. The panoramic view of the Willamette Valley and the Cascades provide the perfect backdrop for your special day all year round.

In the spring, summer or fall, BeckenRidge harmoniously combines the outdoor ceremony with the indoor reception. Choose the lawn or the covered patio for your ceremony – both have a commanding view of the vineyard and beyond. In the winter, choose the fireplace or the window-view to stage your indoor ceremony.

The reception hall is marked by simple elegance in décor, comfort and convenience. The main room has hardwood floors perfect for dancing, a large stone fireplace, and abundant windows to take in the view. This air conditioned building includes kitchen, bar, spacious restrooms, and a private dressing room for the bride. A separate dressing & game room is available for the groom.

Our friendly and knowledgeable staff will help you plan your setup and arrange our furniture according to your wishes, transforming BeckenRidge to be uniquely yours.

Contact
The friendly staff of BeckenRidge are available by phone or email – call for appointment to visit us

Price
Starting at $2,300

Discounts available for mid-week & off-peak season

Capacity
Up to 120 indoors; expands up to 250 utilizing patios

Amenities
- Rental includes private use of the property with the romance of 12 acres of vineyards with astounding views of the Cascades.
- Reception furnishings for 150 are provided & setup by on-site staff.
- Kitchen available to a professional caterer of your choice.
- Expanded collection of rental accessories includes set-up & teardown.

NEW ARRIVALS
Adding groom's room January 2010 ideal with satellite TV, foosball and more.

See page 535 under Rehearsal Dinner

Bravo! Member Since 1998

Visit BravoWedding.com for more information on the best reception & wedding sites

The Benson
A COAST HOTEL@PORTLAND

Four Diamond Award
AAA

309 SW Broadway
Portland, Oregon 97205
p. 503.295.4140
f. 503.241.3757
e. weddings@bensonhotel.com
www.bensonhotel.com

382

About The Benson

Your special day requires a special place. The Benson Hotel, located in the heart of downtown, has a proud 98 year tradition of hosting Portland's most prominent social events. Traditional or trendsetting, intimate or elaborate; our breathtaking rooms along with our highly decorated executive chef and experienced banquet staff will make your wedding celebration truly unforgettable!

Begin your celebration with a reception in front of the fireplace in our grandiose lobby, surrounded by Austrian Crystal, Circassian Walnut and Italian Marble, then move to the stunning Crystal Ballroom. Our largest ballroom, The Mayfair, is exquisitely appointed with Axminster carpets, rich wall coverings, built-in staging, plus state-of-the-art sound and lighting package.

Many other elegant private rooms are available including the Wine Room, Wine Cellar and Little London in the London Grill, perfect for your rehearsal dinner.

The Benson Hotel is a special place to revisit year after year. Contact us today for available dates and to preview our luxurious space and accommodations.

Contact
Sales & Catering Department

Price
Call for personal service

Capacity
Up to 400 seated guests;
Stand-up reception
up to 600

Quick Facts
- AAA Four Diamond Award Winning Hotel
- Fine linen, china, glassware & dance floor at no additional charge
- Elegance atmosphere; convenient location & plenty of parking
- Private dining rooms & award winning Wine Cellar available

Bravo! Member Since 1991

White Glove Photography

BEST WESTERN

OCEAN VIEW
R·E·S·O·R·T

414 North Prom
Seaside, Oregon 97138
p   503.738.3334
p. 800.234.8439
e. catering@oceanviewresort.com
www.oceanviewresort.com

383

Are you dreaming of your wedding or reception on the beach?

Call the Ocean View Resort.

Best Western Ocean View Resort in Seaside is oceanfront on the Prom, on the spectacular North Coast of Oregon. The Ocean View Resort is perfect for rehearsal dinners, wedding ceremonies or receptions from 40 to 340 guests. We offer first-class banquet rooms with a "touch of home" personalized service from our expert staff. Dining options include Salvatore's Cafe, an Italian seafood grille: cozy Sal's Pub for quiet conversation; or catering with our professional staff. The Ocean View Resort is AAA-approved, smoke free and pet-friendly. Enjoy our beautiful indoor pool and spa for year-round recreation.

Ocean View Resort includes 107 guest-rooms and suites, most with a spectacular ocean or coastline view. A wide variety of guestrooms include kitchenettes, private balconies, fireplaces, pillow top mattresses, duvets, and over-size jetted tubs. All guestrooms have been recently renovated and include free internet.

Contact
Donna M. Marx

Price
Group rates available:
Call for details

Capacity
Up to 340 guests

Amenities
- Full service catering offering custom menus, all-inclusive meal plans, & beach events
- Wireless hi-speed internet access property-wide

WHAT'S NEW

- Newly-remodeled oceanfront suites with over-sized, ocean-view, jetted tubs.
- Gift certificates are available: Perfect for birthdays, anniversaries, and weddings.

Bigfoot Lodge

Bigfoot Lodge is the ultimate facility for outdoor lovers' wedding ceremonies, receptions and rehearsal dinners. Bigfoot boasts incredible Mt. Hood views and is set on 64 acres of private forested land and is adjacent to County and National Forest lands. This is it ... if you want the natural beauty, scenery, tranquility of the wilderness and mountains plus total privacy for your reception with no curfews for the entire weekend! Share your love for one another with family and friends in the dramatic but relaxed atmosphere of Bigfoot Lodge and enjoy the 5,000 sq. ft. hand hewn ponderosa pine log lodge.

Custom engineered with soaring 26 foot ceilings, covered decks and porches, expansive green lawn, his/her tile & slate restrooms, dedicated catering staging area, and easy parking. Bigfoot accommodates small wedding groups for Fall, Winter and Spring inside starting at only $500, or Summer weddings with guests up to 250 starting at $1,200. Profess your love for one another at the most inspiring location in the heart of the Hood River Valley. An easy 10 minutes on Hwy 35 from town. Schedule a visit and take in the possibilities...

384

Contact

Mike & Nilsa Zeman

1819 Cascade Avenue
Hood River, Oregon 97031

p. 541.490.7971

e. Mike@LuxurySearch.com

e. Nilsaz@CenturyLink.net

www.Bigfoot-Lodge.com

Price

$500 – $1,200 site fees plus accommodations.

Black Butte Ranch is the wedding destination that is quintessential Oregon. Your special day will be framed with a spectacular ceremony and reception setting of sweeping Cascade mountains, ponderosa pines, glistening aspens and crystal blue waters. Nature's picturesque surroundings compliment the authentic hospitality, outstanding cuisine and a picture perfect wedding location.

Our experienced team will assist you in with your wedding planning, event details, menu selections and arrangements. Complete catering services are available and we can build customized menus for your special day. With several outdoor ceremony locations to choose from and both indoor and outdoor reception venues, Black Butte Ranch is the perfect destination wedding location.

Contact
Aimee Kristine Smith

PO Box 8000
Black Butte Ranch
Oregon 97759

p. 866.976.3548
f. 541.595.1212

e. catering@BlackButteRanch.com

www.BlackButteRanch.com

385

Rates
Rates vary with wedding package, please call for more information.

Included Services
- Destination weddings for up to 175 people. The Ranch features an outdoor ceremony site, with both indoor and outdoor reception areas.

- Central Oregon Cascade Destination with scenic views of the Cascade Mountains.

- Rental Homes and lodging accommodations on site for wedding party, family and guests.

- Recreational activities include 36 holes of golf, full service spa, 19 miles of bike paths, 6 swimming pools, fitness center, horseback riding, fly fishing, trail hiking, kayaking and other outdoor recreational opportunities.

Blackstone Restaurant & Catering, located just over the bridge from Portland in Vancouver, is the perfect Southwest Washington location for your special occasion. Overlooking the Portland city lights, Blackstone offers two private rooms (with the option to join both for one large room) that seat a total of 34. We can accommodate up to 300 guests in the dining room, for any type of occasion: wedding rehearsals, ceremonies and receptions, engagement parties, bachelor/bachelorette parties, and beyond. Whether you are looking to serve passed hors d'oeuvres at your wedding reception or a buffet dinner, Blackstone Catering offers a variety of creative menus for any budget. Have something special in mind? No problem! We are happy to customize a menu to meet your specific needs and budget.

Call us today, and let our expert catering staff at Blackstone make it an event to remember!

BLACK STONE

Contact
Annette Atkinson

p. 360.253.0253

e. annette@blackstonewa.com

www.blackstonewa.com

Rates
Prices vary; please contact us for quotes

Included Services
- 2 Private rooms: Southview Room (up to 14), Blackstone Room (up to 20)
- Blackstone catering available for on or off-site events, by Executive Chef Kevin Kennedy
- Drop-off service, plated dinners, passed hors d'oeuvres or buffet
- Wedding rehearsals, ceremonies & receptions
- Outside patio seating
- Full service bar; Elaborate Northwest wine selection
- Professional and friendly event planning & catering services
- Parking available on-site
- Easy access; just minutes from Portland – Hwy 14, 164th Street Exit

Clients Include
- Burgerville Corporation
- Nautilus
- Linear Technology

BLACK SWAN
The art of hospitality.

p. 360.567.5922
e. g@blackswanevents.net
www.blackswanevents.net

About Black Swan Events

When you dream of your wedding day, what do you see? Is it the casual elegance of a vineyard, lush in the abundance of harvest? Do you envision the classic tradition of a grand ballroom, stately and opulent? Perhaps your dream wedding holds the intimacy of an oceanside ceremony, with the natural whisper of the sea to accompany your vows?

Our featured venues accommodate 10 to 300 guests, and showcase unique properties. These include a private manor estate, an historic ballroom, a private winery in Vancouver, and two stunning ballrooms in Portland. Purchase of the romantic 41 ft classic sailing vessel Moontide harkens back to the era of Bogie and Bacall, and offers a most intimate setting for a sunset vow exchange under sail. Oceanside celebrations are offered in Lincoln City, and may be extended over 2 to 5 days.

Black Swan gathers the very best in the industry, caterers, gown designers, videographers, florists, photographers, bakers, and more, to make your dream wedding, truly, the wedding of your dreams… all within your budget.

Contact
Gabrielle Dowding, Director

Price
$1,000 and up

Quick Facts
- Showcasing 5 breathtaking properties in Vancouver and Portland.
- Custom catering and event design on either our venue or yours.
- Saving clients 20 to 40% on the cost of their celebration.

387

BLOCK 90 BALLROOM
In the heart of Portland's Pearl District

The Block 90 Ballroom

This marvelous space is perfect for your dream wedding of 50, or 1,000! The Block is a perfect mix of old meets new.

Clean lines and a modern feel make this space like no other in Portland. Situated in a converted historical Pearl District warehouse, this newly renovated facility can easily provide space for up to 500 guest for an elegant sit down dinner and up to 1,000 for a standing cocktail reception!

Our company is dedicated to weddings; Our service is complete with a coordinator, full staff, selection of decore items, and nearly all wedding day rentals. Share your dreams with us and together we will turn this amazing facility into your storybook wedding location!

We've spent years looking for a location like this. The Block 90 Ballroom is our dream come true!

www.PowersOregon.com

Weddings, Receptions & Rehearsal Dinners

Contact
Powers Oregon Company
p. 503.478.0997
www.PowersOregon.com

Rates
Please call for info!

Included Services
- A Wedding Planner
- Wedding Day Staff and Management
- A Private Chef
- Gourmet Cuisine Experience
- Exceptional Beer and Wine
- Tables, Chairs & Linens
- Set Up & Tear Down
- Other Various Services

Natural Beauty in Its Most Spectacular Form

Nestled in the heart of the historic Columbia River Gorge, just 30 minutes east of Portland, natural beauty is in its most spectacular form at Bridal Veil Lakes.

Beautiful wildflowers and lush forest are the perfect backdrop for your lakeside wedding. The view of the Columbia River Gorge and the serene lakeside setting add just the hint of romance that will make your wedding memories last a lifetime.

The photo opportunities are endless! Bridal Veil Lakes is protected from the Columbia Gorge east wind and our Lakeside Pavilion is wonderful for weather protection.

Please call 503.981.3695 and make an appointment to visit our exclusive and private setting for the wedding of your dreams.

Other Services

An arch for your ceremony is provided.

We offer four canoes and a number of RV spaces available. We offer ample parking, however parking attendants are strongly suggested. Our facility is fully ADA accessible.

Please visit our website www.bridalveillakes.com for more information.

Contact

Jennifer Miller

PO Box 5
Bridal Veil, Oregon 97010

p. 503.981.3695

www.bridalveillakes.com

Price

Price varies according to event

389

Capacity

Up to 400 outdoors

Amenities

- Tables & chairs provided for 250

- Servers provided by caterer; caterer or renter provides licensed bartender, liquor & liability insurance.

- 800 square feet available in pavilion; 800 square feet covered outdoor patio available for dancing.

- Pavilion & outdoor patio are equipped with decorative lighting.

TYPES OF EVENTS

We are a perfect venue for weddings, receptions, picnics, reunions and anniversaries.

Bravo! Member Since 1998

www.bridgeportbrew.com • events@bridgeportbrewing.com

1313 NW Marshall Street • Portland, Oregon 97209
p. 503.241.7179 ext. 310 • f. 503.241.0625

© Pualani Lobo

390

About BridgePort Brewpub + Bakery

Located in Portland's vibrant Pearl District since 1984, BridgePort brewpub + bakery resides in a hundred and twenty year old brick and timber building, fusing contemporary architecture, modern amenities and historic charm. The brewpub is a Portland landmark, tourist destination and beer lovers paradise. All foods are handcrafted using local, natural and organic ingredients whenever possible. Known internationally for award-winning ales, BridgePort is the oldest craft brewery in Oregon.

Heritage Room

The Heritage Room is a unique venue with rustic brick walls, large windows, wood floors, fir beams and a private full-service bar. This inviting backdrop may be decorated in style for an upscale affair. The Heritage Room can transform to be the perfect venue for your Rehearsal Dinner, Wedding Ceremony and Reception.

Old Knucklehead Room

The Old Knucklehead Room provides privacy amidst the bustle of our busy pub. It is located next to our main bar for an authentic brewpub experience.

Contact

Barbara Lee

Price

Call for price; minimums depend on day of the week

Capacity

Heritage Room:
30 to 110
Old Knucklehead Room:
5 to 25

Amenities

- Coordinator to guide you through all the details of planning

- Extensive menus for all budgets

- Friendly & knowledgeable staff provided

- Sustainable business practices

- On-site artisan bakery

- Private full-service bar in the Heritage Room

- China, glass, silver, linens, tables, chairs & candles provided

- Private Entrance for the Heritage Room

- Breakfast, Lunch & Dinner

- Located on the street car line, close to freeways & downtown

© Pualani Lobo

Bravo! Member Since 1995

© Emily G.

Brookside Inn
ON ABBEY ROAD

8243 NE Abbey Road
Carlton, Oregon 97111
p. 503.852.4433
f. 503.852.0062
e. info@brooksideinn-oregon.com
www.brooksideinn-oregon.com

391

Experience the Magic

Brookside Inn on Abbey Road offers a magical setting for your wedding ceremony and reception in the heart of Oregon's wine country. The pond, brook and gardens with waterfalls offer a variety of settings for your special day. Let your imagination set the stage for both your ceremony and reception.

We would like you and your guests to enjoy the wedding day to the fullest. In addition to all of the amenities offered at our venue, we have teamed with several preferred caterers. They know our property and will work with you to identify your specific needs prior to the wedding and will also provide coordination of your wedding day.

Influenced by the unique character of the Pacific Northwest, the inn features nine guest suites, each with its own private bath. The complimentary breakfast at the inn is a delicious culinary experience inspired by top chefs in the Northwest.

Contact
Susan and Bruce Bandstra

Price
Prices vary according to number of guests. Please email for a personalized proposal.

Quick Facts
- Capacity 200 outdoors.
- Numerous ceremony and reception venues.
- Suggested list of caterers upon request.
- Tables, chairs and catering galley.
- Rehearsal dinner pricing upon request.
- Nine-suite inn for overnight lodging.
- Full breakfast on your schedule.
- Outdoor seating for relaxing, including fire pit area.
- On-site massages available with prior arrangement.

TYPES OF EVENTS
Brookside Inn also hosts both private and wine maker's dinners, corporate meetings, and family reunions.

© Doreen L. Wynja

CAMAS MEADOWS
GOLF CLUB

4105 NW Camas Meadows Drive
Camas, Washington 98607

p. 360.833.2000
f. 360.834.7075
e. jduce@camasmeadows.com
e. sweishaar@camasmeadows.com
www.camasmeadows.com

392

About Camas Meadows Golf Club

Camas Meadows Golf Club promises you a scenic and beautiful location for your special day. Our Event Coordinators will assist you in planning and presenting your event while our outstanding staff will dazzle you with delicious opportunities. Tucked away in the forested wetlands near Lacamas Lake, Camas Meadows Golf Club offers any bride and grooms a unique and spectacular setting in which to celebrate. You and your guests will be surrounded by beautiful towering evergreens and by our extraordinary golf course. While our custom gazebo provides a stunning backdrop to any event, our pavilion tent or spacious Oak room, will provide more than ample room for fine dining and dancing. Rest assured that Camas Meadows Golf Club will offer every effort to ensure that your celebration is filled with unforgettable memories.

Contact
Jenny Duce
Stephanie Weishaar

Price
Call for Quotes

Capacity
Up to 250 people

Quick Facts
- Beautiful outdoor wedding gazebo.
- Large white pavilion tent.
- Spacious indoor and outdoor banquet facilities available.
- Full service catering.
- Full service bar and servers.

TYPES OF EVENTS
Ceremonies, Receptions, Rehearsal dinners, Bridal showers, Bachelor golf outings, & Anniversary celebrations.

Bravo! Member Since 2007

CAMP TURNAROUND

57011 NW Wilson River Highway
Gales Creek, Oregon 97117
p. 503.359.1438
f. 503.359.1438
e. director@campturnaround.com
www.campturnaround.com

About Camp Turnaround

Camp Turnaround is a newly refurbished venue that provides a private and pleasant country setting for your gathering. For decades families have enjoyed this beautifully forested creek-side park. Weddings, church picnics, company picnics and family reunions have all been celebrated here.

Nature provides the gorgeous setting. Landscaping, acres of lawns, pathways with bridges and a pond all add to the great outdoors. The large patios and a deck overlooking the creek provide additional shelter, seating and food service area. The beautiful 3,000 sq. ft. rustic Pavilion has knotty pine paneled walls, a huge rock hearth and wood stove. It will seat 175 – 200 inside. There is also a romantic gazebo nestled into shrubs and flowers with an adjacent lawn area seating 200. The brand new handsome log and cedar stage has an adjacent lawn area that seats 250. Also at the cross there is another smaller lawn area that seats 75 – 100. There is also a playground and lawn game areas for all ages.

Contact
Julie or Gary Morrison

Price
Call for pricing and a complimentary tour

Capacity
175 at table – 250 seated

393

Quick Facts
- Indoor or outdoor ceremony option
- Scenic setting in forest, creek and meadow
- Lawns and shrubbery
- 3000 sq.ft. pavilion for indoor event
- Rustic stage
- Romantic gazebo
- Area at the cross

Caples House Museum

1925 First Street
Columbia City, Oregon 97018
p. 503.397.5390
e. caretaker@capleshouse.com
www.capleshouse.com

About Caples House Museum

The Dr. Charles Caples House Museum was the home of a pioneer doctor, who arrived in the 1844 wagon train, and his family. The grounds feature the 1870's home built upon the original site of his father's log cabin, a view of the Columbia River and Mt. St. Helens, magnificent trees and gardens, the 1870's Heritage Orchard of Apple and Pear trees, a collection of vintage toys and dolls, and a Country Store featuring fine American craft items and collectibles.

The Museum's Knapp Social Center is a cozy indoor meeting venue with views of the Columbia. Seated on its porch, you catch the soft breeze off the river and watch the ships pass by.

Whether you are looking for a large outdoor venue with a stunning river view or an intimate indoor venue, Caples Museum will transport you to another time and a peaceful, happy state of mind.

Contact
Christine Kramer
Caples House Museum
Caretaker

Price
$1,200 Full Day or
call for Short Term rates

Capacity
Up to 300 Outdoors.
51 Seated indoors at tables
or 110 seated in rows.

Amenities
- Ideal for weddings, receptions, corporate retreats, picnics, reunions & other events.
- Beautiful country setting with Columbia River and Mount St. Helens views.
- Expansive, level outdoor spaces under magnificent shade trees.
- Full kitchen facilities.
- Preferred caterers list upon request.

WHAT'S NEW
Catered teas available for 10 to 51 people at $20 each. 48 Hours notice required.

Bravo! Member Since 2008

394

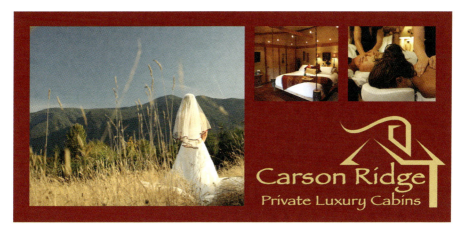

A Carson Ridge Wedding is a cherished memory that everyone will remember. Created by pairing our beautiful setting with unrivaled attention to every detail.

Just imagine your very own luxury cabin to prepare for the big day…wake up to breakfast delivered right to your cabin, soak in the Jacuzzi tub before your in-cabin massage to work away any tension. Then, when the time has come you follow the bridal trail that leads from your cabin to the wedding lawn & pagoda where all your friends and family are waiting to be a part of this special occasion.

Now this is the whole day event that we believe everyone should have. Relaxed, serene, perfect all with the privacy of your own venue!

Let us fulfill your dreams of a truly magical wedding. We can assist you with every aspect of your special day making sure no detail is overlooked.

Voted as the "Best in the West" and the "Top 20 most romantic places"
–bedandbreakfast.com

Contact
Latisha & Pete Steadman

p: 877.816.7908

Capacity
50 indoor & 100 outdoor; lodging: 22

Amenities
- Gorgeous views of the Columbia River Gorge
- Landscaped gardens specially designed for weddings and photos
- Several ceremony/reception sites to chose from
- Cocktail/appetizer garden
- Large Gazebo for ceremony/ reception & dancing
- On site caterer & photographer
- Luxurious Bridal/ Honeymoon cabin with a special trail to the ceremony site
- Private luxury cabins with jetted tubs, fireplaces, log beds, luxury linens, covered decks & log swings
- In cabin spa treatments
- Wedding coordinator & rehearsal included
- Only 45 min from PDX

WHAT'S NEW
3 new custom built cabins & wellness center offering retreats, Yoga, Thai massage & Reiki

395

CATHEDRAL RIDGE WINERY

4200 Post Canyon Drive
Hood River, Oregon 97031

p. 541.386.2882
p. 800.516.8710
f. 541.516.8710

e. crw@cathedralridgewinery.com
www.cathedralridgewinery.com

About Cathedral Ridge Winery

Whether it's one person or a wedding party of 250 people, we love to have people visit our winery and vineyard. Beautiful in virtually every season, you will be amazed by the views of Mt. Adams as you rest on the bench overlooking the vineyards and by Mt. Hood as you tour your way south through the vines. Our charming winery and gift house overlook manicured lawns and beautiful flower gardens, the perfect compliment to these stunning mountain views. Cathedral Ridge exists to provide a perfect event for you and will extend every effort to refer you to appropriate suppliers for whatever you may require. Our friendly and knowledgeable hospitality team is here to help make your wedding or event the most special day of your life!

Types of events: Company meetings, holiday parties, corporate picnics, private lunches, anniversary parties, special event celebrations, Weddings, Weddings and receptions, rehearsal dinners, etc.

Contact
Event Coordinator

Price
Varies depending upon the day of the week & type of event.

Capacity
Up to 200 Guests

Amenities
- Outstanding full-service caterers for all types of events. We offer a list of both Hood River & Portland Caterers with outstanding references.
- We provide seating for 100 & tables to match.
- Staff is included in catering costs.
- We specialize in serving outstanding wines & also provide beer, water & soda as requested.
- Approximately 1200 square feet of dance floor
- Linens, china & glassware: Usually included in catering price.
- Ample free parking.
- All facilities are ADA accessible.

See page 536 under Rehearsal Dinner

396

12353 SE Lusted Road
Sandy, Oregon 97055
p. 503.819.0761
f. 503.663.1750
e. cscountrywedding@gmail.com
www.CedarSpringsCountryEstate.com

A Romantic Country Wedding Park

As if somewhere in time – at the edge of the Sandy River Gorge this beautiful estate is only 40 minutes east of Portland. The Park is nestled in and canopied by old growth trees – a magical location for the wedding of your dreams. The white Victorian gazebo is the perfect setting for your ceremony and dancing under the stars. A spring-fed trout lake rests beside the reception area. With seating on the hillside, your guests enjoy an unobstructed view. In the evening, the lights come on creating a magical wonderland.

Music

The acoustics in the park are lovely; bring in vocalists, harpists, string quartets or DJ's to fill your day with beautiful music.

Availability and Terms

Available July through September for weekday and weekend events. Only one event per day. Reserved with a deposit.

Contact
Patti

Price
Varies on event; please call for quote

Capacity
25 to 300

397

Amenities
- Onsite Wedding Coordinator
- Your choice of caterers or self cater
- Tables, chairs available for amphitheater seating & garden reception
- Champagne, wine or beer possible; bartender & liquor liability required
- Softly-lit Victorian gazebo provides a 350 square foot dance floor
- ADA – limited accessibility

TYPES OF EVENTS

Weddings, anniversaries, private dinner parties, reunions, business meetings & picnics. For elegant occasions or casual events, dine & dance under the stars.

Bravo! Member Since 1991

CEDARVILLE PARK

3800 West Powell Loop
Gresham, Oregon 97030
p. 503.666.7636
e. amelia@cedarvillepark.net
www.clubpaesano.org
www.cedarvillepark.net

398

About Club Paesano - Cedarville Park

An unexpected retreat from the city, and only minutes away. Nestled upon 11.2 acres of lush wooded green space and surrounded by native cedar and fir trees. Cedarville Park the Home of Club Paesano is the true destination site showcasing the heart of the Pacific Northwest's regional natural scenic beauty and the ideal setting for all special occasions.

Our venue facilities and park grounds will meet all expectations and accommodate and care for all your special event needs:

- Weddings: ceremony & reception
- Anniversaries
- Reunions
- Picnics
- Brunches, luncheons, dinner banquets
- Casual to formal affairs

Contact
Larry Cereghino

Price Range for Service
Please contact us for venue & event package rates

Quick Facts:
- Capacity:
  Indoors – Up to 300
  Outdoors – Up to 2,000
- Catering: In-house full-service.
- Provided by: Special Occasions Catering & Events.
- Pre-event planning & onsite coordination.
- Ample & free onsite parking.
- All Set-up & Clean-up included.
- Bar-service available.
- Full sound system available.
- Natural park-like setting.
- Rustic-log cabin lodge motif.
- Spacious dance floor: 2400 square foot
- Outdoor covered Pavilion.
- Garden Courtyard.

© Jim Semlor

Columbia Cliff Villas
LUXURY CONDOMINIUM HOTEL

"Easy to get to. Hard to leave."

3880 Westcliff Drive
PO Box 887
Hood River, Oregon 97031
p. 866.912.8366
p. 541.436.2660
e. info@columbiacliffvillas.com
www.columbiacliffvillas.com

399

Gorgeous Views. Great Memories.

Only One Hour East of Portland on the sunny side of the Cascades, the luxurious new Columbia Cliff Villas provide an unforgettable romantic venue with old-world charm, and breathtaking views of the Columbia Gorge and the historic Columbia Gorge Hotel's lush gardens and 208' waterfall.

Honeymoon Attractions and Photo Ops

The 'easy to get to' ideal location for your honeymoon. So photogenic and memorable that you are sure to return for many future getaways and anniversaries. Enjoy Hood River's award-winning restaurants, galleries and shops. The Columbia River Gorge also now offers 40 wineries, five golf courses, endless hiking and biking, fishing and water sports. Plus, year-round adventure on Mt. Hood.

Wedding Accommodations

Rooms and suites can be joined or separated for your complete privacy. Perfect for your family and friends to gather and make memories as they share in your wedding experience. Spacious suites are perfect for welcoming parties, rehearsal dinners, wedding preparations for the bridal party and even ceremonies or receptions for 50.

Extraordinary Services

Wedding coordination. Private chef dining and catering, as well as limousine and photography services. We can also arrange for music, flowers and wedding cakes. Room service and spa services available in all suites.

Contact
Steve Tessmer
Owner & General Manager

Price
Rooms; $169 – $350
1 – 3 Bedroom Suites;
$295 – $895

Capacity
Indoor seating up to 30
Indoor and outdoor garden and vineyard wedding sites nearby for up to 150

Amenities
- Condo Style Layout
- Kitchens
- Fireplaces
- Private Spa Services
- Nanny Services

Testimonials
"These condos are incredible. If you're looking for a comfortable, spacious, beautiful and special place, with incredible views of the Columbia Gorge, this is the place. My husband and I filled up every available unit for our wedding."
– Lynne; Burbank, CA

OTHER EVENTS
Business meetings, retreats, team building, and wine dinners. Ask us about our extraordinary Columbia Gorge wine tours.

© Jim Semlor

The Columbia Gorge Hotel
4000 Westcliff Drive
Hood River, Oregon 97031
p. 541.386.5566
e. kim.bosch@northp.com
www.columbiagorgehotel.com

400

Since 1921, couples from all over the world have come to the Columbia Gorge Hotel to make vows, create memories and rekindle romances.

Named one of the "Top 10 Places to get Married" by Citysearch.com, our historical Hotel with its stunning 208' waterfall, gorgeous landscapes and sweeping vista of the Columbia River is an idyllic setting for the celebration of your lifetime.

Whether you'd like to have your ceremony performed amidst the gorgeous landscaping or you prefer the romance and ambience of the ballroom, we have a range of venues to suit your style and needs. The Benson Ballroom, our reception area with access to the outdoors and the 208' Wah Gwin Gwin waterfall, can accommodate up to 250 guests. The Falls Room, offers an unparalleled view of the Columbia River and our waterfall. This room provides an intimate setting for smaller receptions up to 30 guests. The lushly manicured grounds, formal gardens, streams and bridges offer a unique and elegant setting for any reception. The Point Lawn overlooks the Columbia River and can accommodate 350 guests.

Let us help you design an unforgettable occasion that will truly capture the emotions and memories of this special time in your life.

Contact
Kim Bosch, CMP

Price
Varies according to wedding package, please call

Amenities
- Seating accommodating up to 250 people
- 39 Guestrooms with historic charm
- Onsite Restaurant & Lounge, full service catering provided by award winning culinary team
- World's Best Travel & Leisure Award Winner – 2007
- Stunning views of the Columbia Gorge
- Located in Hood River, Oregon just minutes from PDX

Columbia RIVER
ADVENTURE CRUISES ®

110 SE Caruthers
Portland, Oregon 97214

p. 503.224.3900
p. 800.224.3901
e. sales@portlandspirit.com

www.portlandspirit.com

The fleet and facilities of the Portland Spirit has an experienced team that offers comprehensive services to help you plan a flawless wedding or special occasion. With the beauty of the Gorge and an abundance of breathtaking views, the Columbia Gorge Sternwheeler and Marine Park provide a unique venue for any event.

Columbia Gorge Sternwheeler
Enjoy an authentic riverboat experience on the Columbia Gorge Sternwheeler as you cruise through the scenic Columbia River Gorge aboard this classic paddle wheel boat. Two levels are fully enclosed and heated, each with an independent sound system. The top Starlight Deck is an open-air viewing deck. Ceremony: up to 150 guests. Reception: up to 300 guests.

Thunder Island
The perfect Northwest "on-land" venue for your wedding offering unparalleled views of the Columbia River Gorge National Scenic Area that are certain to create a breathtaking backdrop to your wedding ceremony. Ceremony: up to 200 guests.

Gorge Pavilion
Complete with tongue and groove woodwork, ambient sconce lighting and a state of the art sound system, the Gorge Pavilion is the perfect location for your special occasion. The Pavilion is a riverside event center that offers phenomenal views of the Columbia River. Ceremony: up to 200 guests. Reception: up to 300 guests.

Contact
Group & Charter Sales

Price
Prices vary – please inquire

Vessel & Facility Amenities
- In-house catering
- Linen tablecloths and napkins provided
- China, glassware & flatware provided
- Servers and bartender included with food and bar service
- Full service cash bar available
- Clean-up provided
- Commercial parking and street parking available
- ADA limited with assistance – please call for more information

TYPES OF EVENTS

Private charter meal and excursion cruises, company picnics, holiday parties, casino cruises, weddings, rehearsal dinners, fundraisers, meetings and conventions.

See page 347 under Boats & page 484 under Reception & Wedding Sites

401

© Alyssa Jul

Bravo! Member Since 1996

402

COOPER SPUR
MOUNTAIN RESORT

10755 Cooper Spur Road
Mount Hood, Oregon 97041

p. 541.352.6692
p. 800.skihood
e. weddings@cooperspur.com
www.cooperspur.com

Share you special day with us!

Cooper Spur Mountain Resort offers a variety of unique and beautiful locations for you to celebrate your wedding. All provide inspiring views surrounded by picturesque forest land. We can host a large outdoor wedding or small wedding with an intimate feeling. Our staff will ensure a smooth and memorable experience.

Event Venues

Grand Lawn – Located at the lodging property the Grand Lawn provides a meadow-like setting surrounded by forestland. The Grand Lawn has enough room for the largest outdoor wedding, yet can be arranged to establish an intimate feeling.

The Log Home – With a magnificent view of Mt. Hood the Log Home sits at the forest edge which provides a stunning and natural back drop for a small wedding. The reception can be presented at the Log Home or on the deck.

Cooper Spur Ski Area Base Lodge – The alpine lodge and sun deck provide a natural setting for a memorable ceremony.

Top of the Spur – Celebrate your occasion at the top of Cooper Spur Ski Area which offers a panoramic view that includes Mt. Hood and the beautiful Hood River Valley. The Homestead Chairlift is used to transport the wedding party and guests.

Lodging

The cabin and lodge structure portray a simple elegance and invite you to relax. Room for lodging for more than 100 people.

Contact
Jodi Gehrman

Price
Moderate to customized events, please inquire

Quick Facts
- Catering menus available
- Servers provided
- Full-service bar available
- Tent, dance floor & other fixtures available-inquire for pricing
- Ample complimentary parking available
- ADA

SPRING AND FALL WEDDING SPECIAL APRIL, MAY, OCT 15 – NOV 15

Host your entire wedding party at Cooper Spur Mountain Resort, including Wedding ceremony, lodging in our Honeymoon Cabin for Bride & Groom, reception dinner, wine, flowers, wedding cake. Price $3500 for up to 40 people (gratuity not included; limited number of dates available.) Call 541.352.6692 to book your date.

1231 North Anchor Way
Portland, Oregon 97217

p. 503.735.1818
f. 503.735.0888

e. tara.blair@marriott.com

www.marriott.com/pdxnh

About Courtyard by – Portland North Harbour

The Courtyard by Marriott – Portland North Harbour is the perfect location for an outdoor celebration. Our 7,500 square foot, seasonally landscaped courtyard patio overlooks the Columbia River channel and has magnificent views of Mount St. Helens and Mount Adams. Complete with gazebo & fountain, the Courtyard by Marriott Portland North Harbour is an ideal setting for ceremonies, receptions, rehearsal dinners, cocktail & holiday parties!

Contact
Tara Blair

Price Range for Service:
$5,000 food
& beverage minimum.

Amenities
- Outdoor venue seats up to 450 people
- All-inclusive package pricing
- Event coordinated by a Marriott Certified Wedding Planner
- Onsite Catering
- Complimentary parking
- Deluxe accommodations for out of town guests
- Honeymoon Suite
- Pricing is inclusive of linens, tables, chairs and a variety of décor

403

Bravo! Member Since 1999

About The Crown Ballroom & Garden Court –
The Ultimate Wedding & Reception Showcase!

A beautiful location for unforgettable weddings! The Crown Ballroom is the resplendent architectural centerpiece of the historic Pythian Building in downtown Portland. Imagine walking down the aisle in a turn-of-the-century Italian Renaissance Ballroom with an intimate theater balcony at one end, majestic gold chandeliers highlighting a cathedral-style ceiling and a grand curtained stage for your ceremony. It's the perfect setting for your dream wedding.

Receptions at The Crown begin in the adjoining Garden Court with cocktails and hors d'oeuvres, then the buffet opens and you lead your guests into the Ballroom for a magical night of dining, friends and dancing.

The Crown is shown by appointment only. Call today and let's get started on making your dream wedding a reality!

Location
The Crown Ballroom is located on the corner of 9th and Yamhill, right across from the new Park Blocks!

Your guests will enjoy convenient parking as well as hotels within walking distance to our Ballroom.

Contact
Raven Wilde, Director

918 SW Yamhill, 5th Floor
Portland, Oregon 97205

p. 503.227.8440
f. 503.210.0267

e. marryme@thecrownballroom.com
www.thecrownballroom.com

Price
$700 to $4,500

Capacity
From 50 to 450

Amenities
- In-house wedding planning services available
- In-house photography services are available, visit: www.julianandraven.com
- Designer decorated VIP rooms for the brides' & grooms' parties
- Ivory Grand Piano for cake cutting
- Full-service in-house catering by Connor Catering at The Crown & complimentary menu planning/tasting for Crown Brides
- DJ services available, includes full light & sound

See page 122 under Full-Service Catering

Bravo! Member Since 1996

404

CROWNE PLAZA®

PORTLAND
CONVENTION CENTER

THE PLACE TO MEET.

1441 NE 2nd Avenue
Portland, Oregon 97232
p. 503.233.2401
f. 503.238.7016
e. sales@cpportland.com
www.cpportland.com

About Crowne Plaza
Downtown/Convention Center

The Crowne Plaza – Downtown/Convention Center offers easy access from I-5 and I-84 and is just 20 minutes from Portland's International Airport. The hotel is just four blocks from the Oregon Convention Center and two blocks from the Rose Quarter and Memorial Coliseum. The Crowne Plaza is located in "Fareless Square" with access to the MAX Light Rail, where passengers can easily explore downtown Portland's incredible shopping, museums, galleries, and restaurants. The Lloyd Center Mall, Oregon's largest shopping mall, is located just seven blocks from the hotel and features an eight screen cinema and an indoor ice skating rink.

So Many Near By Attractions

- Willamette River and the East Esplanade walking path – 4 blocks
- Oregon Museum of Science and Industry – 1 mile
- Chinese Gardens – 1 mile
- Saturday Market – 1 mile
- Oregon Zoo – 6 miles
- Japanese Gardens – 6 miles
- Multnomah Falls – 30 miles

Contact
Trisha Dirks
Executive Meetings & Events Manager

Price
Please inquire

Capacity
9,000+ square feet of meeting & banquet space; seating groups from 10 to 600

405

Quick Fact
- Recently completed a multi-million dollar renovation to become the new Crowne Plaza Portland.

WHAT'S NEW

241 newly remodeled, spacious guest rooms, featuring coffee makers, hairdryers, irons & ironing boards, deluxe-size work desks, microwaves and refrigerators and 42' flat screen TV's. All rooms include the Crowne Sleep Amenities.

Bravo! Member Since 1998

Simple Elegance

Elegant weddings & receptions, rehearsal dinners & special events.

We feature a newly renovated, elegant ballroom to accommodate up to 250 for your reception. Our beautifully remodeled six-story atrium and a dramatic descending entrance in our glass elevator is the perfect venue for your ceremony.

Luxurious Accommodations

Our "Sleep Advantage" program features comfortable new beds with luxurious bedding and sleep amenities for a better night's sleep in our newly renovated guestrooms. We will provide complimentary deluxe accommodations (based on availability) for the bride and groom the evening of the reception, along with a complimentary bottle of champagne. Please ask about our special rates for your out-of-town guests.

406

Contact
Sales & Catering department
14811 Kruse Oaks Drive
Lake Oswego, Oregon 97035
p. 503.624.8400
e. sales@cplakeoswego.com
www.cplakeoswego.com

Price
Price to be determined by event & menu selections

Capacity
Ballroom up to 200 seated; 250 standing reception; Atrium up to 100 seated; 200 standing reception

Catering
Full-service catering, reception packages & custom menus available

Amenities
- Full-service hosted & no host bar; beer, wine & champagne service; we provide all beverages, bartenders & servers
- Complimentary ample parking
- Fully equipped to accommodate ADA requirements

WEDDING SPECIAL
Mention this ad and receive a gift certificate good for a Romance Package on your 1st Anniversary.

Bravo! Member Since 1996

Vineyard Wedding

Domaine Margelle Vineyards offers stunning vistas and quiet woodland settings for your wine country wedding along with Estate grown Pinot Noir and Pinot Gris wine. Included in the package is the use of the property over a two day period. This allows ample time for wedding set-up and rehearsal.

Venue Site

We feature several property sites as possible event locations. Our "La Bastide" woodland setting can accommodate up to 200 guests. Our Vineyard View and Meadow Vista can accommodate up to 400 guests. Special arrangements can be made for the exterior use of the "Manoir" overlooking the vineyard and valley. All venues include the weekend use of "La Bastide" for the Bridal Party. We are happy to work with wedding coordinators and area caterers.

Location

Domaine Margelle is located near Silverton, Oregon, nestled in the foothills of the Cascades. Wedding guests will find ample lodging nearby, including the Oregon Gardens Resort.

Contact

Marci Taylor

20159 Hazelnut Ridge Road
Scotts Mills, Oregon 97375

p. 503.873.0692
f. 503.873.0825

e. info@domainemargelle.com

www.DomaineMargelle.com

Price

Average pricing $3,000 Please contact for more information

Quick Facts

- Outdoor venue featuring several site locations overlooking the Willamette Valley and vineyards
- 2-day use of the property for Rehearsal & Wedding
- Use of vacation rental, "La Bastide" for Bridal Party preparations or overnight accommodations
- Tables & chairs for 150 guests. Site can accommodate up to 400

WHAT'S NEW

Domaine Margelle offers Estate grown Pinot Noir & Pinot Gris Wines for purchase. Contact us today for a private tasting.

See page 537 under Wineries & Vineyards

407

DOUBLETREE® HOTEL
PORTLAND

1000 NE Multnomah Street
Portland, Oregon 97232
p. 503.331.4921
e. jdeuchler@portlanddoubletree.com
www.doubletreegreen.com/weddings

408

Easy, Elegant and Experienced

The Doubletree Hotel is a full-service hotel dedicated to making your wedding day the most amazing day of your life. Our professional wedding coordinators are available to help with every detail. From menu planning to room decor and design, our experienced and friendly staff are there to make planning your wedding a pleasure. Our convenient location and ample parking make attending your wedding easy for your guests. Beautiful ballrooms, a great location and service beyond your expectations make the Doubletree Hotel at Lloyd Center the perfect choice for your special day.

Food and Beverage

Our Executive Chef and outstanding culinary team will create the perfect menu to suit your tastes and preferences. The hotel also offers Kosher weddings and receptions. Let us create a signature menu as unique as you are!

Contact
Julia Deuchler

Price
Customized Wedding
Packages Available

Quick Facts
- Four elegant ballrooms
- Dedicated wedding consultants with more than 20 years of experience
- Award-winning Executive Chef & culinary team
- Kosher weddings & receptions
- Newly renovated deluxe guestrooms for family & friends
- Green wedding specialists!
- Green Seal and Energy Star Certified
- 100 Best Green Companies to Work For

A PERFECT DAY!

From your rehearsal dinner to ceremony, reception to honeymoon suite, the Doubletree Hotel at Lloyd Center will ensure that every detail of your wedding is perfection!

Green Seal Certified, RecycleWorks Award Winner
Portland Composts! Participant, LEED Gold Certified

© Brides' Choice Photography

9957 SE 222nd Drive
Damascus, Oregon 97089
PO Box 104
Gresham, Oregon 97030
p. 503.667.7069
e. karenreed22@comcast.net
www.eastforkestate.com

East Fork Country Estate

East Fork Country Estate was designed for elegant country garden weddings. The Estate is located on 3 acres approximately 3 miles south of Gresham, OR. Floral gardens and terraced lawns surround the Estate House.

Our white Gazebo has a 340-degree view that overlooks a serene farm valley and Mt. Hood. Our Estate house has a large reception room, dance floor, spacious bride and groom's rooms, and is handicap friendly.

Your guests are seated under white canopies for the ceremony and the reception dinner. Our buffet dinners are excellent and we guarantee enough food for second helpings.

We offer horse and carriage service for your ceremony.

East Fork Country Estate offers an atmosphere that is comfortable and elegant. Your family and friends will enjoy a beautiful wedding in a relaxed country setting and will be pampered by our friendly, caring staff.

Our prices are affordable and include gratuities.

Contact
Karen Reed, Owner

Price
Prices are discussed individually depending on number of guests.

Amenities
- Capacity is 225 (invitations sent to 275)
- Open from April 15 through October 15
- Catering and wedding cake are included in package price
- Beer and Wine are available
- Ample free parking on site
- View of Mount Hood

409

Ecotrust Event Spaces

ecotrust

Weddings Celebrated Weekly

Ecotrust Event Spaces serves Portland with two unique green event venues: The Natural Capital Center and the Center for Architecture. Our vintage warehouses beam with modern sophistication, providing the perfect setting for chic ceremonies, smashing receptions or casual rehearsal dinners. Contemporary aesthetics and environmentally astute choices come together here to create weddings that are quintessentially Portland in philosophy and style.

Enjoy a Rooftop Terrace ceremony overlooking the Pearl District, a family-style supper in The Billy Frank, Jr. Conference Center or an intimate reception or rehearsal dinner in the Center for Architecture's creative gallery space.

Availability and Terms

The Natural Capital Center's Billy Frank, Jr. Conference Center is available seven days a week. The Natural Capital Center's Outdoor Terrace is available Monday through Friday after 5 p.m., and all day Saturday and Sunday. The Center for Architecture is available for private rentals on the weekends.

Contact
Sales and Marketing Manager

721 NW Ninth Avenue
Portland, Oregon 97209

p. 503.467.0792

e. experience@ecotrust.org

www.ecotrust.org/events/weddings

Price
Please call for a quote.

Quick Facts
- Two historic, LEED-certified venues available: The Jean Vollum Natural Capital Center & The Center for Architecture. Both are located in the Pearl District.
- Exclusive list of sustainable caterers who offer local, organic & seasonal menus.
- Modern workshop-style furniture is included in the rental fee.
- State of the art audio-visual system is included in the rental fee.
- Electricity use is offset with Green Tag purchases.

Capacity
- The Center for Architecture: 100 standup reception
- The Billy Frank, Jr. Conference Center: 180 standup reception
- The Outdoor Terrace: 200 standup reception

Bravo! Member Since 2001

410

PGE Earth Advantage, RecycleWorks Award Winner, Portland Composts! Participant, LEED Gold Certified

ELK COVE
VINEYARDS

27751 NW Olson Road,
Gaston, Oregon 97119
p. 503.985.7760
p. 877.ELK.COVE
f. 503.985.3525
e. info@elkcove.com
www.elkcove.com

Elk Cove Vineyards

From atop a knoll with commanding views of premier vineyards and buttressing the scenic Oregon Coast Range, the Elk Cove facility is a superb site for that special wedding, yet only 45 minutes from downtown Portland.

The "Roosevelt Room", named after the herds of Roosevelt elk which roam the nearby mountains, will hold up to 150 people. With a full catering kitchen, Italian tiled floors, and a built-in dance floor, the Roosevelt Room's French doors open onto a full-length deck overlooking the vineyard and showcasing the marvelous spectacle that nature displays in one of Oregon's most picturesque locations.

Elk Cove is pleased to offer a wide range of wines, from our award-winning Pinot Gris (the 2005 was honored to be one of Wine Spectator magazine's top 100 wines of the year for 2007) to the much sought-after Pinot Noirs from our La Bohème vineyard, which have been served at two White House state dinners.

Contact
Hospitality Coordinator

Quick Facts
- Capacity up to 150
- Outdoor ceremony location with indoor reception in our Roosevelt Room
- Roosevelt Room opens onto full length deck overlooking vineyards
- Plenty of on-site parking
- Utilize the vendors of your choice
- Tables and chairs in Roosevelt Room included

411

See page 538 under
Wineries & Vineyards

EMBASSY SUITES®

Portland - Downtown

319 SW Pine Street
Portland, Oregon 97204
p. 503.279.9000
f. 503.220.0206
e. pdxps_ds@hilton.com
www.embassyportland.com

About Embassy Suites Hotel Downtown

The Embassy Suites Hotel Downtown provides an elegant, one-of-a-kind backdrop for your special day. This beautifully restored hotel offers boutique style accommodations, exceptional service, exquisite food presentation and ballroom spaces designed for the grandest events.

Originally built in 1912, the Multnomah Hotel was a landmark in Portland and host to royalty and celebrities. After a full restoration, the hotel re-opened as the Embassy Suites and has been dazzling guests for the past 10 years, continuing her reputation for quality and service.

Description of Services:

All tables and chairs provided

Professional and Attentive Service Staff

Full Service Bar and Bartenders

Oak Parquet Dance floor

Damask Linens, Fine China and Crystal Glassware provided

Ample guest parking with valet and self-parking available

Contact
Catering Office

Price
Varies according to event, please call for details

Capacity
Up to 220 sit down
Up to 300 reception

Amenities
- Dedicated wedding specialist with impeccable attention to detail
- All suite accommodations with complimentary breakfast & nightly reception
- Exquisite food presentation inspired by locally grown produce & ingredients
- Luxurious Bridal Suite for the Bride & Groom on their wedding night
- Full service in-house salon & spa

GREAT DOWNTOWN LOCATION

Embassy Suites Downtown is located near Waterfront Park, Max Light Rail, Pioneer Square, and some of Portland's best restaurants.

Bravo! Member Since 1998

EMBASSY SUITES
HOTEL®

9000 SW Washington Square Road
Tigard, Oregon 97223
p. 503.644.4000
f. 503.526.1929
e. kim.mccandlish@wcghotels.com
www.portlandwashingtonsquare.
embassysuites.com

About Embassy Suites Hotel
Portland – Washington Square

The luxuriously renovated Embassy Suites Hotel Portland – Washington Square is Oregon's premier all-suite property featuring 356 beautifully appointed suites, each with separate living room and bedroom. Suites overlook a cascading waterfall in our nine-story atrium and Crossroads Restaurant, which features the finest in Northwest cuisine. The comfort of home awaits your group while staying at Embassy Suites; your guests will enjoy our complimentary, full breakfast buffet and evening Manager's Reception daily. From bridal showers to rehearsal dinners to ceremonies and receptions, our hotel is perfect for your occasion.

Location, Location, Location

Location means everything for your special events, and Embassy Suites is right where you need us. Located in the heart of Washington County and adjacent to Portland's RedTail Golf Course.

Embassy Suites is where you will want to be. Washington Square Mall is also adjacent to the hotel, and we are minutes from Oregon's most prestigious wine country – found right here in Washington County.

All highway arterials are easily accessible to our hotel, offering you close proximity to downtown Portland, Beaverton, Tigard and Lake Oswego.

Contact
Kim McCandlish
Director of Catering

Price
Varies with event size and menu selection

Capacity
Up to 700

413

Amenities
- Complimentary suite for bride and groom on the night of the wedding
- Discounted group rates available for out-of-town guests
- 356 beautifully furnished two-room suites
- Indoor pool and Jacuzzi
- Complimentary use of on-site fitness facility
- Hair dryers, irons and ironing boards in all suites
- Full-service restaurant and lounge open daily

WHAT'S NEW?

Ask us about our current wedding promotion.

Portland Composts! Participant

Bravo! Member Since 1996

An Outstanding Gathering Place

About Events at Copper Hill

Welcome to Events at Copper Hill, where the character of vaulted cedar ceilings, stone fireplaces, bronze chandeliers and detailed finishes merge with modern amenities in a newly renovated building.

This beautifully appointed facility, featuring over 10,000 square feet, has a variety of rooms ideal for gatherings of all sizes. Add to this a central location with ample free parking, state-of-the-art technology, and personalized service, you can expect nothing short of an outstanding event.

The Grand Hall, with soaring cedar ceilings and the "floor to ceiling" fireplace set the style for this immense room that will accommodate the larger events. Make your special event more memorable when held in this grand space.

You'll enjoy the atmosphere of our Lower Meeting Hall, with rough-hewn beams, large projection and flat screens, for presentations or slide shows. Versatility is the focus. Classroom, theater, conferences and receptions are just a sample of the possibilities for this special space.

Contact
Lacey Stark
Event Administrator

3170 Commericial Street SE
Salem, Oregon 97302

p. 503.373.3170
f. 503.373.3171

www.eventsatcopperhill.com

Price
Price is determined by the event & services rendered

Capacity
Up to 250 people in Grand Hall; Up to 140 people in Lower Meeting Hall

Amenities
- Full-service, in-house catering
- Variety of room setups
- Exhibition kitchen, board room & lower gathering area also available for use
- Tables, chairs, white linens, china, flatware, and glasses provided at no additional cost
- On-site audio/visual systems available
- Wireless internet
- Room setup & clean-up provided
- Ample free parking & fully ADA accessible

414

EVERGREEN AVIATION & SPACE MUSEUM
THE CAPTAIN MICHAEL KING SMITH EDUCATIONAL INSTITUTE

500 NE Captain
Michael King Smith Way
McMinnville, Oregon 97128

p. 503.434.4023
f. 503.434.4188
e. events@sprucegoose.org
www.evergreenmuseum.org

Host your next event at the **Evergreen Aviation & Space Museum!** Whether you are planning a small intimate wedding or an extravagant event, Evergreen is the place to visit. We have a variety of venues available, making it easy to find the perfect location for your special day.

The Evergreen Aviation & Space Museum's rental capacity is one of the largest in Oregon. Each building boasts over 121,000 square feet, featuring over 150 historic air and space craft and exhibits, and twelve galleries tracking mankind's journey into space.

These two expansive and elegant steel and glass facilities, with floor-to-ceiling windows, can each accommodate from 10 people up to 3,000 people for standing events and up to 1,500 people when seating is required.

Outdoor venues are also available, with our beautiful Oak Grove which has a capacity of 3,000 people. The West Patio, nestled into the side of the Aviation Museum, provides a gorgeous view of both the Oak Grove and the Evergreen Vineyard. Guests have easy access to all exhibits and aircraft in the Aviation via doors leading directly into the West Gallery.

Let us help you make your wedding one to remember!

Contact
Melissa Grace

Price
$1,000 to $10,000

Quick Facts
- Free parking.
- 72-inch round tables & folding chairs for up to 400 people
- Black, white or ivory table linens included
- More than 150 historic aircraft, spacecraft & exhibits (home of the "Spruce Goose")
- Room for bridal party to gather before event
- Linen upgrades & flowers available
- Indoor & outdoor venues— the Museum, the IMAX Theater Building, or the Museum's Oak Grove

415

WHAT'S NEW

New this year is the Space Museum – a perfect venue for memorable cocktail parties or other events. Call today to inquire about the available options.

2213 NW 23rd Avenue
Camas, Washington 98607

p. 360.834.0861
f. 360.834.5354
e. TheFairgate@aol.com
www.fairgateinn.com

416

The Fairgate Inn is the perfect destination to carry you across the threshold of all your tomorrows. We are a beautiful, private estate and the perfect venue for every season! We cater to the bride who dreams of her Summer Wedding under the stars and also to the bride who wants an elegant, Winter Wedding. Step through the door to your dreams and enjoy an experience of a lifetime that awaits you and your guests. We take pride in our traditional elegance, first class service, and exceptional cuisine. Seeing is believing! We offer new pricing options to make every couple's dreams become a reality.

Contact
Christine Foyt
or Stacey Young

Price
New pricing options for every budget; payment plans available

Capacity
Up to 200 indoors;
250 outdoors

Amenities
- Full-service In-house Catering
- Dedicated, Personal Coordinator to guide you through all the details of planning
- New expanded conservatory for year round events
- China, glass, silver, linens, tables and chairs provided
- Ample free parking

Bravo! Member Since 2000

ELEGANT GEORGIAN ESTATE
The Fairgate Inn possesses many special features found only in this Georgian Colonial-style home. We are open for year-round events.

900 NW 11th Avenue
Portland, Oregon 97209
p. 503.525.2225
f. 503.525.2224
e. info@fenouilinthepearl.com
www.fenouilinthepearl.com

About Fenouil

Fenouil is an Urban Parisian Brasserie located in the heart of the Pearl District. The atmosphere is elegant, warm and inviting.

Our semi-private second floor mezzanine overlooks Jamison Square and is perfect for rehearsal dinners. We offer a variety of customized menus or you may meet with Chef Pascal Chureau to create a menu that is more personalized.

In addition, the entire restaurant is available for weddings and receptions as well as neighboring Jamison Square. It is a lovely setting for an outdoor event.

We also offer offsite, full-service catering for corporate events, rehearsal dinners, wedding receptions, cocktail receptions and many more occasions.

Contact
Janey Clark
JaneyC@fenouilinthepearl.com

Price
Please call for pricing

Capacity
- Full Restaurant:
  120 people + patio
  220 people

- Bar:
  40 people – cocktail reception

- Mezzanine:
  65 people – sit down dinner
  80 people – cocktail reception

- Full Restaurant & Jamison Square Park buyout available

Quick Facts
- Modern Brasserie
- Semi-private dining area available
- Serving lunch, dinner and Sunday brunch
- Seasonal outdoor dining
- Sommelier service
- Valet package available
- Streetcar line access
- Hotel accommodations nearby

See page 525 under Rehearsal Dinner

417

First Unitarian Church of Portland

1011 SW 12th Avenue
Portland, Oregon 97205
p. 503.228.6389
f. 503.228.2676
e. hnicknair@firstunitarianportland.org
www.firstunitarianportland.org

Nestled in the heart of downtown Portland, The First Unitarian Church offers three traditional ceremony spaces and the modern, newly built, LEED Gold Certified, Buchan Reception Hall, perfect for your dream wedding or commitment ceremony and reception.

The Eliot Chapel built in 1924, features Georgian Revival architecture and seats 200 people. For larger events of up to 650, the Sanctuary provides theater style seating, with a balcony and historic 1880's pipe organ and grand piano framed by a walnut and gold leaf presidium arch. Additionally, The Channing Room, a formal parlor, seats up to 30 guests and is ideal for intimate ceremonies and a perfect dressing room for bridal parties.

The Buchan Reception Hall, in our newly built, LEED Gold Certified Buchan Building, offers 2,600 square feet of modern and elegant space for up to 250 guests. Its floor to ceiling windows, city views, adjacent outdoor courtyard and two-story atrium add to its spacious ambiance.

View a virtual tour at www.firstunitarianportland.org

Contact
Holli Nicknair

Price
Between $550 and $2,050

Quick Facts
- Affordable, downtown, LEED Gold Certified venue
- Self cater or choose your own caterer
- Alcohol Permitted
- Our Music Consultants and Ministers are available, though not required for your event
- Onsite Event Coordinator and rehearsal time included in every package
- Two outdoor courtyards perfect for your photo shoot and reception

WHAT'S NEW

The Buchan Building was built in 2008 and is LEED Gold Certified by the US Green Building Council.

See page 353 under Ceremony Sites

Bravo! Member Since 2001

FIVE PINE

HEALTH ✽ BALANCE ✿ ADVENTURE

1021 Desperado Trail
Sisters, Oregon 97759
p. 541.549.5900 ext 107 for Elena
f. 541.549.5200

e. elena.mcmichaels@fivepinelodge.com
e. greg.willitts@fivepinelodge.com

www.fivepinelodge.com

About FivePine Lodge and Spa

For an Enchanted Summer Wedding we invite you to celebrate the most magical day of your life at our pond in the midst of a pine forest at the base of the Cascade Mountains.

For a Magical Winter Wedding come in to the warm fireplaces of the Teresa Reception Center. From Hand Built furniture to the latest audio visual technology we'll create a magical beginning.

We would be honored to be part of your special day. We offer a full range of services with exceptional wine and selected cuisine by our Executive. For your wedding night we will reserve our special romance cottage as the perfect setting to spend your first night as husband and wife. FivePine offers Shibui Spa to relax and rejuvenate in anticipation of your special day combined with complimentary access to our 19,000 square foot Sisters Athletic Club against a backdrop of limitless open space and adventure from our trail kiosk.

Come take a tour

FivePine is a place you have to see to believe. Please call to schedule an appointment to tour our property and visit with our knowledgeable staff.

Contact

Greg Willitts
President

Elena McMichaels
Event Coordinator

Price

Varies; call for details

Amenities

- Exquisite 4,740 square foot full-service Conference Center with beautiful craftsman detailing
- Rich hand hewn maple dance floor
- In house interfaith minister available
- 4,600 square foot creekside patio/lawn space for outdoor ceremonies & receptions
- On-site catering
- Unique Sisters Movie House available for guest entertainment; screening room rental & special events available

419

Bravo! Member Since 2006

Garden Vineyards

12960 NW Dick Road
Helvetia, Oregon
p. 503.547.9046
e. melindawilson@gardenvineyards.com
www.gardenvineyards.com

Welcome to Garden Vineyards
Melinda and Stuart Wilson – Proprietors
Aron Hess – Winemaker

Garden Vineyards is a private vineyard residence, located 15 miles West of Portland. Our vineyards produce world-class Pinot Noir, Pinot Gris and Sparkling wines, which are served at all events. We provide full access to our gardens and event areas for the day.

Our site offers distinctive garden rooms, each affording ideal space for reception, ceremony, dance lounge and after hours.

The reception terrace faces the southern view and is under the protection of shade trees, umbrellas and weatherproof structures. The reception terrace is surrounded by our Tuscan-style home and formal house gardens.

Our lower terrace is ideal for ceremonies and seated dinners. Like the other garden areas, it has magnificent views of the vineyards, valley and mountains in the distance.

The lounge garden is outfitted with a permanent dance floor, lounge seating, band stage and full-time weather protection.

420

Contact
Melinda & Stuart Wilson

Price
Upon request

Capacity
300

Amenities
- Garden Vineyards wines
- Estate quality garden spaces, fully furnished
- Seclusion provided by a paved, scenic mile long driveway
- Expansive views of the Tualatin Valley & Coast Range from each event area
- Ceremony area with seating & clustering of large landscape umbrellas
- Reception area with seating & weather-protected awning structure
- Lounge area with dance floor, band stage, seating & weather-protected awning structure
- Two host suites

GHOST ROCK RANCH
www.ghostrockranch.com

phone: (541) 536-5593

Ghost Rock Ranch
148800 Beal Road
La Pine, Oregon 97739
p. 541.536.5593
f. 541.536.2399
e. info@ghostrockranch.com
www.ghostrockranch.com

With its panoramic mountain views "Ghost Rock Ranch" lends a stunning visual and spiritual backdrop for any wedding or private affair. The Ranch House offers three private guest rooms and there are 5 rustic cabins available for your guests. This Wedding Venue is best utilized with the support of a Wedding Planner. The Ranch can recommend thru your planner a list of experiences to make the wedding celebration worry free. The catering options are endless.

What's New?
Ghost Rock Ranch offers lessons and guided trail rides.

The Ranch features rustic and charming accommodations. Our bunkhouses sleep 3 – 4, and each A-frame cabin sleeps 2.

The Bed & Barn Apartment is charming and warm. It features a large deck, mountain views and privacy, with your own bath and kitchenette.

The fully equipped Ranch House features modern amenities such as 3 luxurious guest rooms, a professional industrial kitchen, and a floor to ceiling river rock fireplace.

Contact
Cherie Appleby

Quick Facts
- Spectacular views for wedding photos
- Deck at the pond
- Deck off the house can serve 100 – 200 guests
- Industrial kitchen suited for caterers and chef
- Western Experience

421

GLENN & VIOLA WALTERS
CULTURAL
ARTS
C · E · N · T · E · R

527 East Main Street
Hillsboro, Oregon 97123
p. 503.615.3485
f. 503.615.3484
e. seanm@ci.hillsboro.or.us
www.ci.hillsboro.or.us/wcac

422

Old-Fashioned Elegance & Romance

Located in the heart of downtown Hillsboro, the Glenn & Viola Walters Cultural Arts Center has quickly become known as one of the most beautiful sites in the area for wedding ceremonies and receptions. The Center's main hall features red stone walls, hardwood floors and custom woodwork and ceiling arches.

The hall accommodates up to 200 seats for ceremonies and 150 seats for receptions. Additional spaces in the facility can be added to your rental to accommodate larger receptions. The terraces and outdoor grounds are beautifully landscaped year-round.

Photo or video presentations can be shown on our 10' screen, and guests can admire the artwork displayed throughout the facility during the event.

Please call for an appointment to discuss your ceremony or reception.

Contact
Sean Morgan

Price
Prices vary according to spaces & amenities requested; please call for details

Capacity
Up to 150 seated for banquet or up to 200 seated for ceremony

Quick Facts
- Air conditioned facility with break out rooms available
- Beautiful hardwood floor throughout the event space is excellent for dancing
- Parking is available on-site and nearby
- Food & beverage arrangements are at the discretion of the renter
- Alcohol service & use of candles permitted with approval

OTHER OPTIONS
Hillsboro Parks & Recreation also has other beautiful and memorable indoor and outdoor wedding and reception sites!

PO Box 100
Underwood, Washington 98651

p. 509.493.2026
f.   509.493.2027

e. info@gorgecrest.com

www.gorgecrest.com

The New Premier event location in the Gorge!

Gorge Crest Vineyards has created the first event site in the Gorge designed specifically for events to cater to your every need. We offer spectacular settings with expansive views of Mt. Hood, the Columbia River Gorge and the Hood River Valley. New traditional winery building with intimate inside settings and a custom rock fireplace. Spectacular views from the indoor and outdoor area, manicured lawns, cobblestone patios, covered porches, built in dance floor, tables & chairs, indoor/outdoor bars, dedicated catering facilities and elegant bathrooms make Gorge Crest the perfect location for your special day!

The grounds were immaculate, the dance floor was beautiful, and the views were right from a postcard! Gorge Crest is the most beautiful venue in the Gorge, and we looked at a lot of places. Plus the fact that there is a beautiful outside and inside area in case of inclement weather is so convenient. They have thought of everything, from the parking placement, to the ability for the bride to arrive without being seen. They were so helpful, available and friendly whenever we had questions or concerns. Our guests have told us that it was the most beautiful wedding they had ever attended! Gorge Crest made our dream come true! – Laura Spinney and Joe Silliman 2008

Contact
Ronda Crumpacker

Quick Facts
- Expansive views of the Columbia River Gorge, Hood River Valley & Mt. Hood
- Exquisite Indoor event room w/stone fireplace (in case of bad weather)
- Extensive manicured lawns w/concrete dance floor
- Dedicated catering facilities
- Elegant bathrooms
- Dressing room
- Covered porches
- Indoor/outdoor bars (including a wine serving area)
- Beautiful cobblestone patios
- Three dedicated band locations w/necessary electrical
- On-site parking facility & Valet Parking turn around
- Chairs & Tables
- Wonderful wine!
- On-site parking facility & Valet Parking turn around

423

© Holland Studios

Gorge-ous Weddings
at the Wind Mountain Ranch

192 Erickson Road
Stevenson, Washington 98648
p. 503.360.4707
f. 509.427.5919
e. info@gorge-ousweddings.com
www.gorge-ousweddings.com

Gorge-ous Weddings at the Wind Mountain Ranch

Located in the heart of the Columbia River Gorge, Wind Mountain Ranch is a private estate specializing in unforgettable weddings, receptions, and Special Events. Offering scenic views of both Wind Mountain and the Columbia River, it is the ideal setting for picture perfect memories. Located in Home Valley Washington, Wind Mountain Ranch truly captures the beauty the Pacific Northwest has to offer.

Hosting only one Celebration at a time, you are truly the center of attention, with our only goal making sure your wedding or event is everything you dreamed it could be.

Wind Mountain Ranch is located 45 minutes East of Portland Oregon. Come celebrate your day in complete privacy.

Contact
Molly Gunn

Pricing
Please call
or email for pricing

Quick Facts
- Beautiful views of both Wind Mountain & the Columbia River
- Overnight accommodations in ranch style home included with most packages
- Ceremony site
- 40 X 82 sent (including side walls, A/C & lighting)
- Tables & chairs
- No restrictions on caterers
- On site parking for up to 500 guests (Parking attendants included)
- RV parking available
- Vintage cars available for bride delivery

WHAT'S NEW
Newly Remodeled Ranch House with Bridal Room. Ranch house rental also available for Family Reunions, Special Events and Vacation Rentals.

424

© Holland Studios

Because you have a life!

Gray Gables
Estate

3009 SE Chestnut Street
Portland, Oregon 97267
p. 503.654.0470
f. 503.654.3929
e. mywedding@graygables.com
www.graygables.com

Business Hours:
M – F, 10a.m. – 5p.m.
By Appointment Only

About Gray Gables Estate

We invite you to share the joy of having your wedding and reception at our two-acre historic estate. Enjoy rich, old-world elegance and discover the beauty of our gardens accented with ponds, waterfalls and statuary. Gray Gables is conveniently located just a few minutes south of downtown Portland.

Special Services

We know that you have a busy life! It takes time to do the research necessary to have a wedding that is memorable and reflective of your good taste. Your style and vision are important to us, and our wedding planners will work hard to bring your wedding day dream to life. Our goal is to make your wedding carefree and stress-free.

Become a Gray Gables' bride...and relax.

Availability and Terms

We accept bookings up to 18 months in advance.

Contact

The Wedding Professionals

Price

Varies depending on time of event, packages & season

Capacity

50 – 300 indoors
or outdoors

Catering

Award-winning caterer; international cuisine available; hundreds of menu suggestions

Amenities

- Two-acre estate with lush gardens & water features
- Indoor & outdoor dance floor
- Tables, chairs, linens, glassware and napkins included
- Exclusivity – only one wedding at a time
- Full bar available
- Setup & clean-up included
- Ample free parking
- ADA accessible Bridal Suite

TYPES OF EVENTS

Weddings, receptions, meetings, trade shows, corporate events, business parties and fundraisers.

425

Bravo! Member Since 1995

20500 Old Highway 99 SW
Centralia, WA 98531
p. 360.347.0027
f. 360.273.8406
e. jpoole@greatwolf.com
www.greatwolf.com/grand-mound/waterpark

Great Wolf Lodge

From the moment you enter our soaring lobby and find yourself surrounded in our north woods theme, you will know you have escaped from the ordinary. Allow us to orchestrate the wedding you've dreamed of! Imagine a majestic resort, a grand entrance, and your first night as a married couple in a romantic suite. Your guests will be entertained and delighted. Your special day will be remembered by all who attend!

Our warm, experienced staff is ready to assist you in planning all the details of your once-in-a-lifetime event. We understand that planning a wedding, while a joyous time in a bride and groom's life, can have its share of ups and downs! We are here to help at all stages of the planning, ensuring that your wedding day is realized exactly as you have imagined.

Give your family and friends the gift of a true vacation, not just a wedding invitation. Our 60,000 square foot indoor waterpark, two full-service restaurants, Elements Spa Salon, Northern Lights Arcade and our proximity to beautiful golf courses and historic downtown Olympia makes it easy to see how Great Wolf Lodge creates excitement for all aspects of your event.

Contact
John Poole

Price
Please inquire

Amenities
- State-of-the-art banquet rooms to accommodate up to 1,050 guests
- Extensive menu selections and catering by masterful chefs
- Full-service Spa Menu for you and your bridal party at our Elements Spa
- Close proximity to beautiful golf courses
- Great Wolf's team of experienced event planners

Bravo! Member Since 2009

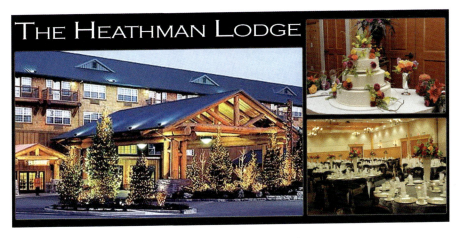

THE HEATHMAN LODGE

About The Heathman Lodge

The Heathman Lodge is Clark County's premiere wedding destination. Inspired by authentic Pacific northwest décor and cuisine, The Heathman Lodge provides each guest with a calm refuge and memorable experience. An unexpected urban retreat, the Lodge offers you and your guests heartfelt service, and rustic mountain lodge comfort.

Guest Rooms

Discover what it means to experience a "Great Day" at The Heathman Lodge in one of our 162 guestrooms or 20 suites. With old-world craftsmanship and hickory peeled furnishings each guestroom captures the beauty of the Pacific NW.

Wedding Facilities

The Lodge features nearly 10,000 square feet of banquet space to accommodate up to 300 for a sit down reception. Our ballrooms are designed with rustic elegance, natural wood wall coverings, and wrought iron chandeliers and are accented with the colors of a Pacific NW forest. Our onsite catering is brought to you by award winning 4-star restaurant Hudson's Bar & Grill.

Contact

Maili Morrison

7801 NE Greenwood Drive
Vancouver, Washington 98662

p. 360.254.3100
f. 360.254.6100

e. weddings@heathmanlodge.com

www.heathmanlodge.com

427

Price

Please inquire

Capacity

Event space: 320

Amenities

- Host & no-host bars available; hotel supplies all liquor & bartender

- Dance floor; up to 21'x21' available complimentary

- Complimentary linen, china, silverware, glassware, cake cutting, mirrored tiles & votive candles

- Guestroom rates available for out-of-town guests

WHAT'S NEW

Complimentary bridal suite when you book your reception at The Heathman Lodge. Mention Bravo! when reserving your dates!

Bravo! Member Since 1998

THE HEATHMAN
RESTAURANT & BAR

1001 SW Broadway
Portland, Oregon 97205

p. 971.404.3141
f. 503.790.7112
e. sosaki@heathmancatering.com
www.heathmanrestaurantandbar.com

This Historic venue is in the heart of Downtown Portland and has over 4,000 sq. ft. of meeting and event space. Our rooms work great for meetings of 6 – 60 people, meals for 6 – 150 and receptions up to 400! Our St. John's board room works great for meetings up to 14. The St. John's has a custom built 'smart' table that is connected to a 50" plasma television, wood cabinetry built from Oregon reclaimed wood; high intensity and low energy consumption lights; custom leather chairs and windows overlooking Broadway! Custom menu creation and working within budgets are our specialty. We offer off-site catering services and are preferred at the Oregon Historical Society.

We specialize in weddings up to 100 and have built in hard wood floors and a fireplace. Remember to reserve your Bridal Shower, Rehearsal Dinner and post-wedding brunch with us!

428

Contact
Sean Osaki, Director of Catering; Kehaulani Petersen, Catering Sales Manager

Price
Food and Beverage Minimums vary, please call for pricing

Quick Facts
- Full Service on and off-site caterer
- Seating for 6 – 150, Receptions for 6 – 400
- 7 private rooms, 5 with windows, 1 with built in fireplace and marble top bar, 1 with glass skylight and 1 state of the art board room
- Complimentary Wi-Fi; Wired internet available
- French Northwest Fare; Custom menus available
- Full service restaurant and bar

WHAT'S NEW?

We offer traditional Afternoon Tea service every day of the week. Renovations of all 150 hotel rooms were completed in April of 2009. James Beard Award Winning Culinary Director, Philippe Boulot.

28005 NE 172nd Avenue
Battle Ground, Washington 98604
p. 360.713.2359
f. 360.666.0890
e. events@heisenhousevineyards.com
www.heisenhousevineyards.com

About the Heisen House

Something old. Something new. Settled in the 1860s by newlywed pioneer homesteaders Alexander and Mary Heisen, this National and State Historic Site offers a truly unique place to begin your life-journey together.

The location features a stunning 1898 Victorian farmhouse surrounded by 5 acres of gardens, vineyards, orchards, and old-growth trees as well as plenty of open lawn space and panoramic rural views, all just 30 minutes from the Portland International Airport and 5 minutes from lodging in nearby Battle Ground, WA.

Pressed for time? Our on-site coordinator, whose services are included in our fee, makes planning your special day easy. Our coordinator will also be there on the day of your event to attend to every detail so you can simply relax and savor the moment with family and friends. Work with your own caterer, florist, photographer, and DJ, or tap into our list of preferred partners for the ultimate in hassle-free planning.

Contact
Event coordinator

Price
$2,000 and up, depending on date, time, and event.

Contact us for details.

Quick Facts
- Complimentary in-house wedding planner
- 30 minutes from Portland International Airport (PDX)
- Unhurried one-event-at-a-time policy
- Catering, your selection or choose from our preferred list
- Date secured with $1,000 non-refundable deposit
- Free parking on site
- ADA accessible

429

See page 540 under Wineries & Vineyards

Heritage House Farm & Gardens
Aurora, Oregon

p. 503.678.5704
p. 888.479.3500
e. heritagehouse@centurytel.net

Shown by appointment;
please call for directions

About Heritage House Farm & Gardens

Heritage House is a 1934 Colonial-style estate home decorated in country elegance. The grounds are lovely, colorful gardens and lush green lawns surrounded by giant trees and rich, green hazelnut orchards. The separate ceremony and reception sites provide a beautiful backdrop for your ceremony, reception and special-moment pictures. Charming dressing rooms in the estate house are furnished for the needs of the bride and bridal party. The groom and groomsmen use the quaint guest house for dressing.

Location

Heritage House is nestled halfway between Portland and Salem (about 25 minutes) in the beautiful Willamette Valley. The historic Aurora Colony is nearby for sightseeing and antique shopping, or take time to golf at two nearby golf courses. Out-of-town guests will enjoy the activities on the Willamette River or a visit to the beautiful Oregon Gardens. Great accommodations, restaurants and recreation are all close for the convenience of your guests.

2010 Summer Dates Still Available

Contact
Bill & Derolyn Johnston

Price
Varies depending on function & size of group; Please call for information

Capacity
From smaller intimate events to 250+

Amenities
- Lovely spring, summer & fall garden events
- Ample convenient parking
- Exclusive full-service catering
- Experienced event planners for weddings, receptions, family parties, business meetings & parties
- See our Photo Gallery at bravowedding.com

430

HERITAGE HOUSE CHOCOLATES

In many areas of the world, hazelnuts are a tradition associated with wedding festivities. We are now offering a delectable selection of fine chocolate and hazelnut products that are available for gifts and your eating pleasure.

Bravo! Member Since 1997

The HIGH DESERT MUSEUM
BEND, OREGON

59800 South Highway 97
Bend, Oregon 97702
p. 541.382.5754 ext. 284
f. 541.382.5256
e. events@highdesertmuseum.org
www.highdesertmuseum.org

About The High Desert Museum

The High Desert Museum is a nationally renowned, unique venue in which to create the perfect event for you & your guests. The Museum's beautiful setting, on 135 pristine acres just 10 minutes from the Old Mill District in Bend, Oregon offers a place for an unparalleled, memorable experience for your guests.

As The New York Times described it, the Museum is an architectural jewel, "nestled into the spare basalt of Central Oregon as if it grew there."

The Museum exudes the natural beauty of the Northwest. Skylights and aspen-filled atria allow natural light to dapple its interior. A peaked, 16-foot Douglas fir-beamed ceiling rises above floors of inlaid Northwest slate. Eye-catching sculptures of wildlife from various artists and rare Western artifacts are on display throughout the spacious Schnitzer Entrance Hall. This premier attraction featuring the wildlife and cultural and living history of the High Desert offers more than 7,000 square feet of event space and can accommodate special event groups of 5 to 500. You can even host an event outdoors at the Museum's beautiful meadow or in the Birds of Prey Pavilion.

Contact
Nancy Lochrie

Price
$300 – $2,500

Quick Facts
- Central Oregon's most unique venue
- 4,000 sq ft in Schnitzer Entrance Hall
- 1,500 square feet in Birds of Prey Pavilion
- 7,200 square feet in Museum Meadow
- Wildly fun place to host an Event!
- Possibilities for Wildlife & Living History encounters

431

WHAT'S NEW?

Our Exhibits change regularly throughout the year, so there's always something new to see and experience.

Bravo! Member Since 2008

Hilton
Portland & Executive Tower

921 SW Sixth Avenue
Portland, Oregon 97204

p. 503.721.2893
f. 503.225.1480
e. kristina.lazos@hilton.com
www.portland.hilton.com

432

About The Hilton Portland & Executive Tower

The Hilton Portland & Executive Tower is a full-service hotel located in the heart of downtown. With a reputation for unparalleled service, our experienced and courteous staff will help you plan your special day.

Our wedding professional works closely with the culinary team to create wedding packages featuring fresh, local cuisine. We feature two of the most elegantly appointed banquet rooms in Portland: the highly sought-after Pavilion Ballroom, unique in its design; and Alexander's, featuring panoramic city views. Your overnight guests will enjoy newly renovated guest rooms with Crabtree & Evelyn® bath products and our signature Suite Dreams beds.

Exceptional Service

Our professional staff draws on years of expertise in the planning and execution of each event. Whether you are planning your rehearsal dinner, ceremony, reception, or farewell brunch, let the Hilton Portland & Executive Tower make this the most memorable event of your lifetime.

Contact
Kristina Lazos

Price
Customized wedding packages at varied prices

Amenities
- Complimentary bridal suite
- Central downtown location
- Full-service catering
- On-site wedding professional
- Two restaurants and bars
- Newly renovated athletic club
- Massage by appointment

Portland Composts! Participant
Green Seal Certified

© Holland Studios

WHAT'S NEW
Newly renovated Plaza Level featuring the Pavilion Ballroom.

Bravo! Member Since 1991

Portland South

25425 SW 95th Avenue
Wilsonville, Oregon 97070

p. 503.682.5598
f. 503.682.5596

e. pwitzleben@hiportlandsouth.com

www.hiportlandsouth.com

About Holiday Inn Portland South

The Holiday Inn in Wilsonville is south Portland's largest full service catering facility. Conveniently located just 12 – 15 minutes from downtown Portland, our close proximity to Highways I-5 and 205 make our property the ideal location for your guests no matter from which direction they may be arriving.

Our newly renovated contemporary Ballroom and indoor sky lit Terrace accommodate up to 450 wedding guests. In addition, one-hundred-sixty-nine elegantly modern guest rooms are available at special rates for your friends and family.

Our years of experience and our professional staff are sure to make your special day one that you and your guests will remember for a lifetime. For further information please contact our catering office.

We would be so pleased to give you tour of our Hotel. Please call to set an appointment to see our Ballroom and Terrace.

Contact
Phyllis Witzleben

Price
$19.95 per person and up

Quick Facts
- Elegant buffet reception packages, affordable prices
- No cake cutting fee
- Group rates for guests attending your wedding
- Convenient location with free parking
- Full service restaurant and bar
- 24 hour pool, spa and fitness facilities
- With the purchase of a full wedding package receive a gift certificate for dinner for two and deluxe accommodations for your anniversary!

433

WHAT'S NEW

The Holiday Inn Portland South has just completed a total renovation. An exceptional setting, exceptional food, and exceptional service can be yours at an affordable price.

Bravo! Member Since 2000

Visit BravoWedding.com for more information on the best reception & wedding sites

HOLOCENE

About Holocene

A gorgeous, airy space with a comfortable and clean urban esthetic – located seconds across the Morrison bridge from downtown. Multiple rooms and modular furnishings let us adapt Holocene to suit your plans perfectly.

Holocene offers a full liquor bar, superb house specialty cocktails, domestic and imported beers and wines – plus espresso, coffee, tea and non-alcoholic drinks. We do wonderful in-house catering (outside catering is welcome, too). And our staff is famously sweet, attentive and charming. Holocene hosts a handful of weddings each season, and is a wonderful alternative to ballrooms and traditional venues – a light, flexible, modern space, with all the amenities, and truly personal service.

Accommodations

Renting our space includes the use of our audio and video equipment, and all furnishings and serviceware. We also have excellent relationships with many artists and vendors, and are more than happy to help you find fantastic musicians, DJs, florists, etc., and plan your perfect party.

Availability

We operate year-round as a restaurant, lounge and performance venue, but can be reserved for weddings and other private events with advance notice. Please drop us an email or give us a ring with any inquiries.

Contact

Jarkko Cain

1001 SE Morrison Street
Portland, Oregon 97214

p. 503.239.7639
f. 206.457.6479

e. weddings@holocene.org

www.holocene.org/events

Price

Reasonable & flexible pricing, according to day, amenities & event size.

Capacity

Up to 300

Amenities

- Plenty of easy & free street parking.
- Outside seating in the nice weather.
- Excellent in-house full band/DJ sound systems & video projection.
- Broadband & Wi-Fi
- Always non-smoking.
- Kids welcome for weddings & receptions!

434

The Hostess House
&
The Bridal Arts Building
Est. 1984

10017 NE Sixth Avenue
Vancouver, Washington 98685
p. 360.574.3284
www.thehostesshouse.com

Introducing The Hostess House: The First Full-Service Wedding Center in the Northwest.

The candle-lit chapel seats 200 guests and looks out onto a beautiful garden with a waterfall. Our reception center is absolutely gorgeous! It has an indoor fountain, oak dance floor, fireplace, lush furnishings and a private landscaped yard with decks and a gazebo.

We offer exquisite catering and bar service. No plastic cups used here. We use long stemmed glassware, linen tablecloths, and silver and crystal serving pieces. Our bridal consultant will assist you with every detail from invitations and flowers to entertainment and photography.

Now you can have the excitement and joy of your perfectly planned wedding with none of the worry, work or frustrations. Let us prepare the exquisite hors d'oeuvres and polish the silver. Let us arrange the flowers and decorate the tables. Let us serve your guests and clean up afterwards. This will let you anticipate, enjoy and remember all the special moments of your wedding day.

Directions

Directions: From I-5 take 99th Street Exit (Exit #5). Go west two blocks, turn right onto 6th Avenue. Open seven days a week. Call for an appointment. The Hostess House... where the bride's wedding dreams come true.

Bravo! Member Since 1990

Contact
Hostess House

Package Prices
$1,995 to $2,995

Capacity
Chapel up to 200
Reception area up to 300

Catering
Full-service, in-house catering & bakery

Amenities
• ADA accessible

ANNOUNCEMENT
In September 09, the Hostess House suffered a devastating fire. All clients were immediately contacted and given their choice of a 100% refund or choosing another venue. The Hostess House paid all additional expenses occurred in relocating and continued to serve as their consultant.

We have rebuilt and reopened, more beautiful and charming than ever before.

We have passed the ultimate test. We have proven that we are truly committed to our brides and grooms.

See page 91 under Bridal Attire & page 358 under Ceremony Sites

435

INDIAN CREEK
G O L F   C O U R S E

3605 Brookside Drive
Hood River, Oregon 97031
p. 866.386.7770
www.indiancreekgolf.com

436

A Spectacular Setting For Your Special Day

Located in Hood River and positioned in the heart of the Columbia River Gorge, Indian Creek Golf Course is the perfect location for your special occasion. With its proximity to Portland, seasoned staff, and remarkable views of both Mt. Adams and Mt. Hood, Indian Creek offers a superior alternative for your wedding or reception.

Availablity And Terms

Reservations are recommended for all groups regardless of size.

Description Of Facility And Services

Full–service in–house catering with servers included. Full–service bar with liquor, beer and wine. Linens and napkins are available. China and glassware are available, please call for quote. Clean–up is included in catering charges. On-site parking, annex lot with shuttle available.

Contact
Indian Creek Golf Course

Price
Varies with menu selections & service options, please call for a quote

Capacity
Indoors up to 100;
Outdoors up to 300

Catering
Full-service, in-house & off-premise catering from our fabulous Divots Restaurant

Amenities
- Special services: ability to accommodate special dietary needs & customized menus
- Audio/Visual: PA system, three television screens
- ADA: yes

TYPES OF EVENTS

Weddings, receptions, fundraising events, golf tournaments, business meetings, birthdays or any special occasion.

Jake's CATERING

611 SW 11th Avenue
Portland, Oregon
p. 503.241.2125
e. lwolfson@jakescatering.com
e. ehight@jakescatering.com
www.jakescatering.com

A Historic Gem

Listed on the National Register of Historic Places, The Governor Hotel is an architectural beauty. Built in 1909, the hotel has been completely restored to its original grandeur. The recently completed renovation of the Heritage Ballroom unveils Portland's best-kept secret, resurrecting this one-of-a-kind grand space for brides and grooms after a hiatus of more than 60 years. The classic design and ornate craftsmanship were preserved in the original Italian Renaissance styling. The room's high vaulted ceilings, marble floors and black-walnut woodwork and walls are truly unique.

Jake's Catering...A Tradition

Jake's Catering is part of the McCormick & Schmick's family of restaurants, including Jake's Famous Crawfish. Jake's is one of the oldest and most respected dining institutions in the Portland area, and Jake's Catering upholds this prestigious reputation.

Known for offering an extensive range of Pacific Northwest menu selections including fresh seafood, pasta, poultry and prime cut steaks, Jake's Catering has the variety, flexibility and talent to cater to your needs.

Availability and Terms

Our Italian Renaissance-style rooms offer variety and flexibility for groups of 25 to 700. The newly renovated Heritage Ballroom, Renaissance Room, Fireside Room, Library and eight additional rooms gracefully complement the charm of The Governor Hotel. We require a 30% deposit to confirm your event and payment in-full 72 hours prior to event for estimated charges.

Contact
Linda Wolfson
Erin Hight

Price
$50 to $100 per person

Capacity
700 reception; 450 sit-down

Amenities
- Tables & chairs for up to 500
- Professional, uniformed servers
- Full-service bar & bartenders
- Cloth napkins & linens in variety of colors
- Fine china & glassware
- A/V available upon request
- Ample parking available

437

TYPES OF EVENTS

From stand-up cocktail and appetizer receptions to fabulous buffet presentations and complete sit-down dinners for groups and gatherings of all sizes.

See page 128 under Full-Service Catering

Bravo! Member Since 1994

© Paul Rubens

Serving Beaverton and the westside since 1955.

8005 SW Grabhorn Road
Beaverton, Oregon 97007
p. 503.629.6355
f. 503.629.6356
e. jenkinsestate@thprd.com
www.thprd.org/facilities/
jenkins/receptions.cfm

438

About the Jenkins Estate

Tualatin Hills Park & Recreation District welcomes you to this tranquil setting, tucked in the wooded niche of Cooper Mountain. The revitalized country Estate consists of natural growth areas in the perimeter, giving way to, cultivated plantings, and a tamed landscape of ornamental trees, shrubs, flowers and winding gravel pathways.

The Main House, built in 1912, has a full-length veranda, beamed ceilings, hardwood floors, ornate light fixtures and stone fireplaces. The refurbished Stable is a charming building with large carriage doors and hardwood floors.

Availability & Terms

Deposit of half the rental fee confirms an event. One building and a location on the grounds for ceremony are included within the time block selected. Balance due 60 days prior to the event, along with a $200 refundable damage deposit.

Rental Includes

Choice of the Main House or Stable for reception including all tables, chairs and table linens within the building; set up and tear down.

Catering

Clients choose from our list of contracted caterers.

Other Notes

Alcohol allowed (bottled beer, wine, champagne only); free parking. The Jenkins Estate invites you to schedule a tour of our facilities and grounds.

Location

Just 10 minutes from Beaverton with views of the Tualatin Valley and Coast Mountain Range.

Contact

Program Coordinator

Price

Varies depending on the time of year & day of the week.

Capacity

The Main House can accommodate up to 175 guests & up to 225 guests in the Stable depending on the event & the time of year.

Features

- Plan a wedding or reception that will always be remembered.
- 68 acre Historic Estate.
- The Garden Tea Room offers a Victorian-style tea for Bridal Showers.

THE PERFECT LOCATION FOR ANY OCCASION

- Weddings & Receptions
- Birthdays
- Anniversaries
- Other Social Celebrations
- Holiday Parties
- Corporate Retreats

PORTLAND'S IRISH RESTAURANT & PUB

112 SW Second Avenue
Portland, Oregon 97204
p. 503.227.4057
f. 503.227.5931
e. tracey@kellsirish.com
e. brad@kellsirish.com
www.kellsirish.com

About Kells Irish Restaurant and Pub

Located on the second floor of the 1889 Historic Glisan building, Kells provides an Irish ambiance with excellent service and outstanding food. Our elegant facility invites your guests to celebrate in the stately Ceili Ballroom and mingle in the Irish Writers, Ulster Bar and Hibernian Rooms.

We provide buffet and formal sit-down service for receptions, rehearsal dinners and more.

Meeting and Banquet Facilities

With more than 2,500 square feet of accommodations, Kells banquet facilities can be modified into separate, more intimate rooms for a rehearsal dinner or one large space for your grand reception.

Both rooms include the latest technology in high-definition, overhead projector televisions, wireless microphones and Internet connectivity.

Kells truly offers all the bells and whistles, along with classic style.

Contact
Tracey Murphy, Brad Yoast

Price
We credit back room fees when minimums are met; call for more information

Capacity
Seated 15 to 120;
Reception 250;
Private banquet facilities on 2nd floor

Amenities
- Full-service, in-house, award-winning catering
- Upgraded air conditioning & heating
- Unique grand ballroom, circa 1889
- Two separate full-bar facilities
- Linens & candles included in service
- China & glassware included in service

GREAT DOWNTOWN LOCATION

Kells is located in the classic Old Town Area, close to the waterfront, Max Light Rail, Convention Center and many upscale hotels.

439

Bravo! Member Since 1997

Kelty Estate
Bed & Breakfast and Wedding Center

PO Box 817 / 675 3rd Street
Lafayette, Oregon 97127
p. 503.883.1262 or
p. 800.867.3740
e. weddings@keltyestatebb.com
www.keltyestatebb.com

440

About Kelty Estate

In the breathtaking beauty of the heart of Oregon's wine country, the Wedding Center at the Kelty Estate is a full-service, exclusive facility. We book only one event per day so you are free to have your idyllic wedding that won't be cut short by the next event coming in. Our on-site wedding planner works with you to help you stay within your budget and still have the wedding you've always dreamed you'd have.

The Kelty's catering menu is so flexible you can virtually create your own menu to fit your wedding theme! And better still…it's totally affordable.

We can arrange for a stylist to do hair and makeup for the big day, a masseuse available for a pre-wedding massage, and several different florists if you need.

Our wedding center will also do reunions, tea parties, birthday parties, rehearsal dinners, wine tasting parties, holiday parties, and brunches.

Contact
Nicci Stokes

Price
Prices will vary on size & type of event

Capacity
Can accommodate groups up to 250

Amenities
- Wedding coordinator included; one hour rehearsal the day prior to your wedding
- Seating for up to 250 guests
- Tables & chairs for up to 250 guests
- White Linens & napkins (Other colors available for an additional fee)
- The Carriage House Dance Floor (indoors); The Starlight Dance Floor (outdoors)
- Changing area for the wedding party

WHAT'S NEW
We have a beautiful Limo that will seat 10 or an SUV that will seat seven. Call or email for details!

11603 South New Era Road
Oregon City, Oregon 97045
Available for viewing by
appointment only
p. 503.784.6298
e. info@kingsravenwine.com
www.kingsravenwine.com

About King's Raven Winery

Twenty minutes south of downtown Portland, King's Raven Winery is located at the gateway to the undiscovered east Willamette Valley viticultural area; halfway between Oregon City and Canby. Our beautiful, three-tier amphitheater is perfect for your most memorable day. Surrounded by our estate vineyard on 35 acres with views from the coastal mountains to the Cascades, you'll find yourself in heaven as you dance the night away.

King's Raven Winery also produces pasture-fed no hormone Black Angus Beef. The farm has been owned and operated by our family since 1942.

Availability and Terms

Space available any day June through September. Deposit required.

More Than Just Weddings

King's Raven Winery offers the space for more than just weddings. Last year we started a movie night series in the vineyard on a giant inflatable outdoor movie screen.

Contact

Darin Ingram
King's Raven Winery, Inc.

– or –

Premiere Catering
503.235.0274

Price

Prices vary depending on the size & amenities of the event

441

Capacity

Up to 300+

Amenities

- Note: We are not a hotel
- Free on-site parking for up to 100 vehicles
- One event booked per weekend
- Property access up to two days before and one day after event
- No corkage fees or exclusive wine requirements
- 1,000 square feet of dance floor
- Electrical hookup
- ADA accessible

See page 542 under
Wineries & Vineyards

© Adams and Faith

Lakeside
Garden

16211 SE Foster Road
Portland, Oregon 97236
p. 503.760.6044
f. 503.760.9311
e. lgardens@easystreet.net
www.lakesidegardensevents.com

About Lakeside Gardens

Lakeside Gardens is a private event facility situated on approximately seven acres. We schedule events year round. As you wind down Lakeside Gardens' magnificent drive, a stunning view of lakes and fountains, meandering paths, charming wooden bridges, flower gardens and a gazebo greet you. Swans glide across the water. A waterfall gently cascades into the lake. It's a place of magical beauty. At the bottom of the drive sits the Grande Estate, a welcoming wedding facility that accommodates up to 240 guests for a seated ceremony. You'll love the Terrace Room with its graceful 17-foot arched ceiling and floor-to-ceiling windows. Views of the upper lake, tall cedars and weeping willows bring in the outdoors. The room spills open to a lovely open-air terrace that sits at the water's edge. Additional inside amenities consist of an elegant oak and marble fireplace, an ebony baby grand piano, and mirrored walls that reflects an inspiring panoramic view of the lake and surrounding gardens.

Contact
Office

Price
Price is determined by the event & menu selected

Capacity
Up to 240 people sit-down wedding at gazebo or inside; up to 300 people hors d'oeuvres buffet reception; up to 200 people special event sit-down buffet dinner

Amenities
- Full-service, in-house catering
- Tables & chairs are provided; terrace & garden seating available
- We offer beer, wine & champagne & provide all beverages & bartenders
- China, glassware & linen tablecloths provided; linen & paper napkins available

WHAT'S NEW

Plenty of free on-site parking, and we provide the clean-up. Please call us for more details and personal assistance as you plan your next event.

© Brides Choice

Bravo! Member Since 1990

442

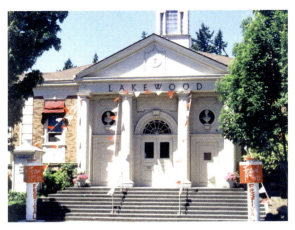

LAKEWOOD
CENTER FOR THE ARTS

368 South State Street
Lake Oswego, Oregon 97034
p. 503.635.6338
f. 503.635.2002
e. center.info@lakewood-center.org
www.lakewood-center.org

443

Description of Facility

Lakewood Center for the Arts is conveniently located on State Street (Highway 43) at the south end of Lake Oswego. The Community Meeting Room, on the lower level at the Center, has windows on two sides and is decorated with a forest green and cream color scheme. A full catering kitchen is attached to the space. The room comes with tables, chairs and place settings for up to 150.

Availability and Terms

Reservations should be made as soon as possible, six months to a year in advance. A security deposit is required to reserve your date. This security fee is non-refundable if you cancel your date. The security deposit is refunded two to three weeks after your event, if there is no damage and the room is clean. Your balance of $550 for the room rental is due one week before your event.

Description of Reception Services

The Lakewood Center is the perfect facility for those who wish to coordinate the details themselves or bring in their own consultant or catering company. The room is ideal for banquets, receptions, reunions, office parties and business meetings.

Place settings of plate, salad plate, coffee cup, water glass and silverware for up to 150 are included. Serving utensils, coffee urns, platters and pots and pans are not included. The room is carpeted. Many groups dance on the carpet or rent a dance floor from outside sources. There is a paved parking lot behind the facility.

Contact
Lakewood Center for the Arts

Price
Starting at $550

Capacity
Up to 150 for
sit down dinner

Up to 225 for cocktail party

Catering
Provided by renter;
kitchen available

Amenities
- Conveniently located on Highway 43
- Full kitchen
- Please inquire about decorations; no tape, tacks or nails please
- Clean-up done by the renter
- ADA accessible.

SPECIAL NOTE

The Center rents only the room, tables and chairs and place settings for up to 150. Items such as linens, silver, crystal, serving utensils, coffee urns and dance floors need to be arranged with other vendors.

Bravo! Member Since 1995

24377 NE Airport Road
Aurora, Oregon 97002
p. 503.678. GOLF (4653)
www.langdonfarms.com

444

About Langdon Farms Golf Club

Nestled among the serenity of Portland's #1 golf course, you will find a peaceful sanctuary. With stunning sunsets and serene surroundings; Langdon Farms is the perfect place to say "I do." Langdon Farms offers close proximity to the city of Portland, yet looks and feels like being in the country. Our white, ranch-style fences and farm-inspired buildings such as The Big Red Barn Clubhouse and Red Shed, all add to the course's historic ambiance. Our Ceremony Lawn overlooks the picturesque 18th hole, which is beautifully framed by emerald green fairways and vibrantly colored flowers. The Red Shed is ideal for wedding receptions and provides the perfect backdrop for your special day. On your wedding a day, rest assured that all of the focus is on the bride and groom.....Congratulations! In addition, we offer pre-wedding golf outings, a bridal party preparation area, and exceptional catering!

Availability and Terms

Reservations can be made anytime, but it is recommended that they be made at least 6 months in advance. A deposit is required to hold a reservation date.

Types of Events

We specialize in hosting weddings, receptions, rehearsal dinners, bridal showers, groomsmen golf outings and lunches.

Contact

Weddings & Events
503.678.4734

Price

Varies according to menu selection

Capacity

Up to 325 (indoor & outdoor facilities available)

Amenities

- Full-service, in-house catering
- Round tables & chairs provided
- Fully trained & licensed servers
- Full-service bar & full selection of liquor, beer, wine & champagne
- Linens, napkins & china provided

SPECIAL NOTE

Langdon Farms Golf Club is open to the public.

Call for current green fees, and tee times.

1203 Commercial Street
Astoria, Oregon 97103
p. 503.325.5922
e. director@liberty-theater.org
www.liberty-theater.org

An elegant site for your wedding

The Liberty Theatre, in the heart of downtown Astoria, was designed to transport you to a Venetian Palace and is one of Oregon's best examples of a 1920's vaudeville-motion picture palace. Opened in 1925, the theater was originally home to vaudeville acts and silent movies.

Recognized by the National Trust for Historic Preservation, the Liberty Theater recently underwent an $8 million renovation. Operating today as a Performing Arts Center, Concert Hall, Conference Center, Town Hall Meeting venue and an elegant site for Weddings. The theater is perfect for large weddings and the McTavish Reception Room is wonderful for smaller weddings, receptions and rehearsal dinners. Available for rent individually or together as a package.

For information on the Liberty Theatre Presents! Series and other current events visit our website at www.liberty-theater.org.

For information about renting the theatre or our beautiful McTavish Reception Room, contact the business office at 503.325.5922 Ext. 33.

Contact
Rosemary Baker-Monaghan
Executive Director

Price
The theater & McTavish Reception Room may be rented individually or together.

Package prices are available when the Liberty Theatre & the McTavish Reception Room are rented together. The McTavish Reception Room rental may also include any or all of the three lobby areas in the theater.

Capacity
- Theatre seats 667 plus 10 wheelchairs
- The McTavish Reception room can accommodate up to 185 persons at a sit down dinner configuration (60″ rounds); more when bistro tables are used & one or more of the lobbies are incorporated

Quick Fact
- The theatre has a Steinway D Concert Grand Piano & the McTavish Room has a Steinway Upright Piano available for an additional cost

© The Daily Astorian

13300 Highway 20
Sisters, Oregon 97759
p. 541.595.2628 Ext. 209 or 283
f. 541.595.2267
e. eventdirector@
   thelodgeatsuttlelake.com
www.thelodgeatsuttlelake.com

About Your Day:

The Lodge at Suttle Lake will make your wedding as timeless as your love. Nestled in the heart of the Deschutes National Forest amid soaring pines, Suttle Lake Resort provides an enchanted wonderland with fairytale back drops to make each moment of your special day as memorable as your first kiss.

Our focus will always lie in the details of your comfort and the quality of your memories.

From "Simple Elegance" to "Suttle Romance" or "Sunset Dreams", your options are limited to your imagination.

The Lodge at Suttle Lake invites you to…
Come find your way…

Availability and Terms

Please see our website or call our Event Director. We prefer a personal touch

Contact
Cynthia Willams or
Kasandra Scevers

Price
Please call for details

Capacity
12 – 80 indoor;
up to 200 outdoor

Amenities
- Several on-site ceremony and reception locations to choose from; including Private outdoor settings and rustic elegant in-door facilities
- 11 lodge rooms, 13 cabins
- Breath taking views
- Spa
- Onsite catering
- Setup and cleanup included
- No cake cutting fee
- Full Service Bar
- Wireless internet

446

Bravo! Member Since 2009

An Historic Oregon Ranch

71105 Holmes Road
Sisters, Oregon 97759
p. 541.923.1901
e. howdy@lhranch.com
www.lhranch.com

About Long Hollow Ranch

Weddings, receptions, honeymoons, anniversaries and family reunions can all happen at LHR. Nestled in a beautiful valley between Sisters and Redmond, we offer a traditional or western wedding option. We are a working ranch with full guest services or B&B and can be reserved partially or fully for your special event.

We can assist you with all your planning needs or let you create your own wedding. Plan a lawn wedding adjacent to the remodeled Victorian era farm house. Outdoor tents and seating for sun protection can be provided, or bring everything yourself.

Or down at the barn with a view of The Three Sisters mountains. Have the wedding ceremony outside on the decked area, with reception inside, or have the entire event indoors. You choose!

We invite you to stay overnight for a B&B visit while you plan – we'll deduct the room charges from your bill when you have your wedding at LHR. Come check us out!

Contact
Dick & Shirley Bloomfeldt

Price
$1,500 to $7,000+ depending on services provided

Quick Facts
- LHR has hosted weddings for almost ten years.
- Formal or informal, the smallest wedding or up to 200+
- Indoor weddings or receptions can be held in the remodeled barn
- Commercial kitchen available and/or bring your own catering
- Tents, tables, benches, decorations etc. are available on request
- Six rooms with private baths for up to 15, including a guest cottage perfect for Bride and Groom

447

WHAT'S NEW

• The barn remodel with indoor seating and dancing floor will completed by Spring 2010 ready for the new season.
• Local accommodations for large groups can be arranged with nearby hotels.
• All forms of dietary needs can be met with advanced notice for food that we prepare.

MAJESTIC INN & SPA

419 Commercial Avenue
Anacortes, Washington 98221
p. 360.299.1400 ext. 110
f. 360.299.8835
e. kristine@majesticinnandspa.com
www.majesticinnandspa.com

Contact
Kristine Ells

Price
Varies by event. Please call
for information.

Quick Facts
- Picturesque setting
  with indoor & outdoor
  banquet facilities
- Accommodates up to 75
  indoor; expands to 200
  using the outside courtyard
- On site catering & event
  coordinating
- Set up/ breakdown,
  bartender, carver, & cake
  cutting service included
- Courtyard gazebo
  and patio – ideal for
  entertainment & dancing
- Custom packages available
- 21 luxurious guest rooms
- Complimentary Majestic
  Suite when booking an
  event of 100 guests
  or more
- Chrysalis Day Spa offering
  massage, facials, body
  treatments, makeup
  application, manicures
  & pedicures
- Ryan Chanel Hair Salon
  – includes complimentary
  consultations

448

Discover a haven of elegance and charm. The Majestic Inn and Spa has been beautifully restored to its original grandeur. The historic Majestic Inn and Spa, located in the heart of downtown Anacortes WA, is your perfect getaway. Nestled in the natural beauty of the Pacific Northwest, surrounded by marinas, evergreen trees and the Puget Sound, Anacortes is the ideal location for shopping, hiking, boating or simply relaxing.

Plan your wedding/reception or rehearsal dinner in the comfort and grace of the Majestic. Your party will appreciate the beautiful building, wonderful courtyard garden and patio, caring staff, elegance and warm ambiance of our Inn and Spa. Our professional event planning staff will guide you every step of the way to ensure an unforgettable experience.

The Chrysalis Day spa invites you to come relax in our eucalyptus steam rooms or schedule an appointment for one of the many euphoric treatments and massages. The Ryan Chanel hair salon offers several services which include a trim, color, cut, style. Group appointments are available for your bridal party in our spacious salon for hair, make-up and nail services. Special food and beverage catering from the Majestic's signature restaurant is available for all group services. Let us pamper you for your memorable day!

The Mansion at Bayou Golf Course

9301 SW Bayou Drive
McMinnville, Oregon 97128
p. 503.435.2500
f. 503.472.3399
e. events@bayougolfcourse.com
www.bayougolfcourse.com

The Mansion at Bayou Golf Course was built in 1946/48 for Dr. B. White and Family, with the Golf Course opening in 1964. We are located in the famous Willamette Valley Wine Country just outside McMinnville.

Towering trees, vast lawns and beautiful gardens surround the impressive white Southern Style Mansion, sitting on a small bluff overlooking the Golf Course.

Very intimate and charming, it lends itself for small and large events like weddings, receptions, meetings and for special celebrations both indoors or combined with the outdoors.

The "Elegant First Floor", with carved Italian Fireplace and winding staircase leads to the upstairs "Starlight Room" with a fireplace and mantel, a small stage and wine bar. Red oak wood floors invite to celebrate and to dance!

The Gazebo, garden and deck are illuminated for evening celebrations.

We invite you to take a tour.

To make your event most memorable, we work closely with you and are flexible.

Contact
Irmi Brown

Price
Varies according to season and time. Weekday hourly rates for inside space starting at $150

449

Capacity
Inside (on two floors) 115
Standing reception 175
Outside 275 guests

Quick Facts
- Tables, chairs and white linen for up to 140 guests, set-up and break-down included
- Licensed to serve wine and beer, staff on site
- Preferred Caterer list
- Bride and Groom dressing rooms
- Ample parking

WHAT'S NEW?
New ownership and upgrades since 2007. Golf discount for wedding party.

9774 Highway 14 West
Goldendale, Washington 98620
p. 877.627.9445
f. 509.773.0586
www.maryhillwinery.com

450

About Maryhill Winery

Established in 1999 by Craig and Vicki Leuthold, Maryhill Winery is one of Washington state's largest family-owned wineries producing 80,000 cases annually. Located in the picturesque Columbia Gorge scenic area in Goldendale, Washington, the winery is perched on a bluff overlooking the Columbia River against the stunning backdrop of Mt. Hood. Nestled among rows of vines, Maryhill is a popular destination for picnics and special events, with an adjacent 4,000-seat outdoor amphitheater that hosts a world-class summer concert series.

Maryhill's 3,000 square foot tasting room draws more than 75,000 wine enthusiasts from around the globe each year, ranking among the top five most visited wineries in the state. Maryhill sources grapes from some of the most highly-regarded vineyards in the state to produce 23 varietals and 28 award-winning wines. Offering something for every palate, Maryhill wines offer tremendous value, with exceptional quality at affordable prices. For more information or to order wines online, visit www.maryhillwinery.com.

Contact
Joe Garoutte
p. 877.MARYHILL ext. 342
e. joeg@maryhillwinery.com

Maryhill provides a selection of 4 sites including:
- Ceremony site on the bluff of the Columbia River
- Amphitheatre & Stage
- Recreation area
- Arbor after hours

Price
Fee is $6,500 & includes the following:

- Selection of sites
- Event Planner Assistance
- Day of event coordination
- 20 tables, 360 chairs

Quick Facts
- "2009 Washington Winery of the Year" – *Winepress NW*
- "Best Destination Winery" – *Seattle Magazine*
- Excellent caterers available for hire
- Personalized Wine labels available for additional charge
- Handicap accessible

See page 543 under Wineries & Vineyards

5350 River Street
West Linn, Oregon 97068
p. 503.655.4268
e. info@mcleanhouse.org
www.mcleanhouse.org

Enjoy Your Special Event in a Beautiful Historic Setting

The grandeur of a gracious 1927 home can be the setting of your memorable event. The McLean House and its 2.4-acre park overlook the Willamette River. The grounds and first floor of the 17-room home have been lovingly restored. Our kitchen is available for your needs or those of your caterer. Dishes, coffee maker, serving pieces and tables are included in the package. White chairs are available for a nominal fee. Wine, champagne and beer are permitted an additional fee is required. Changing rooms are available for the wedding party.

Our Grounds

Many of the plantings on the property are from the 20's. Stroll through the rose garden. The tranquil hillside waterfall and bench provide a place for reflection or a beautiful backdrop for your photos. The grounds are large enough to accommodate your ceremony as well as your reception. We have a separate area suitable for a tent and dance floor.

Availability and Terms

The use of the house and grounds are included in the rental price. Reservations are confirmed upon the receipt in full of the refundable security deposit and the rental and cleaning fees. Please contact our manager for a private tour of the facility and the availability of dates.

Contact
Manager – Shown by Appointment Only

Price
Prices vary based on date. Please contact us for a price quote.

Capacity
Up to 100 (outside)
Up to 60 seated (inside)
75 cocktail reception (inside)

Amenities
- Charming historical home provides an inexpensive setting for your event and allows you control over your food
- Lighted gazebo makes the ideal setting for exchanging your vows
- Our grand lawn will accommodate your ceremony and reception
- Your guests will love the McLean House

451

TYPES OF EVENTS

Weddings, receptions, corporate & private events, business meetings, seminars, retreats, reunions & other private events.

© Resolutions

© Sean McMenamin

McMENAMINS
CORNELIUS PASS ROADHOUSE &
IMBRIE HALL

4045 NW Cornelius Pass Road
Hillsboro, Oregon 97124
p. 503.693.8452
e. salescpr@mcmenamins.com
www.mcmenamins.com

452

Rich in early Oregon heritage, Cornelius Pass Roadhouse & Imbrie Hall is an unexpected and charming setting for weddings, private parties, receptions and more. Hold your special event in the beautiful Octagonal Barn (one of the few such structures left in the nation) or the venerable Roadhouse itself, an 1866 Italianate home full of original artwork, Victorian-era furnishings and ornate fireplaces. Outdoor meadows with lush flora are ideal weddings and summertime parties, and the mid-1850s-era Granary, one of the oldest structures in the area, is the perfect spot for get-togethers. The property offers onsite parking so that your guests are easily accommodated.

About McMenamins

For more than 25 years, McMenamins' historic hotels, pubs and breweries throughout Oregon and Washington have been well known as being friendly, familiar places to enjoy handcrafted ales, wine, spirits and Northwest-inspired pub fare with family and friends. Check out photos, menus, room layouts and rates at mcmenamins.com.

Contact
Group sales office

Price
Food & beverage minimum; varies based on size of room & time of day

Capacity
20 to 600 people

Amenities
- Restaurant
- Small bars
- Onsite brewery
- Outdoor seating
- Beautiful gardens
- Easily accessible from Highway 26

Courtesy of Lyrim Icaz Photography

© Liz Devine

Bravo! Member Since 1991

See page 526 under Rehearsal Dinner

© Liz Devine

McMENAMINS CRYSTAL BALLROOM

1332 West Burnside Street
Portland, Oregon 97209
p. 503.288.3286
e. salescry@mcmenamins.com
www.mcmenamins.com

A Renovated & Historic Ballroom

The Crystal Ballroom is a well-known music and events venue that has drawn national performers since its inception in 1914. You will love the vaulted ceilings, full-length windows, Venetian chandeliers and the famous "floating" dance floor. Gaining inspiration from more than 80 years of history, a team of McMenamins artists added even more color to the ballroom by painting incredible murals throughout the building and onsite brewery. Lola's Room, named for Portland's first policewoman, is a more intimate setting for groups up to 125 people with a full stage and a newer model of the "floating" dance floor. The property's convenient location is ideal for guests staying in downtown hotels or in the nearby Pearl District.

What's New?

Stay tuned to hear about the late 2010 opening of McMenamins Crystal Hotel, just across the street from the Crystal Ballroom! The hotel will offer approximately 50 guestrooms, a restaurant, small bar and more. See mcmenamins.com for updates.

Contact
Group sales office

Price
Food & beverage minimum; varies based on size of group & time of day

Crystal Ballroom Capacity
Accommodates groups from 150 to 1,000 people

Lola's Room Capacity
130 seated;
150 reception-style

Amenities
- Restaurant and bars
- Famous "floating" dance floor
- Sweeping balcony in the Ballroom
- Full bar service
- Original artwork
- Musical history

453

© Liz Devine

Bravo! Member Since 1991

© Liz Devine

MCMENAMINS
EDGEFIELD

2126 SW Halsey Street
Troutdale, Oregon 97060
p. 503.492.2777
p. 877.492.2777
e. salesed@mcmenamins.com
www.mcmenamins.com

454

About Edgefield

The historic 1911 property is surrounded by spectacular gardens and landscaping, making the 74-acre resort a lush paradise that offers stunning backdrops for photographs and video. We offer more than 12 indoor and outdoor event spaces and will be happy to give a tour and discuss your options. Also included onsite are a winery, brewery, distillery, movie theater, gift shop, two par-3 golf courses, the full-service Ruby's Spa, a heated outdoor soaking pool and more. Guests will enjoy the time they have before and after your event to explore all Edgefield has to offer – live music, wine tasting, recent-run films in the theater, massage and more in the spa, strolls throughout the gardens and beyond. The property is 20 minutes east of downtown Portland and only 15 minutes from Portland International Airport.

About McMenamins

For more than 25 years, McMenamins' historic hotels, pubs and breweries throughout Oregon and Washington have been well known as being friendly, familiar places to enjoy handcrafted ales, wine, spirits and Northwest-inspired pub fare with family and friends. Check out photos, menus, room layouts and rates at mcmenamins.com.

Contact
Group Sales Office

Price
Food & beverage minimum; varies based on size of room & time of day

Capacity
Up to 200 people seated; 250 people reception-style (300 people reception-style available in summer).

Amenities
- 114 guestrooms
- Restaurant, pub and small bars
- Ruby's Spa and heated soaking pool
- Indoor and outdoor event spaces
- Two par-3 golf courses
- Movie theater
- Brewery and distillery
- Winery and tasting room
- Gardens grown using organic methods
- Original artwork

© Liz Devine

Bravo! Member Since 1991

See page 527 under Rehearsal Dinner

© Liz Devine

3505 Pacific Avenue
Forest Grove, Oregon 97116
p. 503.992.9530
p. 887.992.9530
e. salesgl@mcmenamins.com
www.mcmenamins.com

About the Grand Lodge

Located in Forest Grove, this elegant 1922 Masonic lodge turned hotel at the entrance to Washington County wine country welcomes you, your wedding party and guests. Relax in cozy guestrooms before the big event, indulge in a massage at Ruby's Spa, take a stroll around the beautifully landscaped grounds and more. There is a wide selection of spaces for your event, party or ceremony, both indoors and out. Enjoy the grandeur of the Compass Room Theater or the quaintness of the Children's Cottage. Your guests who stay onsite will also enjoy the 10-hole disc golf course, movie theater, soaking pool, pubs and beyond.

About McMenamins

For more than 25 years, McMenamins' historic hotels, pubs and breweries throughout Oregon and Washington have been well known as being friendly, familiar places to enjoy handcrafted ales, wine, spirits and Northwest-inspired pub fare with family and friends. Check out photos, menus, room layouts and rates at mcmenamins.com.

Contact
Group Sales Office

Price
Food & beverage minimum; varies based on size of room & time of day

Capacity
Up to 200 indoors; up to 700 outdoors

455

Amenities
- 77 guestrooms
- Two restaurants
- Ruby's Spa and outdoor soaking pool
- Wine bar and other small bars
- Pool tables
- Movie theater
- Disc golf course
- Gardens
- Original artwork

© Liz Devine

See page 528 under Rehearsal Dinner

Bravo! Member Since 1991

© Liz Devine

310 NE Evans Street
McMinnville, Oregon 97128
p. 503.472.8427
e. saleshoto@mcmenamins.com
www.mcmenamins.com

About Hotel Oregon

With its fours stories rising tall above McMinnville's charming downtown district in the center of wine country, Hotel Oregon (built in 1905) is as welcoming as ever! Your guests will enjoy the whimsical artwork, regional wine list, cozy guestrooms and more. Held in Mattie's Room on the second floor, your event will be one to remember. Throughout their stay, your guests can have breakfast, lunch, happy hour or dinner in the inviting McMenamins Pub. They can relax in the Cellar Bar after wandering through the hotel's "gallery" of artwork and historical photographs. Why not book the Rooftop Bar for a morning-after brunch the next day, where your guests will appreciate the spectacular vistas that stretch for miles from the Rooftop Bar – vineyards, orchards and the Coastal Range.

About McMenamins

For more than 25 years, McMenamins' historic hotels, pubs and breweries throughout Oregon and Washington have been well known as being friendly, familiar places to enjoy handcrafted ales, wine, spirits and Northwest-inspired pub fare with family and friends. Check out photos, menus, room layouts and rates at mcmenamins.com.

Contact
Group sales office

Price
Food & beverage minimum; varies based on size of room & time of day

Capacity
From eight to 120

Amenities
- 42 guestrooms
- Restaurant
- Rooftop Bar with lovely views
- Cellar Bar with an extensive wine list
- Original artwork
- Billiards tables
- Set in the middle of Oregon wine country

© Liz Devine

See page 529 under Rehearsal Dinner

Bravo! Member Since 1991

5736 NE 33rd Avenue
Portland, Oregon 97211
p. 503.288.3286
p. 888.249.3983
e. salesken@mcmenamins.com
www.mcmenamins.com

About Kennedy School

This former elementary school turned hotel is an incredible spot for your wedding – your event will be remembered for years to come! The historic 1915 grade school was slated for demolition until the McMenamin brothers purchased the property and renovated it back to its original charm. Today, it's a wonderful hotel and event space offering classrooms-turned-guestrooms (complete with their original chalkboards and coat closets), beautiful artwork by local artisans, the Detention and Honors Bars, an outdoor heated soaking pool and more. Your wedding will be one-of-a-kind, whether it's held indoors in the gymnasium, outdoors in the courtyard or in one of our other intriguing spots. The Kennedy School is located just minutes from downtown Portland and is convenient to the Portland International Airport.

About McMenamins

For more than 25 years, McMenamins' historic hotels, pubs and breweries throughout Oregon and Washington have been well known as being friendly, familiar places to enjoy handcrafted ales, wine, spirits and Northwest-inspired pub fare with family and friends. Check out photos, menus, room layouts and rates at mcmenamins.com.

Contact
Group sales office

Price
Food & beverage minimum; varies based on size of room & time of day

Capacity
From 10 to 200 guests

Amenities
- Restaurant
- Indoor and outdoor spaces
- Several small bars
- Soaking pool
- Onsite brewery
- 35 guestrooms
- Gardens
- Original artwork
- Movie theater

457

See page 530 under Rehearsal Dinner

Bravo! Member Since 1991

700 NW Bond Street
Bend, Oregon 97701
p. 541.330.8567
e. salesbend@mcmenamins.com
www.mcmenamins.com

458

Back to School In Bend

Imagine holding your wedding in this 1936 former Catholic elementary school – what a story you and your new spouse will have to tell and remember for years to come. We encourage all forms of fun and merriment, so no worries about being sent to the head nun's office here. Hold your wedding celebration indoors or out in one of several spaces, adorned with original artwork or lush landscaping. Before or after your ceremony, your guests can enjoy McMenamins handcrafted ales made onsite, Edgefield wines and spirits and more. The movie theater, restaurant and soaking pool are added benefits to those who choose to stay the night at the hotel. Or book a cottage so that a group of friends and family can stay together. Old St. Francis School's convenient downtown Bend location also makes it the ideal spot for those who want to explore the area.

About McMenamins

For more than 25 years, McMenamins' historic hotels, pubs and breweries throughout Oregon and Washington have been well known as being friendly, familiar places to enjoy handcrafted ales, wine, spirits and Northwest-inspired pub fare with family and friends. Check out photos, menus, room layouts and rates at mcmenamins.com.

Contact
Group sales office

Price
Food & beverage minimum; varies based on size of room & time of day

Capacity
Up to 140 indoors and 175 outdoors

Catering
In-house catering only

Amenities
- 19 guestrooms and four guest cottages
- Indoor and outdoor event spaces
- Restaurant
- Small bars
- Pool tables
- Saltwater soaking pool
- Onsite brewery
- Movie theater
- Original artwork

© Liz Devine

Bravo! Member Since 1991

See page 531 under Rehearsal Dinner

© Liz Devine

1157 North Marion Avenue
Gearhart, Oregon 97138
p. 503.717.8502
e. salessandt@mcmenamins.com
www.mcmenamins.com

About the Sand Trap

Whether or not you have a golfer in your party, the Sand Trap is a wonderful spot to hold your big day. Set on the Oregon coast just north of Seaside, our pub and event space looks out over the historic 1892 Gearhart Golf Links, said to be the oldest west of the Mississippi. Just imagine your wedding photos with that velvety green grass in the background! Our event space, Livingstone's, opens up onto a large patio steps away from the links. We also offer a nice outdoor space adjacent to Livingstone's which might better suit your dreams. Throughout it all, we will have McMenamins ales, wines and spirits available to keep your guests happy! Overnight accommodations are available across the street at the Gearhart By the Sea condominiums that look out over the Pacific Ocean or in several small hotels in the area.

About McMenamins

For more than 25 years, McMenamins historic hotels, pubs and breweries throughout Oregon and Washington have served as welcoming, familiar places to gather with family and friends. See updated photos, room layouts, menus and more at mcmenamins.com.

Contact
Group Sales Office

Price
Food & beverage minimum; varies based on size of room & time of day

Capacity
Up to 180 indoors plus an additional 100 outside

Amenities
- Restaurant
- Outdoor seasonal seating
- Overlooking Gearhart Golf Links
- Across the street from the Pacific Ocean

459

© Liz Devine

See page 532 under Rehearsal Dinner

Bravo! Member Since 1991

About The McMinnville Grand Ballroom

The McMinnville Grand Ballroom epitomizes simple, natural elegance. Light floods the room from the north and south facing windows. Beautiful Douglas fir floors stretch from wall to wall throughout the 5,600 square foot ballroom. Turned pillars support high ceilings. The building was designed in 1892 in the Arts and Craft Style for the McMinnville Ballroom Association. This elegant space is located in the heart of downtown McMinnville overlooking historic Third Street.

Location

Central downtown wine-country location. Easy walking distance from hotels and churches. Less than an hour from Portland, Beaverton, Tigard, Wilsonville and Salem.

Rentals

Linens, chair covers, place settings, glassware, napkins, center pieces, dual projection system with large retractable screens, sound system with full set-up and microphones, wedding arch.

Contact

Steven Battaglia

325 NE Third Street
McMinnville, Oregon

p. 503.474.0264

e. info@mgballroom.com

www.mgballroom.com

Price

Starting from $500
up to $2,500

Capacity

From 50 to 350

Catering

Preferred caterer, outside caterer or self-catering & bartending

Amenities

- Tables & chairs
- Changing room
- Set-up & clean-up
- Adjustable chandelier lighting
- Two extra large bars
- Sinks, refrigerator & dishwasher

Bravo! Member Since 1995

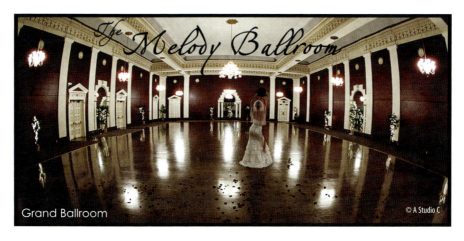

Grand Ballroom

© A Studio C

About The Melody Ballroom

The Melody Ballroom is a unique, historic facility, built in 1925, featuring two beautiful ballrooms. We specialize in producing events that are customized to suit your desires. Our catering staff can produce a diversity of menus, from ethnic, themed, or locally sustainable, to your grandmother's own recipes prepared for you in our kitchen. Our caring staff will provide expert service that will make you and your guests feel well cared for and welcome.

Special Services

The Melody Ballroom rents on a per day basis, giving you the flexibility for decorating and music setup at your convenience. Our on-site event coordinators are always happy to help you plan and execute your event to perfection.

Extraordinary Food and Friendly Service

We offer sit-down, buffet, theme dining, as well as cocktail and hors d'oeuvres styles of celebration.

Our extraordinary food and friendly service will make your event a success!

Contact
Kathleen Kaad

615 SE Alder
Portland, Oregon 97214

p. 503.232.2759
f. 503.232.0702

e. kathleen@themelodyballroom.org

www.themelodyballroom.org

461

Price
Varies, please call

Capacity
Two rooms totaling 1,100 people. Individually, up to 300 or 800 people.

Services
- In-house catering & beverage services only
- Outside catering with some restrictions
- Staff included in catering costs; gratuity on food & beverage
- Full-service bar provided; host or no-host; liquor, beer, & wine
- Fresh flowers, linens & some decorating accessories provided
- 30'x30'; 300 capacity dance floor, plus stage
- Free street parking

Lower Ballroom

Bravo! Member Since 1994

Meriwether's
Restaurant & Skyline Farm

Restaurant:
2601 NW Vaughn Street
Portland, Oregon 97210

Skyline Farm:
12735 NW Skyline Boulevard
Portland, Oregon 97210

p. 503.228.1250

e. info@meriwethersnw.com

www.meriwethersnw.com

462

Portland Composts! Participant

About Meriwether's

Meriwether's Restaurant & Garden (located just 5 minutes from downtown) offers both indoor & outdoor ceremony and/or reception sites. Inside Meriwether's has an elegant, yet comfortable feel. The stone fireplaces, hardwood floors, stained glass and copper accents create a warm & inviting space for year-round wedding events. Outdoors, our all-season covered, heated (and enclosed if needed) patio, garden and gazebo feature fountains, urns & stone paths. Meriwether's gardens are a gorgeous backdrop for your perfect wedding day.

Meriwether's Skyline Farm (a quick 20 minutes from downtown) is an 18-acre oasis on beautiful NW Skyline Boulevard The ceremony is set in front of a "jaw-dropping" panoramic view and the large grass-covered reception site overlooks Skyline Farm where produce is grown and harvested for the restaurant and events menus.

And about our service! Most all of our wedding events are booked through referrals. Our unique "all-inclusive" wedding packages ensure each and every detail will be handled by Meriwether's. If you are trying to find a memorable and worry-free wedding, Meriwether's and Skyline Farm are the perfect fit.

Contact
Events Coordinator

Capacity
From 15 to 400

Types Of Events
Ceremony & reception, rehearsal dinner, cocktail & hors d'oeuvres, bridal shower, wedding brunch, all wedding events either large and small.

Highlights
- "All-Inclusive" weddings (we handle everything!)
- Wedding planning and event coordinators
- Two convenient NW Portland locations
- Urban garden wedding (either indoor or outdoor)
- Skyline Farm wedding (18-acres close to town)
- Menus created from ingredients grown on our own Skyline Farm
- Private parking at both locations

See page 533 under Rehearsal Dinner

Mill Creek Gardens, LLC

4430 Mill Creek Road
Sheridan, Oregon 97378
p. 503.843.4218
p. 971.223.2044
f. 503.843.2469
e. millcreekgarden@onlinemac.com
www.millcreekgardensbb.com

About Mill Creek Gardens LLC

From the planning, to the setup, through the reception and onto the honeymoon travel and accommodations, we arrange it all. Our fun and friendly staff and Wedding Coordinator will make your wedding a memorable, stress-free occasion.

Mill Creek Gardens blends majestic fir and oak trees, beautiful flowers and lush lawns with the peaceful sounds of the rippling creek and the quiet rustle of the trees. If you are planning a fairytale wedding, or a less formal event this is the perfect setting to make your WEDDING DAY DREAMS COME TRUE.

Availability and Terms

We are open daily from 9a.m.–10p.m. We are able to book your event up to one year in advance. A nonrefundable $500 deposit is required to reserve your booking date.

Packages Available

One and three day packages available. Also available is the Bridal Package. Some packages include Event Coordinator, rehearsal, rehearsal dinner, bridesmaid night, ceremony, reception, cake, catering setup to clean-up, honeymoon night. Please see website for details.

Special Services

Also available from Mill Creek Gardens… Honeymoons Cabo Style! We make all your wedding arrangements, leaving you to enjoy a worry-free WEDDING and HONEYMOON in PARADISE. We will arrange the location, photographer, videograhers, caterers, and musicians. www.asunsetwedding.com

Contact
Sheila Herber

Price
$2,500 – $13,000

Capacity
25 to 250 guests

Amenities
- Ceremony Garden
- Reception site creekside
- Bed & Breakfast
- Catering
- Cabo honeymoon
- Site fee only
- Full service

463

WHAT'S NEW

Site fee only $2,500 day, and includes:
– One Hour Rehearsal
– Ceremony Garden
– Creekside Reception
– Guest Chairs
– Arch and Arbor
– Reception Table and chairs
– Catering Table
– Bar Facility
– DJ Area
– Dance Floor.

Winter Sites / Indoor
– Check Website
New Website:
simplydelishcatering.com
– Click on Weddings

Bravo! Member Since 2000

MJCC
MITTLEMAN JEWISH COMMUNITY CENTER

464

About Mittleman Jewish Community Center

Exceeding your Expectations

At the MJCC, we bring a standard of excellence that will ensure the wedding of your dreams. Offering a vast variety of amenities and unmatched flexibility, our caring staff will provide professional service that assures peace of mind for the bridal couple and a memorable reception for everyone. We've spared no expense to make our event space both elegant and inviting. Our in-house caterer will work with you to devise a mouth-watering menu and our friendly and efficient staff will attend to every detail.

Our flexible space can accommodate all of your wedding needs. Take advantage of our on-site spa services including showers, sauna, steam room, whirlpool, and massage. Come experience the best kept secret in Portland!

FIND YOURSELF AT THE J

Contact
Jordana Levenick

6651 SW Capitol Highway
Portland, Oregon 97219

p. 503.535.3555
f. 503.245.4233

e. Jlevenick@oregonjcc.org

www.oregonjcc.org

Price
Please call for more information

Capacity
Ballroom banquet seating for 375. Capacity varies depending on setup style. Call for details.

Quick Facts
- Free on-site parking
- State-of-the-art audio visual system
- Moveable stage
- Dance floor
- Moveable walls (allows the ballroom to be divided into three separate rooms)
- On-site kosher catering
- Podium & Microphones

Bravo! Member Since 2007

**MONARCH
HOTEL
& CONFERENCE CENTER**

12566 SE 93rd Avenue
Clackamas, Oregon 97015
p. 503.652.1515
f. 503.652.5989
e. tthompson@monarchhotel.cc
www.monarchhotel.cc

About the Monarch Hotel

Locally and independently owned and operated for over 25 years, the Monarch Hotel & Conference Center is conveniently located in the heart of Clackamas, just 20 minutes from downtown Portland and Portland International Airport.

Offering over 20,000 sq. ft. of meeting and event space, the Monarch can accommodate intimate receptions for 50 guests to grand affairs of over 600.

With over 30 years of experience, our professional and dedicated Catering staff is committed to creating the event of your dreams. From menu planning to room décor, the Monarch is with you every step of the way to provide the personalized service that you deserve.

Whether you are planning a wedding reception, anniversary party or commitment ceremony, we look forward to sharing in your special day. Please call to schedule your tour and learn more about what the Monarch has to offer.

Contact
Catering Office

Price
$16.95 and up

Capacity
Seating for up to 320 guests in the Pacific Ballroom and up to 600 guests in the Monarch Hall.

Amenities
- On-site Restaurant and Lounge
- Up to 600 people at round table seating
- Ample, complimentary on-site parking
- Complimentary 15' X 15' dance floor
- Tables, chairs, silver, china, glassware and linens included
- Full service, in-house catering
- Complimentary cake cutting
- Full service bar for hosted or no host functions
- 192 newly renovated guest rooms

465

MOUNTAINPARK
Nature's Neighborhood

2 Mt. Jefferson Terrace
Lake Oswego, Oregon 97035
p. 503.635.3561
f.   503.635.0971
e. events@mtparkhoa.com
www.mtparkhoa.com

466

The Mountain Park Clubhouse Hawthorn Room

Consider our building a retreat. A big, warm, beamed hall on a view-endowed city hilltop, easily and quickly accessible, with Lake Oswego arrayed below.

Your guests will find our site gracious and memorable for its groomed landscape, skybridge entrance, exterior decks and long city views.

The Hawthorn Room is quick and easy to decorate. In fact, you'll find it needs little to transform into an individualized, festive space. You can count on our assistance in planning your next event. From room selection to décor, our staff people are here to help with imaginative, energetic and dedicated attention to make your do dazzle. You also get to pick the caterer you want, by the way, a choice people appreciate.

And, you'll have a great time.

Contact
Event Coordinator

Price
Please call for quote

Capacity
300

Amenities
- Tall windows with natural lighting
- Fireplace
- Grand piano
- Outdoor balconies
- Patio furniture
- Parquet dance floor
- Portable bar
- Tables & chairs
- Serving kitchen
- Ice machine
- InFocus projector
- Viewing screens
- Podium & microphone
- WiFi

A PLACE FOR VERY NATURAL EVENTS & CELEBRATIONS

Weddings, receptions, showers, engagements, birthdays, shindigs, retirements, bashes, seminars, bar mitzvahs, reunions, auctions, wine tastings, luaus, presentations, etc.

KEVIN MEYERS PHOTOGRAPHY

MT. HOOD
bed & breakfast, LLC

8885 Cooper Spur Road
Parkdale, Oregon 97041
p. 541.352.6858
e. mthoodbnb@gorge.net
www.mthoodbnb.com

Enchanting Country Setting With Spectacular Mountain Views

Mt. Hood Bed & Breakfast, LLC has everything you need for your wedding and reception. Situated on the north shoulder of Mt. Hood, the facility offers spectacular panoramic views.

Let your mind rest easy. Our professional staff can take care of your every need. We can move indoors if the weather is inclement.

Our grounds are completely private. This means only your guests and people working on your wedding are allowed on site during your event.

We care about you. Yes, we have done hundreds of weddings but our goal is for you to be our "only client" when we work with you for your wedding and reception.

So please call us and tell us your wants and desires. Let us make your wedding day the way you have always dreamed it should be.

Contact
Jackie & Mike Rice, or Betheny Roberts

Price
Available upon request

Capacity
Up to 350

467

Amenities
- Event site from 2:00 p.m. until 10:00 p.m.
- Four (4) complimentary guest rooms
- Overnight accommodations for 8 persons
- Ceremony & reception site
- Cocktail/appetizer garden
- Twinkle lights in reception area
- Outdoor dance floor
- Bar stations
- Stage for band/DJ
- Restrooms – two indoor/ two outdoor
- Parking attendants
- White folding chairs
- Green working B&B farm
- Custom continuous table option available

WHATS NEW

Voted one of the top 10 most romantic places to get away to.
– Sunset Magazine, Feb. 08

© Powers

Bravo! Member Since 1997

Mt. Hood Skibowl
87000 East Hwy 26
Government Camp Oregon
p. 503.272.3206 x 2
www.Skibowl.com

468

Imagine your wedding among the majestic scenery of the Mt. Hood National Forest. Guests will ride the scenic chairlift to mid-mountain where they will enjoy breathtaking views of Mt. Hood as the backdrop for your outdoor ceremony. Following the ceremony everyone will delight in a delicious meal provided by Skibowl's professional catering.

Less than an hour from Portland, Mt. Hood Skibowl is a destination resort featuring spectacular views of Mt. Hood, rare flowers, beautiful natural landscaping and luxury amenities. Whether you are planning an extravagant wedding or a small family ceremony, our goal is to offer you and your guests a memorable experience.

Catering
Our professional chefs are dedicated to working with you to ensure your event is one that is memorable. We are pleased to design a special menu for your event that will fit within your budget.

Lodging
Enjoy the rustic luxury of Mt. Hood's premier accommodations: The Grand Lodges and the Chalets at Collins Lake Resort.. Each beautifully appointed condominium features 2 – 3 bedrooms, 2 – 2.5 bathrooms, gourmet kitchens, and stone fireplaces. Enjoy your choice of a scenic mountain or lake view or the peaceful sound of a cascading creek. Luxurious amenities include the Creekside Lodge, heated pools, hot tubs, oversized leisure pool, and saunas.

Discover an Oregon mountain tradition at Mt. Hood Skibowl.

Contact
Group Events

Price
Prices vary with wedding packages. We'll be happy to provide apersonalized plan and pricing structure that works for you.

Amenities:
- Chairlift/Shuttle access to the Ceremony site
- Tented area for Receptions
- Full-service catering provided by Mt. Hood Skibowl
- Full-service bar available
- Luxury lodging with Mt. Hood's premier accommodations
- Pet-free and pet friendly accommodations available

Mt. Hood Winery

2882 Van Horn Drive
Hood River, Oregon 97031
p. 541.386.8333
f. 541.387.2578
e. linda@mthoodwinery.com
www.mthoodwinery.com

About Mt. Hood Winery

Mt. Hood Winery is conveniently located just 4 miles south of downtown Hood River, off hwy 35. The brand new facility which is surrounded by 16 acres of estate vineyard, along with magnificent views of Mt. Hood and Mt. Adams makes the perfect place to host your wedding and reception. The Northwest Lodge style facility is an architect and designers showcase with its 22' vaulted ceilings and floor to ceiling windows. Additional inside amenities consist of lovely chandeliers, a quarried rock stone fireplace, and a 30 foot long antique replica bar with a mirrored back bar which reflects warmth, light and reflections from the western patio windows.

Types of Events

Mt. Hood Winery offers guests the availability to create a truly unique and memorable event with several different options. We offer everything from a wedding, rehearsal dinner and receptions, business meetings and related events. Our professional and friendly staff are committed to making your special day memorable. Please call to schedule a site visit and consult with our event planner.

Contact
Linda Barber

Price
Varies, depending on event; please call for information.

Capacity
Up to 250 guests

Amenities
- Indoor and outdoor ceremonies and receptions
- Ample complimentary parking on site
- ADA accessible
- Spacious bridal dressing room
- Full kitchen available for catering
- Preferred caterers list upon request
- Tables and chair setup included in site rental
- Estate grown and award winning wines
- Special wine discounts

See page 544 under Wineries & Vineyards

© David Barss

the NINES

525 SW Morrison
Portland, Oregon 97204
p. 503.222.9996
f. 503.222.9997
e. sales@thenines.com
www.thenines.com

Stylish Surroundings In The Heart Of Downtown Portland

Historic splendor. Decadent world-class dining. Every detail executed flawlessly. Picture perfect. Your wedding to the Nines.

DELIGHT – The Nines introduces a new level of service and style to Portland weddings. A made-to-order wedding that will exceed your every whim, with gourmet restaurant-style menus to impress even the most discerning palate, fashionable accommodations for you and your guests and sharp attention paid to every detail. All to ensure that your event will be nothing short of perfection.

IMPRESS – Filled with original art, stylish touches, and beautiful spaces, the Nines embodies classic romantic splendor. The ballroom dazzles with soaring 18-foot ceilings and gleaming Murano glass chandeliers. An elegant wraparound cocktail lounge with panoramic views of Portland effortlessly accommodates up to 500 guests. A sweeping white marble staircase serves as a dramatic backdrop for your grand entrance.

DREAM – Each of the Nines 331 elegantly-appointed guest rooms, including 13 suites, is the ultimate expression of contemporary style. Out of town guests enjoy special room rates and newlyweds bask in stylish suites outfitted with private dining rooms and elaborate bathrooms.

Contact
Shellie Postlewait

Price
Varies depending on event

Capacity
Up to 700 guests for ceremony & standing reception; up to 500 guests for seated reception

Amenities
- 331 luxurious guestrooms, including 13 suites
- Complimentary room for bride & groom based on availability
- Elegant 2-story staircase adds to the grandeur of our spacious ballrooms & event space
- Murano glass chandeliers accentuate the elegant ballroom design
- Over 13,000 square feet of event space
- Full service Audio Visual & production company on site
- Special guest room group rates available for out of town guests

Old McDonald's Farm, Inc.

P.O. Box 326

Corbett, Oregon 97019

503.695.3316

omf@oldmcdonaldsfarm.org

www.oldmcdonaldsfarm.org

About Old McDonald's Farm, Inc.

For a memorable and unusual wedding day, we hope you will think of Old McDonald's Farm, Inc. Nestled among 68 acres of native forest, raspberry fields and a trickling stream in the Columbia River Gorge area, our picturesque Farm is ideal for your special wedding.

The Farm's amenities include a cozy honeymoon suite, rustic schoolhouse, outdoor fire pit, lovely and historic home, restroom facilities, a garden and lots of green space. We are conveniently located just 25 minutes to downtown Portland.

When choosing Old McDonald's Farm, Inc. for your special day, you will also be supporting a local non-profit organization dedicated to providing children in the Portland metropolitan area healthy life experiences utilizing animals, agriculture gardens and natural resources as educational tools.

Contact

Stephanie Rickert
or Kali Moore

Price Range for Service

Varies depending on
your needs

Quick Facts

- Beautiful & scenic 68-acre, raspberry farm
- Picturesque location with a creek, fields, forest, farm animals & off-the-road privacy
- We are located just 1.2 miles off the East Historic Columbia River Highway just a few miles from the Vista House & Crown Point
- We can accommodate a small group or hundreds of people
- Plenty for your family & friends to do between the ceremony & the reception
- Your funds helps us help children as we are a private, non-profit, children's program

471

Have a memorable wedding day…imagine the bride wearing white riding in on a black horse.

Oregon City Golf Club at Lone Oak
Established 1922

20124 South Beavercreek Road
Oregon City, Oregon 97045
p. 503.518.1038
p. 503.518.2846
f. 503.518.1290
e. rose@ocgolfclub.com
www.ocgolfclub.com

472

About Oregon City Golf Club

Beyond Expectations is what our staff is known for at Oregon City Golf Club at Lone Oak.

We offer a highly personalized level of service in a relaxed, lush, and natural environment.

Our unique indoor/outdoor setting has all the amenities you need for an extraordinary wedding experience.

Established in 1922, Oregon City Golf Club at Lone Oak is the third oldest, privately owned, public golf course still in operation in the state of Oregon.

Types of Events:

Weddings; Receptions; Corporate Events; Retirements; Meetings; Tournaments; Seminars; Celebration of Life; All Special Events.

Contact
Rose Holden

Price
Varies according to event

Capacity
150 Winter
250 Summer

Ammenities
- Tables and chairs provided both inside and out
- White table linens and skirting provided
- Tent, tent liner, tent pole covers provided in season
- On-site coordinator provided
- Set up, break down and clean up provided
- Bartender and bar service available
- ADA fully accessible
- Free on-site parking

895 West Main Street
Silverton, Oregon 97381
p. 503.874.2500
f. 503.873.5875
e. tinag@moonstonehotels.com
www.oregongardenresort.com

About The Oregon Garden

The Oregon Garden Resort and Oregon Garden have combined to create one of the premier wedding destinations in the Willamette Valley.

The Oregon Garden Resort features 103 guest rooms, cocktail lounge, restaurant, and full service day spa that is the perfect place to get ready with your party! We have indoor and outdoor venues for both ceremony and reception, and three indoor banquet rooms ideal for rehearsal dinners or farewell brunches.

Directly adjacent to the Resort, the Oregon Garden is a year-round, 80-acre botanical display garden showcasing water features, garden art, and thousands of plants in more than 20 specialty gardens. These elements provide a beautiful setting for your wedding, and an incredible variety of backgrounds for wedding photos. Indoor and outdoor venues are available to accommodate anywhere from 50 to 500 guests any time of year.

Packages and a la carte pricing available. Our properties work seamlessly together to provide a full service experience.

Contact
Tina Garland

Price
Starting at $800

Amenities
- Three outdoor ceremony sites and three reception venues ranging in capacity from 50 to 500 guests
- Full-service catering through the Oregon Garden Resort.
- 103 guest rooms with fireplaces and patios, breakfast included
- On-site day spa with a variety of hair and make-up packages and spa services for your whole party

473

Bravo! Member Since 2006

The Oregon Golf Club

Portland's #1 Ranked Private Country Club

Located atop Pete's Mountain Road in West Linn, 5 minutes from I-205, and only 20 minutes from Downtown Portland, you'll find a private country club with breathtaking views and a tranquil setting... Perfect for your special day.

Upon entering the private driveway, after passing through the rod iron gates, your guests will enjoy the amazing scenery from "above it all", which includes vineyards, trees and an incredible view of Mt. Hood, showcasing Oregon's true beauty. While guests make their way through the professionally manicured grounds, they will find themselves in the award winning Rose Garden where your wedding dreams will come true. After two become one, guests will enjoy butler style served hors d' oeuvres and cocktails on the garden patio that sits above the golf course offering view of the Willamette Valley. When the time has come for dinner service to begin, guests will make their way into the Rose Pavilion. Upon entering the Ballroom, guests will go from impressed to amazed by the beveled chiffon draped 23 foot ceilings, custom made chandeliers and a full wall of windows overlooking the Rose Garden. With specially trained staff and a distinguished Chef, your guests will leave with a lasting impression that will be talked about for years to come.

Perfect Location for any Event

- School Auctions
- Birthdays
- Holiday Parties
- Golf Tournaments
- Corporate Meetings
- Anniversary Parties
- Memorial Services

Call for Details

Bravo! Member Since 1996

Contact
Tara Killinger

25700 SW Pete's Mountain Road
West Linn, Oregon 97068

p. 503.650.7815

e. catering@oregongc.com

www.countryclubreceptions.com

Price
Please call for pricing.

Capacity
100 – 400

Amenities

- All inclusive packages available
- Full service in house catering
- Private Rooms Available for Rehearsal dinners (discount to OGC brides)
- Year round Event Space
- Bridal Suite and Grooms Changing rooms available

WHAT'S NEW?

Year round indoor event space. Mention this ad and receive $500 off room rental or ceremony & site fee for all 2010 events.

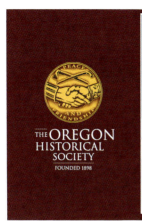

Give your wedding a place in history!

Located in the South Park blocks of downtown Portland, the Oregon Historical Society is surrounded by culture, history and beauty. The Society offers indoor and outdoor venues capable of accommodating a variety of events.

The James F. Miller Pavilion is the ideal location for an elegant downtown event with a unique museum feel. The adjacent outdoor Plaza is a lovely ceremony or reception site on its own, or can be combined with the Pavilion to create a beautiful indoor /outdoor reception.

The Broadway Terrace is the perfect setting for a ceremony or smaller reception, or as an added space for an elegant cocktail hour. Surrounded by boxwoods and encompassing a southern view of the Haas Mural, the Terrace truly emotes urban living.

The Madison Room is designed for smaller groups and is the perfect space for a rehearsal dinner or getting ready on your wedding day. Enjoy a view of the south park blocks from the Madison Room's private terrace.

Contact
Rachael Snow

1200 SW Park Avenue
Portland, Oregon 97205

p. 503.306.5281
f. 503.221.2035

e. events@ohs.org

www.ohs.org

Price
Based on size of event, please call for pricing

Capacity
- **Miller Pavilion,** 150 banquet, 250 reception, 160 theater
- **Plaza 150 banquet,** 200 reception, 200 theater, able to be tented
- **Broadway Terrace,** 60 banquet, 125 reception, 80 theater, able to be tented
- **Madison Room,** 40 banquet, 100 reception, 60 theater

475

WHAT'S NEW!

New flowers and lighting grace our Plaza and our elegant Madison Room and Miller Pavilion have been recently renovated.

OSWEGO LAKE HOUSE

40 North State Street
Lake Oswego, Oregon 97034
p. 503.636.4561
f. 503.636.4871
e. kathy@oswegolakehouse.com
www.oswegolakehouse.com

476

About the Oswego Lake House

Elegant lakeside dining is what you will find at the Oswego Lake House. This historic restaurant is located on State Street in Lake Oswego next to the theater. Our staff of seasoned professionals will provide an effortless event for you, and a memorable experience for your guests. From your first phone call throughout the day of your event you can expect personalized service. Our restaurant is ideal for corporate events, holiday parties and wedding receptions.

The view from our 3,000 square foot deck is spectacular with the lake as a back drop to a wonderful dining experience. We accommodate quite comfortably 250 guests on the deck for any occasion. The comfortable yet elegant main dining room, and adjoining private room with its own bar, also have wonderful views of the lake. Patio includes gas fire pits and heaters, while a fireplace adorns the main dining room.

We understand the success of any event lies greatly in the hands of the staff and simply put, our staff is a cut above. Our entire staff truly looks forward to ensuring the greatness of your event.

Contact
Kathy Krech

Price
Customized by the event, menu choices & services

Capacity
20 – 300

Amenities
- Fireplace
- Cozy lounge
- Private wine lockers
- Three separate bars, including large outdoor bar
- Five decks and patios
- Two firepits
- Stunning views

OFF-SITE CATERING

Consider us for your next event at the location of your choice. Boxed lunches or buffet lunches to go. Light or heavy appetizer platters. Dinner buffets. On-site live cooking (your location). Brunch or breakfast service.

HOTEL VINTAGE PLAZA

PAZZO
R I S T O R A N T E

422 SW Broadway
Portland, Oregon 97205
p. 503.412.6313
www.pazzo.com
www.vintageplaza.com

Italian Romance in the Heart of Portland
From the warm and friendly greetings of the doorman to the pampering from our world class wait staff, we strive to make every event perfect. We feel every event tells a story.. Let Pazzo and the Hotel Plaza tell yours.

Newly renovated and spectacular...
We have truly turned the hotel into a jewel in the middle of the city with our new, updated look. With a focus on wine and the Pacific Northwest, the hotel invites your guests to enjoy the view and natural resources the area has to offer. Stay in one of our local winery themed suites and enjoy a complimentary wine reception at night. We are truly one of Portland's most romantic places to stay..

Italian flare with attention to detail...
Whether you are looking to host your reception for 130 people in our Tuscany room overlooking downtown Portland, or having a rehearsal dinner for 64 in our wine cellar. The service and food are beyond compare. All of our catering comes straight from the award winning Pazzo Ristorante kitchen, so in addition to our venue's elegance and romance, the food will never disappoint.

Contact
Sales and catering at
weddings@pazzo.com

Price
Pazzo can customize a menu to meet your events needs including special needs menus

Capacity
16 – 200

Amenities
- Full-service in-house catering by Pazzo Ristorante
- Custom wedding packages to meet your every need
- Full-service bar available
- Tables, chairs, china, glassware, & linens provided
- Full service bar and dance floor available
- Valet parking available
- In house event manager to make your event flow perfectly

TYPES OF EVENTS
Plated or buffet dinners, cocktail and appetizer receptions, wedding, showers, ceremonies, receptions, and rehearsal dinners

477

RecycleWorks Award Winner

Bravo! Member Since 1996

33180 Cape Kiwanda Drive
Pacific City, Oregon 97135
p. 503.965.3674
p. 866.571.0581
f. 503.965.0061
e. Events@pelicanbrewery.com
www.pelicanbrewery.com

478

About Pelican Pub & Brewery

Located on the oceanfront at the stunning Cape Kiwanda Natural Scenic Area, and only two hours from Portland, the Pelican Pub & Brewery is the perfect place for your most special day.

Our fabulous location provides the memorable opportunity for you to say your vows on the beach, then take ten steps to our beautiful reception/banquet room. From an intimate reception or dinner to a large celebration, you can rely on the Pelican Pub & Brewery to create the wedding day of your dreams. Relax and enjoy your day as every detail will be attended to by our professional and courteous staff.

The award-winning kitchen can prepare meals from simple to extravagant, with the ability to customize menus to your taste and whimsy.

Our in-house brewery has won awards all over the world, and can provide these fresh craft beers directly to your event. In addition, great wines and a full bar are available.

After your celebration, invite your wedding party, friends and family to extend their stay by enjoying our lodging properties – Inn at Cape Kiwanda, The Cottages at Cape Kiwanda, or Shorepine Vacation Rentals, most of which are just steps away from your event. Our properties offer accommodations ranging from beautifully appointed ocean-view rooms to luxuriously furnished cottages and homes.

Pelican Pub & Brewery...the Perfect Place... for your Perfect Day.

Contact
Event Coordinator

Price
Varies based on season & menu

Quick Facts
- Award-winning craft brewery on-site
- First class kitchen prepares meals from simple to extravagant
- Oceanfront
- Private beach for outdoor ceremonies.
- Full bar and attentive service
- Flexible overnight accommodations, from hotel rooms to vacation rentals
- Dedicated wedding planner

See page 534 under Rehearsal Dinner

COUNTRY CLUB

500 SE Butler Road
Gresham, Oregon 97080
p. 503.667.7500
f. 503.667.3885
e. groupsales@persimmoncc.com
www.persimmoncc.com

About Persimmon Country Club

Here at Persimmon, just 30 minutes from downtown Portland, you can relax, eat and drink among the best views nature has to offer. Boasting glorious views of Mount Hood, you will also find rolling manicured lawns, forests and ponds just outside the windows of your perfect setting. With several locations, your ceremony and reception can be all that you have dreamed of.

For a location as special as the occasion, let Persimmon Country Club host your day. From the menu and room arrangements to décor and ambiance, no detail will be overlooked.

Impeccable Service

No matter what the occasion, our personal service, attention to detail and memorable setting are the keys to making your event special.

Contact
Catering Department

Price
Call for pricing

Capacity
Up to 300 dining & 600 theatre-style seating

Amenities
- Spectacular views of Mount Hood
- Outdoor ceremony site over looking the golf course & Mount Hood
- All inclusive catering packages
- Outdoor dining with scenic views
- Only 30 minutes from downtown Portland

479

TYPES OF EVENTS

Business, Bridal, Birthdays, Graduations, Baby Showers, Golf Events, Community Gatherings, Retirement Parties, Fundraisers, Lectures, Holiday Events, Awards Dinners & Weddings

Bravo! Member Since 1995

Pomeroy Farm

20902 NE Lucia Falls Road
Yacolt, WA 98675
p. 360.686.3537
f. 360.686.8111
e. danielbrink@pomeroyfarm.org
www.Pomeroyfarm.org

480

About Pomeroy Farm

Let the serene and beautiful 677 acre Pomeroy Farm, nestled among towering fir trees and situated on the East Fork of the Lewis River, be the setting for your wedding and reception. Located just 45 minutes North of Portland, this picturesque historic farm offers a memorable venue for your wedding. Amenities include the newly renovated "Gathering Place", cavernous 1940's barn, 1920's log home, and expansive fields. The Farm offers colorful seasonal vistas of the remote and beautiful Lucia Valley and the charming herb and flower garden offers an idyllic backdrop for photographs.

Contact
Daniel Brink

Price
$1,500 – $3,500

Quick Facts
- Can accommodate over 500
- Newly remodeled bridal suite
- Various indoor and outdoor settings
- Onsite commercial kitchen

Bravo! Member Since 2009

© Evrim Icoz

PORTLAND ART MUSEUM

1219 SW Park Avenue
Portland, Oregon 97205
p. 503.276.4291
f. 503.276.4377

e. doug.froman@pam.org
www.portlandartmuseum.org

About the Portland Art Museum

Portland's premier event venue for:

- Weddings
- Meetings
- Fundraisers
- Holiday parties
- Elegant receptions

Mingle with the art in newly available gallery reception spaces.

Dance under the stars in the city's most sophisticated outdoor courtyard.

Entertain in style in Portland's most glamorous ballrooms.

Location
Our landmark campus is located in the heart of the beautiful downtown Park Blocks, in the midst of the city's cultural district.

Options
Combine an exhibition viewing or gallery tour in conjunction with your event. Choose from a variety of floor plans.

Contact
Portland Art Museum

Price
Prices vary; please call for details

Capacity
The 9,000 square-foot Kridel Grand Ballroom accommodates 560 for a seated dinner & 1,200 for a reception; the 6,100 square-foot Fields Ballroom accommodates 220 for a seated dinner & 400 for a reception

Amenities
- Rooms fully supported by in-house A/V
- Exclusive caterer offers full-range catering options including bar, décor, floral, and staffing

481

© Evrim Icoz

Bravo! Member Since 1992

PORTLANDCENTERSTAGE

Portland's Newest, Most Exciting Events Venue

The Gerding Theater at the Armory is located in the heart of Portland's fashionable Pearl District. The LEED Platinum rated building's interior is a sophisticated combination of urban contemporary and classic industrial with original brick and basalt walls and a three-story vaulted ceiling exposing the historic, old growth Douglas Fir bow trusses. A "Fire Wall" of flickering lights cascades down the back wall of the Main Lobby, giving the illusion of candlelight in a grand cathedral. A stunning curved, open staircase leads to the Mezzanine level, set underneath the dramatic Starfield Chandelier of 184 tiny bulbs suspended in mid-air. This setting provides an elegant backdrop for a wide range of events, including:

- Wedding Ceremonies and Receptions
- Galas and Fundraisers
- Theatre & Musical Performances (Box Office Services Available)
- Film Premieres & Presentations
- Holiday Parties
- Business Meetings and Presentations of all sizes

Contact

Kavita Jhaveri &
Sarah Mitchell

128 NW Eleventh Avenue
Portland, Oregon 97209

p. 503.445.3824
f. 503.445.3801

e. rentals@pcs.org
www.pcs.org

Price

$250 – $5,000

Amenities

- Seated Dining Capacity of 375; Standing Capacity of 600
- Round & Banquet Tables, Lounge & Bistro Furniture, Folding Conference Chairs included
- Professional Sound System
- Event Lighting Package
- LCD Projection
- Dressing Rooms for Bridal Party
- Day-of Coordination
- Complete on-site Support Staff
- List of Preferred Caterers selected to accommodate all price ranges
- 599-seat Auditorium & 200 seat flexible Black Box Theater with Theatrical Lighting & Audiovisual Services

thesidewalkstudio.com

thesidewalkstudio.com

Bravo! Member Since 2006

蘭蘇園

Portland Classical Chinese Garden

The Most Unique Backdrop to Your Perfect Wedding

The Portland Classical Chinese Garden is perfect for your ultimate dream wedding. Whether an intimate rehearsal dinner, an elegant ceremony or a ceremony followed by a catered reception, the Garden stands alone in being a breathtakingly one of a kind wedding site.

A bridged lake, waterfall, winding pathways, exquisite pavilions and lush flora provide a stunning stage for sharing your romantic moment-in-time with your friends and family.

Located in downtown Portland, the Garden is an easy destination for locals and within walking distance of many hotels for your out-of-town guests.

Our caring, knowledgeable and experienced event staff will assist you in planning the perfect memorable celebration of any size and scope.

We look forward to welcoming you inside the tranquil walls of our peaceful Garden. Please contact us for additional information and to schedule a site visit.

Contact

Gary Wilson & Michele Starry

239 NW Everett
Portland, Oregon 97209

p. 503.228.8131
f. 503.228.7844

e. rental@portlandchinesegarden.org

www.portlandchinesegarden.org

Price
$1,200 – $3,200

Capacity
Up to 300

Amenities

- Exclusive after hour use of the facility
- On-site event management
- Complimentary site visits and rehearsal
- Approved list of caterers to meet your needs
- Chairs (up to 100) available for rent on-site
- Greeter/Security posted at entrance
- Easily accessible via MAX light rail
- ADA accessible

483

© Erin Grace

© Jessica Hill

Consider the Garden for engagement or wedding photos. Call for rates.

484

© Coughlin-Glaser

Portland SPIRIT ®

110 SE Caruthers
Portland, Oregon 97214
p. 503.224.3900
p. 800.224.3901
e. sales@portlandspirit.com
www.portlandspirit.com

The fleet of the Portland Spirit has an experienced team that offers comprehensive services to help you plan a flawless wedding or special occasion.

Portland Spirit
This stylish yacht combines a classic nautical experience with a fine dining atmosphere. Two levels are fully enclosed and climate controlled, each with an independent sound system and baby grand pianos. A built-in marble dance floor is available on the Columbia Deck (2nd level). The top Starlight Deck is an open air viewing deck. Ceremony: up to 200 guests. Reception: up to 400 guests

Willamette Star
Elegance and style has been custom built into the Willamette Star. Features: cherry wood interior, brass accents, two enclosed and climate controlled decks, sound system, piano and two outdoor viewing decks. Ceremony: up to 100 guests. Reception: up to 120 guests.

Crystal Dolphin
This sleek and luxurious vessel provides a bright, contemporary setting for the modern bride. Features: Two enclosed and climate controlled levels, sound system, baby grand piano, and outdoor viewing deck. Ceremony: up to 80 guests. Reception up to 100 guests.

Contact
Group & Charter Sales

Price
Prices vary – please inquire

Vessel & Facility Amenities
- In-house catering
- Linen tablecloths and napkins provided
- China, glassware & flatware provided
- Servers and bartender included with food and bar service
- Full-service cash bar available
- Clean-up provided
- Commercial parking and street parking available
- ADA limited with assistance – please call for more information

© Lau...

See page 347 under Boats & 401 under Reception & Wedding Sites

Bravo! Member Since 1996

12930 Old Pumpkin Ridge Road
North Plains, Oregon 97133
p. 503.647.4747
f. 503.647.2002
e. eventsales@pumpkinridge.com
e. catering@pumpkinridge.com
www.pumpkinridge.com

485

Weddings With Elegance & Class

At Pumpkin Ridge Golf Club, we pride ourselves on creating memorable, lasting events. Set on the edge of the beautiful Willamette Valley, yet convenient to downtown Portland, our Ghost Creek facility offers a gracious 18,000 square-foot clubhouse featuring dramatic architecture and old Portland flavor. Your guests will delight in views of our two championship courses where golf legends have made history on numerous occasions. Our Sunset Room is a spacious banquet facility with open-beam ceilings, skylights, a generous deck and sweeping golf course views. Our expert event staff promise to deliver culinary expertise and an event that far exceeds your expectations. Whether you're planning an intimate gala or a corporate outing, you can relax knowing you and your guests will enjoy nothing less than perfection.

We suggest early reservations, but can accommodate events on short notice if space is available. A deposit is required; payment in full is due seven days prior to your event.

Contact
Event Sales Department
503.647.2507 or
503.647.2527

Price
Varies according to menu selection

Capacity
Up to 300 guests, plus outside seating

Amenities
- Full-service, in-house catering provided
- Tables & chairs provided up to 300 guests
- Full-service bar provided
- Complimentary foursome golf at Ghost Creek
- Parquet dance floor available in a variety of sizes
- China, glassware, linens & napkins provided

TYPES OF EVENTS
Weddings, receptions, rehearsal dinners, showers, formal sit-down, buffet, cocktail and hors d'oeuvres, reunions, anniversary parties, corporate business meetings, holiday parties and groomsmen golf outings.

Bravo! Member Since 1998

Queen anne
victorian mansion

1441 NORTH MCCLELLAN
PORTLAND, OR 97217
T: 503.283.3224

A Magical Storybook Place

Every bride deserves perfection on her wedding day, whether it is formal, informal, or a simple family ceremony. The Queen Anne staff is very detail oriented and will make sure you and your family are at ease knowing everything is taken care of start to finish. Very private setting on over two acres, only 10 minutes from downtown Portland and just across the Interstate Bridge from Vancouver. The mansion is a beautiful and perfect location to create your special day.

The Queen Anne features incredible original woodwork, chandeliers and one of the largest private collections of Povey stained glass windows in the world. Call to set up your appointment and allow our staff to dazzle you with a tour of the grounds and mansion. Appointments are made through the week.

Availability and Terms

The mansion is a 4,300 square-foot beautiful Victorian with a 42' round enclosed gazebo. Reserve as early as possible.

Contact
Event Manager

1441 North McClellan
Portland, Oregon 97217

p. 503.283.3224

e. queenannevictorianmansion@
yahoo.com

www.queenannevictorian-
mansion.com

Price
Rates vary. Please call for specific pricing.

Capacity
Up to 400 seated;
300 reception

Amenities
- All-inclusive
  in-house catering
- Tables & chairs for up
  to 400 provided
- Full bar service available
- Plenty of free parking
- Gazebo is a perfect
  location for dancing
- Completely decorated
  in Victorian-era antiques,
  colorful floral garlands &
  arrangements throughout
  the home; meticulously
  landscaped gardens

Bravo! Member Since 1990

See page 356 under
Ceremony Sites

RED LION HOTEL®
PORTLAND · CONVENTION CENTER

1021 NE Grand Avenue
Portland, Oregon 97232
p. 503.820.4160
f. 503.235.0396
e. kellie.bollinger@gaha.biz
www.redlion.com/conventioncenter

Red Lion Hotel – Portland Convention Center

Imagine being married on a rooftop terrace, surrounded by white lights, overlooking downtown Portland and the West Hills…. Imagine a wedding reception that makes your grandmother happy, as well as your kooky cousin…. Imagine serving food that everyone loves….Imagine specialty cocktails customized to your wedding….Imagine planning a wedding and reception that is practically stress-free….

The Red Lion Hotel across from the Oregon Convention Center has everything you need!

Complete renovation of hotel rooms including bathrooms, event space, lobby, café and lounge. Finished in 2009.

Directly on the MAX light rail line, in fareless square with free transportation to the Lloyd Center district and downtown Portland.

If you already have your wedding and reception location planned…how about guest rooms for your out-of-town guests? Bachelor and bachelorette parties in our Windows Lounge? Rehearsal dinner?

Contact
Kellie Bollinger

Price
Full reception packages range from $32 – $40 per person. Special prices for wedding ceremony space.

Quick Facts
- Picturesque rooftop terrace & event space with panoramic city view, perfect for wedding ceremonies & receptions
- Newly renovated ballroom for receptions of up to 300 people with new carpet, lighting, sound, wall & window coverings
- Special rates for your guests in our renovated guest rooms, including upgraded premium rooms for the bride & groom!
- Packages include traditional foods, buffet or plated; non-alcoholic beverages; champagne toast; décor; tables, chairs & linen; dance floor; room for bride & groom, complimentary parking

WHAT'S NEW

Renovation….the Red Lion is "brand new again"!

487

Bravo! Member Since 1997

RED LION HOTEL ON THE RIVER
JANTZEN BEACH · PORTLAND

909 North Hayden Island Drive
Portland, Oregon 97217

p. 503.283.4466
f. 503.735.4847

e. info@redlionontheriver.com

www.redlion.com/jantzenbeach

About Red Lion On The River

Located on the banks of the Columbia River, yet right here in Portland, the Red Lion Hotel on the River offers a truly unique venue providing the ambience of a resort with the convenience of the city. Create your perfect day in our ballroom with floor to ceiling windows showcasing breathtaking views of the river…imagine standing in your gown on the deck above the river…leave the reception on a boat—possibilities abound.

Just north of downtown, our convenient location and ample parking make attending your event enjoyable for your guests and family as well! Our reputation for exquisite food paired with our unparalleled service make this the ideal location.

A variety of packages are available including limousine service and the perfect bridal suite. Add the convenience of group rates for the family and planning your wedding has just gotten a little easier!

From menu planning to room decor, our experienced and professional wedding team is poised to tend to all of the details and help you design a perfect day filled with memories that will last a lifetime. What you imagine, you can now realize!

Contact
Catering department

Price
Call for pricing

Quick Facts
- Full–service, in–house catering provided by the hotel exclusively
- Now 18 flexible meeting rooms, most with floor to ceiling windows
- Largest pillar free ballroom north of San Francisco
- Spectacular views of the Columbia River in Portland
- Beautiful outdoor River Deck, perfect for ceremonies
- Abundance of outdoor spaces for photos
- Expert catering staff to guide you through your event
- ADA accessible
- Complimentary parking
- Now 100% non–smoking

WHAT'S NEW
Updated public space and guest rooms with private balconies, pillow top mattresses, refrigerators and microwaves.

503 SW Alder Street
Portland, Oregon 97204
p. 503.417.3388
f. 503.417.3386
e. carole.lombardi@redstartavern.com
www.redstartavern.com

489

A Romantic Setting for YOUR Perfect Day

We feature an atmosphere of classic elegance with burgundy carpet with ivory, sage and camel accent colors; apricot and gold wall fabrics; and soft yellow light from unique wall sconces creates a cozy glow in the room. For fun rehearsal dinners, receptions or brunches, try our fabulous Club Room!

Description of Facility

Your choice of eight luxurious private dining rooms. Linens are available in ivory or white. We are pleased to provide special colors on request. White china and all glassware is always included. We provide candles for decoration. We are also delighted to assist you with any floral arrangements and decorations you may need.

Types of Menus and Specialty

Executive Chef Thomas Dunklin focuses his menus around an American Roast House taking full advantage of a wealth of local and regional ingredients from local farmers and sustainable agriculture. The result is such mouthwatering dishes as the infamous Dry Aged Prime Rib with House Made Worcestershire, Sweet Briar Farms Duroc Wood Grilled Pork Chop and the Bourbon Strawberries with Sour Cream Sorbet and Brown Sugar Streusel.

Food

We offer an extensive variety of menu options from formal plated dinners to build-your-own buffet, breakfast/brunch, lunch and standing cocktail receptions. Let us create a menu that will astound and delight you and your guests.

Contact
Carole Lombardi

Price
Contact me for a proposal

Capacity
Up to 130 for banquet & 200 for reception in one of our eight luxurious private dining rooms

Services
- Exquisite new American cuisine served in a magnificent setting
- Hand-crafted cocktails
- Extensive, regional wine list
- Valet parking available
- Eco program includes recycling & composting
- Our menus may be viewed at www.redstartavern.com

SERVING ATTENDANTS

Servers are included with menu costs. Setup fee and room rentals vary.
All food and beverage items are subject to a 15% gratuity and a 6% administrative fee.

Bravo! Member Since 1999

© Shumaker

© Shumaker

THE RESORT
AT THE MOUNTAIN

490

Your wedding event is all about you.
And it deserves the perfect setting.

Your wedding at The Resort at The Mountain will be remembered by how well your guests' five senses – sight, smell, taste, touch and sound – are stimulated. This requires personal, experienced attention to every detail. At The Resort, you will find Catering professionals committed to exceeding your needs, wants and expectations and those of your guests. When it comes to weddings and related events, our associates understand these are more than social occasions – they are deeply personal expressions of you. Allow our wedding coordinator to share your vision and help make it come alive just as you imagined.

The "perfect" wedding day is every young girl's dream. Making that dream come true is an awesome responsibility. And we'll carry it out to the smallest detail. Because when all is said and done, it will be the little things that set The Resort at The Mountain apart. The warmth of a front desk associate's smile, the elegance of a tastefully appointed table, the professionalism of a staff trained to serve with intelligence and grace. You'll be able to enjoy your event as much as your guests!

What's New

The Spa marries healing traditions of indigenous inspired cultures with diverse treatments. Spa-goers embark on journeys of transformative peak experience and personal exploration. Ideal for bridal parties and wedding guests.

Contact

Becca Kolibaba,
Catering & Events Manager

68010 East Fairway Avenue
Welches, Oregon 97067

p. 503.622.2234
f. 503.622.5227

e. becca.kolibaba@theresort.com

www.theresort.com

Price

Moderate to expensive
(package options available)

Capacity

Up to 450

Amenities

- Wedding-related events from 10 to 450 guests including rehearsal dinners, ceremonies, receptions, plated or buffet brunch, lunch, dinners

- Outdoor recreation including 27-holes of golf (The Courses), 18-hole lighted putting course (The Greens), tennis, lawn bowling, croquet, badminton, sand volleyball, outdoor heated swimming pool and whirlpool spa, basketball goal, hiking and nature trails

- The Spa

- Sumptuous on-site dining at Altitude restaurant and lounge or Mallards café & pub (open seasonally)

Bravo! Member Since 1994

RIVER Lodge & Grill

6 Marine Drive
Boardman, Oregon 97818
p. 541.481.6800
f. 541.481.6801
e. sales@riverlodgeandgrill.com
www.riverlodgeandgrill.com

About River Lodge and Grill

We've got a wedding setting that will leave you breathless-the shore of the stunning Columbia River. Once you take your vows, you won't have to leave this gorgeous view behind. Our Washington Room, which can accommodate up to 50 guests for the reception, overlooks this wondrous waterway. We offer a variety of Wedding Packages, which can be tailored to fit your needs-from light hors d'oeuvres to a complete luncheon or dinner. Plus, some packages feature a complimentary room for your wedding night.

Contact
Bob Okeson or
Yolonda Vincent

Price
Call for details

Quick Facts
- Location great for outdoor weddings
- We have a beautiful private beach
- Our restaurant has a lovely view at sunset of the Columbia River
- The hotel has a lodge theme
- We also have a outdoor pool, hot tub & his & hers steam rooms
- We have conference & meeting rooms
- We also offer catering for any of your event needs

491

Bravo! Member Since 2008

The Riverhouse
HOTEL & CONVENTION CENTER

3075 North Business 97
Bend, Oregon 97701
p. 541.617.6278
f. 541.389.0781
e. marketing@riverhouse.com
www.riverhouse.com

492

Imagine the wedding of your dreams nestled along the beautiful Deschutes River in the heart of Bend. At The Riverhouse Hotel & Convention Center, our thoughtful and detailed wedding coordinator and staff will work within your budget to help you turn your vision into reality.

Whether you're looking for an intimate space or a state-of-the-art facility that seats 1000, the Riverhouse has it all; including 220 spacious guest rooms, up to 50,000 square feet of indoor/outdoor event space, Crossings Steakhouse and lounge, and a championship golf course. You will also enjoy the convenience of being in the center of town and just minutes from the airport.

From selecting the right location for your reception, menu planning, decorating the room, and receiving your guests, our staff is there every step of the way. We work with the finest local cake decorators, florists, spas, photographers and decorators and can recommend the right people to join your team.

And for the bride and groom, The Riverhouse offers some of the finest spa and fireplace suites in Oregon. With the sounds of the river flowing outside your room, a bottle of complimentary champagne upon arrival and all the details taken care of, we'll help make your dreams come true.

WHAT'S NEW?
Newly updated public space and remodeled guestrooms, restaurant and lobby await the bride and her party.

Contact
Debra Martyn-Jones

Price Range for service
We are happy to provide a personalized plan and pricing structure that works for you

Quick Facts
- 18 Flexible Meeting Rooms that can host up to 1,000 people for a sit-down dinner – 16,000 sq. ft. ballroom
- State-of-the-art Audio Visual Equipment
- On-site wedding coordinator
- Full-service, in-house catering created by our Executive Chef for both indoor and outdoor spaces
- 220 spacious rooms to lodge friends and family including newly remodeled, fireplace, spa and kitchen suites overlooking the beautiful Deschutes River
- Crossings Steakhouse serving USDA Prime steaks, seafood and other Northwest Favorites. A Wine Spectator Award Winner, Crossings is the ideal setting for your rehearsal dinner party. After dinner, dance under the stars and on the river at Crossings Lounge
- River's Edge 18 Hole Championship Golf Course

Riverside
GOLF AND COUNTRY CLUB

8105 NE 33rd Drive
Portland, Oregon 97211
p. 503.288.6468
f.   503.282.1383
e. rbarta@riversidegcc.com
www.riversidegcc.com

About Riverside Golf & Country Club

A panoramic view of the 18th green and acres of park-like scenery provide a breathtaking backdrop to your special day! Nature's splendor splashes across the course, making each season unique and unforgettable. Classic elegance throughout the clubhouse welcomes your guests as our contemporary and upbeat staff caters to their every need! It's easy to see why Riverside is known as the "Friendliest Club in Town – Where Friends Become Family".

"Laughter is brightest where food is best" ~ Irish Proverb

Nothing will make an event more successful and memorable than incomparable cuisine...we invite you to schedule a menu tasting with our Executive Chef and Staff. Call us today for a tour and more information!!

Contact
Gilbert de Best or
Randy Barta

Price
Please call for our prices
or visit our website
www.riversidegcc.com

Accommodations
- Formal Dining Room
  and Terrace
- Ballroom
- Fireside Room
- Pierre Alarco Board Room
- Private lot with
  porte cochere
- Poolside ceremonies
  (Seasonal)
- Seating for up to 275

Catering Services
- China, glassware & linens
- Full-service Stationary
  and Porta Bars
- Dance Floors (2 sizes)
- Buffet or Plated Meals
- Professional Event Planners
  help with details for your
  Special Day

493

R

Riverview

29311 SE Stark Street
Troutdale, Oregon 97060 (20
minute drive from downtown
Portland)

p. 503.661.3663

e. info@riverview-events.com

www.riverview-events.com

Breathtaking Setting

Riverview's exquisite gardens, towering trees, and waterfront view showcase the serenity and natural beauty of Oregon's landscape. Although located only twenty minutes from downtown Portland, Riverview's manicured grounds, boasting fountains and gazebos, will quickly transport you and your guests to a peaceful world far from the hustle and bustle of the city.

Year-round Events for Small & Large Gatherings

From small, intimate ceremonies to large receptions, our goal is to provide an elegant backdrop for your momentous event. Our indoor and outdoor venues are set on culturally historic property along the Sandy River. Offering gourmet Northwest cuisine, our professional chefs and waitstaff look forward to turning your vision into reality.

Private Room

Our glass-enclosed private room, complete with fireplace and live piano music, is the perfect choice for engagement celebrations, bridal showers, and rehearsal dinners.

Contact
Event Coordinator

Price
Ceremony starts at $500

Capacity
Indoor up to 225 seated;
Outdoor 225+

Quick Facts
- Waterfront view
- Lush gardens & gazebo
- Private room with fireplace
- Full-service bar
- In-house catering by Riverview Restaurant
- Set up & clean up included
- On-site parking

494

5100 NW Neakahnie Avenue
Portland, Oregon 97229

p. 503.645.1115
f. 503.645.1755
e. theclubhouse2@rockcreekcc.com
www.rockcreekcountryclub.com

About Rock Creek Country Club

RCCC offers the finest in professional services, culinary delights, event planning and catering.

Enjoy a classic setting at our clubhouse and impressive 18-hole golf course. Relax and let Rock Creek Country Club ensure your wedding and reception are memorable.

Special Services

Rock Creek Country Club's experienced event planners can assist with all aspects of planning your wedding and reception, whether at the club or off-premise at your business or facility. Our beautiful park-like setting makes us the perfect choice for your joyous day.

RCCC offers extensive full service catering in our clubhouse as well as off-premise catering. Customized menus may be designed to make your time with us truly memorable.

Contact
Catering Department

Price
Price & fees vary according to menu selection & event size

Capacity
Up to 225 guests in our Banquet Room, Second Floor Banquet Room up to 100, Lower Floor up to 275, Seasonal Pavilion Tent up to 300; Clubhouse Bar & Grill up to 65

Amenities
- Professional and courteous staff provided to ensure outstanding service
- Full service, licensed bar available
- 10' x 30' dance floor
- 40' x 80' seasonal pavilion tent
- Ample parking available

495

TYPES OF EVENTS

Weddings & receptions, outdoor ceremonies, rehearsal dinners, holiday parties, corporate meetings, conferences, seminars and fundraising events for groups & gatherings of all sizes.

3839 NE Marine Drive
Portland, Oregon 97211
p. 503.288.4444 ext. 4108
f. 503.281.6353
www.saltys.com/portland

About Salty's

Salty's exceptional Northwest cuisine, warm hospitality, and spectacular views of the mighty Columbia and majestic Mount Hood will make your event a very special occasion! Only 15 minutes from downtown Portland, Salty's has the perfect recipe for engagement parties, bridal showers, rehearsal dinners and wedding receptions up to 170 people. We're easy to get to, and ready to serve you!

Availability and Terms

We recommend reserving your space three to six months in advance. But, if you need assistance with last minute planning, we can help! A deposit is required to reserve your date. Room fees are waived with a minimum purchase of food and beverage.

Description of Facility and Services

We have a variety of table sizes and seating options, with house color linens, restaurant silver, china and glassware available at no additional charge. After gratuity, servers are provided at no charge. A/V equipment available to rent. Salty's staff handles clean-up.

Contact
Dorothy Lane

Price
Call for current pricing

Capacity
Up to 170 guests

Amenities
- Full-service catering; in-house
- First floor ADA accessible; Wine Room & North Shore View Room are on second floor
- Plenty of free parking; complimentary valet service
- Full-service bar provided courtesy of Salty's; host or no-host; liquor, beer & wine

SPECIAL SERVICES

Our catering director works closely with you to ensure your event's success. We print a personalized menu for you and your guests. We are happy to refer you to florists, DJs and musicians. At Salty's, we pride ourselves on catering to your every whim.

496

Bravo! Member Since 1991

Scottish Rite Center

709 SW 15th Avenue
Portland, Oregon 97205
p. 503.226.7827
f. 503.223.3562
e. ceckelly@integra.net
www.aplaceforweddingspartiestheatre.com

About The Scottish Rite Center

The Scottish Rite Center is a unique Northwest landmark. Completed in 1902, the building has been at the center of the area's social and business fabric for decades.

Location

Situated in the heart of downtown Portland, the Scottish Rite Center can make your special occasion a cherished memory that will last for years.

Let the beauty of the Scottish Rite Center add to the grandeur of your event. Next to Hotel deLuxe; convenient for out of town guests.

Terms

A $100 deposit is required to reserve your date. Payment in full is required two weeks prior to event.

Types of Events

Specializing in weddings, receptions, anniversaries, banquets, dances, proms, corporate and private meetings, graduations, award ceremonies, wine tastings, concerts, reunions and theatre productions.

Contact
Cecille Kelly

Price
Varies according to event

Capacity
Up to 300 for receptions;
500 for a dance;
587 seat theatre
Smaller rooms also available

497

Amenities
- Tables, chairs, set-up & clean-up included in rental
- Convenient street parking & commercial lot parking
- ADA accessible
- Piano, pipe & electric organs, podium, whiteboard & easels available
- TV/VCR, In Focus Projector, Large Screens
- Wi-Fi Access
- Air conditioning

KATERING BY KURT

Katering by Kurt, the on-site caterer of the Scottish Rite Center, provides servers, catering and bar service; also linens, china, glassware and flatware.

Settlemier House

355 North Settlemier Avenue
PO Box 405
Woodburn, Oregon 97071
p. 503.982.1897
f. 503.981.6626
e. cst@wbcable.net
www.settlemierhouse.com

About The Settlemier House

The Settlemier House is a 1892 Victorian home located on nearly three acres of beautifully landscaped grounds. The backyard is surrounded by a hedge with a gazebo, offering a romantic and private setting for an outdoor wedding and reception during the late spring, summer and early fall months. Smaller weddings can be held inside during late fall and winter. It is our policy to provide friendly service; we want you and your guests to feel welcome and to have a truly memorable experience.

The Settlemier House is located 30 minutes south of Portland and 20 minutes north of Salem, making it ideally accessible for all your guests.

498

Contact
Peggy Dinges
Event Coordinator

Price
$450 for three hours
$95 each additional hour

Capacity
Up to 300 outside
Up to 75 inside

Amenities
- Available for weddings, receptions & parties
- Convenient mid-valley location
- Beautiful historic house
- Friendly staff on-site to answer questions
- Level grounds
- Free parking

VISIT US
We would love to show you the house. Please call for a daytime, evening or weekend appiontment.
503.982.1897

Bravo! Member Since 1998

SEVENTH MOUNTAIN RESORT

18575 SW Century Drive
Bend, Oregon 97702
p. 800.452.6810 (reservations)
p. 541.382.8711
f. 541.382.3475
e. info@seventhmountain.com
www.seventhmountain.com

About Seventh Mountain Resort

Seventh Mountain Resort is in the heart of Central Oregon, on the Deschutes River, one of Oregon's premier whitewater rivers. The Seventh Mountain Resort is the closest lodging to Mt. Bachelor, Oregon's most celebrated ski and snowboard area.

The resort offers 240 condominium units with fireplaces, living space and private decks. For larger gatherings try one of our two or three bedroom condos.

With 11,000 square feet of meeting space indoors and outdoors, Seventh Mountain Resort can accommodate groups of 10 to 350 for rehearsal dinners, weddings and receptions. We provide a comfortable natural setting in a relaxing atmosphere with the ability to escape into the the Deschutes National Forest.

Contact
Vanessa Berning

Price
Varies, please call

Capacity
Ballroom: 225 guests;
Mt.Bachelor Events Center: 350 guests
Outside: up to 1,000

499

Amenities
- 240 condominium units with fireplaces & private decks
- On-site catering from Season's Restaurant, serving Pacific Northwest Cuisine
- Premier location for recreational activities
- Dedicated wedding coordinator on staff

UNIQUE LOCATIONS

Seventh Mountain Resort is located in the Deschutes National Forest and on the Deschutes River. Ceremony locations include Mt. Bachelor, Cascade Lakes, Fireside, our ice rink, and quaint & expansive lawns. Receptions can be accommodated indoors and outdoors.

Bravo! Member Since 2005

Visit BravoWedding.com for more information on the best reception & wedding sites

8235 NE Airport Way
Portland, Oregon 97220

p. 503.281.2500 ex.858
p. 503.281.2500 ext.853
e. ckillam@sheratonpdx.com
e. mfritz@sheratonpdx.com
www.sheratonportland.com

A Setting Worthy of Your Most Cherished Day

Your wedding day, like a precious diamond, cannot help but be enhanced by a beautiful setting. From beautiful accommodations to elegant surroundings, we make this your most romantic of days.

- Newly renovated, beautiful banquet rooms can accommodate receptions up to 750 people.
- Most reception packages include a complimentary upgrade to bride and groom for the night of their event.
- Handsomely furnished guestrooms are sure to make your out-of-town guests feel at home.
- Our award-winning staff of professionals will ensure all your expectations are not only met but also exceeded.

Wedding Planning

Our professional staff is there to help with every detail, from "I do's" and hors d'oeuvres to limousines and champagne toasts. We have it all for your ceremony, reception, bridal showers or rehearsal dinners as well as fabulous wedding and reception packages.

Catering & Restaurants

Catering by award-winning Sheraton Executive Chef, Barry Handley. Relax and enjoy the regional cuisine in the Columbia Grill & Bar. Ask about our custom menus to enhance your reception.

Contact
Carol Killam or
Michael Fritz

Site Fee
Waived with catering minimums; a small set-up fee applies.

Capacity
50 to 510 seated; up to 750 reception style

Facility & Amenities
- Seating: Full seating or reception style
- Servers: Banquet Captain & full staff of servers included
- Bar Facilities: Private event bar available
- Parking: Spacious complimentary parking lot
- Dance Floor: Included at no charge
- Colored Linens, China, Glassware: Included at no charge
- Cleanup: Provided by Sheraton staff
- Decorations: Linens, lights, candles, greenery, pillars, centerpieces, etc.
- We can bring our catering to you! Ask about our off premise catering pricing

Bravo! Member Since 2007

Skamania Lodge
Scenic Columbia River Gorge

1131 SW Skamania Lodge Way
Stevenson, Washington 98648
p. 800.376.9116
p. 800.221.7117
e. slweddings@destinationhotels.com
www.skamania.com

About Skamania Lodge

Skamania Lodge is a premier resort located just 45 miles east of Portland, Oregon in the scenic Columbia River Gorge.

The Lodge, built in the grand tradition of the elegant lodges of the West's great National Parks, has charm and appeal, yet contains all the guest conveniences of a modern destination resort. With stone fireplaces, plank wood floors, forged iron touches and breathtaking views, the Lodge is an ideal setting for your special day.

Award-Winning Cuisines

Experience excellence in Pacific Northwest dining with award-winning cuisines prepared by our executive Chef and talented culinary staff. Skamania Lodge dining is truly a delectable experience. We offer many dining options including the Cascade Room, the River Rock Restaurant and Lounge and the seasonal Greenside Grille.

What's New at Skamania Lodge

Planning a winter wedding between November and March? Skamania Lodge has developed a Winter Wedding package for you. The Columbia River Gorge area is beautiful all season long. If you hold your wedding between November and March at Skamania Lodge, you'll get beautifully reduced pricing as well. And throughout the winter enjoy the romance of a complimentary horse-drawn carriage ride.

Skamania Lodge, a special location for your special day.

Contact
Jennifer Jeffcott
Danyelle Tinker – Catering
Sales Managers

Price
Rates vary with wedding package, please call for more information

501

Capacity
Memorable weddings for up to 500 people can be accommodated indoors & up to 750 people outdoors during the summer season

Amenities
- Pacific Northwest resort facility located on 175 scenic acres with views of the Columbia River Gorge

- 254 hotel rooms with views; suites & fireplace rooms are available

- On-site recreational facilities including an 18-hole golf course, Waterleaf Spa & Fitness Center, indoor pool, Jacuzzis & dry saunas, outdoor whirlpool & sun deck, hiking trails, tennis & basketball courts

Skamania Lodge is a distinctive experience provided by Destination Hotels & Resorts.

Bravo! Member Since 1995

© Cascade Photography

STONEHEDGE GARDENS

3405 Cascade Avenue
Hood River, Oregon 97031
p. 541.386.3940
e. stonehedge@gorge.net
www.stonehedgegardens.com

The Most Beautiful Terraces in the Gorge

Owned by a winemaker and a chef, Stonehedge Gardens is Hood River's premium wedding venue. The remodeled home, now a restaurant, was built in 1898. The Italian stone terraces were constructed in 2001. Carved into five amazing levels and surrounded by a private six-acre forest and restaurant, the new gardens create the perfect setting for your wedding and reception.

We are less than a mile from the Columbia River. Golf courses, hotels, wineries and downtown Hood River are less than five minutes away.

Host site of the Subaru Gorge Games VIP Dinner (200 people) and the USWA Windsurfing Nationals awards banquet (145 people).

Featured in NW Best Places, Best Places to Kiss, Sunset Magazine and the L.A. Times.

AAA Diamond rated.

Contact
Leilani Caldwell

Price
Varies, please call for quote

Capacity
10 to 250 outside; 6 to 100 inside – seating for up to 200

Amenities
- Servers included; full bars, hosted & no-host
- Hardwood floors indoors, patios outside for dancing
- Linens provided
- Cleanup provided
- Natural setting, floral available; please no rice or confetti
- Very professional, on-site coordination & planning
- Parking & ADA accessible

WHAT'S NEW

New Wedding Grotto features a 10,000 square foot manicured lawn and waterfall with 200 new chairs, stone wedding patio and Tuscan pillars. A new redwood bridal cottage for use before ceremony.

Bravo! Member Since 2001

© Cascade Photography

57081 Meadow Road
Sunriver, Oregon 97707
p. 541.593.4605
f. 541.593.2742
e. weddings@sunriver-resort.com
www.sunriver-resort.com

About Sunriver Resort

Located near the breathtaking Cascade Mountain range, just 15 miles south of Bend, Oregon, Sunriver Resort offers a unique experience for all ages. A unique Northwest resort destination for all seasons that creates togetherness and memories among families and groups, Sunriver Resort provides unmatched activities and experiences in a serene, natural setting.

With more than 44,000 square feet of flexible meeting and banquet space, guests can choose from a wide variety of flexible indoor space featuring Northwest style ambiance, or naturally gorgeous outdoor space, including the scenic Bachelor Lawn or the Great Hall Courtyard.

Whether planning a vacation, corporate meeting or a dream wedding, our state-of-the-art meeting facilities combined with the world-class recreation of Sunriver Resort will help execute your distinct vision with unrestricted flexibility and creativity that exceed your expectations.

Contact
Sunriver Catering Office

Price
Varies

Quick Facts
- Experienced professional staff to attend to every need
- Custom weddings
- Wedding packages are available for ease of planning
- Multiple locations, both indoors and out, that can accommodate weddings and groups of all sizes

503

© Tullis Photography

© Tullis Photography

See page 346 under Accommodations

SURFSAND
resort
Cannon Beach, Oregon

148 West Gower
Cannon Beach, Oregon 97110
p. 503.436.2274
p. 800.797.4666
f. 503.436.2885
e. martha@surfsand.com
www.surfsand.com

504

About The Surfsand Resort

Located just steps away from the Pacific Ocean shores of Cannon Beach, Oregon, the Surfsand Resort is a premier northwest destination resort featuring spectacular views, unparalleled luxury and world-class amenities.

Rooms and suites, which feature breathtaking views of world famous Haystack Rock and Tillamook Lighthouse, offer the ultimate in comfort. Decorated in subtle earth tones inspired by the grandeur of the Pacific Ocean and nearby coastal forests, each room is carefully designed to enhance each guest's beach experience.

Indulge in the luxury of natural finishes and fine furnishings, including gas fireplaces, flat screen televisions with DVD players, iHome audio systems and wet bars in every room. Special touches include Tempur-Pedic mattresses, custom lighting, tile and wood work. Some rooms feature elegant ocean view jetted tubs, separated from the main room by a sliding shoji screen.

The resort provides stunning views of the rugged coastline for storm watching or enjoying the sunset. Our goal is to make the Surfsand Resort your beachfront home-away-from-home.

Contact
Group Events

Price
Call for pricing

Capacity
Seating for 200 guests

Amenities
- Full-service catering provided by The Wayfarer Restaurant & Lounge
- 32 or 37 inch flat-screen LCD televisions in all suites & 15 inch LCD televisions in all bathrooms
- Seasonal Beachfront Cabana Service
- Pet-free and pet friendly accommodations available

ON SITE FACILITIES

- Heated indoor pool and hot tub

- Comprehensive fitness center that features state-of-the-art workout equipment and cedar-lined saunas

- On-site massage rooms and services

Bravo! Member Since 1998

SURFTIDES
LINCOLN CITY

2945 NW Jetty Avenue
Lincoln City, Oregon
p. 541.994.2191 Ext. 128
f. 541.994.2727
e. info@surftideslincolncity.com
www.surftideslincolncity.com

About Surftides

Surftides is an oceanfront resort located in the heart of the Central Oregon Coast. With 141 guestrooms and suites and 5,000 sq. ft. of private event space, we offer an exceptional location for your wedding and reception.

Recently renovated, Surftides offers mid century design – clean lines with touches of bold color along with modern amenities including iPod docking stations and Keurig coffee makers in every room.

Mist, our onsite restaurant offers full service catering featuring comfort food inspired by the sea. A seasonal menu highlights local, organic Northwest ingredients and traditional seafood favorites.

Price

Total wedding packages
$2,500 – $5,000

Amenities

- Newly renovated event space with ocean view for 20 – 120 guests
- Custom menus from award winning chef, Tyson Sanchez
- Private Beach access for ceremonies on the beach
- Full service hotel with oceanfront rooms and suites, Jacuzzi rooms available, indoor pool, hot tub, fitness center, sauna, steam room, fireside courtyard, onsite restaurant and bar
- Centrally located in the heart of Lincoln City

505

WHAT'S NEW

Our fireside courtyard is the latest addition to the Surftides campus. With 4 gas firepits and wood seating for up to 75 guests, it is an ideal gathering spot for guests to enjoy s'mores, wine tasting and each other's company. An ideal location for wedding photos!

Bravo! Member Since 1994

1410 SW Morrison
Portland, Oregon 97205
p. 503.522.4467
f. 503.287.1587
e. events@thetiffanycenter.net
www.tiffanycenter.net
www.rafatiscatering.com

Portland's Premier Event Center

Stunning entrance features local artist's reproduction of Michelangelo's Sistine Chapel, which underscores the historic 1920's elegance of Portland's premier event facility! The Tiffany Center is centrally located in downtown Portland and features expansive ballrooms and cozy foyers together with gilded mirrors, gleaming refinished hardwood floors and emerald green accents which will provide you with an elegant setting for weddings and receptions, business meetings, fundraisers, auctions, corporate dinners or lavish holiday events! Our experienced, professional staff will provide you with everything you need to ensure that your event is a treasured memory.

Catering is available exclusively by Rafati's Elegance in Catering, prepared onsite in their commercially licensed kitchen. Rafati's full service catering can assist you with your selection of the perfect menu for your event, ranging from brunch to casual or formal reception dinner services, all events are customized to reflects each client's individual taste and style. Personalized menu planning in all price ranges.

Contact
Leslie Best

Price
Call for rental rates

Capacity
From 30 up to 1,100; call for specifics

Amenities
- Table & chair set up included in the room rental
- Average six-hour event contract, plus early set up access
- Linens, china, glassware, service staff & bartenders included in catering charges
- Convenient street & commercial lot parking located on MAX line
- Central air conditioning in the second floor ballroom, spot cooling available on the fourth floor for rental

APPOINTMENTS
Appointments are available Monday – Friday, 10:00 a.m. to 5:00 p.m. After hour and Saturday appointments can be arranged as needed. Please call for appointment.

Bravo! Member Since 1994

506

About Timberline Lodge

Timberline Lodge is a year 'round historic lodge on Mt. Hood and considered by many as one of the most unique and romantic settings in Oregon. As the crown jewel of the Cascades, The Lodge's inspirational art, craftsmanship, warmth and majesty make for memories that you and your guests will cherish forever. With 60 rooms on–site as well as luxury condominiums available at The Lodge at Government Camp, you and your guests can enjoy the convenience of your ceremony, reception and overnight accommodations together.

Banquet rooms have massive vaulted ceilings, timber beams, lofts, hand wrought iron, carved wood accents and soaring windows with spectacular views of Mt. Hood and Mt. Jefferson. Let our history be the beginning of your future.

The Lodge is in great demand so make it your first choice and call early to begin your planning and reservations.

Timberline Lodge is a masterpiece of mountain lodges located at the 6,000 ft level on the south side of Mt. Hood just over an hour drive from Portland International Airport. The Lodge has all the amenities and services you would expect from a quality resort with a unique rustic elegance yet a comfortable feel. In addition to weddings and receptions, Timberline is the perfect place of rehearsal dinners, bridal lunches, showers, bachelor parties and engagement dinners.

Timberline, Oregon 97028
p. 503.272.3251
e. weddings@timberlinelodge.com
www.timberlinelodge.com

Contact
Wedding Planner

Price
Inquire for various packages

Capacity
Up to 240 delighted guests

Amenities
- One of the Greatest Historic Lodges in America
- Four indoor wedding & reception settings from 2 – 240
- Patios, decks & amphitheater with spectacular mountain views
- Magnificent photos from Main Lodge & Mt. Hood
- Separate Silcox Hut for smaller more rustic gatherings

Food & Wine
- Nationally recognized, on-premise food & beverage services. Award winning dining room & NW Wine Vault

507

Bravo! Member Since 1993

TOLOVANA INN
CANNON BEACH, OR

3400 South Hemlock
Cannon Beach, Oregon 97145
p. 800.550.5089
f. 360.834.7052
e. pcat1@comcast.net
www.tolovanainn.com

508

Beachfront Setting in Cannon Beach

Imagine a romantic beachfront setting for your upcoming wedding or reception. Tolovana Inn is the perfect venue. Our conference facility features 2,500 square feet of space, accommodating up to 160 in a variety of settings. Our on-site group sales coordinator and experienced staff will help you plan everything to ensure a successful event.

Tolovana Inn offers oceanfront and ocean view lodging with stunning views of Haystack Rock, a fully equipped kitchen, fireplace, private balcony, plus an on-site fitness center, indoor pool, spa and sauna, and masseuse. Other room types are also available.

Tolovana Inn's quiet setting is perfect for creative meetings or social events, yet is within minutes of downtown Cannon Beach, a favorite coastal community filled with art galleries, unique restaurants, and a variety of shopping. A free shuttled into town runs on a regular basis.

Contact
Phyllis Steers

Price Range for Services
Call for pricing

Quick Facts
- 2,500 square feet of meeting space accommodating up to 160
- Oceanfront & ocean view lodging
- Group rates mid September – mid June and Government per diem rates
- On-site catering
- Complimentary Internet Wi-Fi connectivity in all meeting & guest rooms
- Ample free parking

WHAT'S NEW?

• Many of Tolovana Inn's suites have recently been remodeled for your enjoyment.

• Tolovana Inn is a "Green" Hotel Association's partner member, with programs, such as green laundry and cleaning products and energy efficient lighting.

Peter Paul Rubens

THE TREASURY

326 SW Broadway Street
Portland, Oregon 97204
p. 503.226.1240
e. events@treasuryballroom.com
www.treasuryballroom.com

About the Treasury Ballroom

The elegant, historic Treasury Ballroom is located conveniently downtown near some of Portland's finest hotels. A grand staircase descends into the Ballroom, which features neo-classical architecture, arches, and floors and columns of Italian marble. The turn-of-the-century bar, restoration light fixtures, stained glass, steel vault door and rich velvet curtains complete the extraordinary and unique atmosphere.

With a seating capacity of 200, the Treasury is ideal for weddings or rehearsal dinners. The lounge is perfect for bridal preparations and the Rooftop Terrace is a nice added addition to your rental of the Ballroom, for a breath of fresh air, an outdoor ceremony and a view of downtown Portland.

Contact
Kurt Beadell

Price
Options include all-inclusive packages. Please contact us for a free consultation.

Capacity
Ballroom up to 225

Amenities
- We offer full event planning services including: customized menu, décor, floral, entertainment and day-of event management
- Vibrant Table Catering & Events
- Tables, mahogany chiavari chairs, china, linens & glassware are just some of the elements included in your package when you book the Treasury

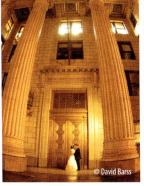

© David Barss

TOUR THE TREASURY

Take a virtual tour of the Treasury on the Bravo! website www.bravoevent.com/virtualtours

The Troutdale House
by the Sandy River

411 East Historic Columbia River Highway
Troutdale, Oregon 97060
p. 503.481.9449
e. thetroutdalehouse@gmail.com
www.thetroutdalehouse.com

510

The perfect place for your wedding, reception, event or business meeting!

Have your wedding, ceremony, reception, reunion, anniversary party or business meeting at the beautiful Troutdale House by the Sandy River. Enjoy the cozy and rustic charm of this historic property surrounded by the spectacular Sandy River and Depot Park. We are located in Troutdale, just twenty minutes from downtown Portland.

Be one of the happiest brides to get married at a place that your friends and family will enjoy and remember forever!

The Troutdale House by the Sandy River can accommodate 200 guests for your event or formal dining. It can be configured for ceremony, reception or both. After the ceremony, the chairs and tables will be moved to the reception area.

We invite you to bring caterers or prepare your own food in our large kitchen. You can set up the food in the banquet room for your guests to enjoy.

Contact
Laura

Pricecs
$2,100 Friday – 10 hours
$2,400 Saturday – 10 hours
$2,100 Sunday – 10 hours

Quick Facts
- 10 hours for your wedding & reception
- Bring your own food or caterers!!
- Outside patio & garden area
- Your choice of three ceremony sites
- White wedding arch, tables & chairs
- Free parking for your guests
- Bride's dressing room & lounge
- Groom's room & recreational area
- White aisle runner or grey carpet runner
- 47" LCD TV for slideshows & presentations
- Play your own music through our sound system

WHAT'S NEW?
Say "I do!" outside in our newly landscaped patio area.

URBANSTUDIO

206 NW 10th Avenue
Portland, Oregon 97209
p. 503.860.0526
e. via@urban-restaurants.com
www.urbanstudiopdx.com

About Urban Studio

Urban Studio is an event facility located in the heart of the trendy Pearl District. Ideal for wedding rehearsals, ceremonies and receptions, Urban Studio is the quintessential contemporary event location. Light and airy, Urban Studio features a sunken banquet room accented in soaring radiant walls of pewter, chocolate brown and pearly white. Guests are first greeted with a slightly raised reception area trimmed in chandeliers, natural stone and large windows that usher in natural light. The 5,000 square-foot space offers a flexible floor plan which can accommodate your guests in a variety of ways such as a stand-up reception, lounge-style cocktail party, or sit-down dinner. Our experienced event staff will meet your needs in planning and coordinating the perfect wedding.

Pearl Catering, our exclusive in house full service caterer, delivers a menu of crowd pleasing favorites richly influenced by Northwest ingredients, beautifully presented and full of flavor!

Contact
Via Hersholt

Price
Please call for quotes

Quick Facts
- 5,000 square-foot; flexible floor plan with built-in wrap around bar
- Capacity: 250 seated, 375 reception style
- Bridal loft available for changing, storage
- Wedding/reception packages available
- Movable walls allow for the grand floor to be broken up/divided
- Audio/visual system includes: wireless mic, projector, iPod hookup
- Ample parking, with valet service available
- Full service & licensed in-house caterer for both food & alcohol service
- ADA accessible
- On the Portland Streetcar line

WHAT'S NEW?

Space rental is waived with a minimum food and beverage purchase with Pearl Catering. Call for more information 503.860.0203

511

THE VIEW POINT INN

40301 East Larch Mountain Road
Corbett, Oregon 97019
p. 503.695.5811
e. events@theviewpointinn.com
www.theviewpointinn.com

About The View Point Inn

Quite possibly the most romantic, charming and elegant place on earth...The View Point Inn is just 22 miles from downtown Portland, near Crown Point, situated on a one-acre bluff with a panoramic view of the entire Columbia River Gorge, the city lights of Portland and Vancouver. During its heyday in the 20's and 30's, it boasted such guests as President Roosevelt, Charlie Chaplin, even kings and queens. The View Point Inn was placed on the National Register of Historic Places in 1984. This historic private boutique hotel and fine dining restaurant built in 1924, is exclusively yours for your event and closed to the public. Most recently used for the prom scene in the move "Twlight".

Location

From Portland: I-84 East, exit #22 (Corbett). Go right up Corbett Hill Road. At top, go left onto the Historic Columbia River Highway East. Follow signs to Crown Point, three miles. Veer right onto Larch Mountain Road. The View Point Inn is the first property on the left: 40301 East Larch Mountain Road, Corbett, Oregon 97019.

© Altura

Price
Please inquire

Capacity
Up to 125

Amenities

- This wonderful, historic inn requires little decoration as the gardens, grounds & view are abundant with fragrance & color
- World class service and cuisine provided by The View Point Inn Restaurant
- On site event coordinator
- Linens, flatware, stemware china provided
- Overnight lodging available
- 1,200 square foot dance floor indoors
- Lunch, dinner, Saturday & Sunday brunch service to the public
- Is exclusively yours for your event & closed to the public
- Unforgettable sunsets

TYPES OF EVENTS

Weddings, destination weddings receptions, corporate and private celebrations, business meetings, seminars, retreats, reunions, and any private event.

512

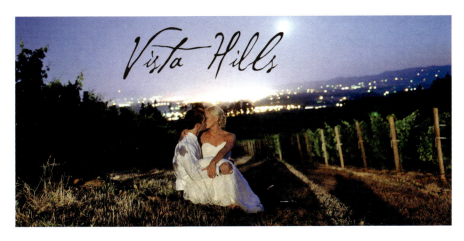

Weddings, Receptions & Rehearsal Dinners

Vista Hills is Oregon's most exciting new wedding venue and one of the most beautiful places on Earth to get married!

Views and Vista await you, from our quiet little stand atop the breathtaking Dundee Hills in Oregon's Willamette Valley. This picturesque site is a magical place to celebrate your wedding day. Let our expert staff and planning team help you create the wedding experience of your dreams.

Give us a call to learn more or set up a time to visit our Portland Downtown showroom and view albums and videos from this site. You can also learn more at www.PowersOregon.com.

Contact
Erin or Kat
p. 503.478.0997
www.PowersOregon.com
www.VistaHillsVineyard.com

Included Services
- Pre event planning
- Event day management
- Guest count range of 5 to 225
- Set up & tear down of event
- All tables chairs & linens
- All flatware
- Menu design, cake service
- Bar management
- At cost beverage service
- Powers Photography Studios credit

513

Bravo! SPECIAL!

Book within 2 weeks of your first site visit
and save $250!

www.PowersOregon.com

Vista Hills Vineyard – Dayton, Oregon
503.478.0997

See page 545 under
Wineries & Vineyards

Weatherford's
fine cuisine • wine • cocktails

602 7th Street
Oregon City, Oregon 97045
p. 503.723.9253
e. events@weatherfordsgrandlodge.com
www.weatherfordsgrandlodge.com

514

Historic Charm and Amenities

Weatherford's is located in the historic Oregon City IOOF building – originally built in 1922 for the Odd Fellows as their Oregon Grand Lodge. The building features high ceilings, wood floors and beautiful historic details. The facilities offer charm and elegance to any event.

Fine Cuisine

Our Executive Chef has prepared a catering menu featuring a large variety of cuisine. Much attention has been placed on utilizing fresh local and seasonal ingredients. In addition to selections from our catering menu we welcome the opportunity to create a custom dish just for you.

Event Coordination

Our Event Manager will work closely with you to create an event that meets your needs. Whether you are looking for a large gathering, a small and intimate celebration, or a lavish, romantic affair – leave the details to us!

Contact
Event Manager

Price
Catered wedding/reception packages for 80 guests starting at $2,495.

Please call event manager for details.

Quick Facts
- Banquet seating for up to 200 in our Grand Ballroom
- Pre-event and day of event coordination available
- Smaller private spaces available for events, dinners and meetings
- Billiards Room adds entertainment to your Grand Ballroom event
- Our fine dining restaurant located downstairs from the ballroom is perfect for rehearsal dinners and bridal showers

The West End Theater
www.PowersOregon.com   503-478-0997
DOWNTOWN PORTLAND

New in 2009!

The West End Theater is Portland's newest wedding, reception and event facility. This historic downtown theater sits a few blocks off Broadway, near all downtown hotels, Pioneer Square, the Max and bus lines and all downtown destinations!

This beautiful ballroom boasts very tall ceilings, hardwood floors, large windows and an elegant clean design. As you and your guests enter the building you are greeted by our doorman, past the coat check and up the double banister staircase you enter the fireside lounge. With so many ballrooms available in Portland we wanted the West End to be different!

Once in the main ballroom you will find a mix of old and new. A large plasma screen monitor hangs from a wall (for your slideshows, videos or a movie)and our state of the art computer controlled lighting system will amaze you with style options! In addition to the lighting, the ballroom comes wired with a top notch sound system for your use.

Give us a call to set up a showing or register on this website for more information.

www.www.PowersOregon.com

West End Theater
1220 SW Taylor, Portland, Oregon 97205
503-478-0997

Weddings, Receptions & Rehearsal Dinners
Contact
Erin or Kat

p. 503.478.0997

www.PowersOregon.com

www.WestEndBallroom.com

Price
$1,995 – $3,995
up to 225 guests

515

Included Services
- Pre event planning
- Event day management
- Set up & tear down of event
- All tables chairs & linens
- All flatware
- Menu design, cake service
- Bar management
- At cost beverage service
- Credit if you book with Powers Studios
- Live web camera for out-of-town guests

13315 NE Airport Way
Portland, Oregon 97230
p. 503.224.0134
www.wildbills.com

516

About Wild Bill's
Host your next party in our new 2,000 sq. ft. event space!

Its a great space for:
- Company Parties and Meetings
- Birthday and Anniversary Parties
- Wedding Receptions
- Bar/Bat Mitzvahs
- Graduation Parties
- Charity Fundraising

Our Specialties:
- Casino Nights
- Murder Mystery Dinners
- The Great American Game Show
- A Vegas Wedding in Portland
- And Much More!

Contact
Shannon Walker

The Room Includes:
- 14ft Bar
- Built in Sound System
- Catering Room
- Bartender
- Private Lounge
- Tables & chairs
- Custom lighting
- LED Projector & Screen
- On-Site Free Parking
- Your Caterer or Choose from our Preferred List

Wilfs

800 NW 6th Avenue
Portland, Oregon 97209
p. 503.223.0070
f. 503.223.1386
e. candace@wilfsrestaurant.com
www.wilfsrestaurant.com

About Wilfs Restaurant & Bar

Wilfs Restaurant & Bar at Union Station, minutes from downtown, offers a unique, convenient location for all your events: lunch, dinner, meetings, wine tasting, family celebrations, to the perfect wedding! Our catering options range from informal cocktail parties to a formal sit-down affair with live entertainment.

Weddings as Easy as 1-2-3

Wilfs offers coordinating services to help unravel the complexities of event planning. Expert staff offers personal service and attention to the details, and Candace, our event coordinator, will create a seamless event. Our experience in asking the "right" questions from the start, assures you, your event for 10 – 1,000, will be effortless.

The Perfect Plan for your Perfect Day

Our packages are created for your moment. We offer reception-style, sit-down, or a cocktail party atmosphere; either at the restaurant or an event site. We source our ingredients from our NW backyard, creating contemporary cuisine with a classic touch for every palate.

Contact
Candace McDonald

Price
Starting at $15 per person

Quick Facts
- Capacity from 2 – 1,000
- Settings include Union Station depot lobby, Rose garden, entire restaurant
- Outdoor urban roof top venue over looking the city
- Off-site catering services
- Event coordinator
- Easy parking
- A sustainable company.
- Open warehouse seating up to 800
- Vegan & vegetarian options

517

©ROBERT MCNARY

WILF'S RESTAURANT & BAR

- Unique location
- Outdoor urban roof top venue
- Locally grown products from the NW
- Live Entertainment

Bravo! Member Since 1992

© TithJerod Photography

Windrose, llc
conference & meeting center

809 West First Street
Newberg, Oregon 97132
p. 503.701.7273
e. lynn@windrosecenter.com
www.windrosecenter.com

518

About Windrose Conference & Meeting Center

Located just 25 miles from Portland or Salem in the heart of Oregon wine country, Windrose has gorgeous facilities and would be a perfect setting for your smaller and more intimate wedding. It has a European flair with a touch of wine country flavor.

Outside boasts a large brick courtyard surrounded by flowers that can seat 70 people and is perfect for weddings, receptions, wine and hors d'oeuvre functions. The smaller courtyard has a water fountain and can be used as the bar area or for socializing. The back lawn area overlooks the canyon and creek and the ceremony site has an arbor on Italian stamped concrete. Inside has the feel of an old English library, with 2 fireplaces, kitchenette, reception area, and meeting space for up to 50 people. We have an exclusive use policy, which means we cater to only one group at a time and you have use of the entire facility and grounds.

Windrose is available for weddings any day of the week and bookings are confirmed with a deposit and signed agreement. Ample free parking is provided. Tours are encouraged so you can see all that Windrose has to offer.

Contact
Lynn Weygandt – Owner & Manager

Price
$100 – $1,500, depending on event & size of group

Quick Facts
- Price includes all tables, chairs, linens
- Capacity is 50 indoors/70 outdoors
- Ceremony site overlooks the canyon & creek with white archway, or inside by the fireplace (for indoor weddings)
- Private, large dressing area for bride & her party
- Price includes 1 full day, plus 2 hours during the week for rehearsal
- Bring in your own caterer, choose from our preferred list, or do it yourself (requires clean up & rental of china & silver)

WHAT'S NEW
Price now includes a full service 'Day of' Coordinator to handle all the details of your wedding so that you will have a stress free day, including the rehearsal.

Bravo! Member Since 2005

6855 Breyman Orchards Road
Dayton, Oregon 97114

p. 503.864.3446
p. 800.261.3446
f. 503.864.3109
e. jld@winecountryfarm.com
www.winecountryfarm.com

Welcome to a
B&B, Winery, Tasting Room & Carriage Rides

A beautiful wine country estate at the top of the Dundee Hills providing a spectacular year round location for your wedding. Surrounded by our vineyards, enjoy breathtaking views of the Willamette Valley and Cascade Mountain range.

Outdoor weddings can be arranged on our grounds with beautiful lawns, flowers, gazebos, views and a large covered dance floor. Inside weddings are offered in our spacious tasting room with a fireplace and baby grand piano. Changing rooms are provided for the wedding party. Horse and carriage rides available for the bride and grooms' entry and exit.

Snuggle down in our romantic bed & breakfast in the vineyards. Nine bedrooms all with private bath, air-conditioning and views; some with fireplaces.

Wine Country Farm is less than an hour drive from Portland and just a half-hour from Salem. We are featured in the New York Times #1 Best Seller, "1,000 Places To See Before You Die" by Patricia Schultz.

Contact
Joan Davenport

Price
Varies depending on size & type of event

Capacity
Weddings for up to 130 inside or 300 in an outside venue; 18 overnight guests at B&B.

519

Amenities
- Wedding Coordinator included; one hour rehearsal, day before wedding

- Spacious yet intimate room for inside weddings with fireplace, baby grand piano & kitchen

- Beautifully landscaped lawns & gardens filled with flowers & spectacular sweeping vineyard & valley views for outside weddings

- Catering – we can recommend or bring your own caterer

- Winery & Cellar – we offer our fine wines & beer with our OLCC licensed servers; No hard alcohol

- Ample parking on–site, out of view of your wedding

See page 546 under Wineries & Vineyards

Wooden Shoe Gardens

33814 South Meridian Road
Woodburn, Oregon 97071
p. 503.201.2847
f. 503.634.2710
e. susie@woodenshoe.com
www.woodenshoe.com

About Wooden Shoe Gardens

Wooden Shoe Gardens offers landscaped gardens, open fields and stunning views.

Located just 45 minutes from downtown Portland, there is plenty of outdoor space and parking for all your friends and family. This lovely country setting is home to the Wooden Shoe Tulip Festival, Wine Down Wine Tasting Event and The Firehouse Cook-off, which draw thousands of visitors every year.

The Wooden Shoe Gardens is the perfect setting for celebrations small to large. Our reception areas accommodate up to several hundred people making this a perfect setting for weddings, receptions and many other types of events. If you are searching for a lush location with a charming feel, this is the place for you. To enhance your festivities, our facility provides a food preparation area and cooler, accommodating to the caterer of your choice.

Contact
Susie Schriever

Price
Please call for pricing

Capacity
Up to 100 inside; unlimited outdoor seating

Services
- Several on-site locations to choose from
- Outside areas available for more than 800 guests
- Spacious bridal dressing room
- Food preparation area with walk-in cooler
- One event per day – allowing for flexible set up
- Unlimited parking
- Kids play area
- Horse shoe ring

WHAT'S NEW?
Free bulbs with rental.

Bravo! Member Since 2007

The Woods

6637 SE Milwaukie Avenue
Portland, Oregon 97202

p. 503.890.0408

e. heatherofthewoods@gmail.com

www.thewoodsportland.com

The Woods, a Private Event Rental Space and Music Hall, is located in the classic Sellwood neighborhood. The hardwoods, chandeliers and spacious elegance evoke the glamour of an Old West hotel. The 3000 sq ft. venue houses a beautiful chapel, as well as several lounges and partially-covered outdoor seating.

Eccentric yet stately, The Woods has everything you could wish for in a wedding location: modern sound equipment, two bars, two kitchens, and a spacious dressing-room for the Bride , and best of all it's competitively priced! Call today to arrange a tour.

Contact
Heather Bryse-Harvey

Price
Varies

Capacity
Currently 125

Amenities

- Beautiful light and bright rooms with hardwood floors, raised stage and gorgeous Art Deco lighting
- Parking for 26 cars plus an adjacent Public Parking Lot
- Private Bridal Dressing Room with attached bathroom
- Large covered patio with auxiliary bar and plenty of outdoor space
- Kitchen(s) available
- If you do not have an Officiant of your own we can provide a non-denominational Minister for your Ceremony
- We also offer our Prize-Winning Cake Designer's skills as an option
- You can use the Caterer of your choice or we can recommend
- For virtually 'One-Stop Shopping', but uniquely your own style, come and see us at "The Woods" in Sellwood

521

© Paul Rich

WORLD FORESTRY CENTER

4033 SW Canyon Road
Portland Oregon 97221

p. 503.488.2101
f. 503.228.4608

e. amorrison@worldforestry.org

www.worldforestry.org

RecycleWorks Award Winner

About World Forestry Center

You will remember your wedding day for the rest of your life, and we want to help make it absolutely perfect. We offer a natural and relaxed setting with all the modern amenities, and our extensive preferred caterer list gives you the opportunity to choose from some of the finest establishments in town for your banquet needs.

Whether you choose to have just your reception or both your wedding and reception in either Cheatham Hall or Miller Hall, the natural wood tones and large, open ceilings create an elegant and comfortable atmosphere for you and your guests.

Our 10,000 square-foot plaza can be enjoyed on a star-studded evening or tented to create a stylish and protected outdoor event. Combined with Cheatham Hall, the possibilities are endless for designing a day to remember.

Located only ten minutes from downtown and right off the Washington Park MAX tunnel stop, the World Forestry Center is conveniently located for both in-town and out-of-town guests.

Contact
Amber Morrison

Price
Call for quote

Capacity
Miller Hall: up to 250 people for a dinner; Cheatham will comfortably seat 150

Amenities
- We are conveniently located in Portland's beautiful Washington Park – ideal for both in-town & out-of-town guests
- Our professional & courteous staff will make sure your room is setup is perfect for your special day
- Our list of preferred caterers gives you many menus choices & budget flexibility
- Free onsite parking & on the Max line

GIVE US A CALL

Whether you are planning a wedding for 50 or 250, please give us a call. We believe in providing you with excellent customer service so you don't have to worry about a thing.

© Paul Rich

Bravo! Member Since 1994

© Holland Studios

WORLD TRADE CENTER PORTLAND

Two World Trade Center Portland
25 SW Salmon Street
Portland, Oregon 97204
p. 503.464.8688
www.wtcpd.com

Distinctive Urban Elegance

A distinctive site for your wedding ceremony and reception, a professional staff ready to cater to your every need, and an exceptional downtown location make the World Trade Center the perfect choice for an elegant Portland wedding. The magic of the day is yours at Portland's own World Trade Center!

Availability and Terms

The World Trade Center is an ideal location for weddings. The center can easily accommodate both indoor and outdoor functions. Unique to Portland is our Sky Bridge Terrace, which is completely surrounded by angled windows and has a spectacular view of the river. Also exclusive to downtown is our 11,000 square-foot European-style Outdoor Plaza surrounded by trees dressed in twinkle lights. Our Mezzanine level offers a bird's-eye-view of the plaza and the city below. A 25% deposit of anticipated total expenses is required at the time of booking.

Contact
Danya Minyan

Price
Please contact for pricing & availability

Capacity
Sky Bridge Terrace: 600 reception, 300 seated; Outdoor Plaza: 800 reception, 600 seated

Amenities
- Table & chair setup included in rental price
- Linens, glassware, silverware & china included in rental price
- Full beverage service provided
- Building is available prior to the event for decorating; schedule can be arranged with your bridal consultant
- Flat rate evening & weekend parking available in the building
- ADA accessible

523

Bravo! Member Since 1995

Youngberg Hill has the Most Spectacular View in the Heart of the Wine Country

Sitting high atop the vineyard hills of the Willamette Valley, Youngberg Hill Vineyards & Inn has a striking panoramic view of the Cascades, Costal Range, and Willamette Valley that will distinguish any occasion. Nestled in the middle of 50 acres, including 22 acres of award winning Pinot Noir and Pinot Gris vineyards surround the estate; there are photo opportunities galore. The natural beauty of the site is complemented by the private, quiet tranquility.

We will provide personal attention to you and your guests to ensure that every detail is attended to. In fact, you will feel that you are having your wedding at home surrounded only by family and friends. This is a place where dreams and love stories come together.

Special Services

The eight room inn on the property accommodates your wedding party, including honeymoon suite. Youngberg Hill is the highest rated inn in the valley, and the area's most elegant accommodations.

Contact
Wedding Coordinator

10660 SW Youngberg Hill Road
McMinnville, Oregon 97128
p. 888.657.8668
www.youngberghill.com

Price
Prices vary on size & amenities of the event

Amenities
- Can host up to 400 guests
- Unparalleled views
- 40 x 60 tent with lights
- Wine, beer & champagne provided
- Preferred catering available
- 1,000 square foot dance floor with electrical hookups
- Ample free parking
- ADA accessible

TYPES OF EVENTS

Youngberg Hill Vineyards and Inn is a perfect venue for weddings, receptions, reunions, concerts and celebrations of any event.

See page 547 under Wineries & Vineyards

Bravo! Member Since 2006

524

900 NW 11th Avenue
Portland, Oregon 97209
p. 503.525.2225
f.   503.525.2224
e. info@fenouilinthepearl.com
www.fenouilinthepearl.com

About Fenouil

Fenouil is an Urban Parisian Brasserie located in the heart of the Pearl District. The atmosphere is elegant, warm and inviting.

Our semi-private second floor mezzanine overlooks Jamison Square and is perfect for rehearsal dinners. We offer a variety of customized menus or you may meet with Chef Pascal Chureau to create a menu that is more personalized.

In addition, the entire restaurant is available for weddings and receptions as well as neighboring Jamison Square. It is a lovely setting for an outdoor event.

We also offer offsite, full-service catering for corporate events, rehearsal dinners, wedding receptions, cocktail receptions and many more occasions.

Contact
Janey Clark
JaneyC@fenouilinthepearl.com

Price
Please call for pricing

Capacity
- Full Restaurant:
  120 people + patio
  220 people

- Bar:
  40 people – cocktail reception

- Mezzanine:
  65 people – sit down dinner
  80 people – cocktail reception

- Full Restaurant & Jamison Square Park buyout available

Quick Facts
- Modern Brasserie
- Semi-private dining area available
- Serving lunch, dinner and Sunday brunch
- Seasonal outdoor dining
- Sommelier service
- Valet package available
- Streetcar line access
- Hotel accommodations nearby

See page 417 under Reception & Wedding Sites

525

© Liz Devine

4045 NW Cornelius Pass Road
Hillsboro, Oregon 97124
p. 503.693.8452
e. salescpr@mcmenamins.com
www.mcmenamins.com

526

This historic property just 20 minutes west of downtown Portland is a beautiful and unique spot to hold your rehearsal dinner. Settled in the 1850s by the Imbrie family, the estate resonates with Oregon history and includes a few of the original buildings. Hold your dinner in the elegant 1866 Roadhouse itself, or perhaps stage a more casual and fun affair in the unusual Octagon Barn, one of the few such structures left in the nation. If the weather allows, we offer outdoor meadows or tree-filled glades for a lovely, under-the-sun-or-stars dinner. Meet with one of our sales coordinators to discuss your options on setting, menus and more.

About McMenamins

For more than 25 years, McMenamins historic hotels, pubs and breweries throughout Oregon and Washington have served as friendly, familiar places to enjoy handcrafted ales, wines and spirits and Northwest-inspired pub fare with family and friends. See photos, room layouts, menus and more at mcmenamins.com.

Contact
Group sales office

Price
Food & beverage minimum; varies based on size of room & time of day.

Capacity
35 to 400; larger groups available with multiple spaces.

Amenities
- Restaurant
- Onsite brewery
- Beautiful gardens
- Ample parking

© Liz Devine

Bravo! Member Since 1991

See page 452 under
Reception & Wedding Sites

© Liz Devine

McMENAMINS
EDGEFIELD

2126 SW Halsey Street
Troutdale, Oregon 97060
p. 503.492.2777
e. salesed@mcmenamins.com
www.mcmenamins.com

About Edgefield

At McMenamins Edgefield, there are several spaces, both indoors and out, from which to choose! Host a small gathering of family and friends in one of our side rooms adorned with original artwork, or perhaps take over the elegant ballroom for a larger, more polished affair. Weather permitting, host a casual barbecue outdoors on the front lawn of the Administrator's House. Once your guests have arrived, they will enjoy McMenamins handcrafted ales, wines and spirits, all made onsite, paired with Northwest-inspired menus. Or they could come early for a round of golf or a treatment in the full-service spa! The possibilities are many – and we look forward to going through all your options with you.

About McMenamins

For more than 25 years, McMenamins' historic hotels, pubs and breweries throughout Oregon and Washington have been well known as being friendly, familiar places to enjoy handcrafted ales, wine, spirits and Northwest-inspired pub fare with family and friends. Check out photos, menus, room layouts and rates at mcmenamins.com.

Contact
Group Sales Office

Price
Food & beverage minimum; varies based on size of room & time of day.

Capacity
Indoors, 200 seated, 250 reception-style; outdoors, 250 seated, 300 reception-style.

Amenities
- Onsite brewery & distillery
- Winery & tasting room
- Ruby's Spa
- Original artwork
- Beautiful gardens
- Ample parking
- 114 guestrooms

527

See page 454 under Reception & Wedding Sites

© Liz Devine

Bravo! Member Since 1991

Visit BravoWedding.com for more information on wonderful rehearsal dinner locations

© Liz Devine

3505 Pacific Avenue
Forest Grove, Oregon 97116
p. 503.992.9530
p. 887.992.9530
e. salesgl@mcmenamins.com
www.mcmenamins.com

528

About the Grand Lodge

The Grand Lodge is a truly elegant location to hold a rehearsal dinner for friends and family. Perhaps a cozy get-together in a side parlor complete with a roaring fire sounds ideal. Or maybe you and your partner would prefer an outdoor evening picnic, with stars overhead? These are just a few suggestions. Once your guests have arrived, they will enjoy McMenamins handcrafted ales, wines and spirits, paired with Northwest-inspired menus. Located about 30 minutes from downtown Portland, your guests will appreciate being able to stay the night in one of the hotel's 77 guestrooms. The possibilities are many – and we look forward to going through all your options with you.

About McMenamins

For more than 25 years, McMenamins' historic hotels, pubs and breweries throughout Oregon and Washington have been well known as being friendly, familiar places to enjoy handcrafted ales, wine, spirits and Northwest-inspired pub fare with family and friends. Check out photos, menus, room layouts and rates at mcmenamins.com.

Contact
Group Sales Office

Price
Food & beverage minimum; varies based on size of room & time of day.

Capacity
Indoors, seated 200, reception-style 250;

Outdoors, seated 800, reception-style 1,000

Amenities
- Original artwork
- Beautiful gardens
- Ample parking
- 77 guestrooms
- Restaurant & small bars
- Ruby's Spa

© Liz Devine

© Liz Devine

Bravo! Member Since 1991

See page 455 under Reception & Wedding Sites

© Liz Devine

310 NE Evans Street
McMinnville, Oregon 97128
p. 503.472.8427
e. saleshoto@mcmenamins.com
www.mcmenamins.com

About Hotel Oregon

What better place to hold your rehearsal dinner than right in the middle of beautiful Oregon wine country? Your guests will appreciate our convenient location, just an hour south of Portland and within an hour of more than 200 Pacific Northwest wineries. Host an intimate, mid-week affair in the hotel's speakeasy-style Cellar Bar, which boasts an extensive regional wine list. Or book Mattie's Room, which offers space to mingle and celebrate with your entire wedding party plus guests. Encourage your friends and family to stay a night with us after your rehearsal dinner in one of our 42 cozy guestrooms. The possibilities for your rehearsal dinner are many – and we look forward to going through all your options with you.

About McMenamins

For more than 25 years, McMenamins' historic hotels, pubs and breweries throughout Oregon and Washington have been well known as being friendly, familiar places to enjoy handcrafted ales, wine, spirits and Northwest-inspired pub fare with family and friends. Check out photos, menus, room layouts and rates at mcmenamins.com.

Contact
Group sales office

Price
Food & beverage minimum; varies based on size of room & time of day.

Capacity
Seated 80, reception-style 120

Amenities
- Restaurant & small bars
- Original artwork
- 42 guestrooms

529

© Liz Devine

Bravo! Member Since 1991

See page 456 under Reception & Wedding Sites

© Liz Devine

5736 NE 33rd Avenue
Portland, Oregon 97211

p. 503.288.3286
p. 888.249.3983
e. salesken@mcmenamins.com
www.mcmenamins.com

530

About Kennedy School

Why not hold your rehearsal dinner in one of Portland's most unusual spots – a 1915 former elementary school turned hotel, complete with onsite brewery, restaurant, bars and more. The Kennedy School invites fun and merriment – imagine telling your guests they'll be gathering in a former classroom for dinner (no need to raise your hand if you have something to say, either)! Or perhaps you'd like a quieter, more formal affair in the library? Then gather afterwards for fresh-juice cocktails or whiskeys at the Honors Bar or Detention Bar (depending on how good or bad you've all been…). The possibilities are endless – and throughout it all, your guests will enjoy McMenamins handcrafted ales brewed in-house, along with wines, spirits, Northwest-inspired menus and more.

About McMenamins

For more than 25 years, McMenamins' historic hotels, pubs and breweries throughout Oregon and Washington have been well known as being friendly, familiar places to enjoy handcrafted ales, wine, spirits and Northwest-inspired pub fare with family and friends. Check out photos, menus, room layouts and rates at mcmenamins.com.

Contact
Group sales office

Price
Food & beverage minimum; varies based on size of room & time of day.

Capacity
Indoor & outdoor, 112 seated, 120 reception-style

Amenities
- 35 guestrooms
- Onsite brewery
- Restaurant and small bars
- Original artwork
- Soaking pool
- Movie theatre

© Liz Devine

© Liz Devine

Bravo! Member Since 1991

See page 457 under
Reception & Wedding Sites

© Liz Devine

700 NW Bond Street
Bend, Oregon 97701
p. 541.330.8567
e. salesbend@mcmenamins.com
www.mcmenamins.com

Back to School In Bend

Your friends and family will be charmed by this unusual event space – a 1936 former Catholic school turned destination hotel set in downtown Bend. Host an elegant outdoor dinner in O'Kanes Square or perhaps book Father Luke's Foundation Room to accommodate your entire wedding party, plus family and out-of-town guests. No matter which space you choose, your guests will no doubt enjoy the McMenamins handcrafted ales brewed onsite along with our own wines, spirits and Northwest-inspired menus. Encourage your guests to stay the night in one of our 19 guestrooms or 4 cottages.

About McMenamins

For more than 25 years, McMenamins' historic hotels, pubs and breweries throughout Oregon and Washington have been well known as being friendly, familiar places to enjoy handcrafted ales, wine, spirits and Northwest-inspired pub fare with family and friends. Check out photos, menus, room layouts and rates at mcmenamins.com.

Contact
Group sales office

Price
Food & beverage minimum; varies based on size of room & time of day.

Capacity
100 seated, 120 reception-style indoors; outdoors, 100 seated, 150 reception-style

Catering
In-house catering only

Amenities
- 19 guestrooms and 4 cottages
- Onsite brewery
- Restaurant and small bars
- Original artwork
- Mosaic tiled soaking pool
- Movie theatre

531

© Liz Devine

Bravo! Member Since 1991

See page 458 under Reception & Wedding Sites

© Liz Devine

1157 North Marion Avenue
Gearhart, Oregon 97138
p. 503.717.8502
e. salessandt@mcmenamins.com
www.mcmenamins.com

About the Sand Trap

Got a golfer or two in your wedding party? Then look no further – the Sand Trap is an ideal spot for your rehearsal dinner, set overlooking the historic 1892 Gearhart Golf Links. Book your wedding party a round of golf and then meet up for a casual dinner on the outdoor terrace. Or make it a more formal affair indoors at Livingstone's, which opens up onto a patio next to the links. No matter which venue you choose at the Sand Trap, your guests will undoubtedly appreciate our McMenamins handcrafted ales, wines and spirits, all paired with Northwest-inspired menus and seasonal seafood specials.

About McMenamins

For more than 25 years, McMenamins historic hotels, pubs and breweries throughout Oregon and Washington have served as friendly, familiar places to enjoy handcrafted ales, wines and spirits and Northwest-inspired pub fare with family and friends. See photos, room layouts, menus and more at mcmenamins.com.

Contact
Group Sales Office

Price
Food & beverage minimum; varies based on size of room & time of day

Capacity
Up to 180 indoors plus an additional 100 outside

Amenities
- Restaurant and small bars
- Original artwork
- Across the street from the ocean

© Liz Devine

Bravo! Member Since 1991

See page 459 under Reception & Wedding Sites

Meriwether's
Restaurant & Skyline Farm

Restaurant:
2601 NW Vaughn Street
Portland, Oregon 97210

Skyline Farm:
12735 NW Skyline Boulevard
Portland, Oregon 97210

p. 503.228.1250

e. info@meriwethersnw.com

www.meriwethersnw.com

About Meriwether's

Meriwether's Restaurant & Garden (located just 5 minutes from downtown) offers both indoor & outdoor ceremony and/or reception sites. Inside Meriwether's has an elegant, yet comfortable feel. The stone fireplaces, hardwood floors, stained glass and copper accents create a warm & inviting space for year-round wedding events. Outdoors, our all-season covered, heated (and enclosed if needed) patio, garden and gazebo feature fountains, urns & stone paths. Meriwether's gardens are a gorgeous backdrop for your perfect wedding day.

Meriwether's Skyline Farm (a quick 20 minutes from downtown) is an 18-acre oasis on beautiful NW Skyline Boulevard. The ceremony is set in front of a "jaw-dropping" panoramic view and the large grass-covered reception site overlooks Skyline Farm where produce is grown and harvested for the restaurant and events menus.

And about our service! Most all of our wedding events are booked through referrals. Our unique "all-inclusive" wedding packages ensure each and every detail will be handled by Meriwether's. If you are trying to find a memorable and worry-free wedding, Meriwether's and Skyline Farm are the perfect fit.

Contact
Events Coordinator

Capacity
From 15 to 400

Types Of Events
Ceremony & reception, rehearsal dinner, cocktail & hors d'oeuvres, bridal shower, wedding brunch, all wedding events either large and small

Highlights
- "All-Inclusive" weddings (we handle everything!)
- Wedding planning and event coordinators
- Two convenient NW Portland locations
- Urban garden wedding (either indoor or outdoor)
- Skyline Farm wedding (18-acres close to town)
- Menus created from ingredients grown on our own Skyline Farm
- Private parking at both locations

533

Portland Composts! Participant

See page 462 under Reception & Wedding Sites

33180 Cape Kiwanda Drive
Pacific City, Oregon 97135
p. 503.965.3674
p. 866.571.0581
f.   503.965.0061
e. Events@pelicanbrewery.com
www.pelicanbrewery.com

About Pelican Pub & Brewery

Located on the oceanfront at the stunning Cape Kiwanda Natural Scenic Area, and only two hours from Portland, the Pelican Pub & Brewery is the perfect place for your most special day.

Our fabulous location provides the memorable opportunity for you to say your vows on the beach, then take ten steps to our beautiful reception/banquet room. From an intimate reception or dinner to a large celebration, you can rely on the Pelican Pub & Brewery to create the wedding day of your dreams. Relax and enjoy your day as every detail will be attended to by our professional and courteous staff.

The award-winning kitchen can prepare meals from simple to extravagant, with the ability to customize menus to your taste and whimsy.

Our in-house brewery has won awards all over the world, and can provide these fresh craft beers directly to your event. In addition, great wines and a full bar are available.

After your celebration, invite your wedding party, friends and family to extend their stay by enjoying our lodging properties - Inn at Cape Kiwanda, The Cottages at Cape Kiwanda, or Shorepine Vacation Rentals, most of which are just steps away from your event. Our properties offer accommodations ranging from beautifully appointed ocean-view rooms to luxuriously furnished cottages and homes.

**Pelican Pub & Brewery...the Perfect Place...
for your Perfect Day.**

Contact
Event Coordinator

Price
Varies based on
season & menu

Quick Facts
- Award-winning craft brewery on-site
- First class kitchen prepares meals from simple to extravagant
- Oceanfront
- Private beach for outdoor ceremonies
- Full bar and attentive service
- Flexible overnight accommodations, from hotel rooms to vacation rentals
- Dedicated wedding planner

See page 478 under
Reception & Wedding Sites

© Kris Stalnaker

BeckenRidge
VINEYARD

300 Reuben Boise Road
Dallas, Oregon 97338
p. 503.831.3652
f. 503.831.3279
e. info@beckenridge.com
www.beckenridge.com

Celebrate Your Special Occasion Nestled In the Beauty of the Vineyard.

BeckenRidge Vineyard was specifically designed for weddings, receptions and special occasions. The beautiful and private setting of the vineyard together with the friendly staff offers a warm, welcoming atmosphere for you and your guests. The panoramic view of the Willamette Valley and the Cascades provide the perfect backdrop for your special day all year round.

In the spring, summer or fall, BeckenRidge harmoniously combines the outdoor ceremony with the indoor reception. Choose the lawn or the covered patio for your ceremony – both have a commanding view of the vineyard and beyond. In the winter, choose the fireplace or the window-view to stage your indoor ceremony.

The reception hall is marked by simple elegance in décor, comfort and convenience. The main room has hardwood floors perfect for dancing, a large stone fireplace, and abundant windows to take in the view. This air conditioned building includes kitchen, bar, spacious restrooms, and a private dressing room for the bride. A separate dressing & game room is available for the groom.

Our friendly and knowledgeable staff will help you plan your setup and arrange our furniture according to your wishes, transforming BeckenRidge to be uniquely yours.

Contact
The friendly staff of BeckenRidge are available by phone or email – call for appointment to visit us

Price
Starting at $2,300

Discounts available for mid-week & off-peak season

535

Capacity
Up to 120 indoors; expands up to 250 utilizing patios

Amenities
- Rental includes private use of the property with the romance of 12 acres of vineyards with astounding views of the Cascades

- Reception furnishings for 150 are provided & setup by on-site staff

- Kitchen available to a professional caterer of your choice.

- Expanded collection of rental accessories includes set-up & teardown

NEW ARRIVALS
Adding groom's room January 2010 ideal with satellite TV, foosball and more

See page 381 under Reception & Wedding Sites

Bravo! Member Since 1998

CATHEDRAL
□ RIDGE □
WINERY

4200 Post Canyon Drive
Hood River, Oregon 97031

p. 541.386.2882
p. 800.516.8710
f. 541.516.8710

e. crw@cathedralridgewinery.com
www.cathedralridgewinery.com

About Cathedral Ridge Winery

Whether it's one person or a wedding party of 250 people, we love to have people visit our winery and vineyard. Beautiful in virtually every season, you will be amazed by the views of Mt. Adams as you rest on the bench overlooking the vineyards and by Mt. Hood as you tour your way south through the vines. Our charming winery and gift house overlook manicured lawns and beautiful flower gardens, the perfect compliment to these stunning mountain views. Cathedral Ride exists to provide a perfect event for you and will extend every effort to refer you to appropriate suppliers for whatever you may require. Our friendly and knowledgeable hospitality team is here to help make your wedding or event the most special day of your life!

Types of events: Company meetings, holiday parties, corporate picnics, private lunches, anniversary parties, special event celebrations, Weddings, Weddings and receptions, rehearsal dinners, etc.

Contact
Event Coordinator

Price
Varies depending upon the day of the week & type of event.

Capacity
Up to 200 Guests

Amenities
- Outstanding full-service caterers for all types of events. We offer a list of both Hood River & Portland Caterers with outstanding references
- We provide seating for 100 & tables to match.
- Staff is included in catering costs
- We specialize in serving outstanding wines & also provide beer, water & soda as requested
- Approximately 1,200 square feet of dance floor
- Linens, china & glassware: Usually included in catering price
- Ample free parking.
- All facilities are ADA accessible

See page 396 under Reception & Wedding Sites

536

WINES, WEDDINGS & SPECIAL EVENTS

Vineyard Wedding

Domaine Margelle Vineyards offers stunning vistas and quiet woodland settings for your wine country wedding along with Estate grown Pinot Noir and Pinot Gris wine. Included in the package is the use of the property over a two day period. This allows ample time for wedding set-up and rehearsal.

Venue Site

We feature several property sites as possible event locations. Our "La Bastide" woodland setting can accommodate up to 200 guests. Our Vineyard View and Meadow Vista can accommodate up to 400 guests. Special arrangements can be made for the exterior use of the "Manoir" overlooking the vineyard and valley. All venues include the weekend use of "La Bastide" for the Bridal Party. We are happy to work with wedding coordinators and area caterers.

Location

Domaine Margelle is located near Silverton, Oregon, nestled in the foothills of the Cascades. Wedding guests will find ample lodging nearby, including the Oregon Gardens Resort.

Contact

Marci Taylor

20159 Hazelnut Ridge Road
Scotts Mills, Oregon 97375

p. 503.873.0692
f. 503.873.0825

e. info@domainemargelle.com

www.DomaineMargelle.com

537

Price

Average pricing $3,000.
Please contact for
more information

Quick Facts

- Outdoor venue featuring several site locations overlooking the Willamette Valley and vineyards

- 2-day use of the property for Rehearsal & Wedding

- Use of vacation rental, "La Bastide" for Bridal Party preparations or overnight accommodations

- Tables & chairs for 150 guests. Site can accommodate up to 400

WHAT'S NEW

Domaine Margelle offers Estate grown Pinot Noir & Pinot Gris Wines for purchase. Contact us today for a private tasting.

See page 407 under Reception & Wedding Sites

ELK COVE
VINEYARDS

27751 NW Olson Road
Gaston, Oregon 97119
p. 503.985.7760
p. 877.ELK.COVE
f. 503.985.3525
e. info@elkcove.com
www.elkcove.com

Elk Cove Vineyards

From atop a knoll with commanding views of premier vineyards and buttressing the scenic Oregon Coast Range, the Elk Cove facility is a superb site for that special wedding, yet only 45 minutes from downtown Portland.

The "Roosevelt Room", named after the herds of Roosevelt elk which roam the nearby mountains, will hold up to 150 people. With a full catering kitchen, Italian tiled floors, and a built-in dance floor, the Roosevelt Room's French doors open onto a full-length deck overlooking the vineyard and showcasing the marvelous spectacle that nature displays in one of Oregon's most picturesque locations.

Elk Cove is pleased to offer a wide range of wines, from our award-winning Pinot Gris (the 2005 was honored to be one of Wine Spectator magazine's top 100 wines of the year for 2007) to the much sought-after Pinot Noirs from our La Bohème vineyard, which have been served at two White House state dinners.

Contact
Hospitality Coordinator

Quick Facts
- Capacity up to 150
- Outdoor ceremony location with indoor reception in our Roosevelt Room
- Roosevelt Room opens onto full length deck overlooking vineyards
- Plenty of on-site parking
- Utilize the vendors of your choice
- Tables and chairs in Roosevelt Room included

See page 411 under Reception & Wedding Sites

538

PO Box 100
Underwood, Washington 98651
p. 509.493.2026
f. 509.493.2027
e. info@gorgecrest.com
www.gorgecrest.com

Contact
Ronda Crumpacker

The New Premier event location in the Gorge!

Gorge Crest Vineyards has created the first event site in the Gorge designed specifically for events to cater to your every need. We offer spectacular settings with expansive views of Mt. Hood, the Columbia River Gorge and the Hood River Valley. New traditional winery building with intimate inside settings and a custom rock fireplace. Spectacular views form the indoor and outdoor area, manicured lawns, cobblestone patios, covered porches, built in dance floor, tables & chairs, indoor/outdoor bars, dedicated catering facilities and elegant bathrooms makes Gorge Crest the perfect location for your special day!

The grounds were immaculate, the dance floor was beautiful, and the views were right from a postcard! Gorge Crest is the most beautiful venue in the Gorge, and we looked at a lot of places. Plus the fact that there is a beautiful outside and inside area in case of inclement weather is so convenient. They have thought of everything, from the parking placement, to the ability for the bride to arrive without being seen. They were so helpful, available and friendly whenever we had questions or concerns. Our guests have told us that it was the most beautiful wedding they had ever attended! Gorge Crest made our dream come true! – Laura Spinney and Joe Silliman 2008

Quick Facts
- Expansive views of the Columbia River Gorge, Hood River Valley & Mt. Hood
- Exquisite Indoor event room w/stone fireplace (in case of bad weather)
- Extensive manicured lawns w/concrete Dance Floor
- Dedicated catering facilities
- Elegant bathrooms
- Dressing room
- Covered porches
- Indoor/outdoor bars (including a wine serving area)
- Beautiful cobblestone patios
- Three dedicated band locations w/necessary electrical
- On-site parking facility & Valet Parking turn around
- Chairs & Tables
- Wonderful wine
- On-site parking facility & Valet Parking turn around

539

28005 NE 172nd Avenue
Battle Ground, Washington 98604
p. 360.713.2359
f. 360.666.0890
e. events@heisenhousevineyards.com
www.heisenhousevineyards.com

About the Heisen House

Something old. Something new. Settled in the 1860s by newlywed pioneer homesteaders Alexander and Mary Heisen, this National and State Historic Site offers a truly unique place to begin your life-journey together.

The location features a stunning 1898 Victorian farmhouse surrounded by 5 acres of gardens, vineyards, orchards, and old-growth trees as well as plenty of open lawn space and panoramic rural views, all just 30 minutes from the Portland International Airport and 5 minutes from lodging in nearby Battle Ground, WA.

Pressed for time? Our on-site coordinator, whose services are included in our fee, makes planning your special day easy. Our coordinator will also be there on the day of your event to attend to every detail so you can simply relax and savor the moment with family and friends. Work with your own caterer, florist, photographer, and DJ, or tap into our list of preferred partners for the ultimate in hassle-free planning.

540

Contact
Event coordinator

Price
$2,000 and up, depending on date, time, and event.

Contact us for details.

Quick Facts
- Complimentary in-house wedding planner
- 30 minutes from Portland International Airport (PDX)
- Unhurried one-event-at-a-time policy
- Catering, your selection or choose from our preferred list
- Date secured with $1,000 non-refundable deposit
- Free parking on site
- ADA accessible

See page 429 under
Reception & Wedding Sites

23269 NW Yungen Road
Hillsboro, Oregon 97124
p. 503.647.7596
e. info@helvetiawinery.com
www.helvetiawinery.com

Winery Tours And Events

Your country farm and winery experience just 25 minutes from downtown Portland and 10 minutes from high-tech Hillsboro. Our cozy, historic farmhouse, and the grounds surrounding it are available for wine tastings, private winemaker dinners, meetings, and picnics with a minimum wine purchase. Take a break from the business at hand and tour the Christmas tree farm, vineyards and winery. A perfect setting to learn about wine and winemaking in a relaxed and friendly atmosphere.

Wine Catering

Helvetia Winery will bring a variety of fine vintage wines from local vineyards, at special case prices, for wine tasting at your event in your location. An expert server will assist you and your guests in learning the finer points of Oregon wines, such as the importance of vintage, winemaking styles and aging.

Custom Labels

Your logo, your photo, a wine named after you: we can provide cases of wine with custom labels to serve at your event, or as gifts, mementos, motivational awards, and party favors.

"The north wind howls here every time it frosts. However, the grapes often ripen full and wonderful."

– Jakob Yungen writing to his Swiss relatives in 1917

Contact
John Platt

Price
Call for quotes

Quick Facts
- 25 minutes from downtown Portland
- Enjoy a fine wine tasting with your offsite, dinner, party, meeting, wedding or any event
- Custom labels for events, gifts, & souvenirs

541

We're open every weekend from noon to five year-round. Come visit and see for yourself.

Bravo! Member Since 2001

11603 South New Era Road
Oregon City, Oregon 97045
Available for viewing by
appointment only
p. 503.784.6298
e. info@kingsravenwine.com
www.kingsravenwine.com

About King's Raven Winery

Twenty minutes south of downtown Portland, King's Raven Winery is located at the gateway to the undiscovered east Willamette Valley viticultural area halfway between Oregon City and Canby Oregon. Our beautiful, three-tier amphitheater is perfect for your most memorable day. Surrounded by our estate vineyard on 35 acres with views from the coastal mountains to the cascades, you'll find yourself in heaven as you dance the night away.

King's Raven Winery also produces pasture fed no hormone Black Angus Beef. The farm has been owned and operated by our family since 1942.

Availability and Terms

Space available any day June through September. Deposit required.

More Than Just Weddings

King's Raven Winery offers the space for more than just weddings. Last year we started a movie night series in the vineyard on a giant inflatable outdoor movie screen.

542

Contact
Darin Ingram
King's Raven Winery, Inc.

– or –

Premiere Catering
503.235.0274

Price
Prices vary on size &
amenities of the event

Capacity
Up to 300+

Amenities
- Note: We are not a hotel
- Free on-site parking for up to 100 vehicles
- One event booked per weekend
- Property access up to two days before and one day after event
- No corkage fees or exclusive wine requirements
- 1,000 square feet of dance floor
- Electrical hook-up
- ADA accessible

See page 441 under
Reception & Wedding Sites

9774 Highway 14 West
Goldendale, Washington 98620
p. 877.627.9445
f. 509.773.0586
www.maryhillwinery.com

About Maryhill Winery

Established in 1999 by Craig and Vicki Leuthold, Maryhill Winery is one of Washington state's largest family-owned wineries producing 80,000 cases annually. Located in the picturesque Columbia Gorge scenic area in Goldendale, Washington, the winery is perched on a bluff overlooking the Columbia River against the stunning backdrop of Mt. Hood. Nestled among rows of vines, Maryhill is a popular destination for picnics and special events, with an adjacent 4,000-seat outdoor amphitheater that hosts a world-class summer concert series.

Maryhill's 3,000 square foot tasting room draws more than 75,000 wine enthusiasts from around the globe each year, ranking among the top five most visited wineries in the state. Maryhill sources grapes from some of the most highly-regarded vineyards in the state to produce 23 varietals and 28 award-winning wines. Offering something for every palate, Maryhill wines offer tremendous value, with exceptional quality at affordable prices. For more information or to order wines online, visit www.maryhillwinery.com.

Contact

Joe Garoutte

p. 877.MARYHILL ext. 342
e. joeg@maryhillwinery.com

Maryhill provides a selection of 4 sites including:

- Ceremony site on the bluff of the Columbia River
- Amphitheatre & Stage
- Recreation area
- Arbor after hours

Price

Fee is $6,500 & includes the following:

- Selection of sites
- Event Planner Assistance
- Day of event coordination
- 20 tables, 360 chairs

Quick Facts

- "2009 Washington Winery of the Year" – *Winepress NW*
- "Best Destination Winery" – *Seattle Magazine*
- Excellent caterers available for hire
- Personalized Wine labels available for additional charge
- Handicap accessible

543

See page 450 under Reception & Wedding Sites

Mt. Hood Winery

2882 Van Horn Drive
Hood River, Oregon 97031
p. 541.386.8333
f. 541.387.2578
e. linda@mthoodwinery.com
www.mthoodwinery.com

About Mt. Hood Winery

Mt. Hood Winery is conveniently located just 4 miles south of downtown Hood River, off hwy 35. The brand new facility which is surrounded by 16 acres of estate vineyard, along with magnificent views of Mt. Hood and Mt. Adams makes the perfect place to host your wedding and reception. The Northwest Lodge style facility is an architect and designers showcase with its 22' vaulted ceilings and floor to ceiling windows. Additional inside amenities consist of lovely chandeliers, a quarried rock stone fireplace, and a 30 foot long antique replica bar with a mirrored back bar which reflects warmth, light and reflections from the western patio windows.

Types of Events

Mt. Hood Winery offers guests the availability to create a truly unique and memorable event with several different options. We offer everything from a wedding, rehearsal dinner and receptions, business meetings and related events. Our professional and friendly staff are committed to making your special day memorable. Please call to schedule a site visit and consult with our event planner.

Contact
Linda Barber

Price
Varies, depending on event; please call for information.

Capacity
Up to 250 guests

Amenities
- Indoor and outdoor ceremonies and receptions
- Ample complimentary parking on site
- ADA accessible
- Spacious bridal dressing room
- Full kitchen available for catering
- Preferred caterers list upon request
- Tables and chair setup included in site rental
- Estate grown and award winning wines
- Special wine discounts

544

See page 469 under
Reception & Wedding Sites

Weddings, Receptions & Rehearsal Dinners

Vista Hills is Oregon's most exciting new wedding venue and one of the most beautiful places on Earth to get married!

Views and Vista await you, from our quiet little stand atop the breathtaking Dundee Hills in Oregon's Willamette Valley. This picturesque site is a magical place to celebrate your wedding day. Let our expert staff and planning team help you create the wedding experience of your dreams.

Give us a call to learn more or set up a time to visit our Portland Downtown showroom and view albums and videos from this site. You can also learn more at www. PowersOregon.com.

Bravo! SPECIAL!

Book within 2 weeks of your first site visit and save $250!

www.PowersOregon.com

Vista Hills Vineyard – Dayton, Oregon
503-478-0997

Contact
Erin or Kat

p. 503.478.0997

www.PowersOregon.com

www.VistaHillsVineyard.com

Included Services
- Pre event planning
- Event day management
- Guest count range of 5 to 225
- Set up & tear down of event
- All tables chairs & linens
- All flatware
- Menu design, cake service
- Bar management
- At cost beverage service
- Powers Photography Studios credit

545

See page 513 under Reception & Wedding Sites

6855 Breyman Orchards Road
Dayton, Oregon 97114

p. 503.864.3446
p. 800.261.3446
f. 503.864.3109

e. jld@winecountryfarm.com

www.winecountryfarm.com

Welcome to Wine Country Farm
B&B, Winery, Tasting Room & Carriage Rides

A beautiful wine country estate at the top of the Dundee Hills providing a spectacular year round location for your wedding. Surrounded by our vineyards, enjoy breathtaking views of the Willamette Valley and Cascade Mountain range.

Outdoor weddings can be arranged on our grounds with beautiful lawns, flowers, gazebos, views and a large covered dance floor. Inside weddings are offered in our spacious tasting room with a fireplace and baby grand piano. Changing rooms are provided for the wedding party. Horse and carriage rides available for the bride and grooms' entry and exit.

Snuggle down in our romantic bed & breakfast in the vineyards. Nine bedrooms all with private bath, air-conditioning and views; some with fireplaces.

Wine Country Farm is less than an hour drive from Portland and just a half-hour from Salem. We are featured in the New York Times #1 Best Seller, "1,000 Places To See Before You Die" by Patricia Schultz.

Contact
Joan Davenport

Price
Varies depending on size & type of event

Capacity
Weddings for up to 130 inside or 300 in an outside venue; 18 overnight guests at B&B.

Amenities
- Wedding Coordinator included; one hour rehearsal, day before wedding
- Spacious yet intimate room for inside weddings with fireplace, baby grand piano & kitchen
- Beautifully landscaped lawns & gardens filled with flowers & spectacular sweeping vineyard & valley views for outside weddings
- Catering – we can recommend or bring your own caterer
- Winery & Cellar – we offer our fine wines & beer with our OLCC licensed servers; No hard alcohol
- Ample parking on–site, out of view of your wedding

See page 519 under Reception & Wedding Sites

10660 SW Youngberg Hill Road
McMinnville, Oregon 97128
p. 888.657.8668
www.youngberghill.com

Youngberg Hill has the Most Spectacular View in the Heart of the Wine Country

Sitting high atop the vineyard hills of the Willamette Valley, Youngberg Hill Vineyards & Inn has a striking panoramic view of the Cascades, Coastal Range, and Willamette Valley that will distinguish any occasion. Nestled in the middle of 50 acres, including 22 acres of award winning Pinot Noir and Pinot Gris vineyards, there are photo opportunities galore. The natural beauty of the site is complemented by the private, quiet tranquility.

Special Services

The eight room inn on the property accommodates your wedding party, including a honeymoon suite. Youngberg Hill is the highest rated inn in the valley, and boasts the area's most elegant accommodations.

Contact
Wedding Coordinator

Price
Prices vary on size & amenities of the event

Amenities
- 40 x 60 tent
- Wine, beer & champagne provided
- 1,000 square foot dance floor with electrical hookups
- Shaded gazebos, ceremony gazebo, unparalleled views
- Ample free parking
- ADA accessible

547

TYPES OF EVENTS

Youngberg Hill Vineyards and Inn is a perfect venue for weddings, receptions, reunions, concerts and celebrations of any event.

See page 524 under Reception & Wedding Sites

Helpful Hint

Planning Your Outdoor Wedding

Whether you're planning a backyard bash at your parent's house, your local park or a picturesque setting by a lake or river – remember it's more complicated to host a wedding outdoors.

HERE SRE SOME THINGS TO KEEP IN MIND...

Before anything – figure out the best time to wed. It's pretty rainy here till mid-July sometimes - and then it can be blistering hot! We have the luxury of a beautiful fall season - just keep in mind those home football games that might conflict with schedules of your bridal party.

Put a tent in your budget and keep in mind fans, air conditioning or heat lamps cost extra, as do sidewalls and lighting.

If you're in a backyard, several months before the wedding, have the yard evaluated. You may need a landscaper to fill in uneven ground and plant grass seed or lay sod.

Meet with your Wedding Coordinator to go over the best places for an aisle - which you can create with rose petals, potted plants or large stones.

Think of where you want to say your vows...perhaps a terrace, a majestic tree or mom's prize rosebushes. Let your florist know where you are getting married and supply them with photos – they will have suggestions of what you can use from wedding to reception.

Don't forget to inform neighbors ahead of time about your event, ask the police about any noise ordinances or curfews. Remember neighbors can be guests too...unless you want them mowing the lawn during the ceremony!

Look into a local hotel to hold your guests. Your parents house can hold only so many people and it's best to have extra space so you don't feel overwhelmed.

Don't let anyone that comes to the house early park in the driveway – keep that area clear for deliveries.

Hire a professional valet service (remember "Father of the Bride"?)

Find out when trash day is and call them to find out about special pick-ups.

If you're in someone's backyard, think about how guests will access the yard without traipsing through the home.

Don't block the street – depending upon the neighborhood, you may need a special permit from the local police precinct or city/county office to allow so many cars to park on the street. Consider having guests park at a local school or community center and hire a shuttle service.

Remember those pesky bugs (mosquitoes love dusk) and if you're by water, they can reak havoc – so plan ahead with hidden bee traps, keep the food close to the house or facility so the catering staff can keep on top of keeping them away.

Allergies - pollen peaks in early Spring and late Summer.

Suggested list of "must haves" for a backyard wedding - tables, chairs, linens (that drop to the ground to cover the legs), portable restrooms if there's only one or two on-site, dance floor, generator, speakers, lighting, microphones, a tent.

If you're working with a facility with an outdoor space – check to see which items they have on-site and which ones need to be rented.

Ask your caterer for suggestions with the warm weather. Remember that cold, crisp food works well, but try to stay away from anything in heavy cream, mayonnaise dressing, cheese displays, heavy or braised meats or cake frosted in buttercream.

© Studio 190

Central Oregon Businesses

Bella Brides
800 NW Wall Street #202
Bend, Oregon 97701
p. 541.330.7090
e. nicole@bellabridesbend.com
www.bellabridesbend.com
See page 89

Ghost Rock Ranch
148800 Beal Road
La Pine, Oregon 97739
p. 541.536.5593
e. info@ghostrockranch.com
www.ghostrockranch.com
See page 421

Black Butte Ranch
PO Box 8000
Black Butte Ranch, Oregon 97759
p. 541.595.1267
e. catering@blackbutteranch.com
www.blackbutteranch.com
See page 385

High Desert Museum
59800 South Highway 97
Bend, Oregon 97702
p. 541.382.5754
e. events@highdesertmuseum.org
www.highdesertmuseum.org
See page 431

Celebrations Magazine
PO Box 3111
Bend, Oregon 97707
p. 541.598.8766
e. becky@centraloregonevents.net
www.centraloregonevents.net
See page 49

The Lodge at Suttle Lake
13300 Highway 20
Sisters, Oregon 97759
p. 541.595.2628
e. eventdirector@thelodgeatsuttlelake.com
www.thelodgeatsuttlelake.com
See page 446

FIVEPINE
HEALTH • BALANCE • ADVENTURE

FivePine Spa & Resort
1021 Desperado Trail
Sisters, Oregon 97759
p. 541.549.5900
e. elena.mcmichaels@fivepinelodge.com
www.fivepinelodge.com
See page 419

Long Hollow Ranch
71105 Holmes Road
Sisters, Oregon 97759
p. 877.923.1901
e. howdy@lhranch.com
www.lhranch.com
See page 447

550

McMenamins Old St. Francis School
700 NW Bond Street
Bend, Oregon 97701
p. 541.330.8567
e. salesbend@mcmenamins.com
www.mcmenamins.com
See pages 458, 531

SunRiver Resort
57081 Meadow Road
Sunriver, Oregon 97707
p. 541.593.4605
e. weddings@sunriver-resort.com
www.sunriver-resort.com
See pages 346, 503

**The Riverhouse Hotel
& Convention Center**
3075 North Highway 97
Bend, Oregon 97701
p. 541.617.6278
e. marketing@riverhouse.com
www.riverhouse.com
See page 492

551

Seventh Mountain Resort
18575 SW Century Drive
Bend, Oregon 97702
p. 800.452.6810
e. info@seventhmountain.com
www.seventhmountain.com
See page 499

Stott Shots Photography
912 NW Canyon Drive
Redmond, Oregon 97756
p. 541.526.0563
e. info@stottshotsphotography.com
www.stottshotsphotography.com
See page 296

Notes

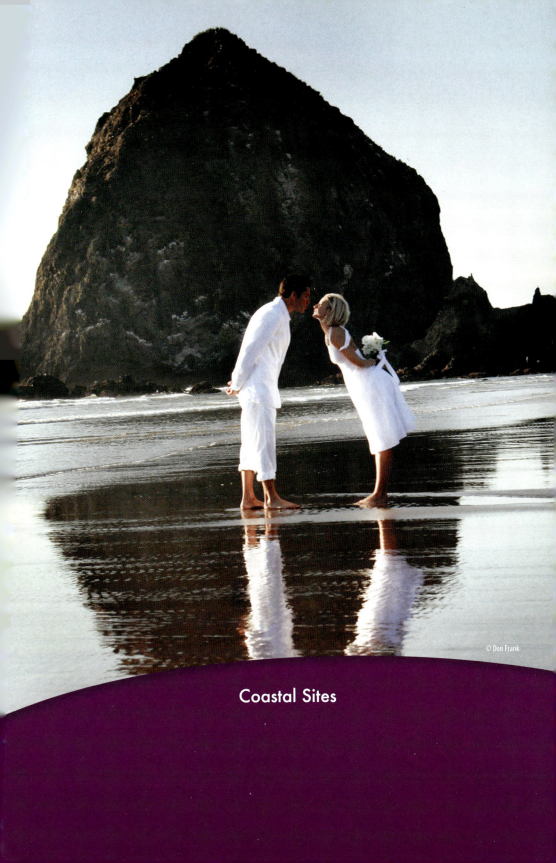

© Don Frank

Coastal Sites

The Banker's Suite

The Banker's Suite
1215 Duane St.
Astoria, Oregon 97103
p. 425.417.6512
e. bankerssuite@bluemars.com
www.thebankerssuite.com
See page 379

Liberty Theater
1203 Commercial Street
Astoria, Oregon 97103
p. 503.325.5922
e. director@liberty-theater.org
www.liberty-theater.org
See page 445

**Cannon Beach Florist –
Basketcase Inc.**
123 South Hemlock
Cannon Beach, Oregon 97110
p. 800.611.5826
e. cbflorist@theoregonshore.com
www.cannonbeachflorist.com
See page 150

McMenamins Sand Trap
1157 North Marion Avenue
Gearhart, Oregon 97138
p. 503.717.8502
e. salessandt@mcmenamins.com
www.mcmenamins.com
See pages 459, 532

Best Western Oceanview Resort
414 North Prom
Seaside, Oregon 97138
p. 800.234.8439
e. catering@oceanviewresort.com
www.oceanviewresort.com
See page 383

Pelican Brewpub
33180 Cape Kiwanda Drive
Pacific City, Oregon 97135
p. 503.965.3674
e. Events@pelicanbrewery.com
www.pelicanbrewery.com
See pages 478, 534

Don Frank Photography
PO Box 2641
Gearhart, Oregon 97138
p. 503.738.5118
e. don@donfrankphotography.com
www.donfrankphotography.com
See page 270

Surfsand Resort
148 West Gower
Cannon Beach, Oregon 97110
p. 800.797.4666
e. martha@surfsand.com
www.surfsand.com
See page 504

554

SURFTIDES
LINCOLN CITY

Surftides Hotel & Conference Center
2945 NW Jetty Avenue
Lincoln City, Oregon 97367
p. 541.994.2191
e. info@surftideslincolncity.com
www.surftidesinn.com
See page 505

Tolovana Inn
3400 South Hemlock
Cannon Beach, Oregon 97145
p. 800.550.5089
e. pcatl@comcast.net
www.tolovanainn.com
See page 508

555

Weddings at the Beach Bridal Show
p. 503.738.5332
e. contact@weddingsatthebeach.org
www.weddingsatthebeach.org
See page 79

Notes

© FS Photographers

Mt. Hood & Columbia River Gorge Businesses

A Majestic Mountain Retreat
38250 Pioneer Boulevard #602
Sandy, Oregon 97055
p. 503.686.8080
e. becca1st@gmail.com
www.amajesticmountainretreat.com
See page 344

Carson Ridge Luxury Cabins
1261 Wind River Road
Carson, Washington 98610
p. 877.816.7908
e. info@carsonridgecabins.com
www.carsonridgecabins.com
See page 395

Bigfoot Lodge
1819 Cascade Avenue
Hood River, Oregon 97031
p. 541.490.7971
e. Mike@LuxurySearch.com
www.Bigfoot-Lodge.com
See page 384

Cathedral Ridge Winery
4200 Post Canyon
Hood River, Oregon 97031
p. 800.516.8710
e. crw@cathedralridgewinery.com
www.cathedralridgewinery.com
See pages 396, 539

Bridal Veil Lakes
PO Box 5
Bridal Veil, Oregon 97010
p. 503.981.3695
www.bridalveillakes.com
See page 389

Cedar Springs Country Estate
12353 SE Lusted Road
Sandy, Oregon 97055
p. 503.819.0761
e. cscountrywedding@gmail.com
www.CedarSpringsCountryEstate.com
See page 397

Busy Bee Catering
P.O. Box 295
Welches, Oregon 97067
p. 503.622.6743
e. busybeecatering@hotmail.com
www.busybeecatering.com
See page 119

Columbia Cliff Villas
3880 Westcliff Drive
Hood River, Oregon 97031
p. 866.912.8366
e. info@columbiacliffvillas.com
www.columbiacliffvillas.com
See page 399

558

Columbia Gorge Hotel
4000 Westcliff Drive
Hood River, Oregon 97031
p. 541.386.5566
e. kim.bosch@northp.com
www.columbiagorgehotel.com
See page 400

Falcon's Crest Lodge – Mt. Hood Vacations
Government Camp, Oregon
p. 503.686.8080
www.falconscrestlodge.com
See page 345

Columbia Gorge Sternwheeler
110 SE Caruthers
Portland, Oregon 97214
p. 503.224.3900
p. 800.224.3901
e. sales@portlandspirit.com
www.portlandspirit.com
See pages 347, 401

Gorge Crest Vineyards
PO Box 100
Underwood, Washington 98651
p. 509.493.2026
e. info@gorgecrest.com
www.gorgecrest.com
See pages 423, 539

Columbia River Gorge Visitors Association
p. 800.984.6743
e. info@crgva.org
www.crgva.org
See page 51

Gorge-ous Weddings
192 Erickson Road
Stevenson, Washington 98648
p. 503.360.4707
e. info@gorge-ousweddings.com
www.gorge-ousweddings.com
See page 424

Cooper Spur Mountain Resort
10755 Cooper Spur Road
Mount Hood, Oregon 97041
p. 541.352.6692
p. 800.skihood
www.cooperspur.com
See page 402

"I Do" Artistic Hair Design
p. 503.250.0871
e. idoweddinghair@gmail.com
www.portlandweddinghair.com
See page 27

I Do Events
Hood River, Oregon 97031
p. 541.387.5502
e. leith@idoevents.com
www.idoevents.com
See page 64

Maryhill Winery
9774 Highway 14 West
Goldendale, Washington 98620
p. 877.627.9445
e. joeg@maryhillwinery.com
www.maryhillwinery.com
See pages 450, 543

Indian Creek Golf Course
3605 Brookside Drive
Hood River, Oregon 97031
p. 866.386.7770
www.indiancreekgolf.com
See page 436

Mt. Hood Bed and Breakfast
8885 Cooper Spur Road
Parkdale, Oregon 97041
p. 541.352.6858
e. mthoodbnb@gorge.net
www.mthoodbnb.com
See page 467

560

Lucy's Informal Flowers
311 Oak Street
Hood River, Oregon 97031
p. 541.386.3666
e lucy@informalflowers.com
www.informalflowers.com
See page 165

Mt. Hood Ski Bowl
87000 East Highway 26
Government Camp, Oregon 97028
p. 503.272.3206
e. knorton@skibowl.com
www.skibowl.com
See page 468

Martin's Gorge Tours
PO Box 18177
Portland, Oregon 97218
p. 503.349.1323
e. martin@martinsgorgetours.com
www.martinsgorgetours.com
See page 323

Mt. Hood Winery
2882 Van Horn Drive
Hood River, Oregon 97031
p. 541.386.8333
e. linda@mthoodwinery.com
www.mthoodwinery.com
See pages 469, 544

Old McDonald's Farm
PO Box 326, Corbett, Oregon 97019
p. 503.695.3316
e. omf@oldmcdonaldsfarm.org
www.oldmcdonaldsfarm.org
See page 490

Sikora Photography
p. 503.866.2645
e. info@sikoraphotography.com
www.sikoraphotography.com
See page 295

The Resort at the Mountain
68010 East Fairway Avenue
Welches, Oregon 97067
p. 503.622.2234
e. becca.kolibaba@theresort.com
www.theresort.com
See page 490

Skamania Lodge
Scenic Columbia River Gorge

1311 SW Skamania Lodge Way
Stevenson, Washington 98648
p. 800.376.9116
e. slweddings@destinationhotels.com
www.skamania.com
See page 501

561

River Lodge & Grill
6 Marine Drive
Boardman, Oregon 97818
p. 541.481.6800
e. sales@riverlodgeandgrill.com
www.riverlodgeandgrill.com
See page 491

STONEHEDGE GARDENS

Stonehedge Gardens
3405 Cascade Avenue
Hood River, Oregon 97031
p. 541.386.3940
e. stonehedge@gorge.net
www.stonehedgegardens.com
See page 502

Sea to Summit Adventure Tours
PO Box 83916
Portland, Oregon 97217
p. 503.286.9333
e. seatosummit@qwest.net
www.seatosummit.net
See pages 45, 325

Timberline Lodge
Timberline, Oregon 97028
p. 503.272.3251
e. weddings@timberlinelodge.com
www.timberlinelodge.com
See page 507

The Troutdale House
411 East Historic Columbia River Highway
Troutdale, Oregon 97060
p. 503.481.9449
e. thetroutdalehouse@gmail.com
www.thetroutdalehouse.com
See page 510

Weddings & Other Bloomin' Occasions
67211 E Highway. 26 Space D
Welches, Oregon 97067
p. 503.380.9891
e. bloominoccasions@peoplepc.com
www.weddingsbloominoccasions.com
See page 167

562

Viewpoint Inn
40301 East Larch Mountain Road
Corbett, Oregon 97019
p. 503.695.5811
e. events@theviewpointinn.com
www.theviewpointinn.com
See page 512

© Powers

Southwest Washington Businesses

AJ's Studio
Vancouver, Washington 98664
p. 360.694.6684
www.ajsstudio.com
See page 257

Black Swan Events
p. 360.567.5922
e. g@blackswanevents.net
www.blackswanevents.net
See page 387

Alderbrook Resort & Spa
10 East Alderbrook Drive
Union, Washington 98592
p. 360.898.2200
e. sales@alderbrookresort.com
www.alderbrookresort.com
See page 373

Camas Meadows Golf Club
4105 NW Camas Meadows Drive
Camas, WA 98607
p. 360.833.2000
e. jduce@camasmeadows.com
www.camasmeadows.com
See page 392

564

Anderson Lodge
18410 NE 399th Street
Amboy, Washington 98601
p. 360.247.6660
e. lodge@andersonlodge.com
www.andersonlodge.com
See page 375

David Cooley Band
p. 800.364.1522
e. info@davidcooleyweddings.com
www.davidcooleyweddings.com
See page 178

BLACKSTONE

Blackstone Restaurant & Catering
3200 SE 164th Avenue, Suite 204
Vancouver, Washington 98683
p. 360.253.0253
e. info@blackstonewa.com
www.blackstonewa.com
See page 386

Dippity Doodads
Chocolate Fountain Rentals

Dippity DooDads
8205 NE 91st Street
Vancouver, Washington 98662
p. 360.798.7395
e. shirley@dippitydoodads.com
www.dippitydoodads.com
See page 106

Dream Capture Media
p. 360.608.9415 or
  360.921.9718
e. info@dreamcapturemedia.com
www.dreamcapturemedia.com
See page 336

Flowers Exclusively by Wendy
PO Box 257
Vancouver, Washington 98665
p. 360.993.4749
e. toflowersbywendy@aol.com
www.flowersbywendy.com
See page 157

**Dreams Come True Elegant
Entertaining & Events**
p. 360.600.7279
keangelo@comcast.net
www.dreamscometrueelegantentertaining.com
See page 61

Gigi Floral Design
p. 360.909.1209
e. natalie@gigifloraldesign.com
www.gigifloraldesign.com
See page 162

565

"The Finest in Espresso Catering"

Espresso Elegance
p. 206.282.8155
e. holly@espressoelegance.com
www.espressoelegance.com
See page 116

Great Wolf Lodge
20500 Old Highway 99SW
Centralia, Washington 98531
p. 360.273.7718
e. jpoole@greatwolf.com
www.greatwolf.com
See page 426

The Fairgate Inn
2213 NW 23rd Avenue
Camas, Washington 98607
p. 360.834.0861
e. thefairgate@aol.com
www.fairgateinn.com
See page 416

Heisen House
28005 NE 172nd Avenue
Battle Ground, Washington 98604
e. events@heisenhousevineyards.com
See pages 429, 440

The Heathman Lodge
7801 NE Greenwood Drive
Vancouver, Washington 98662
p. 360.254.3100
e. maili.morrison@heathmanlodge.com
www.heathmanlodge.com
See page 427

Majestic Inn & Spa
419 Commerical Avenue
Anacortes, WA 98221
p. 360.299.1400
www.majesticinnandspa.com
See page 448

The Hostess House
&
The Bridal Arts Building
Est. 1984

Hostess House & Bridal Arts
10017 NE Sixth Avenue
Vancouver, Washington 98685
e. 360.574.3284
www.thehosteshouse.com
See pages 91, 358, 435

Paradox Productions
7806 E. 24th Court
Vancouver, WA 98665
p. 360.909.6700
e. info@djpdx.com
www.djpdx.com
See page 197

Laszlo Photography
p. 360.896.2367
e. plaszlo@spiritone.com
www.laszlophoto.com
See page 286

Parke Avenue
Limousine

Parke Avenue Limousine
1819 NE 49th St
p. Vancouver, WA 98663
p. 503-750-3891
www.parkeavenuelimousine.com
See page 324

Le Paperie (Petite BonBon)
p. 360.954.5032
e. thu@le-paperie.com
www.le-paperie.com
See pages 215, 216, 226

Party Outfitters
PO Box 8489
Lacey, WA 98509
p. 800-853-5867
e. justin@partyoutfitters.com
partyoutfitters.com
See page 200

Pomeroy Farm
20902 NE Lucia Falls Road
Yacolt, WA 98675
p. 360-686-3537
e. danielbrink@pomeroyfarm.org
www.pomeroyfarm.org
See page 480

Swingline Cubs
1414 NE 115th Avenue
Vancouver, WA 98684
p. 360.254.3187
e. joe@swinglinecubs.com
www.swinglinecubs.com
See page 181

Reverend Robert Thomas
12820 NW 33rd
Vancouver, WA 98685
p. 360-573-7725
e. charbobthomas@juno.com
See page 244

Taylor Events

Making your event memorable

Taylor Events
PO Box 822158
Vancouver, Washington 98668
p. 360.882.6074
e. taylorevents@live.com
e. your.nw.dj@live.com
www.ataylorevent.com.
www.yournwdj.com
See page 74

San Juan Island Weddings
640 Mullis Street, Suite 211
Friday Harbor, Washington 98250
p. 888.468.3701 x1
e. info@visitsanjuans.com
www.visitsanjuans.com
See page 362

Uncommon Invites
14300 NE 20th Avenue, Suite D102-175
Vancouver, WA 98686
p. 800.676.3030
e. info@uncommoninvites.com
www.uncommoninvites.com
See page 229

Simply Thyme Catering
14020 NE 4th Plain Road, Ste E
Vancouver, WA 98682
p. 360.891.0584
e. kelly@simplythymecatering.com
www.simplythymecatering.com
See page 134

Uniquely Yours

Chair Covers
Table Styling Linens

Uniquely Yours
7405 NE 87th Circle
Vancouver, WA 98662
p. 360.624.0781
e. lou@uniquely-yours.biz
www.uniquely-yours.biz
See page 314

567

Notes

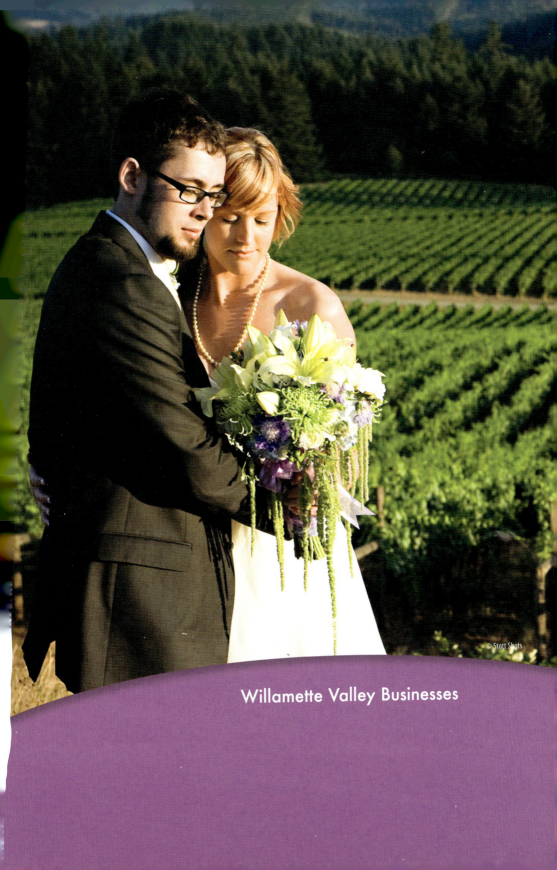

Willamette Valley Businesses

© Stott Shots

Abiqua Country Estate
18401 Abiqua Road NE
Silverton, Oregon 97381
p. 503.829.9280
e. jude@molalla.net
www.abiquacountryestate.com
See page 367

Class Act Event Coordinators
Salem, Oregon
p. 503.371.8904
e. events@classactevents.net
www.classactevents.net
See page 59

An Event to Remember
3325 Felina Avenue NE
Salem, Oregon 97301
p. 888.652.0115
e. info@aneventtoremember.info
www.aneventtoremember.info
See page 239

Domaine Margelle Vineyards
20159 Hazelnut Ridge Road
Scotts Mills, Oregon 97375
p. 503.873.0692
e. info@domainemargelle.com
www.domainemargelle.com
See pages 407, 537

570

Antonia Ballroom
221 North Grant Street
Canby, Oregon 97013
p. 503.263.2085
e. info@antoniaballroom.com
www.antoniaballroom.com
See page 377

Events at Copper Hill
3170 Commercial Street SE
Salem Oregon 97302
p. 503.373.3170
www.eventsatcopperhillcom
See page 414

Beckenridge Vineyards
300 Reuben Boise Road
Dallas, Oregon 97338
p. 503.831.3652
e. info@beckenridge.com
www.beckenridge.com
See pages 381, 535

Heritage House Farm & Gardens
Aurora, Oregon

Heritage House Farm & Gardens
Aurora, Oregon 97002
p. 503.678.5704
e. heritagehouse@centurytel.net
See page 430

Honey Bucket
1685 McGilchrist Street SE
Salem, Oregon 97301
p. 800.966.2371
www.honeybucket.com
See page 309

The Oregon Garden
895 West Main St.
Silverton, Oregon 97381
p. 503.874.2500
e. tinag@moonstonehotels.com
See page 473

In The Lens Photography
Albany, Oregon 97322
p. 541.974.5855
e. inthelens@comcast.net
www.inthelensphotography.com

The Oregon Wedding Showcase
PO Box 153, Monmouth, Oregon 97361
p. 800.317.6589
e. judy@oregonweddingshowcase.com
www.oregonweddingshowcase.com
See page 76

571

Langdon Farms Golf Club
24377 NE Airport Road
Aurora, Oregon 97002
p. 503.678.4653
www.langdonfarms.com
See page 444

Reverend Laurel Cookman
p. 503.807.7927
e. willgables@wmconnect.com
www.aweddingyourway.com
See page 239

Lights in the Attic Creative Media
645 Judson Street SE
Salem, Oregon 97302
p. 503.990.8669
e. lightsintheattic@mac.com
www.litacreative.com
See page 337

Robert Renggli M.A.
2115 Cunnigham Lane South
Salem, Oregon 97302
p. 503.363.3156
e. brenggli@comcast.net
www.bobrenggli.com
See page 243

Settlemier House

Settlemier House
355 N. Settlemier Avenue
Woodburn, Oregon 97071
p. 503.982.1897
e. cst@wbcable.net
www.settlemierhouse.com
See page 498

Wooden Shoe Gardens

Wooden Shoe Gardens
33814 South Meridian Road
Woodburn, Oregon 97071
p. 503.201.2847
e. susie@woodenshoe.com
www.woodenshoe.com
See page 520

BEGIN TO IMAGIN *with*
STUDIO 190

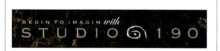

Studio 190 Photography
1923 NW Kenard Street NW
Salem, Oregon 97304
p. 503.510.9623
e. s190image@gmail.com
www.s190image.com
See page 297

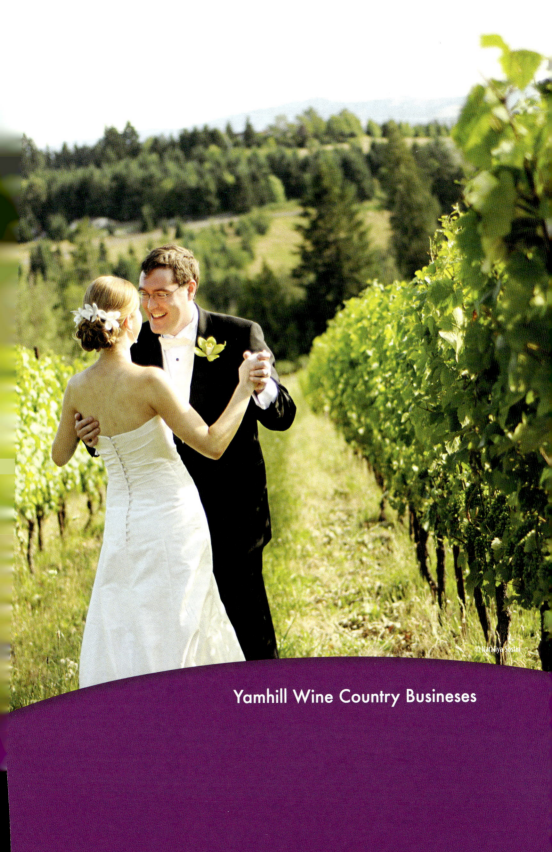

© Nataliya Sostni

Yamhill Wine Country Busineses

5 Rock Ranch
23800 NW Flying M Road,
Yamhill, Oregon 97148
p. 503.662.5678
e. christy@5rockranch.com
www.5rockranch.com
See page 365

Evergreen Aviation Museum
500 NE Captain Michael King Smith Way
McMinnville, Oregon 97128
p. 503.434.4023
e. events@sprucegoose.org
www.evergreenmuseum.org
See page 415

Brookside Inn
8243 NE Abbey Road
Carlton, Oregon 97111
p. 503.852.4433
e. info@brooksideinn-oregon.com
www.brooksideinn-oregon.com
See page 391

Five Gables Photography
p. 503.550.7385
e. fivegablesphoto@comcast.net
www.fivegablesphotography.com
See page 273

574

CAMP TURNAROUND
Camp Turaround
57011 NW Wilson River Highway
Gales Creek, Oregon 97117
p. 503.359.1438
e. director@campturnaround.com
www.campturnaround.com
See page 391

Kelty Estates
675 3rd Street
Lafayette, Oregon 97127
p. 503.883.1262
e. weddings@keltyestatebb.com
www.keltyestatebb.com
See page 440

ELK COVE
VINEYARDS

Elk Cove Vineyards
27751 NW Olson Road
Gaston, Oregon 97119
p. 503.985.7760
e. info@elkcove.com
www.elkcove.com
See pages 411, 538

The Mansion at Bayou Golf Course

The Mansion at Bayou Golf Course
9301 SW Bayou Drive
McMinnville, Oregon 97128
p. 503.435.2500
e. events@bayougolfcourse.com
www.bayougolfcourse.com
See page 449

McMenamins Hotel Oregon
310 NE Evans Street
McMinnville, OR 97128
p. 503.472.8427
e. saleshoto@mcmenamins.com
www.mcmenamins.com
See pages 456, 529

Vista Hills
p. 503.478.0997
www.PowersOregon.com
www.VistaHillsVineyard.com
See pages 513, 545

McMinnville Grand Ballroom
325 NE 3rd Street
McMinnville, Oregon 97128
p. 503.474.0264
e. info@mgballroom.com
www.mgballroom.com
See page 460

Windrose Conference & Meeting Center
809 W First St.
Newberg, Oregon 97132
p. 503.701.7273
e. lynn@windrosecenter.com
www.windrosecenter.com
See page 518

575

Mill Creek Gardens, LLC

Mill Creek Gardens
Sheridan, Oregon 97378
p. 503.843.4218
www.millcreekgardensbb.com
See page 463

Wine Country Farm
6855 Breyman Orchards Road
Dayton, Oregon 97114
p. 503.864.3446
e. jld@winecountryfarm.com
www.winecountryfarm.com
See pages 519, 546

No Ordinary Affair

No Ordinary Affair
PO Box 423
McMinnville, Oregon 97128
p. 503.868.9455
e. info@noordinaryaffair.com
www.noordinaryaffair.com
See page 67

Wine Country Wedding Professionals

Wine Country Wedding Professionals
PO Box 423
McMinnville, Oregon 97128
p. 503.868.9455
e. becky@winecountrywedding professionals.com
www.winecountryweddingprofessionals.com
See page 53

Youngberg Hill
10660 SW Youngberg Hill Road
McMinnville, Oregon 97128
p. 888.657.8668
www.youngberghill.com
See pages 524, 547

576

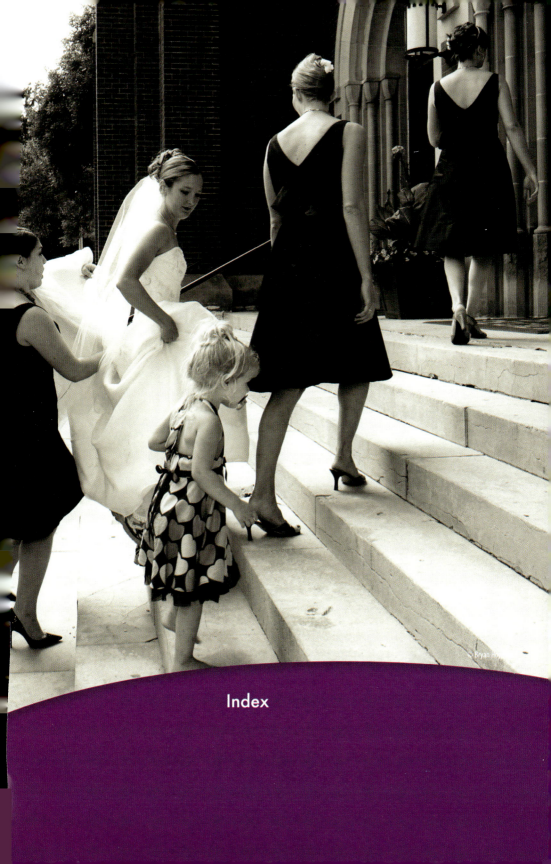

Index

D

E

579

580

581

Q

R

S

T

583

Notes